GLORY NOT DISHONOR

Francis J. Moloney, S.D.B.

GLORY
NOT
DISHONOR

Reading John 13–21

Wipf & Stock
PUBLISHERS
Eugene, Oregon

Wipf and Stock Publishers
199 W 8th Ave, Suite 3
Eugene, OR 97401

Glory Not Dishonor
Reading John 13-21
By Moloney, Francis J.
Copyright©1998 Augsburg Fortress
ISBN: 1-59244-791-0
Publication date 8/6/2004
Previously published by Fortress Press, 1998

Mary (née O'Connor) and Denis Moloney
1899–1996
In Memoriam

Contents

Preface

¶ THE TITLE OF THIS FINAL VOLUME of my narrative commentary on the Fourth Gospel was inspired by a sermon of the eighth-century abbot St. Theodore the Studite on the adoration of the cross: "Indeed an unheard of exchange! We are given life instead of death, incorruptibility instead of corruption, glory instead of dishonor."[1] The Johannine account of the death and resurrection of Jesus (John 18–20), with its lengthy introduction (chaps. 13–17), reads Jesus' death as a departure by means of a "lifting up." God is made known, and a community of believers is founded. Its members will love as he has loved—guided, strengthened, and taught by the Paraclete. As the cross draws together the threads of the story, the traditional climax to the story of Jesus, the resurrection (20:1-31), has a different function in the Johannine narrative strategy. My study of the Gospel will close with a brief reflection on the place of John 21.

Some recent scholarship has withdrawn approval for the approach I have adopted for my reading of the Fourth Gospel.[2] A postmodern

[1] For the Greek text, with a Latin translation, see St. Theodore the Studite, *Oratio II—In Adorationem Crucis* (PG 99:696B). The earlier volumes are F. J. Moloney, *Belief in the Word: Reading John 1–4* (Minneapolis. Fortress Press, 1993); idem, *Signs and Shadows: Reading John 5–12* (Minneapolis Fortress Press, 1996).

[2] See especially S. D. Moore, *Poststructuralism and the New Testament· Derrida and Foucault at the Foot of the Cross* (Minneapolis. Fortress Press, 1994), 65–81; The Bible and Culture Collective, *The Postmodern Bible* (New Haven: Yale University Press, 1995), 20–

reading of the Bible can no longer privilege the biblical text. The Bible, like all other imposed "canons," is a collection of moments in the endless play of intertext that has been frozen and then imposed as a "rule" within a culture. In a parallel fashion, the reader is also an unstable text, the result of the interweaving of many texts, none of which should be taken as the norm. Yet I have pursued my project to its conclusion. One of the many important contributions of postmodern scholarship is its focus on context. My context is critical scholarship of the Christian tradition *from within the Christian tradition*. One of my difficulties with scholars who demand that the Bible be removed from its canonical position is their apparent neglect of their own context: academics who are who they are and do what they do because of the Christian tradition.

Fernando Segovia rightly asks in his gracious review of *Belief in the Word:* "Do all readers come up with the same implied reader?"[3] My implied reader will not be everyone's implied reader, as factors outside the text inevitably influence my reading. Yet every attempt is made to respond to the perceived strategies of an author in the text to create a reader in the text, in the hope that it will speak to real readers of the text. Unlike many narrative critics, I regard the original readers of the Gospel as an important point of reference in following the interplay between the author and reader in the text. Thus, I hope to trace an implied reader that would have spoken eloquently to a Christian community at the close of the first century.[4] My implied reader is only one of the many possible because there is no interpretative context that can ever claim to have exhausted all the potential of a given text.[5]

118; and J. L. Staley, *Reading with a Passion: Rhetoric, Autobiography and the American West in the Gospel of John* (New York: Continuum, 1995), with specific reference to my work on pages 9–10. I suggest that approval has been "withdrawn" because Staley and some members of The Bible and Culture Collective were pioneers in the development of the narrative approach to biblical texts.

[3] *CBQ* 56 (1994): 803.

[4] This concern has led me to maintain a scholarly dialogue with traditional, historical interpretation. See J. Ashton, "Narrative Criticism," in *Studying John* (Oxford: Clarendon, 1994), 141–65; D. F. Tolmie, *Jesus' Farewell to the Disciples: John 13:1—17:26 in Narratological Perspective,* (BibIntS 12 Leiden: E. J. Brill, 1995), 34–39. For a thought-provoking recent historical study of the diverse Johannine understandings of the death of Jesus, see M. C. de Boer, *Johannine Perspectives on the Death of Jesus,* (CBET 17 Kampen: Kok Pharos, 1996).

[5] The defense of the objectivity of text, along with an insistence that the interplay of text and reader is never finished but always leaves a "remainder," comes from Paul Ricoeur. As he says so well: "Perhaps we should say that a text is a finite space of interpretations: there is not just one interpretation, but, on the other hand, there is not an infinite number of them. A text is a space of variations that has its own constraints;

"Comprehension is limited by the capacity of the comprehender, and inexhaustibility is one of the marks of a work of art."[6] The limited comprehension created by context is not detrimental until one pretends to be free from it.

This book has been written in the spaces I have been able to create around my busy role as the Foundation Professor of Theology at Australian Catholic University. I have been encouraged and supported throughout this three-volume project by the staff at Fortress Press, especially by Dr. Marshall Johnson, who guided it from the beginning, Dr. K. C. Hanson, and Deborah Finch Brandt. Dr. Cynthia Thompson and Lois Torvik edited and produced the second volume. Dr. Mary Coloe, P.B.V.M., my colleague at Australian Catholic University, read the final draft of this study and made valuable suggestions. Above all, I am indebted to Nerina Zanardo, F.S.P., whose assiduous reading of the many versions of this script has made it a better book than I ever could have produced on my own.

My first published book was dedicated to my parents.[7] I also offer this completion of my reading of the Fourth Gospel to their memory. They taught me: "No one has ever seen God; if we love one another, God lives in us, and his love is perfected in us" (1 John 4:12). Now each of them is able to address God with words of the Johannine Jesus: "I glorified you on earth, having accomplished the task which you gave me to do" (John 17:4).

---

and in order to choose a different interpretation, one must always have better reasons" ("World of the Text, World of the Reader," in M. Valdés, ed., *A Ricoeur Reader: Reflection and Imagination* [Toronto: University of Toronto Press, 1991], 496). As C. R. Koester, *Symbolism in the Fourth Gospel: Meaning, Mystery, Community* (Minneapolis: Fortress Press, 1995), 268, puts it: "The text means many things, but it does not mean just anything."

[6] H. Gardner, *The Business of Criticism* (Oxford: Oxford University Press, 1959), 14. See also R. A. Culpepper, "The Gospel of John as a Document of Faith in a Pluralistic Culture," in F. F. Segovia, *"What Is John?" Readers and Readings of the Fourth Gospel*, SS 3 (Atlanta: Scholars Press, 1996), 109–27.

[7] F. J. Moloney, *The Johannine Son of Man*, 1st ed., BibScRel 14 (Rome: LAS, 1976). A second edition appeared in 1978.

Abbreviations

The abbreviations for the biblical books follow those provided by the *NJBC*, xxxi–xxxii. References to the Mishnah name the tractate, without any prefix, while references to the Babylonian Talmud have the prefix *b* before the tractate and references to the Jerusalem Talmud have the prefix *j* before the tractate. The Midrashim Rabbah are indicated by the abbreviation of the biblical book followed by R (e.g., *ExodR*). All other references to Jewish, intertestamental and patristic literature not mentioned below are given in full.

AB	Anchor Bible
ABD	D. N. Freedman, ed., *The Anchor Bible Dictionary*, 6 vols. New York: Doubleday, 1992.
ABRL	The Anchor Bible Reference Library
AGSU	Arbeiten zur Geschichte des Spätjudentums und Urchristentum
AnBib	Analecta Biblica
AnGreg	Analecta Gregoriana
ANRW	W. Haase and H. Temporini, eds., *Aufstieg und Niedergang der römischen Welt: Teil II: Principat—Religion*. Berlin: Walter de Gruyter, 1979–84.
Ant	*Antonianum*
Art	Article
AusBR	*Australian Biblical Review*

BAGD	W. Bauer, W. F. Arndt, and F. W. Gingrich. *A Greek-English Lexicon of the New Testament and Other Early Christian Literature.* 2d ed. Rev. and augmented by F. W. Gingrich and F. W. Danker. Chicago: University of Chicago Press, 1979.
BDF	F. Blass and A. Debrunner. *A Greek Grammar of the New Testament and Other Early Christian Literature.* Rev. and trans. R. W. Funk. Chicago: University of Chicago Press, 1961.
BETL	Bibliotheca Ephemeridum Theologicarum Lovaniensium
BGBE	Beiträge zur Geschichte der biblischen Exegese
Bib	*Biblica*
BibInt	*Biblical Interpretation*
BibIntS	Biblical Interpretation Series
BibOr	*Bibbia e Oriente*
BibScRel	Biblioteca di Scienze Religiose
BJ	Bible de Jérusalem
BK	*Bibel und Kirche*
BTB	*Biblical Theology Bulletin*
BU	Biblische Untersuchungen
BWANT	Beiträge zur Wissenschaft vom Alten und Neuen Testament
BZ	*Biblische Zeitschrift*
CahRB	Cahiers de la Revue Biblique
CBAA	Catholic Biblical Association of America
CBET	Contributions to Biblical Exegesis and Theology
CBQ	*Catholic Biblical Quarterly*
CBQMS	Catholic Biblical Quarterly Monograph Series
CCSL	Corpus Christianorum Series Latina (Turnhout: Brepols)
CultBib	*Cultura Biblica*
DRev	*Downside Review*
EB	Études bibliques
EstBib	*Estudios Biblicos*
ET	English translation
EThSt	Erfurter Theologische Studien
ETL	*Ephemerides Theologicae Lovanienses*
ETR	*Études théologiques et religieuses*
EuntD	*Euntes Docete*
EvTh	*Evangelische Theologie*
FB	Forschung zur Bibel
FRLANT	Forschungen zur Religion und Literatur des Alten und Neuen Testaments

FThSt	Frankfurter theologische Studien
HeyJ	*The Heythrop Journal*
HKNT	Handkommentar zum Neuen Testament
HTCNT	Herder's Theological Commentary on the New Testament
HUT	Hermeneutische Untersuchungen zur Theologie
IBS	*Irish Biblical Studies*
ICC	International Critical Commentary
ILBS	Indiana Literary Biblical Studies
Int	*Interpretation*
IRM	*International Review of Mission*
JB	Jerusalem Bible
JBL	*Journal of Biblical Literature*
JSNT	*Journal for the Study of the New Testament*
JSNTSS	Journal for the Study of the New Testament Supplement Series
JSOT	*Journal for the Study of the Old Testament*
JTS	*Journal of Theological Studies*
ktl.	Greek: *kai ta loipa* = et cetera
LAS	Libreria Ateneo Salesiano
Laur	*Laurentianum*
LD	Lectio Divina
LSJ	H. Liddell, R. Scott, and H. S. Jones, *A Greek-English Lexicon*. Oxford: Clarendon, 1968.
LTP	*Laval théologique et philosophique*
LXX	Septuagint
MNTC	Moffatt New Testament Commentary
MüTZ	*Münchener theologische Zeitschrift*
NAB	New American Bible
NCB	New Century Bible
NEB	New English Bible
NEchtB	Die neue Echter Bibel
Neot	*Neotestamentica*
NICNT	The New International Commentary on the New Testament
NJB	*New Jerusalem Bible*
NJBC	*The New Jerome Biblical Commentary*, ed. R. E. Brown, J. A. Fitzmyer, and R. E. Murphy. Englewood Cliffs, N.J.: Prentice Hall, 1989.
NovT	*Novum Testamentum*
NovTSupp	Supplements to Novum Testamentum
NRSV	New Revised Standard Version

NRT	*Nouvelle Revue Théologique*
NT	New Testament
NTAbh	Neutestamentliche Abhandlungen
NTS	*New Testament Studies*
NVB	Nuovissima Versione della Bibbia
ÖTK	Okumenischer Taschenbuchkommentar zum Neuen Testament
OT	Old Testament
PG	*Patrologiae cursus completus, series graeca,* ed. J. P. Migne.
PL	*Patrologiae cursus completus, series latina,* ed. J. P. Migne.
PNTC	Pelican New Testament Commentaries
RB	*Revue Biblique*
RivBib	*Rivista Biblica*
RSR	*Recherches de science religieuse*
RSV	Revised Standard Version
RTL	*Revue Théologique de Louvain*
Sal	*Salesianum*
SANT	Studien zum Alten und Neuen Testament
SB	Studi Biblici
SBFA	Studium Biblicum Franciscanum Analecta
SBLDS	Society of Biblical Literature Dissertation Series
SBS	Stuttgarter Bibelstudien
ScEs	*Science et Esprit*
SCM	Students' Christian Movement
SDB	*Dictionnaire de la Bible Supplément,* ed. L. Pirot, A. Robert, H. Cazelles, and A. Feuillet. Paris: Letouzey, 1928–.
SE	*Studia Evangelica.* Texte und Untersuchungen. Berlin: Akademie-Verlag, 1959–82.
Sem	*Semeia*
SJT	*Scottish Journal of Theology*
SNTSMS	Society for New Testament Studies Monograph Series
SPCK	Society for the Propagation of Christian Knowledge
SS	Symposium Series
ST	*Studia Theologica*
Str-B	H. Strack and P. Billerbeck. *Kommentar zum Neuen Testament aus Talmud und Midrasch.* 6 vols. Munich: C. H. Beck, 1922–61.
SuppRivB	Supplementi alla Rivista Biblica
s.v.	sub voce
SVTQ	*St. Vladimir's Theological Quarterly*
Tanh	*Midrash Tanhuma*
Targ	Targum

TDNT	G. Kittel and G. Friedrich, eds., *Theological Dictionary of the New Testament.* 10 vols., Grand Rapids: Eerdmans, 1964–76.
Test	*Testament*
TOB	Traduction Oecuménique de la Bible
TT	*Theology Today*
TW	Theologie und Wirklichkeit
TynBul	*Tyndale Bulletin*
TZ	*Theologische Zeitschrift*
UBSGNT	*The Greek New Testament.* United Bible Societies.
WBC	Word Biblical Commentary
WMANT	Wissenschaftliche Monographien zum Alten und Neuen Testament
WUNT	Wissenschaftliche Untersuchungen zum Neuen Testament
ZGB	M. Zerwick, *Biblical Greek Illustration by Examples.* Rome: Biblical Institute Press, 1963.
ZNW	*Zeitschrift für die neutestamentliche Wissenschaft*
ZTK	*Zeitschrift für Theologie und Kirche*

Chapter One

Making God Known
John 13:1-38

¶ JOHN 13:1-38 forms part of a larger literary unity, a so-called last discourse (13:1—17:26), which is marked by a number of well-known literary tensions.[1] A scholar who has devoted great energy to the study of John 13-17, Fernando Segovia, once wrote: "Nowadays hardly any exegete would vigorously maintain that John 13:31—18:1 constitutes a literary unity as it stands."[2] If 13:1—17:26 as a whole presents literary problems for the interpreter, severe tensions are also found within John 13:1-38.[3] There appears to be a double interpreta-

---

[1] For a survey, see R. E. Brown, *The Gospel according to John* (2 vols.; AB 29, 29A; Garden City, N.Y.: Doubleday, 1966–70) 2:581–604. For attempts to resolve these difficulties, see F. F. Segovia, *Love Relationships in the Johannine Tradition: Agapē/Agapan in I John and the Fourth Gospel* (SBLDS 58, Chico: Scholars, 1982) 81–97; idem, *The Farewell of the Word: The Johannine Call to Abide* (Minneapolis. Fortress Press, 1991) 1–58; A. Dettwiler, *Die Gegenwart des Erhöhten. Eine exegetische Studie zu den johanneischen Abschiedsreden (Joh 13,31–16,33) unter besonderer Berücksichtigung ihres Relecture-Charakters* (FRLANT 169, Göttingen. Vandenhoeck & Ruprecht, 1995) 14–33.

[2] Segovia, *Love Relationships*, 82. See also M. Rodriguez Ruiz, *Der Missionsgedanke des Johannesevangeliums: Ein Beitrag zur johanneischen Soteriologie und Ekklesiologie* (FB 55; Wurzburg: Echter, 1987) 164. On John 13, see R. Schnackenburg, *The Gospel according to St John* (3 vols., HTCNT 4/1–3; London: Burns & Oates; New York: Crossroad, 1968–82) 3:7.

[3] See G. Richter, *Die Fusswaschung im Johannesevangelium: Geschichte und Deutung* (BU1; Regensburg: Pustet, 1967) 3–284, and the briefer synthesis of F. F. Segovia, "John 13:1-20. The Footwashing in the Johannine Tradition," *ZNW* 73 (1982) 31–37.

tion of the footwashing scene. The first of these, from vv. 6-11, speaks of the disciples having a part in Jesus' death. This interpretation has possible baptismal contacts, but the theme disappears in v. 12. Verses 12-20 encourage the imitation of Jesus. Judged as moralistic in tone, vv. 12-20 are often read as a later addition to an original reflection on Jesus' gift of himself to his disciples in love, and as an invitation that the disciples join him in the loving gift of themselves.[4] Many scholars accept that vv. 31-38 should be separated from the more narrative accounts of the footwashing and the gift of the morsel of vv. 1-30. The proclamation of the glorification of the Son of Man (vv. 31-32) is judged to be the beginning of the discourse proper.[5] Some scholars understand vv. 31-38 as the introduction to 13:31—14:31, the original form of the discourse,[6] while others see it as an introductory summary to the whole discourse in its final form.[7]

It is almost universally accepted that John 13:1—17:26 is a final collection of many traditions remembered and told in various times and situations throughout the life of the Johannine church.[8] A close

---

[4] For recent attempts to construct a source for vv. 1-20, see C. Niemand, *Die Fusswaschungerzahlung des Johannesevangeliums: Untersuchungen zu ihrer Entstehung und Uberlieferung im Urchristentum* (Studia Anselmiana 114; Rome: Pontificio Ateneo S. Anselmo, 1993) 81–256.

[5] Among many, see Segovia, *Love Relationships*, 136–79; M. J. J Menken, "The Translation of Ps 41.10 in John 13:18," *JSNT* 40 (1990) 75–76 n 19; D. F. Tolmie, *Jesus' Farewell to the Disciples. John 13:1–17.26 in Narratological Perspective* (BibIntS 12; Leiden: Brill, 1995) 28–29. X Léon-Dufour, *Lecture de l'Évangile selon Jean* (3 vols.; Parole de Dieu; Paris: Seuil, 1988–93) 3.23–24, argues that 13:1-32 is a unit which closes 13:1-30, and that the discourse proper begins with vv 33-38. See also I. de la Potterie, *La Vérité dans Saint Jean* (2 vols., AnBib 73, Rome: Biblical Institute Press, 1977) 1:249–53. G. Segalla, *Giovanni* (NVB; Rome: Edizioni Paoline, 1976) 362–63, reads 13:1-35 as a unit, and vv. 36-38 as a "brief introduction" to 14:1-31. See also C. H. Talbert, *Reading John: A Literary and Theological Commentary on the Fourth Gospel and the Johannine Epistles* (New York: Crossroad, 1992) 189–90.

[6] See, e g , Brown, *John*, 2:605–16.

[7] See, e.g., R. E Brown, *The Gospel according to John* (2 vols.; AB 29, 29A; Garden City, N Y. Doubleday, 1966–70) 449–53.

[8] Many argue that the final discourse (synchronic reading) cannot be understood without a prior discovery of the prehistory of its parts (diachronic reading). See, e.g., U. Schnelle, "Die Abschiedsreden im Johannesevangelium," *ZNW* 80 (1989) 64–65. But there is little or no consensus among those who claim to have uncovered the prehistory. Compare J. Schneider, "Die Abschiedsreden Jesu· Ein Beitrag zur Frage der Komposition von Johannes 13.31—17:26," in *Gott und die Gotter: Festgabe für E. Fascher* (Berlin: Evangelische Verlagsanstalt, 1958) 103–12, J. Becker, "Die Abschiedsreden Jesu im Johannesevangelium," *ZNW* 61 (1970) 215–46; J. Painter, "The Farewell Discourses and the History of Johannine Christianity," *NTS* 27 (1980–81) 525–43; J. Ph. Kaefer, "Les discours d'adieu en Jean 13.31—17:26," *NovT* 26 (1984) 251–82.

reading of the discourse in its present shape indicates that, on the basis of literary form alone, 13:1-30 (a narrative) and 17:1-26 (a prayer) stand apart. The remaining discourse is also marked by contradictions and tensions, highlighted by Jesus' words in 14:31. Themes in 14:1-31 are repeated in 16:4-33, with the material in chap. 16 restating chap. 14's themes of Jesus' departure, its motivation and its consequences.[9] The metaphor of the vine with its theme of abiding and Jesus' contrasting words on hatred and violence found in 15:1—16:3 are unique. Only Jesus speaks. He is never interrupted, as in chaps. 14 and 16, by questions and statements from the surrounding disciples. Thus, 15:1—16:3 appears to some as having little logical link with the discourses that now form chaps. 14 and 16. For many scholars, this section of the discourse reflects a collection of earlier discourses, and most see 15:1-17 and 15:18—16:4a as originally independent units.

A Johannine story of words and events that took place at a final meal (see 13:1-38), several discourses dealing with Jesus' departure, the future mission, sufferings and obligations of his disciples, the gift of the Paraclete (see 14:1—16:33), and a prayer of departure (see 17:1-26) had their own history in the storytelling of the Johannine community. A process of telling and retelling produced a Gospel that is thoroughly Johannine in all its parts.[10] Various elements from the recorded memories of the community are laid side by side to form 13:1—17:26 as we now have it. Segovia, once pessimistic about such a reading, can now see the need "to address the character of 13:31—16:33 as an artistic and strategic whole with a highly unified and coherent literary structure and development, unified and coherent strategic concerns and aims, and a distinctive rhetorical situation."[11] However obvious the seams (see especially 13:31-32; 14:31; 17:1), the

---

[9] See Brown, *John,* 2:589–91

[10] On the process of "Relecture," see Dettwiler, *Die Gegenwart,* 44–52, and especially the recent study of Dettwiler's *Doktorvater,* J Zumstein, "Der Prozess der Relecture in der johanneischen Literatur," *NTS* 42 (1996) 394–411. The Gospel as a whole has a unified style and language. See R. E. Brown, *The Gospel according to John* (2 vols.; AB 29, 29A; Garden City, N.Y.: Doubleday, 1966–70) 5–15, M. Hengel, *Die johanneische Frage: Ein Losungsversuch mit einem Beitrag zur Apokalypse von Jorg Frey* (WUNT 67; Tubingen: J C. B. Mohr 1993) 238–48.

[11] Segovia, *Farewell,* 284. On this change of "reading strategies," see F. F. Segovia, "The Tradition History of the Fourth Gospel," in R. A. Culpepper and C C. Black, eds., *Exploring the Gospel of John: In Honor of D. Moody Smith* (Louisville: Westminster John Knox Press, 1996) 178–89. C. C. Black, "'The Words That You Gave to Me I Have Given Them': The Grandeur of Johannine Rhetoric," in ibid., 224, suggests that this is not the case, but that "John 14–17 appears not to be a tightly argued exercise in formal logic but rather a ceremonial elaboration (13:1) of topics."

reader of 13:1—17:26 strives "even if unconsciously, to fit everything together in a consistent pattern."[12]

A FINAL DISCOURSE AND THE TESTAMENT TRADITION

There is an increasing interest in the shape and message of John 13:1—17:26 "as an artistic and strategic whole."[13] The recognition of the relevance of Israelite testamentary literature, roughly contemporary with the emergence of a Christian literature, has contributed to this interest.[14] The peculiarly Johannine final discourse has a function within the rhetoric of the Fourth Gospel that parallels a well-established Israelite literary form. The reader who emerges from 1:1—12:50 is prepared for the account of the end of Jesus' life.[15] The narrative has produced a reader not surprised to find Jesus gathering with his intimate disciples for a discourse, during which, in word and deed, he bequeaths to them his final testament. But the reader is also aware that Jesus' testament must continue and develop themes that have emerged during the story of his ministry.

The practice of placing a "farewell speech" on the lips of a great person approaching death was common in a number of religious writ-

[12] W. Iser, *The Implied Reader: Patterns of Communication in Prose Fiction from Bunyan to Beckett* (Baltimore: Johns Hopkins Univ. Press, 1978) 283. There is always the possibility that an author loses control of sources, abandons a rhetorical strategy, and leaves fragments scattered in an unrelated fashion. Although historical-critical scholarship has sometimes resorted to this hypothesis (outstandingly present in Bultmann's spectacular rearrangement of the traditional text [see R. Bultmann, *The Gospel of John: A Commentary* (trans. G. R. Beasley-Murray; Oxford: Blackwell, 1971) 457–61]), these are desperate measures, and should only be resorted to when all else fails. See R. Alter, *The Art of Biblical Narrative* (New York: Basic Books, 1981) 131–54, and M. Sternberg, *The Poetics of Biblical Narrative: Ideological Literature and the Drama of Reading* (ILBS; Bloomington: Indiana Univ. Press, 1985) 7–23, on what Alter calls "composite artistry."

[13] Segovia shares my conviction that 13:1—17:26 is "a coherent and self-contained narrative section of the Gospel," and a "clear example of a farewell type scene." See *Farewell*, 1–24. The citations are from 20.

[14] For more detailed studies, see J. Becker, *Das Evangelium des Johannes* (2 vols.; OTK 4/1–2; Gutersloh: Gerd Mohn; Wurzburg: Echter, 1979–81) 2.440–46; W. S. Kurz, *Farewell Addresses in the New Testament* (Zacchaeus Studies: New Testament; Collegeville, Minn.: Liturgical Press, 1990) 9–32, 71–120; E Cortès, *Los Discursos de Adiós de Gen 49 a Jn 13–17* (Colectanea San Paciano 23; Barcelona: Herder, 1976); E. Bammel, "The Farewell Discourse of the Evangelist John and Its Jewish Heritage," *TynBul* 44 (1993) 103–16, Segovia, *Farewell*, 2–20, and Dettwiler, *Die Gegenwart,* 14–33.

[15] See F J. Moloney, *Signs and Shadows: Reading John 5–12* (Minneapolis: Fortress Press, 1996) 202–9.

ings from the first three centuries of the Christian era[16] and was already widespread in the biblical literature. Farewell speeches, or testaments, are found in Gen 47-50 (Jacob), Deut 31-34 (Moses), Josh 23-24 (Joshua), 1 Kgs 2:1-10 (David), Tob 14:3-11 (Tobit), and in 1 Macc 2:49-70 (Mattathias). In the New Testament, outside the Fourth Gospel, Jesus delivers a farewell speech in Luke 22:14-38; Paul, in Acts 20:17-35; and Peter, in 2 Peter 1:12-15. At 13:1-2 Jesus gathers at table with "his own" for a final encounter. The reader of the Fourth Gospel is about to share in a testament, which in many ways parallels contemporary testaments popularly associated with the last moments of great figures from Israel's past. Care must be taken however, in drawing parallels across various testaments. The Israelite testaments were produced at different times and places, from the second century B C.E. (e.g., *Testament of the Twelve Patriarchs*) till the third century C.E. (e.g., *Testament of Solomon*) or even later (parts of the *Testament of Adam*), and have come to us in interpolated translations. As such, the Jewish testaments are not unified by a discrete literary model, yet "one can discern among them a loose format."[17] The following features are regularly found in the testament tradition.

1. *Prediction of death and departure.* The speech is understood by the figure who is about to depart as his "farewell" to his disciples. The setting for these testaments is sometimes a meal (see *Testament of Naphtali* 1:2-5; 9:2).[18] There is some indication or prediction of an oncoming death in all the testaments. In some cases, death is unexpected (*Testament of Levi* 1:2; *Testament of Naphtali* 1:2-4; *Testament of Asher* 1:2). Whether expected because of extreme old age, or unexpected, the prediction of death and departure is the reason for the gathering that forms the background to

---

[16] For Greco-Roman texts, see W. S. Kurz, "Luke 22:14-38 and Greco-Roman and Biblical Farewell Addresses," *JBL* 104 (1985) 253-55. For a collection of Jewish texts, with introductions and in English translation, see J. H. Charlesworth, ed., *The Old Testament Pseudepigrapha* (2 vols.; London: Darton, Longman & Todd, 1983) 1:773-995. On communal meals in the ancient schools, see R. A. Culpepper, *The Johannine-School Hypothesis Based on an Investigation of the Nature of Ancient Schools* (SBLDS 26; Missoula, Mont.: Scholars, 1975) 78; (Plato and the Academy), 167-68, (Qumran, 192-94; (Hillel), 225-26; (Jesus), and the summary on 250-52. On communal meals in the Johannine School, see 279.
[17] Charlesworth, *Pseudepigrapha*, 1:773.
[18] Bammel, "The Farewell Discourse," 106-7, regards the meal setting in John 13 as more influenced by Greek background than by the Jewish testaments. See also B. Witherington III, *John's Wisdom: A Commentary on the Fourth Gospel* (Louisville: Westminster/John Knox, 1995) 231-34.

the testament (*Testament of Reuben* 1:3-4; *Testament of Levi* 1:2; *Testament of Dan* 2:1; *Testament of Moses* 1:15).

2. *Predictions of future attacks on the dying leader's disciples.* This feature is also fundamental to the structure of the testaments. One of the motivations for the testament is to forewarn disciples that they are in danger (*Testament of Simeon* 3:1-2; *Testament of Gad* 4:1-7). There are frequent references in the testaments to the future failings of the disciples generally associated with the end time (see, e.g., *Testament of Levi* 4:1; 10:1-5; 14:1-8; *Testament of Isacchar* 6:1-4; *Testament of Dan* 5:7-8; *Testament of Naphtali* 4:1-5), but there are also references to present sinfulness (see *Testament of Judah* 23:1).

3. *An exhortation to ideal behavior.* The testaments devote attention to the difficulties to be endured in the future. They are to be met with behavior that will both protect the members of the group around the patriarch and help them to overcome their difficulties. These exhortations are always closely linked to the narrative of the hero's experience, both sinful and virtuous. It is the life and experience of the dying figure that serve as the basis for the instruction of the surrounding disciples. All of the testaments found in the *Testament of the Twelve Patriarchs* are highlighted by this feature (see, e.g., *Testament of Reuben* 4:1, *Testament of Judah* 14:1; *Testament of Zebulon* 5:1-5; *Testament of Joseph* 18:1-4; *Testament of Benjamin* 3:1-3). The later *Testament of Job* is predominantly a midrashic expansion of the story of Job told for the edification of the bystanders.[19]

4. *A final commission.* The departing hero gives instructions to his disciples concerning their reconstitution after his departure. Central to these instructions is the command to love one another (see *Testament of Reuben* 6:9; *Testament of Simeon* 4:7; *Testament of Zebulon* 5:5; *Testament of Gad* 6:1-7; 7:7; *Testament of Joseph* 17:1-8).[20] Various further directions are given to the disciples that they might successfully survive the many difficulties they must face (see *Testament of Levi* 18:1-14; *Testament of Judah* 24:1—25:5; *Testament of Dan* 5:7-13; *Testament of Naphtali* 8:1-8; *Testament of Benjamin* 10:2-11).

5. *An affirmation and a renewal of the never-failing covenant promises of God.* This understanding of God's never-failing presence to the chosen people undergirds much of the narrative, exhortation,

[19] See Bammel, "The Farewell Discourse," 111–12, for this feature of the testaments.
[20] See J. F. Randall, "The Theme of Unity in John 17," *ETL* 41 (1965) 377–78

and praise of all the testaments. It is understandably expressed strongly and explicitly in the *Testament of Moses* (see 1:8-9; 3:9; 4:2-6; 12:7-13).[21]

6. *A closing doxology.* Although not present in the *Testament of the Twelve Patriarchs,* all of which close with notice of the patriarch's death and burial, other testaments close with a brief prayer of praise, rendering glory to God (see *Testament of Job* 43:1-17; *Testament of Isaac* 8:6-7; *Testament of Jacob* 8:6-9).

The reader of the Fourth Gospel will not be surprised to find reminiscences of a well-known testament tradition as Jesus' life story draws to an end. But, as the testaments were determined by biblical and popular traditions that had gathered around the dying patriarch, so will John 13:1—17:26 be determined by the Johannine traditions that surrounded the life, and especially the death, of Jesus of Nazareth.[22]

THE SHAPE OF THE NARRATIVE

After the reflections of the narrator (see 12:37-43) and Jesus (see 12:44-50), which conclude the Johannine account of the public ministry, 13:1 points the narrative in a new direction. Jesus is alone with his disciples in the upper room. It is "the most significant transition in the Gospel, introducing not only the scene of the footwashing but the entire second half of the Gospel."[23] The material in vv. 31-38, widely regarded as part of the first discourse (13:31—14:31), is not only discourse. There is also the report of an encounter between Simon Peter and Jesus in vv. 36-38, where the future denials of Simon Peter are foretold. This passage matches the similar earlier prophecies that told of Judas' betrayal of Jesus (vv. 10-11, 21-22). It also reminds the reader

---

[21] Although he does not consider the extra-biblical Jewish testaments (on these, see the extensive treatment [including a study of the Targums on Gen 49 and Deut 33] of Cortès, *Los Discursos,* 106–384), this feature of the farewell genre has been identified and described by Kurz, "Luke 22:14-38," 251–68. Especially useful is the chart of elements common to Greco-Roman, Old Testament and New Testament testaments, on 262–63.

[22] For Witherington, *John,* 245–46, the testament is strongly influenced by the Johannine understanding of Jesus as a Jewish sage. See also idem, *Jesus the Sage: The Pilgrimage of Wisdom* (Minneapolis: Fortress Press, 1994) 378–79.

[23] R. A. Culpepper, "The Johannine *hypodeigma:* A Reading of John 13:1-38," *Sem* 53 (1991) 135. On the narrative-chronological sequence of 12:1-50 and 13:1—19:41, see S. van Tilborg, *Imaginative Love in John* (BibIntS 2; Leiden: E. J. Brill, 1993) 128–30.

of Peter's earlier misunderstanding of Jesus' gesture in the footwashing (see vv. 6-9).[24]

A feature of 13:1-38 is the regular appearance of the Johannine expression: "Amen, amen, I say to you" (see vv. 16, 20, 21, 38). This expression occurs only in the Fourth Gospel, where it appears twenty-four times.[25] It is found in 13:1-38 more times (four uses) than in any other chapter of the Gospel, and it occurs only three times in the rest of the last discourse (14:12; 16:20, 23).[26] The second reference to Judas' betrayal (v. 21) opens with this Johannine expression, while the prophecy of Peter's denials closes with it (v. 38). The use of this Johannine expression at the beginning and end of the betrayal and denial prophecies (vv. 21-38) suggests that vv. 31-38 are more closely associated with 13:1-30 than with the discourses in chaps. 14–16. The theme of the failure of both Judas and Peter plays no further role in the discourse proper.[27]

Attention to the strategic positioning of double "amen" sayings indicates the possibility of the following literary shape:

1. *Verses 1-17:* This section is formed by the narrative of the footwashing and the discussions that surround that narrative. It features narrator's comments (see vv. 1-5), dialogue between Jesus

---

[24] For this suggestion, see G. Ferraro, "'Pneuma' in Giov. 13,21," *RivBib* 28 (1980) 190–93.

[25] The double use of the "amen" is unique to John. "Amen, I say to you" is found in the Synoptic Gospels, especially in Matthew (31 times). On the Johannine expression, see de la Potterie, *La Vérité,* 1:57–58.

[26] The double "amen" will play a structural role wherever it appears in 13:1—17:26. See Y. Simoens, *La gloire d'aimer. Structures stylistiques et interprétatives dans la Discours de la Cène (Jn 13–17)* (AnBib 90; Rome: Biblical Institute Press, 1981) 115–29, 151–73. Its importance is noted by J. Neugebauer, *Die eschatologischen Aussagen in den johanneischen Abschiedsreden: Eine Untersuchung zu Johannes 13–17* (BWANT 140; Stuttgart: Kohlhammer, 1995) 74, but inconsistently applied to the text. On John 13:1-38 as a literary unit, see A Niccaci, "L'unità letteraria di Gv 13,1–38," *EuntD* 29 (1976) 291–323; D. Cancian, *Nuovo Commandamento Nuova Alleanza Eucaristia nell'interpretazione del capitolo 13 del Vangelo di Giovanni* (Collevalenza: Edizione "L'Amore Misericordioso," 1978) 63–72; F. Manns, *L'Evangile de Jean à la lumière du Judaïsme* (SBFA 33; Jerusalem: Franciscan Printing Press, 1991) 321–37; K. T. Kleinknecht, "Johannes 13, die Synoptiker und die 'Methode' der johanneischen Evangelienuberlieferung," *ZTK* 82 (1985) 361–88; Culpepper, "The Johannine *hypodeigma*," 133–52. For H. A. Lombard and W. H. Oliver, "A Working Supper in Jerusalem. John 13:1-38 Introduces Jesus' Farewell Discourses," *Neot* 25 (1991) 357–78, 13:1-38 forms a unit and contains an introduction to the themes of the subsequent discourses. G. Mlakuzhyil, *The Christological Literary Structure of the Fourth Gospel* (AnBib 117; Rome: Biblical Institute Press, 1987) 221–23, regards vv. 31-38 as a bridge, closing vv. 1-30 and opening 14:1-31.

[27] See also Culpepper, "The Johannine *hypodeigma*," 133–34.

and Peter (vv. 6-9), and Jesus' words on Judas (vv. 10-11) in the midst of the failure and ignorance of the disciples. The section concludes with the double "amen" in vv. 16-17.

2. *Verses 18-20:* This section contains only words of Jesus, directed to the disciples, which may serve as the literary center of 13:1-38. It concludes with the double "amen" in v. 20.

3. *Verses 21-38:* Returning to the same form as vv. 1-17, narrative and dialogue reappear. The narrative tells of Jesus' gift of the morsel in the midst of the disciples' questions and discussion. The context of betrayal and denial intensifies (vv. 21-30, 36-38). This section opens and closes with a double "amen" in v. 21 and v. 38.

In vv. 1-17 the double "amen" appears in v. 16, introducing two statements from Jesus, one concerning the relationship between servant and master (v. 16) and another about knowing and doing (v. 17). The reader senses closure, as themes from the narrator's introduction in vv. 1-5 return. Vv. 1-5 play upon the themes of Jesus and "his own," his "knowing," and his "doing": "When Jesus *knew* that his hour had come. . . . Having loved *his own* who were in the world, he loved them to the end. . . . Jesus, *knowing* that the Father had given all things into his hands . . . *rose* from the supper, *laid aside* his garments, and *girded himself* with a towel." Jesus' "knowing" that his hour had come and that the Father had given all things into his hands led to an active "doing": He loved his disciples and washed their feet.[28] The reader learns from vv. 1-5 that Jesus' "knowing" and "doing" touch the disciples' lives. The narrative of Jesus washing his disciples' feet and calling them to have part with him follows. At the close of the section, after the solemn double "amen," Jesus tells the disciples that, in their relationship to him as his servants and sent ones (v. 16), they are called to repeat exactly what "the master" has done:[29]

If you *know* THESE THINGS,
blessed are you
if you *do* THESE THINGS (v. 17).[30]

[28] The "knowledge" of Jesus is central to the message of 13:1-38. See Culpepper, "The Johannine *hypodeigma,*" 134–37; R. H. Lightfoot, *St John's Gospel* (ed. C F. Evans, Oxford: Oxford Univ. Press, 1956) 263–64.

[29] See also Talbert, *Reading John,* 193–94; B. G. Schuchard, *Scripture Within Scripture: The Interrelationship of Form and Function in the Explicit Old Testament Citations in the Gospel of John* (SBLDS 133; Atlanta. Scholars, 1992) 110–11.

[30] This translation reflects the Greek: *ei TAUTA oidate makarioi este ean poiēte AUTA.*

The verb "to know" appears again in v. 18, but another theme emerges. Not only is Jesus' knowledge stressed, but also the fact that he has "chosen" his disciples. The theme of Jesus choosing disciples is developed in v. 20: "He who receives any one whom I send receives me." The "chosen ones" are described as "any one whom I send." Jesus both chooses (v. 18) and sends (v. 20) his disciples. The closely linked themes of being chosen and being sent highlight the beginning and the end of vv. 18-20, marked by the use of the double "amen" in v. 20.[31] The double "amen" both opens and closes vv. 21-38. The section is also framed by Jesus' prophecies concerning the failure of members of his innermost circle of friends, the disciples with whom he is sharing his table: Judas (vv. 21-30) and Peter (vv. 36-38). The theme of the gift of the morsel winds through the passage dealing with the betrayal of Judas. On receiving the morsel, Judas leaves the upper room, and the Passion is set in motion. This is the significance of the introduction to Jesus' exultation in v. 31a: "When he had gone out. . . ." The action of Judas is crucial to an understanding of the glorification of Jesus through the cross. One should not make a major break in the narrative between Judas' exit into the night in v. 30 and Jesus' words in vv. 31-32. The reference to Judas in v. 31a (*hote oun exēlthen*) is there because the author wants the reader to link the two. The use of *oun* must be given its full weight.[32] John 13:1-38 thus unfolds as follows:

Part One: The Footwashing (vv. 1-17)
   a. Verses 1-5:   The narrator indicates the perfection of Jesus' love for his own (v. 1), but this is followed immediately by reference to Judas' betrayal of Jesus (v. 2), which does not deter Jesus from going ahead with his preparations for the footwashing. Love and knowledge flow into action (vv. 3-5).
   b. Verses 6-11:   A dialogue between Peter and Jesus (vv. 6-10b) leads to the first public hint of Judas' betrayal of Jesus (vv. 10c-11).
   c. Verses 12-17:   Jesus provides in word and deed the gift of his example. The lifestyle of Jesus (vv. 1-5) is now demanded of the disciple (vv. 16-17).

---

[31] The use of the double "amen" suggests that vv 18-20 form the center of the passage, and much depends on the relationship between the *pantōn humōn* and the *tinas* of v. 18ab. In my interpretation Jesus' words "I know whom I have chosen" refer to the disciples at the table who are involved in the raising of the heel. Jesus may not be referring to all of them (*pantōn humōn*) but he is referring to some (*tinas*) whom he has chosen. The singular of v. 18d is determined by the use of the OT quotation.

[32] See BDF, para 451

Part Two: To Make God Known (vv. 18-20)
Jesus tells of his knowledge of these fragile disciples whom he has
chosen (v. 18) and the identity between himself, who *sends,* and these
same disciples who are his *sent ones* (v. 20). Between these two affir-
mations he informs his disciples that he is telling them these things
before they happen so that when they do happen, they might believe
that he is the revelation of God (v. 19: *hina pisteusēte hotan genētai hoti
egō eimi*).

Part Three: The Gift of the Morsel (vv. 21-38)
   a. Verses 21-25: Jesus is troubled in spirit and he gives witness (v.
21a), but this is followed immediately by reference to the betrayal (vv.
21b-25).
   b. Verses 26-30: A dialogue between Judas and Jesus (vv. 26-27)
leads to Jesus' unequivocal reference to Judas' betrayal (vv. 28-30).
   c. Verses 31-38: Jesus teaches, in word and deed, the new commandment of love. As 13:1-38 opened with reference to Judas' betrayal of Jesus (see v. 2), it closes with reference to the future denials
of Peter (see vv. 36-38).

   The narratives of vv. 1-17 and vv. 21-38 stress the love, knowledge,
and action of Jesus as he gives himself in symbolic gestures to his
disciples in the midst of their failure: ignorance, betrayal, and denial.
The centerpiece of the narrative, vv. 18-20, is made up entirely of Jesus' words, highlighting the themes of his knowledge of his own, the
traitor, and the choosing and sending of the disciples.

READING THE NARRATIVE

1. The Footwashing (13:1-17)
On arrival at 13:1, the reader is asking important questions: How is it
possible that crucifixion can be glorification, gathering, the revelation
of God? The narrator opens the account of Jesus' final encounter with
his disciples with words that begin to answer those questions: On the
eve of Passover, Jesus, knowing that the hour has come to depart from
this world to the Father, loves his own to the very end (13:1). Ulrich
Busse has commented, "In 13:1 a short, vivid summary is found of
what the reader actually can and should know about the passion of
Jesus."[33] But this demands too much of the reader. Further explanation is necessary, as the link between Jesus' consummate love for "his

---

[33] U. Busse, "The Beloved Disciple," *Skrif en Kerk* 15 (1994) 220.

own" and his departure from this world to the Father has no prece-
dent in the story.

a. Verses 1-5: Jesus' Knowledge, Love, and Action   The reader knows that
"the hour," which throughout the public ministry had not yet come
(see 2:4; 7:30; 8:20), has now arrived, and that it is associated with the
celebration of the Passover (see 11:55-57; 12:20-24, 27-33).[34] There
have been two "times" running through the story: the feasts of "the
Jews" (see 2:13, 23; 4:45; 5:1, 9; 6:4; 7:2; 10:22; 11:55-57; 12:1) and
"the hour" of Jesus, determined by God (2:4; 4:21, 23; 7:30; 8:20;
12:23, 27). Now they coalesce: There is a feast of "the Jews" that is
also the hour of Jesus. "The hour" is to be a moment when Jesus will
depart from the sphere of the everyday story of human events.[35] Earlier, more veiled comments about Jesus' going away (see 7:32-36; 8:14,
21-27) are now made more explicit for the reader. The one who has
been sent by the Father (see 3:17, 34; 4:34; 5:23-24, 30, 36, 37; 6:38-
39, 44, 57; 7:16, 28, 29, 33; 8:16, 18, 26, 29, 42; 9:4; 10:36; 11:42) will
go back to the Father. However, during the course of the ministry,
Jesus has gathered disciples, a group of people who can be called "his
own" (*hoi idioi;* see also 1:11-12; 10:3, 4, 12). The reader has learned
from chaps. 11–12 that Jesus' "going away" through death is not for
himself. This theme is repeated here, but the introduction of the use
of the verb *agapaō* to describe his self-gift for others has only been
hinted at earlier in the narrative (see 3:16-17; 10:14-18). Jesus' hour is
to be a supreme demonstration of his love for his own. The use of the
expression *eis telos* is open to two meanings, and both are intended.
On the one hand, the expression has a *chronological* significance: Jesus
loved his own until the end of his life (*eis telos*). It is in his death
that love can be seen. On the other hand, the same expression has a
qualitative sense: that he loved them in a consummate fashion, in a
way that surpassed all imaginable loving, the perfection of love (*eis
telos*). The marriage of both meanings produces one of the major
themes for the rest of the story: Jesus' death makes known his love for
his own and thus makes God known (see 3:16-17).[36]

[34] On the use of the Passover, see T. Knoppler, *Die theologia crucis des Johannesevangeliums: Das Verstandnis des Todes Jesu im Rahmen der johanneischen Inkarnations- und Erhohungschristologie* (WMANT 69; Neukirchen-Vluyn: Neukirchener Verlag, 1994) 119–21.

[35] The Johannine use of the expression *kosmos* is open to several interpretations. On
this, see F. J. Moloney, *Belief in the Word: Reading John 1–4* (Minneapolis: Fortress Press,
1993) 37 Here it has a neutral meaning: the time and place of human activity.

[36] See Brown, *John,* 2:550; B. Lindars, *The Gospel of John* (NCB, London: Oliphants,
1972) 448. It is not only temporal, as Witherington, *John,* 235–36, claims.

But all of this is said in the past tense: Jesus knew (*eidōs*) . . . loved (*agapēsas*) his own . . . and loved (*ēgapēsen*) them to the end. The narrator states the program for both chap. 13 and the rest of the Gospel: Jesus' death was the hour of his passing over to the Father and the moment of a consummate act of loving self-gift.[37] The second half of the Gospel (chaps. 13–20) begins in a parallel way to the opening of the first half (chaps. 1–12), with a statement of what Jesus is and does. Both 13:1 and 1:1-18 inform the reader of *what* Jesus was and did, but the reader needs to know *how* Jesus passed over to the Father, loving his own "to the end" (*eis telos*).[38] Within the context of the intimacy of a supper, the reader is informed of the design of the devil: Judas will betray Jesus (v. 2).[39] The narrator has set the scene by informing the reader of two designs: the design of God in and through Jesus' love for his own, and the design of Satan that one of these would betray Jesus. This information does not come as a surprise to the reader (see 6:71; 12:4-6) but, apart from Jesus, the characters in the story are unaware of the betrayal.

Jesus, acting out of his union with the Father, knowing both his origin and his destiny, moves into action (v. 3). After all that has been said and done throughout the public ministry (1:19—12:50), the reader might expect the disciples to be aware of these truths, but such does not appear to be the case. Jesus' origins and destiny were spelled out as programmatic for the reader in 1:1-18 and were stated and re-stated many times, especially during his debates with the Jews during their feasts (5:1—10:42).[40] They have proved to be the stumbling block for a proper understanding of Jesus throughout the narrative. The memory of this relentless conflict, which led to the decision that Jesus must die for the nation and gather into one the children of God scattered abroad (11:49-53), enhances the dramatic setting of the Pass-

---

[37] The aorist tense should be taken as gnomic. See BDF, para. 333.

[38] For the suggestion that 13:1-3 serves as a "minor prologue" to the Book of the Passion, see W. K. Grossouw, "A Note on John XIII 1–3," *NovT* 8 (1966) 124–31

[39] Reading the Semitic expression "to put in mind" as "to make up one's mind" (*bebléketos eis tēn kardian; see 1 Sam 29:10; Job 22:22*), and applying it to Satan, not Judas Thus, v. 2 reads: "The devil had already made up his mind that Judas would betray him (Jesus)." See E. Delebecque, *Évangile de Jean: Text Traduit et Annoté* (CahRB 23; Paris: Gabalda, 1987) 183.

[40] As throughout this study, I will continue to place "the Jews" in quotations to indicate that "the Jews" are not the Jewish people, but one side of a christological debate One must "recognise in these hot-tempered exchanges the type of family row in which the participants face one another across the room of a house which all have shared and all call home" (J. Ashton, *Understanding the Fourth Gospel* [Oxford: Clarendon Press, 1991] 151).

over, which is "the hour," Jesus' passing over to the Father, and a consummate and final act of love (see v. 1). Jesus rises from the table, prepares himself to act as a servant, and begins washing his disciples' feet (vv. 4-5).[41] Jesus' knowledge (v. 1), even of his betrayer (vv. 2-3), and his love for "his own" (v. 1), are expressed through actions (vv. 4-5).

b. *Verses 6-11: Jesus and Peter*   The dialogue between Simon Peter and Jesus opens with Simon Peter's objection to Jesus' washing his feet (v. 6). However incongruous Jesus' actions may appear, the information already provided for the reader by the narrator in vv. 1-5 links Jesus' action with "the hour" of the departure (v. 1a), Jesus' consummate love for his own (v. 1b), the oneness of knowledge that exists between the Father and Jesus, and Jesus' subsequent knowledge that everything has been given into his hands by the Father (v. 3). The footwashing is part of God's design for Jesus, and Simon Peter's objections indicate that he is imposing his understanding on Jesus' actions. There is a lack of openness to the revelation of God's ways in Jesus' words and deeds. Jesus' response balances Simon Peter's ignorance in the "now" of story time against the "afterward" of plotted time, when he will understand. Something will happen between "now" and "afterward" that will change Simon Peter. A gap has been created, but the reader has been provided with sufficient information to suspect that "the hour" and Jesus' loving his own to the end (*eis telos*, see v. 1) are part of the intervening events.

The conflict between Jesus and Peter deepens as the latter refuses to allow Jesus to wash his feet (v. 8a). Jesus' warning response connects the footwashing with the hour of Jesus' consummate loving. What is at stake is "having part" with Jesus (v. 8b: *ouk echeis meros met'emou*). The Christian reader of the Johannine story recognizes a veiled reference to the practice of baptism in the early church.[42] The author is

---

[41] Culpepper, "The Johannine *hypodeigma*," 137, rightly points to contacts between Jesus' laying aside of his garments (v. 4: *tithēsin*) with other uses of the verb for the Good Shepherd (see 10:11, 15, 17, 18). Similarly, the verb describing his taking up of his clothes (v 12 *elaben*) is used for the Good Shepherd's taking up his life again (see 10:17, 18). See also C R. Koester, *Symbolism in the Fourth Gospel: Meaning, Mystery, Community* (Minneapolis· Fortress Press, 1995) 10–11, and J. D. G. Dunn, "The Washing of Disciples' Feet in John 13:1-20," *ZNW* 61 (1970) 248.

[42] See de Boer, *Johannine Perspectives on the Death of Jesus* (CEBT 17; Kampen: Kok Pharos, 1996) 283–92, for a stong emphasis on the baptism theme. It reflects de Boer's third stage in the community's growth Baptism "removes a disciple from jeopardy, from the danger of sin and the devil "

not concerned with the rite, but with the relationship baptism has with Jesus' death (see Rom 6:3). To "have part with Jesus" through washing also means to be part of the self-giving love that will bring Jesus' life to an end (see v. 1) and is being symbolically anticipated in the footwashing (v. 8). Peter's desire to "have part" in this way reflects his false understanding of the ritual of washing, as if the number of parts of the body mattered (v. 9). It leads to Jesus' further words on the privileges of those who have bathed[43] and thus have no further need of washing.[44] Jesus' knowledge, which flows from his union with the Father and the Father's design (see v. 3), extends to a knowledge of who will betray him (vv. 10-11). In the midst of ignorance (v. 6), misunderstanding (vv. 8-9), and the threat of betrayal (vv. 10-11), Jesus indicates the depths of his love for his own by washing their feet. The explanatory remark of the narrator in v. 11 insists on Jesus' knowledge of the betrayer and gives the reader privileged "inside information," while the disciples struggle with their misunderstanding. The recipients of the footwashing, a symbolic action that reveals Jesus' limitless love for his own, are ignorant disciples, one of whom Jesus knows will betray him.

c. *Verses 12-17: A New Example: Disciples Must Know, Love, and Act*
Despite the apparent contradiction between Jesus' words on Peter's lack of understanding in v. 7 and his question concerning the disciples' understanding in v. 12, there is no break in the narrative at v. 12. There is a unity of place, characters, and theme across vv. 1-17. Peter cannot, as yet, understand the link between Jesus' action of washing his disciples' feet and his unconditional love for them (v. 7). Jesus' interrogation concerning the disciples' understanding of what he has done for them is of a different order. It is closely linked to the footwashing, which has just been reported, but Jesus' question looks

---

[43] In v. 10a the expression *ho leloumenos* (in contrast to the use of *nipsasthai* in v. 10b, which means a partial washing) means a total immersion and is a further hint of both Baptism and the association of the disciple with the death of Jesus. See Schnackenburg, *St John*, 3.21-22; A. J. Hultgren, "The Johannine Footwashing (13.1-11) as Symbol of Eschatological Hospitality," *NTS* 28 (1982) 544

[44] The *ei mē tous podas nipsasthai* of v. 10b was added by later copyists to solve the problem of further forgiveness of sin after baptism. See F. J. Moloney, *The Johannine Son of Man* (2d ed.; BibScRel 14; Rome: LAS, 1978), 192–93. Recent scholarship has questioned this. See, e.g., J. C. Thomas, *Footwashing in John 13 and the Johannine Community* (JSNTSS 61; Sheffield: JSOT Press, 1991) 19–25, C. Niemand, *Die Fusswaschungerzahlung*, 252–56. I remain convinced by P. Grelot, "L'interprétation pénitentielle du lavement des pieds," in *L'homme devant Dieu: Mélanges H. de Lubac* (2 vols., Paris Aubier, 1963) 1:75–91.

away from the symbol of his self-gift for them toward his new example, which reverses established patterns of behavior. A link exists
between Jesus' question to his disciples in v. 12 and Peter's question
to Jesus in v. 6. Peter understood that accepted practice was being
subverted, and he objected to this subversion. However, his objections
have been overcome, and this is what Jesus points out to his disciples
in the question of v. 12, which he answers in vv. 13-14. The Teacher
and Lord has washed their feet (v. 13).

Jesus pursues his program of instruction through word and deed.
The disciples may have witnessed the footwashing and taken part in
it, but even Simon Peter's enthusiastic acceptance of Jesus' warnings
(see vv. 8b-9) is not motivated by a proper understanding of Jesus'
actions. More instruction is needed so that their correct understanding of their Teacher and Lord might be lived in a way that shows what
it means to have Jesus as Teacher and Lord (v. 13). Jesus' action is
recalled as he tells the disciples that they are to repeat among themselves what he has done for them (vv. 14-15). Whatever may have
been the historical and ritual background to this instruction,[45] within
its present literary context, Jesus' instruction is a call to his disciples
to repeat in their lives what he has done for them. He has given them
the example of a loving gift of self in love, symbolized in the footwashing, which they must now repeat (v. 15). The theme of death is
caught up in the author's use of the hapax legomenon, *hypodeigma*
("example"). This term is found in well-known Jewish texts (see LXX 2
Macc 6:28; 4 Macc 17:22-23; Sirach 44:16) associated with exemplary
death. Jesus is not exhorting his disciples to better moral performance,
but to imitate his self-gift. "Jesus' death . . . as it is here interpreted
through the footwashing, is the norm of life and conduct for the believing community."[46] The reader knows that the command to lose

[45] See the possibilities canvassed by Thomas, *Footwashing*, 126–185, who associates
footwashing with the forgiveness of sins in the Johannine community, and Niemand,
Die Fusswaschungerzahlung, 320–402, who argues that the footwashing (found in vv. 9,
10abc) reflects a discussion in the early Church over the need for a partial or full initia-
tion rite for ex-disciples of the Baptist who became Christians.

[46] Culpepper, "The Johannine *hypodeigma*," 144. The association of the footwashing
with the death of Jesus has long been proposed, although the connection has been
made in different ways. See, e.g., J. Beutler, "Die Heilsbedeutung des Todes Jesu im
Johannesevangelium nach Johannes 13,1-20," in K. Kertelge, ed., *Der Tod Jesu: Deutungen im Neuen Testament* (Quaestiones Disputatae 74; Freiburg; Herder, 1976) 188–204;
J. A. T. Robinson, "The Significance of the Footwashing," in *Twelve More New Testament
Studies* (London: SCM, 1984) 77–80; Dunn, "The Washing," 247–52, and Koester, *Symbolism*, 111–18. Against, among many, Schnackenburg, *St John*, 3:23, who claims that
the link between the footwashing and the death of Jesus in vv. 6-11 disappears in
vv. 12-17.

oneself in loving self-gift unto death, in imitation of the *hypodeigma* of Jesus, has been ritualized in baptism. Baptism, a summons to total self-gift in love, repeats the example given by Jesus, which takes place within the Christian community. The passage is not "about baptism," but presupposes the ritual within the life of the Johannine community (see 3:5; 19:34),[47] as the Johannine Christians are called to do as Jesus has done for them (v. 15). Entrance into the Johannine community meant taking the risk of a commitment to love even if it led to death.[48]

The first section of Jesus' brief discourse draws to a close with the use of "Amen, amen, I say to you" in v. 16. This section of the narrative began with the narrator's insistence that Jesus' *knowledge* flowed into *action* (see vv. 1-5). The disciples are to *know* certain things, and to *do* certain things. The footwashing is not an end in itself, but an instruction of servants by the master, the sent ones by the one who sent them. They must maintain their place as servants, followers, and sent ones of the master and the one who sent them (v. 16). This means that blessedness can be theirs (v. 17b: *makarioi este*), but only by *knowing* the things Jesus has said and done (v. 17a: *ei tauta oidate*), and by *doing* them (v. 17c: *ean poiēte auta*). The reader experiences a sense of closure on arrival at vv. 16-17, which look back across what has been done and said so far. As the knowledge and love of Jesus flowed into action (vv. 1-5), so must the knowledge and love of the disciple flow into action. Therein lies blessedness (v. 17).

2. To Make God Known (13:18-20)

The reader is aware that Jesus knows a great deal about his followers: He knows that one of them will betray him (v. 10), and he knows the identity of the betrayer (v. 11). He also knows that a change of heart between the failure of Peter's "now" will lead to understanding "afterward" (v. 7). This knowledge makes his choosing of *these* disciples surprising. Why choose disciples who are ignorant, who do not understand, and who are betrayers? It is so that Scripture might be fulfilled:

---

[47] See F. J. Moloney, "When is John Talking about Sacraments?" *AusBR* 30 (1982) 10–33. See also R. H. Lightfoot, *St. John* 261–62, C. K. Barrett, "Sacraments," in *Essays on John* (London: SPCK, 1982) 80–97, D Rensberger, *Johannine Faith and Liberating Community* (Philadelphia: Westminster Press, 1988) 64–86, and the important remarks of D. E. Aune, *The Cultic Setting of Realized Eschatology in Early Christianity* (NovTSup 28; Leiden: Brill, 1972) 16–18, on the need for a proper understanding of baptism and Eucharist in the early centuries.

[48] See Culpepper, "The Johannine *hypodeigma*," 144 See also H. Weiss, "Footwashing in the Johannine Community," *NovT* 41 (1979) 298–325; Dettwiler, *Die Gegenwart*, 68–74.

One of the people who shares Jesus' table will strike at him (v. 18b; see Ps 41:10). Jesus informs his disciples of a logic that defies all human logic *before* the events foretold by the Scriptures take place so that when they do take place, the disciples might come to know and believe that Jesus is the unique revelation of God (v. 19b: *hina pisteusēte hotan genētai hoti egō eimi*). The absolute use of *egō eimi*, taken from the prophetic tradition, points to Jesus as the unique revelation of God, over against all others who might make such a claim.[49] Part of this revelation is his choice of a group of ignorant, failing disciples, one of whom will betray him. When this betrayal occurs, the wonder of a God who does such things will be seen. Then disciples might believe that Jesus' choice of them makes God known.

Not only has Jesus knowingly *chosen* fragile (v. 18), failing disciples, but he *sends them out* as his representatives (v. 20). This central section of the story of the footwashing and the gift of the morsel closes with another use of a double "amen" and Jesus' telling the disciples that they are his privileged "sent ones." To receive the disciple means to receive Jesus, and to receive Jesus means to receive God, the one who sent Jesus (v. 20). Something of Jesus' earlier words to Peter returns in vv. 18-20. Earlier he told Peter there would be a difference between his ignorance and failure "now" and his understanding "afterward" (see v. 7). Jesus is not speaking of all of them, as they are not all clean (v. 18; see v. 10). Yet Jesus has chosen (v. 18) and will send out (v. 20) disciples who are ignorant, who misunderstand him, and who will betray him. His loving knows no bounds (see v. 1: "to the end," *eis telos*), and as proof of that truth, he tells them that in the near future one of them will strike out against him. The reader knows that these future events refer to the betrayal, suffering, and death of Jesus. Then Scripture will be fulfilled and God will be revealed (vv. 18b-19) in a remarkable gift of self unto death for those whom he chose and those whom he will send, despite the fact that these very disciples fail and betray him. God is revealed in a love that surpasses all imaginable ways of loving.[50] The narrative promises that Jesus' death will be a

[49] For this understanding of the absolute use of *egō eimi*, see Moloney, *Signs and Shadows*, 100–101. D. M. Ball, *'I Am' in John's Gospel. Literary Function, Background and Theological Implications* (JSNTSS 124; Sheffield: Sheffield Academic Press, 1996) 110–19, 198–200, sees the importance of the "I am" in 13:19 and suggests that it pushes the reader further into the narrative to discover *who Jesus is*.

[50] S. M. Schneiders, "The Footwashing (John 13:1-20): An Experiment in Hermeneutics," *CBQ* 43 (1981) 84–86, presents three models of service. She claims that Jesus' washing his disciples' feet is a model of service between friends. I am suggesting that there is a further quality of love shown here that surpasses the model of service between friends· Jesus' love of friends who fail and betray the one who gives his life out of love for them.

moment of self-gift in love that will both reveal God and transform failing disciples into the sent ones of Jesus and his Father.[51]

3. The Gift of the Morsel (13:21-38)
a. Verses 21-25: Jesus' Witness   In v. 21 Jesus' words open with "Amen, amen, I say to you." The same expression has marked the closure of vv. 1-17 and vv. 18-20. Here we find it opening Jesus' words as he raises the question of the betrayer and begins a dialogue with his own that will lead to the revelation of the identity of the betrayer at the table (v. 26; see v. 18). A double "amen" will close the narrative of Jesus' final words on Peter's future denials (v. 38). There is also a parallel between v. 1, where the narrator reports Jesus' knowledge and love, and v. 21a, where another emotional experience is mentioned: Jesus is troubled in spirit.[52] A link with the cross was established in v. 1 through words that spoke of Jesus' love for his own *eis telos*. The cross is again close at hand in the words *etarachthē tō pneumati,* which echo Pss 42–43—already used by the author to make oblique reference to the passion (see 11:33; 12:27).[53] The solemn nature of the verb *emartūrēsen* ("troubled") indicates a break between vv. 18-20 and what follows. The earlier brief discourse has come to a close, and Jesus testifies to the betrayal in a way that will lead to a dialogue (vv. 23-30), as his earlier approach to wash Simon Peter's feet led to dialogue (vv. 6-11). The earlier dialogue had taken place within the context of a footwashing, while the present dialogue takes place within the context of the gift of a morsel.

Jesus' words on the betrayal highlight that one of the disciples present at the table (see vv. 12, 18) will betray him (v. 21b: *hoti eis ex humōn paradōsei me*). These words set off a reaction among the disciples around the table, who continue to show that they are not moving in the world of Jesus. They are "uncertain (*aporumenoi*) of whom he spoke." This use of *aporeō* is a hapax in the Fourth Gospel, but each of its other (rare) uses in the New Testament, refers to perplexity (see Mark 6:20; Luke 24:4; Acts 25:20; 2 Cor 4:8; Gal 4:20). Ignorance, con-

---

[51] G. R. O'Day, "'I Have Overcome the World' (John 16:33): Narrative Time in John 13–17," *Sem* 53 (1991) 153–66, points to the collapsing of the present and future narrative moment. But the element of expectation is never eliminated, as the reader still waits for a future time when "these things" will take place.

[52] Ferraro, "'Pneuma' in Giov 13.21," 185–211, sees the structural importance of v. 21, and makes a good case for a possible reference to the spirit in v. 21 as the Spirit of God, driving Jesus on in the face of rejection.

[53] See J. Beutler, "Psalm 42/43 im Johannesevangelium," *NTS* 25 (1978–79) 34–37; C. H. Dodd, *Historical Tradition in the Fourth Gospel* (Cambridge: Cambridge Univ Press, 1965) 37–38, 69–71.

fusion, and misunderstanding continue (see vv. 6, 7, 9, 12-13). For the first time in the narrative, the Beloved Disciple is mentioned, lying at the table in a position of affectionate closeness: "on Jesus' chest" (*en tǭ kolpǭ tou Iēsou*, v. 23; see 1:18). Yet, despite his position of honor, he is included in the perplexity. As will happen regularly from this point on in the story, Peter is subordinated to the Beloved Disciple. Peter's request of the Beloved Disciple indicates that the latter already knows the answer: "Tell us who it is of whom he speaks" (v. 24). But this special disciple, like all the other disciples at the table, is ignorant of the full meaning of Jesus' words. The Beloved Disciple must ask Jesus, and his question triggers the words and actions that follow: "Lord, who is it?"[54]

b. Verses 26-30: Jesus and Judas   The one who is to betray Jesus will be part of an intimate human gesture: dipping the morsel at table and sharing it with him (v. 26a). With stark brevity, the narrator describes Jesus' actions by repeating his words: "So when he had dipped the morsel, he took it and gave it to Judas, the Son of Simon Iscariot" (v. 26b).[55] It is only after the reception of the morsel that Satan enters into Judas (v. 27a). In v. 2 the reader was told that the devil had decided that Judas was to betray Jesus, but in v. 27a Satan enters into Judas. He now is part of a satanic program, diametrically opposed to the program of God revealed in Jesus. Yet, in a final gesture of love, Jesus shares the dipped morsel with his future betrayer (v. 26), only to be totally rejected as Satan takes possession of Judas (v. 27a). Is it possible that the evil disciple (6:70-71; 12:4-6; 13:2) shares a eucharistic morsel (13:26)?[56]

In the immediately previous reference to Judas' presence with Jesus at the table in v. 18, Jesus claims that the events about to happen

---

[54] There is no reason to see the Beloved Disciple's use of *kyrie* as an elevated Christology. It is a respectful question

[55] Because of the possibility that the morsel given to Judas might be regarded as eucharistic, this text is notoriously disturbed. For the textual problem as a whole, and the reasons for my inclusion of the words "he took it" (*lambanei kai*) see below.

[56] For the discussion, see M.-J. Lagrange, *Evangile selon Saint Jean* (EB; Paris: Gabalda, 1927) 362–63. Most modern scholars either regard the use of the morsel as a method of eliminating Judas from the upper room (e.g., Schnackenburg, *St John*, 3:30; Cancian, *Nuovo Commandamento*, 140–49), an indication that here Judas chooses Satan rather than Jesus (e.g., Brown, *John*, 2:578). Because Jesus' love for his failing disciples *eis telos* has not been given full weight scholars shy clear of a eucharistic interpretation. Those who have seen the passage as eucharistic (e.g., W. Bauer, *Das Johannesevangelium erklärt* [3d ed.; HKNT 6, Tubingen: J. C. B. Mohr, 1933] 175) use 1 Cor 11.29 to claim that Satan enters the sinful Judas because he takes the eucharistic morsel without discerning.

fulfill Ps 41:10b: "He who ate my bread has lifted his heel against me." The LXX translation of the first part of the Psalm ("He who ate my bread") reads: *ho esthiōn artous mou*. However, the Johannine author renders the text as: *ho trōgōn mou ton arton*. There appears to have been a deliberate replacement of the more "proper" word for eating (*esthiein*) that is found in the LXX. The verb that has been used to replace it (*trōgein*) is a less delicate term. It means "to munch," or "to crunch with the teeth."[57] The reader recalls four earlier uses of the same physical verb in the eucharistic passage of 6:51c-58:

> 6:54: The one who eats (*ho trōgōn*) my flesh and drinks my blood.
> 6:56: The one who eats (*ho trōgōn*) my flesh and drinks my blood.
> 6:57: The one who eats (*ho trōgōn*) me will live because of me.
> 6:58: The one who eats (*ho trōgōn*) this bread will live forever.

Framed between uses of the verb *phagein* (see 6:51, 52, 53 and 6:58), the verb *trōgein* dominates the most explicit eucharistic material in the Gospel. The only other use of this verb is at the gift of the morsel in 13:18.[58] The use of Ps 41:10 may have been part of the early Church's traditional explanation of what happened at the Last Supper (see Mark 14:18; Luke 22:21). The Johannine author refashions this Old Testament passage, linking the gift of the morsel to Judas with Christian traditions that surrounded the Last Supper. The morsel is linked with the flesh and blood of the Son of Man referred to in the clearest eucharistic material in the Gospel: the discourse by the lake

---

[57] There has been some discussion on the significance of the two verbs in the late Greek of the New Testament. For the position taken above, see C. Spicq, "*Trōgein*: Est-il synonyme de *phagein* et d'*esthiein* dans le Nouveau Testament?" *NTS* 26 (1979–1980) 414–19.

[58] In a study claiming that 13:18 represents a translation of Ps 41:10 from the Hebrew influenced by Johannine use of current exegetical techniques, Menken, "Ps 41.10," 65, notes the five appearances of *trōgein*, and argues that 6:51c-58 and 13:18 indicate a typically Johannine use of the verb especially in the light of the use of *esthiein* in 6:53. See also A. Obermann, *Die christologische Erfüllung der Schrift im Johannesevangelium: Eine Untersuchung zur johanneischen Hermeneutik anhand der Schriftzitate* (WUNT 2. Reihe 83; Tübingen: J. C. B. Mohr 1996) 255–58, 263–65. The eucharistic contexts are not mentioned. *Phagein* is well used in other Johannine contexts (see 4:31, 32, 33; 6:5, 23, 26, 31, 49, 50, 51, 52, 53, 58; 18:28). Why alternate it with *trōgein* in 6:51-58, and why does it not appear in 13:18? The eucharistic contexts influence the choice of the verb Schuchard, *Scripture Within Scripture*, 108–10, 112–17, argues, against Menken, that the Johannine use of Ps 41:10 is from the Old Greek, influenced by the Old Greek of 2 Sam 20:21. Although agreeing with Menken that there is no distinction between *phagein* and *trōgein* (112), he accepts that the Johannine author may use the latter verb to associate 13:18 with 6:51-58 (112–13). For a recent updated re-publication of Menken's article, see his *Old Testament Quotations in the Fourth Gospel: Studies in Textual Form* (CBET 15; Kampen: Kok Pharos, 1996) 123–38.

of Tiberias (John 6:51c-58). These eucharistic hints would not be missed by the reader.

One of the many textual difficulties in v. 26b can now be resolved.[59] The words *lambanei kai* recall Jesus' deliberate action of taking bread in the bread miracles of all four Gospels (Mark 6:41; 8:6; Matt 14:19; 15:36; Luke 9:16; John 6:11), all of which reflect the eucharistic thought and practice of the early church.[60] The same expression is found in the Synoptic and Pauline reports of the Last Supper (Matt 26:26; Mark 14:22; Luke 22:19; 1 Cor 11:23). Given the eucharistic hints involved in the use of the verb *trōgein*, the originality of the words indicating that Jesus took the morsel before giving it to Judas should be maintained.[61] This expression should not be eliminated from the text as evidence of a scribal accommodation to other eucharistic passages,[62] but included because 13:26b is a eucharistic text. There is intertextuality between the gift of the morsel and eucharistic traditions the Johannine community held in common with the early church.[63] Eucharist is a subtheme to the morsel, just as baptism is a subtheme to the footwashing. Within the context of a meal indicated as eucharistic, Jesus gives the morsel to the most despised character in the Gospel's narrative: Judas. The reader in the narrative and all

[59] The words *lambanei kai* are missing in some important early manuscripts, e.g., P[66], first hand of Sinaiticus, Bezae, and Koridethi.

[60] As well as the commentaries, see J.-M. van Cangh, *La Multiplication des Pains et l'Eucharistie* (LD 86, Paris: Editions du Cerf, 1975); B. van Iersel, "Die Wunderbare Speisung und das Abendmahl in der synoptischen Tradition (Mk VI 35–44 par., VIII 1–20 par.)," *NovT* 7 (1964) 167–194, F. J. Moloney, *A Body Broken for a Broken People· Eucharist in the New Testament* (2d ed., Peabody, Mass.· Hendrickson, 1996) 37–44, 62–77, 86–90.

[61] The editors of *UBSGNT* thought that it should be included. See also, Bauer, *Johannesevangelium*, 174; Schnackenburg, *St John*, 3:30.

[62] As many commentators would claim. See, e.g., C. K. Barrett, *The Gospel according to St John* (2d ed. London: SPCK, 1978) 447; Brown, *John*, 2:575; E. Haenchen, *John* (2 vols ; Hermeneia: Philadelphia: Fortress Press, 1984) 2:113 and Lindars, *John*, 459. The difficulties which the gift of the morsel created for the scribes can be sensed in the confusion of the textual tradition for the whole of v. 26, not only for the inclusion of the *lambanei kai* For a summary, see B. M. Metzger, *A Textual Commentary on the Greek New Testament* (2d ed., Stuttgart: German Bible Society, 1994) 205

[63] The Greek word used for "morsel" (*psōmion*) could refer to a morsel of either bread or meat. I am taking it for granted that bread is referred to here. See, however, M.-J. Lagrange, *Saint Jean*, 362, who argues that it was meat. R. Kysar, *John* (Augsburg Commentary on the New Testament; Minneapolis: Augsburg, 1986) 214, suggests that it was bitter herbs. J N Suggit, "John 13:1-30: The mystery of the incarnation and of the eucharist," *Neot* 19 (1985) 64–70, claims that 13:1-30 would naturally recall Jesus' death and Eucharist, so closely associated with it. See also Cancian, *Nuovo Commandamento*, 311–23, for a similar understanding of 13:1-38 on the basis of John 6 and the Johannine understanding of a new covenant.

subsequent Christian readers of the Gospel are aware that disciples always have and always will display ignorance, fail Jesus, and deny him, and that some may even betray him in an outrageous and public way. But Jesus' never-failing love for such disciples, a love that reached out even to the archetype of the evil disciple, reveals a unique God (see vv. 18-20).

Jesus knows Judas' intentions. Jesus has reached out in a gift of love, but Satan's designs for Judas, already made clear to the reader in v. 2, begin to happen: Satan enters into Judas (v. 27a). Jesus knows this and sends Judas on his way, recommending that he do his task as quickly (*tachion*) as possible (v. 27b). There are no subtle allegories behind these words of Jesus; they are dramatic words that lead to the information of vv. 28-29: The reader is told of the overwhelming and universal ignorance of the disciples. Not one of the people at the table understood (*oudeis egnō*). The *oudeis* includes the Beloved Disciple (v. 28). The reader finds it hard to grasp how it is possible that no one understands, after the clarity of the question and the response to the question in word and deed in vv. 25-26. One would expect understanding from the Beloved Disciple, who was so close to Jesus (v. 23), and who asked the question from his position lying against Jesus' breast (v. 25). Ignorance and confusion reign, and the best some of the disciples can do is guess that Jesus is telling Judas, the guardian of the money box, to make some purchases for the feast or to give something to the poor (v. 29). After receiving the morsel, Judas immediately (*euthus*) goes out, and it is night (v. 30). Now controlled by Satan, Judas walks away from the Light of the world (see 8:12; 9:5) into the night and the darkness of those who reject Jesus and plan to kill him (see 1:5; 3:2; 8:12; 9:4; 11:10; 12:35, 46). The reader recalls that, at the beginning of Jesus' ministry, one of "the Jews" moved from the night toward Jesus (3:2). That journey is still in progress (see 7:50-51).[64] Now, as Jesus' life comes to an end, one of "his own" moves away from the light into the night (13:30).

c. Verses 31-38: A New Commandment: Disciples Must Love One Another
Judas' action leads to a "shout of triumph" from Jesus.[65] The author links Jesus' proclamation in vv. 31-32 with Judas' departure: "when he went out" (*hote oun exēlthen*). This connection is generally ignored

---

[64] On this passage, and its function in the story of Nicodemus in the Fourth Gospel, see Moloney, *Signs and Shadows*, 90–93
[65] The expression comes from G H C. Macgregor, *The Gospel of John* (MNTC; London Hodder and Stoughton, 1928) 283.

by commentators who read vv. 31-32 as the opening statement of the first discourse (13:31—14:31).[66] Crucial to Jesus' self-gift in love will be his being "lifted up" to make God known (see 3:13-14; 8:28), to draw everyone to himself (12:32-33). The reader knows but does not yet fully understand that the lifting up is both an exaltation and a physical lifting up on a stake, as Moses lifted up the serpent (see 3:14). Within the Johannine rhetoric, Judas' departure into the darkness to betray Jesus unto death leads logically to Jesus' statement of vv. 31-32. The hour has come (see 12:23, 27, 31; 13:1); now is the time for the Son of Man to be lifted up for his glorification, and through it, for God to be glorified. Jesus' use of the expression "the Son of Man" throughout the Gospel has pointed the reader forward to the crucifixion (see 1:51; 3:14; 6:27, 53; 8:28; 12:23). On the cross Jesus is glorified, but his death will also reveal the "glory of God" (*doxa tou theou*). Consistent with the author's use of *doxa* throughout the story to refer to revelation (see 1:14; 2:11; 5:44; 7:18; 11:4, 40; 12:41, 43), as the *doxa* of God was made visible at Sinai,[67] the cross is the time and the place where God is to be revealed. As earlier the arrival of the Greeks led to Jesus' first announcement that the hour had come for the Son of Man to be glorified (see 12:20-33), so now it is *because* Judas has been taken over by Satan after receiving the morsel, in a radical rejection of the love of God revealed in and through Jesus' gift of the morsel, that actions are in motion that will lead to Jesus' being lifted up (v. 31a). Jesus can thus proclaim that *now* the Son of Man will be glorified, and the glory of God will be seen in the glorification of Jesus on the cross (vv. 31b-32b). The glorification of Jesus and the revelation of God, so intimately associated with the crucifixion, will take place now (v. 32c: *euthus*).[68] Judas' exit sets in motion the events promised by Jesus in vv. 18-20 as the time and the place when the disciples, chosen and sent by Jesus, might come to believe that Jesus is the revelation of God (v. 19: *hoti egō eimi*).

Jesus introduces a theme that will dominate the final discourses. Opening with a term of endearment, "little children" (*teknia*), which reinforces the reader's impression of Jesus' unconditional commitment of love for his failing disciples, he looks back to words spoken

---

[66] E.g., Schnackenburg's detailed commentary on vv. 31-32 (*St John*, 3:49-52) does not give one word to v. 31a. But see de Boer, *Johannine Perspectives,* 208.

[67] See Moloney, *Belief,* 55–57.

[68] For a detailed study of 13:31-32, see Moloney, *Son of Man,* 194–202. See also de Boer, *Johannine Perspectives,* 186–89. De Boer understands this association of Jesus' death with glorification as reflecting the final stage of the Johannine community's theological development; see 53–82.

to "the Jews." Within the context of a possible violent arrest of Jesus by officers of the Pharisees (*hupēretai*) on the occasion of the Feast of Tabernacles, Jesus told "the Jews" he would be with them a little longer (7:33). That moment, also marked by conflict and danger, is recalled as Jesus tells his disciples that they will seek him but not find him because, as he told "the Jews": "Where I am going you cannot come" (v. 33; see 7:34). The reader finds in one verse a term of endearment (*teknia*), a statement from Jesus that a time is close at hand when he will no longer be with his disciples, and a close association of the disciples with "the Jews." As "the Jews" will not and cannot understand who Jesus is and where he is going in his return to the Father, so it is also with Jesus' ignorant and failing disciples. Yet they remain his disciples, his "little children," lost yet loved in their misunderstanding, failure, and ignorance (v. 33).

Jesus' relationship with "the Jews" has deteriorated to such an extent that he has called them "children of the devil" (see 8:39-47), and they have decided that he must be slain (see 11:49-50). To his own, whom he calls "little children," he gives a new commandment (vv. 34-35). Within the context of the footwashing, Jesus gave the disciples an example (v. 15a: *hypodeigma gar edōka humin*), and within the context of the gift of the morsel he gives them a new commandment (v. 34a: *entolēn kainēn didōmi humin*). Both the example and the commandment are closely associated with Jesus' demand that his disciples follow him into a loving self-gift unto death. This was implied in the command that the disciples do to one another, *as Jesus had done for them* (v. 15b: *kathōs egō epoiēsa humin*). It becomes more explicit in the new commandment that they love one another, *even as Jesus has loved them* (v. 34b: *kathōs ēgapēsa humas*). The link between the example and the commandment is clear.[69] This unique quality of love among human beings will single out the followers of Jesus.[70] They will be universally recognized as disciples of Jesus (*en toutō gnōsontai pantes hoti emoi mathētai este*) because they love one another as Jesus has loved them (v. 35). There will shortly be a time when Jesus will no longer be with them, and they will not be able to go where Jesus is (see v. 33). In that

[69] See Dettwiler, *Die Gegenwart*, 74–79. It is seldom noticed by scholars who separate vv. 31-38 from vv. 1-30. Schnackenburg, *St John*, 3.12, 52–54, uses it as one element in his claim that vv. 34-35 are an editorial addition.

[70] The presence of the command to mutual love in the testaments leads R. F. Collins, "A New Commandment I Give You . . . (Jn 13:34)," *LTP* 35 (1979) 238, to claim: "The appearance of the exhortation to fraternal charity in the Farewell Discourses of the Fourth Gospel is to be expected." Collins points to the specifically Christian "newness" in the link between the command and the love of Jesus (see 249–52).

time of absence, they are to repeat the love of Jesus and thus render present the lifestyle of Jesus (vv. 34-35). This lifestyle calls the disciple to the gift of self unto death. This, in turn, reveals the oneness of purpose and mission that exists between Jesus and the Father.[71]

In v. 7a Jesus told Peter: "What I am doing you do not know now." In proof of Jesus' statement, Peter now asks what is meant by the proximate absence of Jesus caused by his going to a place where they cannot come (v. 36a). Jesus first repeats to Peter the words he said to all the disciples in v. 33: He is going to a place where Peter cannot follow "now." But harking back to the prolepsis of v. 7b, "but afterward you will understand," Jesus tells Peter that even though he cannot follow him "now" (v. 36b), he shall follow "afterward" (v. 36c). The reader again finds a tension between the "now" of the story time, with failing and misunderstanding disciples at the center of the action (vv. 7a, 36b), and the plotted time of "afterward" when this situation will be transformed (vv. 7b, 36c; see 2:22; 12:16). The reader is reading in the "in-between time" and looks confidently forward to the resolution of the tension created by the prolepses and only partially resolved by Jesus' words in v. 19: "I tell you this now, before it takes place, that when it does take place you may believe that I am he."

But Peter claims there is no tension. As earlier he attempted to dictate terms to Jesus both about whether he should have his feet washed (vv. 6-8) and about how he should be washed (v. 9), so now he asks Jesus a question that indicates that there is no journey he is not prepared to make with Jesus (v. 37). Peter is thinking of human journeys into some dangerous place and time; Jesus is speaking of his return to the Father. As so often throughout this Gospel, a character in the story and Jesus are working on two planes. Peter claims he is prepared to lay down his life for Jesus, as the Good Shepherd had earlier said that he would lay down his life for his sheep (see 10:11, 15, 17). This is exactly what Jesus asks of his disciples in the gift of his example (v. 15) and the gift of the new commandment (vv. 34-35), but such love flows from a radical following of Jesus and never from an imposition of one's own worldview upon God's designs. Jesus prophesies that Peter will be thwarted by his own ignorance. He will fail as he denies Jesus three times before the cock crows (v. 38). The "now" of Peter's ignorance and failure is to be further demonstrated, and Jesus' knowledge

---

[71] See Collins, "A New Commandment," 252–61. Although intensified and more theological, this can be understood as an exhortation to a quality of life that flows from the life story of a departing hero, as in the testaments. See Cancian, *Nuovo Commandamento*, 275–76

will be highlighted. The reader is aware that the narrative ahead will tell of Judas' betrayal of Jesus (see vv. 2, 10-11, 18, 21-30, 31a) and Peter's denials (vv. 36-38).

CONCLUSION

As the first events in the Johannine account of Jesus' final night with his disciples began (vv. 1-5), they were marked by three major themes: the arrival of "the hour" of Jesus; Jesus' love for his own, no matter how sinful they might be (vv. 1-3); and Jesus' bringing to perfection his task by means of a consummate act of love (v. 1). As they came to an end, one of those themes returns: Jesus' love for his own (vv. 34-35), no matter how frail they might be (vv. 36-38). Another theme is added: the glorification of Jesus and the revelation of the glory of the Father (vv. 31-32). This theme has also been present at the center of the passage, in Jesus' claim that his disciples would come to recognize him as the unique revelation of God (v. 19: *egō eimi*). But John 13 is a description of the glory shown by unconditional love. Jesus asks, by both deed and word, that his disciples live and love in imitation of him. This is the example (v. 15), the new commandment (v. 34). In the end, the example and the new commandment coalesce.

Many themes adumbrated during the ministry have now come to the fore: the frailty of the disciples (see 1:35-49; 4:27-38; 6:1-15; 9:1-5; 11:5-16), the betrayal of Judas (see 6:70-71; 12:4-6), the denials of Peter (see 1:40-42; 6:67-69), the departure of Jesus (see 7:33-34; 8:21), the impossibility to follow him to the Father "now" (see 7:33-34), an upcoming event that will transform the lack of faith and knowledge of the "now" into an "afterward" when the disciples will know and follow him (see 2:22; 12:16), the knowledge of Jesus (see 2:24-25; 4:1; 5:42; 6:15; 10:14-15), his love for his own (see 3:16-17, 34-35), the cross as the moment of Jesus' glorification (see 1:51; 11:4; 12:23, 33), and the revelation of the glory of God in and through the cross (see 3:13-14; 8:28; 12:32). Puzzles produced by the story of Jesus' public ministry converge, and in this sense 13:1-38 introduces the reader to 14:1—20:31.

John 13:1-38 tells of the ignorance, betrayal, and denial of Jesus by the disciples with whom he shares his table. But Jesus commits himself to these disciples, "his own," loving them until death (13:1), washing their feet (vv. 4-11) and sharing bread, even with his betrayer (vv. 21-30). The center of the narrative (vv. 18-20) is crucial for its overall message. Here we find the careful presentation of a fundamen-

tal Johannine concept. Jesus knows whom he has chosen: these disciples, whose feet he has washed (vv. 1-17) and who have received the
morsel (vv. 21-38), and who will turn against him (see v. 18). The cruel
reality of their turning against him (vv. 2-3, 10-11, 21-30, 36-38), their
lifting their heel against their host (v. 18b), alters nothing. Indeed, he
will send them forth as his representatives and as the representatives
of his Father (vv. 18a, 20). In the acceptance of these failed yet loved
disciples, one will receive both Jesus and the Father (v. 20). In Jesus'
choosing and sending ignorant and failing disciples, dramatically portrayed in the failure of both Judas and Peter, Jesus' uniqueness and
oneness with God can be seen. His love for his failing disciples is,
above all, the final proof for his claim to be the one who makes God
known (see v. 19: *hoti egō eimi*). Revealed here is God's love, which
transcends and challenges all human criteria and human experience.
Equally surprising is that, despite their ignorance, failure, betrayals,
and denials, the disciples are to imitate Jesus, loving one another as
he loved them, so that the world might recognize them as disciples
and those sent by Jesus Christ (vv. 15, 20, 34-35).

Chapter Two

Departure
John 14:1-31

¶ THE DIALOGUE predicting the denials of Peter in 13:36-38 brings to a close the parallel stories of the footwashing (see vv. 1-17) and the morsel (see vv. 21-38). Jesus spoke to Peter in the second person singular (see v. 38: *sou . . . thēseis . . . soi . . . phōnēsę . . . arnēsę*). Although the question of Jesus' departure was raised by Peter in 13:33, 36, a broader audience is addressed in 14:1 through imperatives (1a: *mē tarassesthō;* 1b: *pisteuete;* 1c: *pisteuete*) and a change in form.[1] Jesus adopts a magisterial role, peppering his words to his disciples with imperatives (see vv. 1 [3 times], 9, 11 [twice], 27 [twice], and 31 [twice]), as they struggle to follow his words and promises (vv. 5 [Thomas], 8 [Philip], 22 [Judas]). This first section of Jesus' final discourse concludes with the enigmatic words of v. 31c: "Rise, let us go hence." Despite widespread scholarly opinion that "13:31-38 functions as an introduction to chapter 14,"[2] the reader senses a new stage in the story at 14:1: "Only with Chapter 14 do we actually begin the farewell proper."[3]

---

[1] For many (e.g., W. Bauer, *Das Johannesevangelium erklart* [3d ed.; HKNT 6; Tubingen: J. C. B. Mohr, 1933] 176) 13:33, 36 link 13:31-38 with 14:1-31. Not all interpreters would read the three verbs as imperatives.

[2] F. F. Segovia, *Farewell to the Word: The Johannine Call to Abide* (Minneapolis: Fortress Press, 1991) 64

[3] G.-M. Behler, *The Last Discourse of Jesus* (trans. R. T. Francover; Helicon: Baltimore, 1965) 75. See also J. Beutler, *Habt keine Angst: Die erste Johanneische Abschiedsrede (Joh 14)* (SBS 116, Stuttgart: Katholisches Bibelwerk, 1984) 9–19.

THE SHAPE OF THE DISCOURSE

There is widespread disagreement among scholars concerning the internal articulation of the passage.[4] A variety of syntactic elements and details of content suggest a threefold division of the material. The imperative "believe" in 14:1 dominates vv. 1-14. Belief is explicitly mentioned in vv. 1, 10, 11, and 12, and Jesus' words throughout this section are related to the content and the consequences of belief in Jesus. The recommendation to "love" appears in v. 15 for the first time in 14:1-31. It reappears in vv. 21, 23, and 24, and the section is framed by statement and restatement of the same point, at first positively: "If you love me, you will keep my commandments" (v. 15), and then negatively: "He who does not love me does not keep my words" (v. 24a). The section that runs from vv. 25-31 is dominated by the theme of communication by means of the word: "speaking" (v. 25: lelalēka), "teaching" (v. 26b: didaxei), "saying" (v. 26c: eipon), "saying" (v. 28: eipon), "telling" (v. 29: eirēka), and "speaking" (v. 30: lalēsō).

Vv. 1-6 are highlighted by the themes of Jesus' departure (vv. 2, 3a, 4), the theme of faith (see v. 1) and words of encouragement (vv. 1-4, 6). Jesus' words in v. 1, "Do not let your hearts be troubled" (mē tarassethō humōn hē kardia), set the mood. The same association of themes is again found as the discourse closes in vv. 27b-31: departure (vv. 28, 31), faith (v. 29), and encouragement (vv. 27b-29, 31). Jesus' instruction to his disciples in v. 1 is repeated in v. 27b.[5] When one notices the steady rhythm of Jesus' command to love him, through the keeping of his commandments and his word, across the central section of the discourse (vv. 15-24) in vv. 15, 21, 23, and 24, a threefold division emerges: vv. 1-14, vv. 15-24, and vv. 25-31.[6] It unfolds in the following fashion:

---

[4] Segovia, Farewell, 64–65, nn. 6–13, lists thirty scholars who have divided the material into two to nine major sections. See also A. Niccací, "Esame letterario di Gv 14," EuntD 31 (1978) 209–14; S Migliasso, La presenza dell'Assente: Saggio di analisi letterario-strutturale e di sintisi teologico di Gv 13,31–14,32 (Rome: Pontificia Universitas Gregoriana, 1979) 64–73.

[5] This obvious repetition in v. 1 and v 27b is often accepted as indicating an inclusion between v. 1 and v. 27b. See, e.g., R. Bultmann, The Gospel of John: A Commentary (trans. G. R. Beasley-Murray, Oxford· Blackwell, 1971) 599; J Schneider, "Die Abschiedsreden Jesu: Ein Beitrag zur Frage der Komposition von Johannes 13:31—17:26," in Gott und die Gotter: Festgabe fur E. Fascher zum 60. Geburtstag (Berlin: Evangelische Verlagsanstalt, 1958) 106. Rather than an inclusion, I am regarding both v. 1 and v. 27b as statements of encouragement, introducing subsections (vv. 1-6 and vv. 27b-31) that deal with Jesus' departure.

[6] This macro-structure follows that proposed by (among others) Beutler, Habt keine Angst, 21–22, 51–53, 87–88, Simoens, La gloire L'aimer: Structures stylistique et interpreta-

Verses 1-14: Jesus speaks encouragingly of his departure. There is no need to be troubled (v. 1: *mē tarassesthō humōn hē kardia*), since Jesus goes to prepare a place for them. His disciples know the way, and Thomas's question is a rhetorical device that allows Jesus to reveal himself[7] through an *egō eimi* statement with a predicate: He is the way leading to the Father (vv. 1-6). The mention of the Father in v. 6b closes one subsection and opens another. Jesus points beyond himself; he is the revelation of the Father. Once again a question from a disciple, this time Philip, acts as a rhetorical device that allows Jesus to state that to see him is to see the Father, and that his words and works manifest his oneness with the Father (vv. 7-11). The mention of "the works" in v. 11b closes one subsection and opens another. A solemn use of the double "amen" introduces the development of this theme. Jesus makes a link with the revelation of the Father through his works to point beyond the story time of his life to a future time when the disciples, who will ask in his name, will do even greater works. Anyone who asks in Jesus' name will continue the task of manifesting the Father's oneness with the Son (vv. 12-14).

Verses 15-24: Jesus instructs on the fruits of belief and love. The first of four statements (*ean agapate me*) demanding the disciples' love and leading to the keeping of Jesus' commandments is intimately linked with Jesus' request to the Father, who will give "another Paraclete" to abide with the disciples, setting them apart from "the world," which cannot receive the Spirit (vv. 15-17). The dwelling of the other Paraclete assures the continuation of the presence of the departed Jesus, the former Paraclete.[8] Jesus instructs his disciples, who love him (*ekeinos estin ho agapōn me*) and keep his commandments. He is with them in the endless presence of the Paraclete, giving life among disciples loved by both the Father and Jesus (vv. 18-21). Judas' question enables Jesus to return to the exclusive nature of a discipleship that receives the revelation of Jesus, and "the world," which does not (see vv. 15-17). Jesus' response again takes up the theme that has dominated this section of the discourse: *ean tis agapa me* (see v. 15). The one who loves receives the word, while *ho mē agapōn me* does not hear the word which, as the reader knows, is the revelation of the Father who sent him (vv. 22-24).

Verses 25-31: Jesus speaks encouragingly of his departure. The close relationship between Jesus and the Paraclete returns as Jesus informs his disciples that he has told (perfect tense: *lelalēka*) them all he has to tell them during the

---

tives dans la *Discours de la Cine (Jn 13–17)* (AnBib 90, Rome: Biblical Institute Press, 1981) 107–12; D F Tolmie, *Jesus' Farewell to the Disciples: John 13:1—17 26 in Narratological Perspective* (BibIntS 12; Leiden: Brill, 1995) 29–30.

[7] On this device, see J. Becker, *Das Evangelium des Johannes* (2 vols; OTK 4/1–2, Gutersloh: Gerd Mohn; Wurzburg: Echter, 1979–81) 2.462; M. W G. Stibbe, *John* (Readings: A New Biblical Commentary; Sheffield: JSOT Press, 1993) 156–58.

[8] The first Paraclete passage refers to the Paraclete as *allon paraklēton* (v. 16), indicating that Jesus has already exercised a paraclete ministry See especially, R E. Brown, "The Paraclete in the Fourth Gospel," *NTS* 13 (1966–67) 113–32.

"now" of his ministry, but "later" the Paraclete will recall everything Jesus has said and expand that by instructing (future tense: *didaxei*) them in all things (vv. 25-26). The theme of this section is the communication of the truth, both in the presence of Jesus and after his departure, through the Paraclete who recalls and continues the word of Jesus. This revelation lies behind the unique peace Jesus leaves with his disciples (v. 27a). They are not to be troubled (v. 27b: *mē tarassesthō humōn hē kardia*). Jesus is returning to the Father, but he tells them of this essential aspect of God's design before it happens, so that when he does depart, the disciples will come to a greater faith. The clash between the ruler of "this world" and Jesus' revelation of the love of God is at hand, but the conflict will only make clear to "the world" that Jesus loves the Father. It is time to depart (vv. 27b-31).

The impression created over the latter stages of Jesus' public ministry, that his departure will be through the experience of death, is reinforced. Jesus commands his disciples to avoid all consternation. His words recall the midrashic use of Pss 42–43, already found in 11:33, 35, 38; 12:27, and 13:21, and point the reader forward to the Passion.[9] His promise that he will not leave his disciples "orphans" (v. 18: *orphanous*) indicates that he is about to leave them through death.[10] The first section of the discourse concludes with the affirmation, "The ruler of this world is coming" (v. 30), and the reader recalls that Jesus has already explained that this ruler will be cast out as Jesus is lifted up on a cross (see 12:31-33). After a narrative that spoke openly of a gift of self in love within the context of betrayal, denial, and death (13:1-38), the discourse proper of 14:1—16:33 opens with Jesus' teaching his disciples the *fact* of his imminent departure through death, (14:1-31) and the *consequence* of the departure for those who love and believe: the gift of a peace that "the world" can never give (v. 27a).

READING THE DISCOURSE

1. The Departure of Jesus (14:1-14)
a. Verses 1-6: Departure to the Father   However caring the symbolic gestures of footwashing and sharing the morsel have been, they also carry a foreboding sense of Jesus' willingness to give himself unto death for his disciples (13:1-38). Jesus' words to his fragile disciples both increase their reasons for fear and offer comfort. Their understandable

---

[9] See J Beutler, "Psalm 42/43 in Johannesevangelium," *NTS* 25 (1978–79) 33–57. On 14:1-9, 27, see 46–54. See also G. R. Beasley-Murray, *John* (WBC 36; Waco: Word Books, 1987) 249

[10] On John 14 as an example of the Jewish testament form, as a hero leaves his disciples through death, see Beutler, *Habt keine Angst,* 15–19.

consternation after the events and prophecies of 13:1-38 must be overcome through a renewal of their faith and trust in God and their faith and trust in Jesus (v. 1). Death is in the air. Faith and trust in God are still reasonable requests to make of the disciples, but the imperative "believe also in me" may involve a risky association with a doomed man, which is more than they are prepared to give. To go on believing and trusting in Jesus is a difficult command, thus he must further explain his upcoming departure through death. Jesus is going to the home (*oikia*) of his Father, where there are many dwelling places (*monai*). The house of the Father of Jesus is the realm of God. Within this realm, there are many places for the disciples to dwell. It will be so, as Jesus has *said* it will be so, and disciples are to believe in the word of Jesus (v. 2b; see 2:1—4:54).[11] The expression *monai* has numerous possible sources,[12] but the key to its understanding is the Johannine use of the verb *menein*, which refers to a permanent dwelling or abiding. The reader has already encountered this idea in John the Baptist's description of the Spirit remaining upon Jesus (1:32) and Jesus' teaching on the life-giving and permanent presence of the gift of the Son of Man (6:27), a dwelling in the Son (6:56, 12:46) and in his word (8:31). It was used negatively of dwelling in darkness and sin (9:41; see also 12:46) and positively to indicate the never-ending presence of the Son, the Christ (8:35: Jesus; 12:34: "the Jews"). The link made between "my Father's home" (*oikia tou patros mou*) and Jesus' going to prepare a place (*topon*) informs the disciples of a permanent, life-giving dwelling among the many *monai*.[13] Jesus' departure should

[11] Verse 2b has a disturbed textual tradition. The *hoti* is wrongly omitted by the first hand of P66, Mt Athos, Old Latin, and it is not clear whether a stop should be made after *humin*, or whether the sentence should run on with *hoti*. For a good survey of possibilities, concluding that the *hoti* should be omitted, see R E. Brown, *The Gospel according to John* (2 vols., AB 29, 29A, Garden City, N.Y.: Doubleday, 1966–1970) 2·619–20. Given the fact that Jesus has never before told his disciples of the Father's house and the many dwelling places, I am reading v. 2b, including the *hoti*, as an insistence upon the importance of the word of Jesus, building upon the imperative of v. 1c It should be read (following, among many, C. K. Barrett, *The Gospel according to St John* [2d ed. London: SPCK, 1978] 457): "There will be many abiding places (and if it had not been so I would have told you), for I am going to prepare a place for you " For a fuller discussion, see G Fischer, *Die himmlischen Wohnungen: Untersuchungen zu Joh 14,2f* (Europäische Hochschulschriften XXIII/38; Bern: Herbert Lang, 1975) 35–36; J McCaffrey, *The House with Many Rooms: The Temple Theme of Jn. 14, 2–3* (AnBib 114; Rome: Biblical Institute Press, 1988) 138–40.

[12] For surveys, see Fischer, *Wohnungen*, 105–290; McCaffrey, *The House*, 49–75 Both affirm Johannine originality.

[13] R. Gundry, "In My Father's House are many *Monai* (John 14:2)," *ZNW* 58 (1967) 68–71, uses the Johannine language of abiding to conclude that 14:2 indicates that the believers already dwell in Christ, and await his final coming. See also W. H Oliver and

not be a cause for sorrow, but for comfort and trust (v. 1). He is going away to prepare for them the universal and permanent possibility of communion with his Father (v. 2).

The Johannine tension between end-time and realized eschatology (see 5:25-29; 6:35-40, 44-48) returns in v. 3. The use of *palin erchomai* (present tense) with *kai paralēmpsomai humas* (future tense) is grammatically clumsy but is generally regarded as determined by Jesus' future coming to take his own unto himself. The concluding *hina* clause (*hina hopou egō eimi kai humeis ēte*) demands a future meaning for both verbs. Jesus is departing to prepare a place for his own in the Father's house, but his departure will be matched by a future return when he will take his disciples to himself, to the place where he is. Is that return wholly determined by a traditional eschatology, the final encounter between Jesus as Lord and the individual or the nations (see Matt 25:13-15, 31-46; Mark 13:24-27; Luke 19:11-27; 1 Thess 4:17)? Jesus' words point toward a final coming, but the expression hints that the Jesus who is about to depart (*ean poreusthō kai hetoimasō*) is also coming to the disciples (*erchomai*). Too much of Jesus' earlier preaching has insisted on the present gift of life to the believer for the reader to collapse Jesus' promise of 14:3 into a time scheme *totally* conditioned by an end-time eschatology.[14] He is going away, and he will return at

---

A. G. van Aarde, "The Community of Faith as Dwelling Place of the Father. *Basileia tou theou* as 'Household of God' in the Johannine Farewell Discourses," *Neot* 25 (1991) 379–400. Some commentators link the use of *oikia* and *topos* with the Jerusalem Temple, and Jesus' words which look to the transcending of that "place" (see 4:20-24). This looks back to Jesus' body as a temple (see 2:21), and thus 14:2-3 promises "universalism in religion" (J. Marsh, *Saint John* [PNTC; Harmondsworth: Penguin, 1968] 501) through the departure of Jesus.

[14] As do, e.g., J. H. Bernard, *A Critical and Exegetical Commentary on the Gospel according to St John* (2 vols.; ICC; Edinburgh: T & T. Clark, 1928) 2:534–36; E. Delebecque, *Evangile de Jean: Text Traduit et Annoté* (CahRB 23; Paris: Babalda, 1987) 187. Recent, more sophisticated, approaches to the question are exemplified by Becker, "Die Abschiedsreden Jesu," 219–28 (*Johannes*, 2 460–61). He (among others) claims that vv. 2-3 contain a primitive Son of Man Christology and eschatology, which is corrected later in the discourse, in vv. 6-10, 12-17, and 18-24. Others, (e.g. Marsh, *John*, 503; B. Lindars, *The Gospel of John* [NCB; London: Oliphants, 1972] 471; Fischer, *Wohnungen*, 299–348) attempt to read vv. 2-3 in a more realized sense, looking further into the last discourse for support. There is no need to resolve this tension at this stage of the discourse, as does, e.g., B. Witherington III, *John's Wisdom: A Commentary on the Fourth Gospel* (Louisville: Westminster/John Knox, 1995) 249· "Heaven begins on earth." See E. C. Hoskyns, *The Fourth Gospel* (2d ed.; ed. F. N. Davey; London: Faber & Faber, 1947) 454, for a better balance. On the importance of maintaining the traditional end-time eschatological perspective here, see Gundry, "In My Father's House," 71–72; Beutler, *Habt keine Angst*, 37–40. McCaffrey, *The House*, 35–45, also leaves open the "when" of Jesus' return. For

some future time, but there is also the promise of an ongoing presence of Jesus. For the moment, the reader wonders how Jesus' going away and his coming relate to the earlier teaching that the time is coming, *and is already present,* when those who believe in the Son have eternal life (see, 3:15, 16, 36; 4:14, 36; 5:24-25; 6:27, 35, 47, 56, 63; 10:10, 28; 11:25-26; 12:50). There is no solution for the reader in the immediate context; further clarification is called for, but this is no ordinary departure.[15]

The departure remains central as Jesus reminds the disciples that they already know the way to where Jesus is going (v. 4).[16] They have been instructed on the way of Jesus and his destiny. Jesus is returning to his Father (see 10:38; 12:27-28) by means of an experience of death, which is at the same time his glorification, and renders glory to God (see 11:4, 40; 12:23, 32-34; 13:31-32). The reader is even better informed, as the narrator has linked the return to the Father with Jesus' total gift of self in love in 13:1. Aware that there can be no avoiding the "end" of Jesus' story, and his "way" to the Father, the reader senses in Thomas' question an ongoing unwillingness to face the inevitable end of Jesus' story (v. 5; see also 13:33, 36). They should know where Jesus is going (*pou hupageis*), but a request for further instruction on "the way" (*tēn hodon*) is justifiable.

Jesus responds with his self-revelation: "I am the way" (v. 6a: *egō eimi hē hodos*). Jesus points to himself as the way to the Father (see v. 6b) and explains *how* he is the way by means of the two words used

a survey of this debate, see J. Neugebauer, *Die eschatologischen Aussagen in den johanneischen Abschiedsreden* (BWANT 140; Stuttgart: Kohlhammer, 1995) 14–34

[15] See A. Dettwiler, *Die Gegenwart des Erhohten: Eine exegetische Studie zu den johanneischen Abschiedsreden (Joh 13,31—16,33) unter besonderer Berucksichtigung ihres Relecture-Charakters* (FRLANT 169; Gottingen: Vandenhoeck & Ruprecht, 1995) 141–57. McCaffrey, *The House,* suggests that 14:2-3 is deliberately open to two readings In the upper room, the disciples sense their oncoming separation from Jesus and, along with 14:23, the passage looks toward an end-time solution (see 137–176). Only later in the narrative will the disciples be aware that Jesus returns continually to take believers "along the way of his passion-resurrection into the heavenly sanctuary of the Father's house" (see 177–221; citation from 220). A. Stimpfle, *Blinde Sehen: Die Eschatologie im traditionsgeschichtlichen Prozess des Johannesevangeliums* (BZNW 57; Berlin: de Gruyter, 1990) 147–216, argues that the passage is open to a misunderstanding of the departing and returning Jesus as end-time oriented, and thus serves to single out true and false believers. The true believers have life *now* as the predestined children of God in the world. For M. C. de Boer, *Johannine Perspectives on the Death of Jesus* (BET 17, Kampen: Kok Pharos, 1996) 130–32, the return of Jesus refers to the coming of the Paraclete.

[16] The English "the way where" reflects the clumsy Greek *hopou egō hupagō oidate tēn hodon,* found in P66, Sinaiticus, Vaticanus, the first hand of the Ephraem Rescript, Freer Gospels. See Segovia, *Farewell,* 85–86 n. 49.

after an epexegetical *kai:* "the truth and the life" (*kai hē alētheia kai hē zōē*).[17] Jesus is the way to the Father because he is the truth and the life. The earlier use of these two Johannine expressions, from their use in the prologue (see 1:4, 14, 17) through the story itself, points to Jesus as the authoritative and saving revelation of God to the world (*alētheia:* 1:14, 17; 5:33; 8:32, 40, 44-46; *zōē:* 1:4, 6:33, 35, 48, 63, 68; 8:12; 10:10; 11:25).[18] But Jesus' claim to be "the way" is more than self-revelation. As with all the *egō eimi* statements with a complement, it not only tells the reader who the Johannine Jesus is, but also what he does. The way leads somewhere (see 10:7, 9), and v. 6b informs the reader that Jesus, the way, leads to the Father. As in earlier claims for the absolute nature of his revealing and mediating role (see 1:18, 51; 3:13; 5:37-38; 6:46; 10:1, 7, 11, 14), Jesus claims that there is only one way to the Father: through him. Jesus is the unique saving revelation of God (v. 6a), and he is the only way to the Father (v. 6b). God is revealed in the life and word of Jesus, and the disciples should know that Jesus' departure to go to the Father will be through a lifting up (see 3:14; 8:28; 12:32) and a death (see 10:16-18; 11:4, 49-53; 12:23-24; 32-33; 13:18-20). This is the revelation (v. 6a): The way of Jesus is a loving and total gift of himself unto death (see 13:1). It must also become the way of his followers (v. 6b; see 13:34-35). It is the only way to join Jesus in the place he has prepared with the Father for his followers. A passage that began with a strong exhortation to the disciples to trust and believe in both God and Jesus (v. 1) has taught the disciples of *their* departure, the consequence of Jesus' own (vv. 2-4). It closes with the reason why the disciples' faltering belief in Jesus must hold firm. Belief and trust in Jesus are the only way to their goal: oneness with the Father (vv. 5-6; see v. 1).

b. Verses 7-11: To See the Father and His Works   The reference to "the Father" links the first subsection (v. 6) and the central subsection (vv. 7-11) of vv. 1-15. To know Jesus is to know the Father (v. 7a), and from the time of Jesus onward (*ap'arti*),[19] anyone who knows the Father through seeing Jesus has also seen the Father (v. 7b). The promise of

---

[17] See I de la Potterie, *La Vérité dans Saint Jean* (2 vols.; AnBib 73; Rome: Biblical Institute Press, 1977) 1·252–53.

[18] The fundamental study, insisting that v. 6a is a statement on Jesus as the unique revelation of the Father, is that of de la Potterie, *La Vérité,* 1:241–78. For Bultmann, *John* 604–7 (and others) Jesus is the way (*hodos*) to the heavenly realities of truth and life (*alētheia* and *zōē*).

[19] See de la Potterie, *La Vérité,* 1:263–65. The revelation of the Father in the Son has been present throughout the time of Jesus.

1:18 is fulfilled.[20] From Jesus' defense of his Sabbath activity in 5:19-30 through the remainder of his public ministry (see especially 8:19, 38, 58; 10:30, 38), his claim to be the presence of the Father has been boldly made, despite the mounting conflict generated by such a claim (see, e.g., 8:20; 10:31, 39). He speaks the word of the Father, who sent him (see 3:34, 7:16; 8:28-29; 12:49-50); he and the Father are one (10:30). Jesus' statement (*ei egnōkate me . . . gnōsesthe*) is a promise: "If you have come to know me, as you have done, you shall know my Father also."[21] The perfect tense (*ei egnōkate me*) indicates a knowledge already attained. As in vv. 4-5, Jesus' statement on the disciples' knowledge (v. 7) leads to a question from one of them that shows that his hopes for his disciples' knowledge are misplaced. Philip asks Jesus to show them the Father so that they might be satisfied (v. 8).[22] There is irony in the fact that this same disciple earlier wondered about the "satisfaction" Jesus could provide. The verb *arkein* ("to be enough") is found only twice in the Fourth Gospel, and both times it is Philip who uses it. In 6:7 he wondered about Jesus' ability to provide satisfaction for the hungry crowd by the lake, and in 14:8 he asks to see God so that the disciples might be satisfied. The disciples are ignorant of truths that are fundamental for the author's understanding of who Jesus is, what he is doing, and where he is going.

Jesus' response looks back across the long period of time during which he has been with the disciples (*meth' humōn*). To know Jesus is to know the Father, and Philip is exasperatingly ignorant in asking Jesus to show the Father (v. 9). The problem lies in the disciples' lack of faith.[23] They have heard and been taught the way to the Father (v. 6): Jesus is in the Father and the Father is in Jesus (10:38). But they have not come to belief in this oneness (v. 10a).[24] Turning patiently

[20] Bernard (*St John,* 2:539–40) points to the different levels of "seeing" in John. Not all who "see" Jesus see the Father, but verbs are used indiscriminately. The identical claim for the seeing of God ("the one who sent me") in seeing Jesus in 12:45 uses *theōrein,* while 14:9 uses *horaō.*

[21] Reading *ei egnōkate . . . gnōsesthe,* with P⁶⁶, Sinaiticus, Bezae, as a promise, rather than, with Vaticanus, *ei egnōkeite . . . an ēideite,* as a reproach. See, among many, Barrett, *St John,* 458–59. For the opposite view, see Segovia, *Farewell,* 87 n. 52.

[22] It is often pointed out that Philip's request articulates the spiritual search of humankind, perhaps reflecting Moses' request in Exod 33:18 (see also Exod 24:9-11; Isa 6:1; 40:5).

[23] The shift from a singular to a plural audience in vv. 9-10 indicates that Jesus' response to Philip addresses all the disciples.

[24] As R. Schnackenburg, *The Gospel according to St John* (3 vols.; HTCNT 4/1–3; London: Burns & Oates; New York: Crossroad, 1968–82) 3:69, points out, this oneness is "a linguistic way of describing . . . the complete unity between Jesus and the Father." It is not metaphysics.

from accusation to teaching, Jesus repeats truths from the earlier part
of the story: the words Jesus speaks are the words of the Father (see
3:34; 5:23-24; 8:18, 28, 38, 47; 12:49), and the deeds of Jesus are the
works (*ta erga*) of the Father (v. 10b; see 5:20, 36; 9:3-4; 10:25, 32, 37-
38).[25] This central subsection (vv. 7-11) of the first major division (vv.
1-14) concludes with an appeal from Jesus to his unbelieving disciples.
Belief is crucial (v. 11; see v. 1). One must believe that Jesus is in the
Father and the Father is in him. Flowing from this oneness and making it known are the works Jesus does.[26] If the disciples as yet are unable to commit themselves to a saving belief in the oneness between
Jesus and the Father, then they should start at the place where such
oneness is reflected: in Jesus' works (*ta erga*) (v. 11).

c. Verses 12-14: To Believe, and to Do the Works of the Father The theme
of "the works" is introduced as the second subsection closes (v. 11),
linking the central and final subsection (vv. 12-14).[27] The double
"amen" links what has gone before with what follows. Belief in Jesus
will enable the believer (*ho pisteuōn*) to do the works of Jesus and to
excel in the works of Jesus (v. 12ab). The issue close to the surface
throughout vv. 1-14, Jesus' departure, motivates the increased greatness of the works of the believer (v. 12c). The absence of Jesus created
by his departure will not lead to the end of the works of the Father by
which Jesus has made God known (see 5:41; 7:18; 8:50, 54). The return
of Jesus to the Father (see 13:1; 14:2, 6) will lead to disciples doing
greater works. They are exhorted to ask in the name of Jesus so that

[25] The "words" and the "works" of Jesus are not to be collapsed into one reality called
"revelation," as do Bultmann (*John*, 610–11) and others. Both reveal God, but there is
a close association between what Jesus does (*ta erga*) and the revelation of the *doxa tou
theou* (see 2:11, 11:4, 40) which must be respected. See Brown, *John*, 2:622.
[26] The oneness between Jesus and the Father has its roots in the Jewish concept of
"the sent one" who completely identifies with the "one who sent." See especially P.
Borgen, "God's Agent in the Fourth Gospel," in *Logos Was the True Light and Other Essays
on the Gospel of John* (Relieff 9; Trondheim. Tarın, 1983) 121–32, J.-A. Buhner, *Der Gesandte und sein Weg im 4. Evangelium: Die kultur- und religionsgeschichtlichen Grundlagen der
johanneischen Sendungschristologie sowie ihre traditionsgeschichtliche Entwicklung* (WUNT
2 Reihe 2; Tubingen: J. C. B. Mohr, 1977). However, in the Johannine view, Jesus' dependence upon the Father is total (see 5:19–30). See D. A. Carson, *The Gospel According
to John* (Grand Rapids: Eerdmans, 1991) 494–95.
[27] Verse 14 is omitted by some manuscripts. Despite the clumsy *aitēsēte me*, and its
repetition, it should be retained. For detail, see B. M. Metzger, *A Textual Commentary on
the Greek New Testament* (2d ed.; Stuttgart: German Bible Society, 1994) 208; Carson,
John, 497–98. For Becker, *Johannes*, 2:465, vv 14-15 are clumsy Johannine paraenesis,
and disturb the link between v. 13 and v. 16. This ignores the important relationship
between v. 15 and v. 24 which separates vv. 15-24 from vv. 12-14. See Dettwiler, *Die
Gegenwart*, 125–26.

works will continue to be done. The greatness of the works lies in
their being done in his name, after his departure. Jesus affirms that
his works, and even greater works, will continue in the life of the
believers after his departure. There will be a difference between the
works of Jesus, done during his ministry, and the works of the disciples
after Jesus' departure. Jesus' departure opens a new era when the works
of the disciples surpass those of Jesus.[28] Jesus will be present in his
absence as the disciples do the works he is doing (v. 12: *ha egō poiō*),
and *he* will do (vv. 13-14: *egō poiēsō*) what the disciples request.[29] The
reader wonders *how* this will take place.[30] There is a logic to Jesus'
exhortation. He has done the works of the Father during his time with
the disciples (see v. 9) because of his oneness with the Father (vv. 10-
11). He is now departing to the house of the Father (v. 2), and he will
come again (v. 3). There will be an in-between time during which the
disciples must ask in Jesus' name, and he will continue the works of
the Father among them.[31] The ongoing presence of the absent Jesus
will be found in the worshiping community. Its members will associate themselves with the departed Jesus, asking in his name. Jesus, the
former Paraclete, doing whatever is asked in his name (vv. 13a, 14),
glorifies the Father in the Son (v. 13b). The glory of God, once seen in
the deeds of Jesus (see 2:11; 5:41; 7:18; 8:50, 54; 11:4, 40), will be seen
in the deeds of worshiping disciples, deeds done as a result of their
asking in Jesus' name (vv. 13-14).[32]

[28] See C. Dietzfelbinger, "Die grosseren Werke (Joh 14 12f.)," *NTS* 35 (1989) 27–32
[29] See Schnackenburg, *St John*, 3:72; D. E. Aune, *The Cultic Setting of Realized Eschatology
in Early Christianity* (NovTSup 28; Leiden: Brill, 1972) 104–5.
[30] Becker, *Johannes*, 2:464–65, rightly claims that vv 12-13 present Jesus as a Paraclete,
and thus prepare the way for the "other Paraclete" of v. 16. On vv. 12-14 as a preparation for vv. 15-27, see Segovia, *Farewell*, 90–93
[31] To ask *en tō onomati* ("in the name") probably reflects the practice of the earliest
communities who called upon the name of Jesus in prayer. This practice, which is not
a repetition of the practice of the magical cults, reflected a prayer in union with Jesus,
accordance with his will, and acceptance of his mission. See W. Heitmuller, *"Im Namen
Jesu": Eine sprach- u. religionsgeschichtliche Untersuchung zum Neuen Testament, speziell zu
altchristlichen Taufe* (FRLANT 2; Gottingen Vandenhoeck & Ruprecht, 1903) 53–65, 77–
80, 264–65; H. Bietenhard, *"onoma ktl,"* *TDNT* 5 (1968) 258–61.
[32] There is no need to have recourse to the subsequent missionary successes of early
Christianity to explain the "greater works" (see, e.g , Bauer, *Johannesevangelium*, 181;
Hoskyns, *Fourth Gospel*, 457, Rodriguez Ruiz, *Der Missionsgedanke*, 171–84) Dietzfelbinger, "Die grosseren Werke," 22–47, points to the uniqueness of the Johannine situation. Unable to call upon founding witnesses to the Jesus tradition, and in a situation
of conflict and rejection, the community develops a confident theology of its post-
Easter situation, surpassing the works of Jesus, directed and inspired by the Paraclete.
See also C. Dietzfelbinger, "Paraklet und theologischer Anspruch im Johannesevangelium," *ZTK* 82 (1985) 394–408.

2. The Fruits of Belief and Love (14:15-24)
a. Verses 15-17: The Paraclete and the World
While vv. 12-14 demanded faith and dependence, v. 15 asks for love, and the theme of love holds vv. 15-24 together. The disciple who loves Jesus shows this union by holding fast to his commandments (v. 15).[33] Jesus has received a commandment from the Father to make God known. The way he loves (see 10:14-18) and the way he speaks (see 12:49-50) reveal this life-giving commandment. On the evening before his death Jesus exhorts his disciples to match his love (13:34-35; 14:15a) by holding fast (*tērēsete*) to his revealing word (v. 15b).[34] Jesus will pray, asking his Father to send "another Paraclete" (*allon paraklēton*) to be with them forever. Jesus' description of his ongoing presence to the believers in vv. 12-14, and especially in v. 13, indicates that he performs the role of a Paraclete (see also 1 John 2:1). But there will be "another Paraclete." This Paraclete will not be lifted up in death to reveal the love of God in a consummate act of love for the disciples (see 12:32-33; 13:1), but will remain with the disciples *eis ton aiōna* (v. 16).[35] The Paraclete is the Spirit of truth (*to pneuma tēs alētheias*), "the

---

[33] The future *tērēsete*, following Vaticanus, rather than the imperative (Bezae, Koridethi) or the subjunctive (P66, Sinaiticus), makes best sense. See Barrett, *St John*, 461

[34] This section (vv. 15-24) is marked by Jesus' demand that the disciple keep the "word," "words," and "commandments" (see vv. 15, 21, 23, 24). There is widespread agreement that these expressions all ask for faith in the revelation of God in and through the word of Jesus. See Segovia, *Farewell*, 94–95. X Léon-Dufour, *Lecture de l'Evangile selon Jean*, (3 vols., Parole de Dieu; Paris: Seuil, 1988–93) 3:112–16, has shown the close link that exists between the demands of Jesus and the demands of the Covenant, especially as they are found in Deuteronomy (see Deut 5:10; 6:5-6; 7:9; 10:12-13, 11:13, 22). See also Beutler, *Habt keine Angst,* 55–83.

[35] There is a voluminous discussion of the background for the term *paraklētos,* and of the possible source from which the Fourth Evangelist may have taken the Paraclete material. For a survey, see Brown, "The Paraclete," 115–26; G. M. Burge, *The Anointed Community: The Holy Spirit in the Johannine Tradition* (Grand Rapids: Eerdmans, 1987) 3–45; de la Potterie, *La Vérité,* 1 330–341; Dettwiler, *Die Gegenwart,* 181–89. The primary meaning of the Greek word is forensic: "legal assistant, advocate" (LSJ, 1313, s.v.). This meaning is also found, transliterated, in Hebrew and Aramaic documents. On this, see the discussions of N. Johansson, *Parakletoi: Vorstellungen von Fursprechern für die Menschen vor Gott in der alttestamentlichen Religion, im Spatjudentum und Urchristentum* (Lund Gleerup, 1940), who looks to the widespread Jewish idea of an intercessor, and O Betz, *Der Paraklet: Fursprecher im haretischen Spatjudentum, im Johannesevangelium und in neu gefundenen gnostischen Schriften* (AGSU 2; Leiden: E. J. Brill, 1963) 36–116, who uses Qumran to point to an angelic being (Michael) behind the interceding Paraclete. See also F. Manns, *L'Evangile de Jean à la lumière du Judaisme* (SBFA 33; Jerusalem: Franciscan Printing Press, 1991) 360–73. Such views are generally regarded as not best responding to the *overall* Johannine use of the term. De la Potterie, *La Verité,* 1:336–39, argues for the forensic nature of the Paraclete sayings by setting them within the Fourth

Spirit who communicates truth,"[36] the ongoing presence of the revelation of God in the world, which "the world" is unable to recognize. One cannot live in "the world of Jesus" if one thinks that it can be determined by the realities of "this world." Jesus' *origin* with the Father has always been the stumbling block (see 1:35-51; 3:1-21, 31-36; 4:10-15; 5:19-30, 36-38, 43-44; 6:41-51; 7:25-31, 40-44; 8:12-20, 21-29; 9:24-34; 10:31-39). His *return* to the Father continues "the world's" inability to recognize the ongoing presence of the revelation of God (v. 17a).

The disciples are part of the "world of Jesus." As such, the Spirit of truth already dwells with them (v. 17cα: *par' humin menei*), and there will be another Paraclete who will be in them (v. 17cβ: *en humin estai*). The interplay between Jesus as Paraclete (see v. 13) and the gift of another Paraclete (see v. 16) continues. Jesus is the gift of the truth (see 1:17), the way who is the truth (see 14:6) who dwells with them (*par' humin menei*).[37] His departure to the Father will not bring that revealing presence to an end. It will be in them (*en humin estai*).[38] The

---

Gospel understood as a trial between Jesus and "the world." Bauer (*Johannesevangelium*, 182–83) and others suggest that the Johannine expression is best linked with the use of *parakalein* and *paraklēsis* in early Christianity and with uses of *parakalōn* in LXX Greek (see Job 16:2, but not elsewhere) for the concept of consolation (see Isa 40:1) This position has been throughly developed by U. B. Muller, "Die Parakletenvorstellung im Johannesevangelium," *ZTK* 71 (1974) 31–77. For Muller, "Die Parakletenvorstellung," 43–52, the earliest Johannine concept was "the Spirit of truth," and this notion was then associated with the Paraclete as the guide, comfort and teacher The originally separate traditions of "Holy Spirit" and "Paraclete" have been joined in the Fourth Gospel (see 14 16-17, 26). On the fundamentally Johannine nature of the expression, see G. Johnston, *The Spirit-Paraclete in the Gospel of John* (SNTSMS 12; Cambridge: Cambridge Univ. Press, 1970) 3–58; J. L Martyn, *History and Theology in the Fourth Gospel* (2d ed.; Nashville. Abingdon, 1979) 143–51. The classical presentation of the case for the Paraclete passages as interpolations is found in H. Windisch, *The Spirit-Paraclete in the Fourth Gospel* (Facet Books: Biblical Series 20, Philadelphia· Fortress Press, 1968) 1–26 (original German, 1927).

[36] Barrett, *St John*, 463. The identification of the Paraclete with the Spirit links what may have originally been two traditions. The link had probably been made before the Gospel came into existence.

[37] See de la Potterie, *La Vérité*, 1:345–56, on the link between faith in Jesus and the gift of the Paraclete, impossible for "the world," but present to the disciples.

[38] Copyists and scholars have attempted to smooth out the two uses of the present tense (*ginōskete . . . menei*) and the final future (*estai*). Manns, *L'Evangile*, 352, claims that it represents a Rabbinic practice, where both verbs simultaneously mean present and future. See the discussion in J E. Morgan-Wynne, "A Note on John 14.17b," *BZ* 23 (1979) 93–96. Morgan-Wynne correctly insists, "The future *estai* points to the post-cross era" (96). Copyists have made the *menei* future (it only requires a change of accent), while some scholars who rightly accept the present tense argue that it has a future meaning. See, e.g., Beasley-Murray, *John*, 243.

Paraclete, a new character in the narrative, is the ongoing presence of the truth as "the Spirit who communicates truth." These first words on the Paraclete introduce the figure as the ongoing presence of the revelation of God to those who love Jesus and keep his command- ments (see v. 15). The presence of the Paraclete will ensure that the ongoing revelation of the truth will continue among Jesus' disciples.[39] Despite the absence of the physical Jesus, his revealing mission is not coming to an end; it is moving toward a new era when the role of the former Paraclete, Jesus, will be taken over by another Paraclete, the Spirit of truth. The reader recalls the narrator's comment as Jesus promised the gift of living water during the celebration of Tabernacles: "Now he said this about the Spirit, which those who believed in him were to receive; for as yet the Spirit had not been given, because Jesus was not yet glorified" (7:39). The moment of glorification is at hand (see 11:4, 51-53; 12:23, 32-33; 13:1, 31-32), and Jesus' gift of the Spirit is associated with it. *That* such a gift will take place is now an estab- lished part of the narrative; *how* it will happen is yet to be discovered.[40]

b. Verses 18-21: The Revelation of the Oneness of Jesus and the Father
Jesus' departure (see vv. 2-3, 4-5, 18) will not leave the disciples, known to the reader as "children" (see 1:12; 11:52: *tekna tou theou*), orphans (*orphanous*). This situation should follow the death of a par- ent, and Jesus' departure is associated with his death; yet it leads to his coming. The departure and the return coalesce (v. 18)! Jesus' physical departure will not be the end of his presence. This theme dominates vv. 18-21. Jesus' departure ends all "sight" of the revelation of the truth for "the world." As he warned "the Jews": "The light is with you for a little while (*eti mikron*). Walk while you have the light, lest the darkness overtake you" (12:35ab). That "little while" (14:19a: *eti mi- kron*) is now coming to an end for "the world," as Jesus will depart definitively from its midst.[41] But the disciples, the ones who believe

[39] Many scholars (see, e.g., Schnackenburg, *St John*, 3:76; Manns, *L'Evangile*, 352) ex- plain the tenses as a reflection of the later experience of the Johannine community, experiencing the Spirit, and confident of the future presence of the Spirit. Schnacken- burg distinguishes between the prepositions to make this point: *par' humin* refers to the present experience of the community, and *en humin* stresses the disciples' future knowledge of the Spirit's "inner presence."

[40] There is a *temporal* distance between Jesus and the Paraclete that must be main- tained, despite O'Day's claims ("'I Have Overcome'," 160–61), that the Paraclete is not time-bound. Jesus departs before the gift of the Spirit.

[41] The use of *eti mikron* in 12:35, warning "the Jews" as well as the more positive use of the expression with the disciples in 13:33, is involved in 14:19. It still contains an "oppressive element" denied by Schnackenburg, *St John*, 3:77–78.

in Jesus (see vv. 1, 11, 12), who love him and hold fast to his com-mandments (v. 15), are promised the sight of the departed Jesus and a life that will flow from the fact that he lives beyond the departure of his death (v. 19).

When will this be? Most scholars opt for the resurrection, while others refer to different forms of a life-giving presence of the risen Christ among the believers.[42] The distinction between the physical Jesus, who is departing, and the "other Paraclete," who will be given (see v. 16), must be maintained. They are two different characters in the narrative, however closely their roles may be linked. The reader is aware that Jesus' departure will be through death (see 12:32-33) and that the Paraclete is a gift of the departed Jesus (v. 16). Although Jesus is going away (v. 18a), he is coming to his disciples (v. 18b: *erchomai*) and they will see him (v. 19b: *theōreite*). The death and departure of Jesus will lead to his life with the Father (v. 19cβ) and life for the disciples (v. 19cγ). Because Jesus still lives, a consequence of his depar-ture from the world is his life-giving presence to the disciples (v. 19b: *hoti egō zō kai humeis zēsete*).[43] Jesus' departure and the gift of the Para-clete, the Spirit of truth, necessitate a distinction between Jesus and the Spirit. But what the Spirit does for the disciples is the prolongation and the perfection of what Jesus does for them. In the Spirit-Paraclete, the absence of the physical Jesus is overcome.[44] How is this possible? David Aune has shown that there can be no notion of the departed

---

[42] For a survey, see Aune, *Cultic Setting*, 128-29. See also Migliasso, *La presenza*, 207-26, who unites the going, the coming and the life-giving presence of the absent Jesus to the redemptive event of the cross.

[43] This "life" is linked to the gift of the Paraclete. See Muller, "Die Parakletenvorstel-lung," 51. On the disciples as "successor-agents" of the working of Jesus and the bearers of the presence of the Father and the Son, see D. B. Woll, "The Departure of 'the Way': The First Farewell Discourse in the Gospel of John," *JBL* 99 (1980) 231-39.

[44] The Greek Fathers, especially Cyril of Alexandria, identified Jesus with the Paraclete. See A. Casurella, *The Johannine Paraclete in the Church Fathers: A Study in the History of Exegesis* (BGBE 25; Tubingen: J. C. B. Mohr, 1983) 43-45, 143-44. This position is nowa-days universally rejected. See, e.g., Hoskyns, *Fourth Gospel*, 458-60 I am arguing for a position between that of the Fathers, who *identified* Jesus and the Paraclete, and most contemporary scholarship which argues that *Jesus returns* in the post-resurrection pe-riod. One must distinguish yet associate Jesus, the Paraclete (v. 13), and "the other Paraclete" (vv. 16-17). See Becker, *Johannes*, 2:464-65, 466-67; J. Zumstein, "Mémoire et relecture pascale dans l'évangile de Jean," in D. Marguerat, and J. Zumstein, eds., *Le mémoire et le temps: Mélanges offerts a Pierre Bonnard* (Genève: Labor et Fides, 1991) 165; Neugebauer, *Die eschatologischen Aussagen*, 113-15; H. Weder, "*Deus Incarnatus:* On the Hermeneutics of Christology in the Johannine Writings," in R A Culpepper and C. C. Black, eds., *Exploring the Gospel of John* (Louisville: Westminster/John Knox, 1996) 336-39.

Jesus' return in any physical form. It is in the community's "experi-ence of the presence of the exalted Jesus in the midst of the worship-ping community" that the absent one is present to those who love him and keep his commandments.[45] Jesus' departure is not leaving them orphans (v. 18), as he comes to them in a gift of a living presence (v. 19). Jesus is leaving his disciples. This affirmation must be taken seriously. It no doubt reflected the experience of the Johannine read-ers, for whom the fleshly Jesus of Nazareth was no longer present.[46] But the experience of the living Jesus, exalted and thus no longer available in and through the physical Jesus, continues in and through the permanent presence of the Spirit-Paraclete. In the worshiping community, and especially in baptism and Eucharist, those who love and believe experience the presence of the absent one.[47] The "coming" of the exalted—and therefore absent—Jesus in the worship of the community is a proleptic experience of a final "coming" made pos-sible in the in-between time by the Spirit's presence.

Jesus promises a knowledge that will be granted to the believer on the day of his departure (*en ekeinę tę hēmerą*), the time of his coming and his gift of new life (v. 20).[48] This knowledge, a fruit of the presence of the Spirit, is the revelation of the oneness that exists between the Father and the Son and the mutual oneness that exists between Jesus and the believer. The oneness between the Father and the Son has been at the heart of much of Jesus' teaching and has been the basis of his authority (see, e.g., 5:19-30), but the introduction of the believer into that oneness is new. The resolution of the search for knowledge and union with God has been promised to those who believe in Jesus (see vv. 1, 11, 12), who love him and keep his commandments (v. 15). They will not be left orphans through the departure of Jesus (v. 18), but granted life (v. 19), a knowledge of God, his Son, and themselves (v. 20). The departure of Jesus unleashes something hitherto unknown and unspoken among his disciples.

---

[45] Aune, *Cultic Setting,* 126–33. For the quotation, see 133.

[46] See Muller, "Die Parakletenvorstellung," 40–43. See also F Porsch, "Der 'andere Par-aklet,'" *BK* 37 (1982) 134

[47] See Aune, *Cultic Setting,* 16–18, 112–14. F. J. Moloney, *Belief in the Word: Reading John 1–4* (Minneapolis: Fortress Press, 1993) 109–14 (on John 3:3-5); idem, *Signs and Shadows: Reading John 5–12* (Minneapolis: Fortress Press, 1996) 55–59 (on John 6:51-58).

[48] Taking the traditional eschatological expression *en ekeinē tē hēmerą* as a reference to Jesus' "hour" and departure (see E. Haenchen, *John* [2 vols.; trans. R. W. Funk, Hermen-eia; Philadelphia: Fortress Press, 1984] 2:126–27), producing what Brown (*John,* 2:640) rightly describes as "the period of Christian existence made possible by 'the hour.'" Most read it as indicating the resurrection.

As v. 21 opens, Jesus shifts from the intimacy of the second person address to his disciples to the wider audience of the Gospel's readership: "Anyone who has my commandments." All potential recipients of the promise of v. 20 are told that oneness with God is to be understood in terms of love. The reader is aware that Jesus' departure to the Father will be highlighted by his love for his own (13:1), having read how this will shortly take place in the midst of the disciples' ignorance, betrayal, and denial (13:1-38). But disciples must transform their response to the revelation of God in Jesus by a commitment to loving Jesus and holding fast to his commandments. They are now called to a parallel life of love in the in-between time after the departure of Jesus (13:34-35), enlivened by the gift of the Paraclete (14:16), communicating life to the disciples that flows from the departed but living Jesus (v. 19). This love will lead to being loved by the Father and by Jesus (v. 21b), and to the ongoing revelation of Jesus (*emphanizein autō hemauton;* see Exod 33:13, 18; Wis 1:2; 17:4), even after his departure (v. 21c).[49] Jesus' departure is not a departure in the sense in which "the world" would understand the experience of death. On the contrary, as a consequence of the gift of the Paraclete, the Spirit of truth (vv. 15-16), it leads to the intimacy of being loved by both the Father and Jesus, and to the ongoing revelation of God in and through Jesus as disciples experience the presence of the absent one in their worship.

c. Verses 22-24: Loving Jesus and Keeping His Word   The theme of loving Jesus and holding fast to his commandments opened the first subsection of vv. 15-24. Judas' question, asking further clarification of a revelation to the disciples, which will not be given to "the world" (v. 22), enables this subsection of the discourse to close with the same themes (vv. 23-24). As with earlier questions (see vv. 5, 8), Judas asks for information already obvious to the reader.[50] Jesus' revelation of himself, which is the sight of God's glory (see 1:14, 2:11; 11:4, 40), can only be given to those who are open to his word. Judas wonders about a revelation that will startle the world (see 7:3-4). From the beginnings of the story, the author has instructed the reader that the sight of the revelation of God in Jesus is the consequence of belief (see 1:9-13; 1:19-51; 2:1—4:54). The present discourse, uttered on the eve before Jesus' consummate act of love for his own (see 13:1), has opened with

---

[49] As Barrett, *St John*, 465, points out, the use of *emphanizein*, a hapax legomenon, "is an appropriate word since it is used of theophanies."

[50] On "Judas, not Iscariot," see Schnackenburg, *St John*, 3:80–81.

a strong insistence on the need for belief (see 14:1, 11, 12) but has made a further demand from the disciples: Disciples are not only to believe in the word of Jesus, but also to love him (see 14:15, 21, 23-24). The departed Jesus will manifest himself to the disciples because they believe in his words and love him. He will not manifest himself to "the world," because it refuses both belief and love. The reader knows of the hostility, rejection, and increasing threat of a violent end that marked the public life of Jesus. But during that period of time he was physically present. Such a situation will no longer exist in the in-between time, after the departure of Jesus. The absent Jesus will be present only to those who, gifted with the Spirit, believe and love.

Jesus reaffirms the positive results of a disciple's loving him and keeping his word: the Father of Jesus *will love* that disciple, and both Father and Son *will come* and *will set up* their abode in him or her (v. 23). As with vv. 18-21, the question arises: When will this "coming" take place? In v. 23 the departure is coupled with the promise of the coming of the Father and the Son to make their home (*monēn*) with the disciple who loves Jesus and keeps his word. But unlike vv. 18-21, which promised the experience of the presence of the absent Jesus after his departure (see v. 18: *erchomai pros humas*), in v. 23 every verb is in the future: the Father and the Son *will love,* they *will come,* and they *will establish* a dwelling place (see v. 23: *pros auton eleusometha*). The temporal setting of the meal must be kept in mind. Jesus opened his discourse speaking of a time between his departure and the promise of his future coming (vv. 2-3). This period will be filled by the presence of the Paraclete (vv. 15-17) and the life-giving presence of the departed and exalted Lord in the worshiping community (vv. 18-21). In v. 23 the presence of the absent one is restated in a way that assures the disciple of *both* a proximate future and a final outcome. Jesus' promise in vv. 18-21 continues into v. 23. The love of the Father and the presence of the Father and the absent Jesus will be part of the in-between time for those who love Jesus and keep his word. But there are two details in v. 23 that also point the reader toward the end of the in-between time. First, the use of the present tense (v. 18: *erchomai*) and the future (v. 23: *eleusometha*) in proximate contexts indicates that the author is suggesting different possibilities for the "coming" in vv. 18-21 and v. 23.[51] Second, the resumption of an image from vv. 2-3, where *monē* was used, suggests the definitive and permanent

[51] The *erchomai* in v. 18 cannot be put down to the use of the present with a future meaning, unlike the use of *palin erchomai* in v. 3 where a future meaning is likely within the general context and after *palin*.

presence of the Father and the Son, establishing their *monēn* with the one who loves Jesus and holds fast to his word (v. 23).[52] The departed Jesus comes to those who love and believe as they experience the presence of the absent one (v. 18-21), and they can also look forward to a final coming, when Jesus and the Father will set up their dwelling with them (v. 23).[53] The person who does not love Jesus and does not keep his words is rejecting the words of the Father who sent Jesus. It is not the sent one who is being rejected, but the one who sent him (v. 24). The promise of the dwelling of the Father and the Son is in the future, but the rejection of the one who does not love Jesus or keep his commandments (*mē agapōn . . . ou tērei*) is an action that takes place in the present. This is a rejection of the ongoing revelation of God that took place in the words and works of Jesus and is continued in the Spirit-filled community. It restates a theme that has appeared repeatedly during Jesus' public ministry (see 3:34; 5:23-24; 8:18, 28, 38, 47; 12:49). In a short time Jesus will be physically absent, but the revelation of God continues in and through the Spirit-filled community of disciples, enlived by the presence of the absent one.[54] It can be rejected by those who refuse to love Jesus and keep his commandments, but such rejection is nothing less than a rejection of God (v. 24).

The theme of Jesus' departure is present across vv. 1-14, especially in vv. 1-6. It is a fundamental presupposition for all that is said in vv. 15-24. The situation of the disciples after Jesus' departure (see vv. 18-19) is dealt with. While some of Jesus' instructions are based

---

[52] Here I depart from Aune, *Cultic Setting*, 130–31, who associates the *monē* of v. 23 (where *oikia* does not appear) with the use of *oikia* and *monē* in v. 2, claiming that they both refer to "an individual believer who is the locus for the pneumatic dwelling of the Father and the Son."

[53] I am questioning the widespread interpretation of v. 23 as "in terms of the mystical abiding of God with the believer" (Barrett, *St John*, 466), or a collapsing of history into a totally realized eschatology (see Bultmann, *John*, 613). The almost universal agreement that vv. 18-24 refers to the *present* coming of Jesus (and the Father) to the believer does away with the need for the Paraclete. Dettwiler, *Die Gegenwart*, 191–202, interprets vv 18-24 as addressing the Easter-coming of Jesus. But he dehistoricizes Easter, claiming that it does not refer to an event in the past, but is "die Erfahrbarkeit der Liebe Gottes in Jesus" (195). This leads to an unsatisfactory explanation of the distinction between Jesus and the Paraclete: "Die damit angezeigte Differenzierung zwischen Jesus und dem Geist ist allerdings nicht eine Differenz zweier voneinander getrennter Entitäten, sondern zweier Modi der Anwesenheit Jesus" (204) There is, therefore, no Johannine eschatological expectation, nor any real distinction between Jesus and the Paraclete.

[54] See Aune, *Cultic Setting*, 103–5.

on the reader's knowledge and experience of the story of his public ministry (see vv. 16-17, 19, 24), they increasingly look forward to the inevitable end of the Gospel, known to the reader as his glorification and the revelation of the glory of God (see 11:4; 12:23; 13:31-32), the moment in the future when the Spirit will be given to the believer (see 7:37-39). This feature of the story has led to the insinuation of a theme that has not been present earlier in the story: love (vv. 15, 21, 23-24: "love me") and loyalty (vv. 15, 21, 23-24: "keep my word/ words/commandments"). The association of belief, love, and loyalty leads to a new promise: disciples who, in the presence of the Paraclete, love Jesus and keep his commandments in the in-between time, will come to know God and be loved by God and Jesus. Because the exalted Jesus lives, gifted by the Spirit-Paraclete (see vv. 16-17), they will experience the life-giving presence of the absent one (see v. 19). They will experience the life of love that unites the Father and the Son (vv. 20-21), until the Father and the Son finally come to establish their dwelling with them (v. 23).

3. The Departure of Jesus (14:25-31)
a. Verses 25-26: The Paraclete and the Disciples The theme of Jesus' departure (see vv. 1-6, 18-24) returns in Jesus' closing words (vv. 25-31). There are two "times" in the experience of the disciples. At the moment, as Jesus speaks to them, he is still *with them* (v. 25), but there will be a time in the future when the Paraclete, the Holy Spirit, *will be with them*, sent by the Father in the name of Jesus (see vv. 16-17), replacing the physical presence of Jesus,[55] teaching them all things, and recalling for the disciples everything he has said to them (v. 26). As Jesus is the sent one of the Father (see 4:34; 5:23, 24, 30, 37; 6:38–40; 7:16; 8:16, 18, 26; 12:44-49), so is the Paraclete sent by the Father, in the name of Jesus.[56] The one mission and purpose of Jesus, a Paraclete who speaks and teaches "his own," and the "other Paraclete" (see vv. 13, 16), who teaches and brings back the memory of all that Jesus has said, links the "time of Jesus" with the "time after the departure of Jesus."[57] The accepted meaning of a departure has been

[55] This is the only place in the NT where the expression "the Holy Spirit" is found. It probably passed into the Johannine text from the tradition, which had already associated it with the Paraclete. See Schnackenburg, *St John*, 3:83.

[56] In 14:16 the Father is said to send the Paraclete *at Jesus' request*. In v. 26 the Father sends the Spirit *in Jesus' name*. The latter expression carries with it the idea of union and ongoing revelation. See de la Potterie, *La Vérité*, 1:363–67.

[57] The verbs *didaxei* and *hupomnēsei* are joined with an explicative *kai*. The *teaching* of the Holy Spirit *recalls* what Jesus has said, taking it deeper and further into the memory

undermined. The reader recalls two moments during the ministry of Jesus when the narrator looked beyond the story time to a period "when he was raised from the dead" (2:22), "when Jesus was glorified" (12:16). The inability of the disciples to understand the words and deeds of Jesus will be overcome as they "remember" what Jesus had said (2:22) and what had been written of him and done to him (12:16). The reader now knows that this "remembering" will be fruit of the presence of the Paraclete with the disciples in the in-between time.[58] Jesus' words on the Paraclete in vv. 16-17 and v. 26 are related, but the later teaching (v. 26) adds to what was said in vv. 16-17. The Paraclete will do what Jesus has done: make God known through word and teaching. In v. 16 Jesus focused on the inability of "the world" to know the Paraclete, but in v. 26 the gift of the Paraclete to the disciples is his major concern. As Jesus was *with* the disciples (see v. 25), so will the Paraclete be *with* the disciples (v. 16). As the story has insisted that Jesus' teaching has revealed God to the disciples, so will the Paraclete recall and continue Jesus' revelation of God to the disciples (v. 26).[59]

b. Verse 27a: The Gift of Peace   There is a further fruit of the departure of Jesus and the presence of the Paraclete: peace. Matching Jesus' earlier insistence that hearts not be troubled because of his departure (v. 1), Jesus now informs the disciples that he is leaving a precious gift with them, a peace "the world" can never give (v. 27a).[60] The peace Jesus offers is *his* peace (*eirēnēn tēn emēn*), and the qualification makes it something that can never be matched by the peace of "the world." The peace of Jesus flows from his oneness with the Father, his return to the Father from whence he came, and the authority he has with the Father, so that whatever is asked in his name will be given (see vv. 13-14, 16). The gift of peace, therefore, is intimately associated

---

and consciousness of the disciples of Jesus during the in-between time. See de la Potterie, *La Vérité*, 1:367–78.

[58] The earlier passages (2:22; 12:16) have the verb *mimnēskō*, while 14:26, speaking of the action of the Paraclete, strengthens this with the use of *hupomimnēskō*. On "remembering" as part of the Jewish testament tradition, see Bammel, "The Farewell Discourse," 108.

[59] Muller, "Die Parakletenvorstellung," 52–65, draws a large number of parallels between the consoling, teaching presence of the Paraclete, and the period after the death of the hero envisioned by the Jewish testamentary traditions See *Assumption of Moses* (post-Moses); *Antiquitates Biblicae* (post-Moses); *Syriac Baruch 77* (post-Baruch); *4 Ezra 14* (post-Ezra).

[60] On the gift of peace as something "left" by the departing Jesus, a "parting gift" (NEB), see B. F. Westcott, *The Gospel According to Saint John* (London: John Murray, 1908) 209.

with the gift of the Spirit Paraclete, the ongoing presence of Jesus in his absence (see vv. 16-17, 26), the source of the disciples' being loved by the Father and the Son, the agent for the ongoing revelation of both Jesus and the Father to the one who loves Jesus and keeps his commandments in the in-between time (see vv. 20-21). But it would be a mistake for the reader to regard the gift of the Spirit and the gift of peace as identical. Jesus' departure leads to a oneness between the believer, Jesus, and the Father that transcends the Spirit, however much it may be a result of the abiding presence of the Spirit. Jesus' gift of peace is "from God," a gift the quantifiable and fragile peace produced by the politics of this world can never match.[61] In this peace (v. 27b), inspired and enlightened by the Spirit of Truth, the other Paraclete (vv. 16-17, 26), a community of disciples will perform "greater works" (v. 12) than Jesus himself, continuing the revelation of the Father and the Son (vv. 18-21).[62]

c. Verses 27b-31: Departure to the Father   Recalling his earlier words, Jesus commands the disciples not to be troubled; nor should they be stricken with fear (see v. 1). One could expect such responses from disciples faced with the announcement that their master and model is about to depart, especially when they suspect the departure will be the result of violence (v. 27b). Jesus has insisted that the disciples are to love him and to hold fast to his word (see vv. 15, 21, 23-24). Their love is now tested as he reminds them of his words by means of a brief paraphrase of vv. 3-4: "I go away, and I am coming [*erchomai*] to you" (v. 28a). Untroubled hearts, without fear in face of his departure, are the guarantee that they have heard his words and are holding fast to them. If they loved Jesus, therefore, they would rejoice at his departure, but they still have much to learn.[63] A new era is dawning, and there is reason for joy. Their love for Jesus should lead them to rejoice in what will happen *for Jesus* in his departure to the Father who is greater than him.[64] Jesus is the obedient sent one of the Father (see 4:34; 5:19, 23, 24, 30, 37; 6:38-40; 7:16; 8:16, 18, 26, 29, 55; 12:44-49), and it is as the lesser figure, the sent one, that he delights in his

[61] On peace, see Isa 9:6-7; 52 7, 57:18-19; Ezek 37:26; Hag 2:9, Acts 10:36; Rom 14:17.
[62] See Dietzfelbinger, "Die grosseren Werke," 32–34.
[63] Accepting with Brown, *John*, 2:654, and others, that the conditional tense of *ei ēgapate me* is unreal, indicating that their love is at the moment possessive, and thus could lead to sadness at Jesus' departure.
[64] C. K. Barrett, "The Father is Greater than I' (John 14:28). Subordinationist Christology in the New Testament," in *Essays on John* (London: SPCK, 1982) 28.

return to the greater figure, the sender (v. 28b).[65] But the coming of
the sent one into the world, and his return to the one who sent him
is not irrelevant to the disciples. Thus, even these words of Jesus are
"less concerned with the relation between the Father and the Son,
than with the relation between the Father and the Son and the Disciples."[66]

The theme of "before and after" the departure returns. Jesus recalls
his words to the disciples at the heart of the footwashing and the gift
of the morsel (see 13:19). He is telling them all these things while he
is still with them (*nun*) so that afterward (*hotan genētai*) they might
believe (v. 29). There is an inevitability about the events that lie in the
proximate future that must not be cause for fear or distress. Love for
Jesus and belief in his word should make them occasions for further
belief. The departure of Jesus will not be a moment of tragic desolation
for the disciples (see vv. 1, 18, 27b), but the beginning of the time of
the Paraclete (vv. 16-17), a time of love (vv. 15, 21, 23-24, 28), belief
(vv. 15, 21, 23-24, 29), joy (v. 28), and peace (v. 27a). Jesus' words to
the disciples are coming to an end as the departure is nigh (v. 30a).
The indications throughout the narrative so far, that Jesus' departure
would be through violence, are reinforced as he tells his disciples that
he will not speak to them much longer, as the ruler of this world is
coming (v. 30b). No doubt the reference to *ho tou kosmou archōn* refers
to the power of evil that opposes Jesus at a metahistorical level, the
darkness, in the midst of which the light shines (see 1:5).[67] But the
reader has met a series of *archontes* throughout the story, and they all
come from the world of "the Jews" (see 3:1; 7:26, 48; 12:31[!], 42).[68]
Throughout the Gospel the reader has followed a presentation of Jesus' increasingly intense clash with "the Jews," leading inevitably toward violence (see 5:18; 7:1, 19-20, 25; 8:37; 40; 11:53, 57). But the
reader is aware that Jesus' moment of violent death and departure
must be understood differently. He will be "lifted up" in death (see

[65] See Brown, *John*, 2:655. On the difficulties that 14 28 created in the early Church,
especially during the Arian crisis, see Schnackenburg, *St John*, 3 85–86, and Patristic
discussions of Jesus' subordination in Westcott, *St John*, 213–16. See also Barrett, "'The
Father is Greater," 19–36.

[66] Hoskyns, *Fourth Gospel*, 464.

[67] See, most recently, J. I. Kovacs, "'Now Shall the Ruler of This World Be Driven Out'.
Jesus' Death as Cosmic Battle in John 12:20-36," *JBL* 114 (1995) 228–40.

[68] For my suggestion that, as in 14:30, the *ho archōn tou kosmou toutou* ("the ruler of
this world") of 12:31 is an oblique reference to "the Jews," see Moloney, *Signs and Shadows*, 191–92. A link with the cult of Heracles, as suggested by J E. Bruns, "A Note on
John 16:33 and I John 2:13-14," *JBL* 86 (1967) 451–53, is unlikely.

3:13-14; 8:28; 12:32-33), overcoming the powers of darkness (see 1:5; 11:50-53; 12:7, 10, 23-24, 31-33) to return to the Father (see 13:1; 14:28). The departure of Jesus is unlike any other departure. Despite all appearances to the contrary, the disciples and the reader should know that the prince of this world has no power over Jesus, whose departure is the result of his loving response to his Father (v. 30c; see 4:34; 5:30; 6:38; 10:15, 17-18). Despite the ultimate impotence of the prince of this world, Jesus accepts his departure at the violent hands of his opponents to reveal to the world his love for his Father. He has spoken of the Father's love for him (see 3:35; 5:20; 10:17), and now he announces his reciprocation of that love.[69] The time for words appears to have come to an end. Jesus' violent departure will make known to the world—by deeds rather than words—how much Jesus loves the Father (v. 31a), and it will be a final demonstration of his unconditional acceptance of the will of his Father (v. 30b).[70]

Jesus announces a departure: "Rise, let us go hence" (v. 31c).[71] The reader expects the action of the violent encounter between the prince of this world and Jesus, announced in v. 30, to begin, but no such events follow upon Jesus' summons to leave the table. This is a notorious problem and doubtless reflects an earlier stage in the development of the discourse before the addition of chapters 15–17, when 14:31 ran into the opening words of the Passion in 18:1. But what does the reader make of this summons to go forth, which leads nowhere? Perhaps the very frustration felt by historical-critical scholars supplies the answer,[72] as the reader is also frustrated. The frustration has a rhetori-

---

[69] 14:31 is the only passage in the New Testament that mentions Jesus loves the Father

[70] The use of *ho kosmos* ("the world") in v. 31a does not have the negative connotations of vv. 17, 19, and 22. It refers to God's creation offered life and salvation through the revelation of God in Jesus (see 3 16; 4:42).

[71] Commentators make reference to the close parallel between 14:31c and Mark 14:42, but this does not explain its clumsiness

[72] Most scholars settle for the literary explanation, seeing the words as the original ending of the discourse, leading directly into 18:1. Some (e.g., Bultmann, *John*, 631; Bernard, *St John*, 2 557) eliminate the problem by rearranging the sequence of the chapters. More ingenious have been the suggestions of Westcott, *St John*, 211, that 14:31 has Jesus and the disciples leaving the room, and chaps. 15–17 are uttered before they cross the Kidron (see also Haenchen, *John*, 2·128; Delebecque, *Jean*, 189; Carson, *John*, 478–79). Behler, *Last Discourse*, 131–32 (following Cyril of Alexandria), suggests that the words are addressed to all Christians, as well as the disciples, summoning them to conversion (see also Hoskyns, *Fourth Gospel*, 465; T. L. Brodie, *The Gospel according to John: A Literary and Theological Commentary* [New York· Oxford Univ. Press, 1993] 470–71). C. H. Dodd, *The Interpretation of the Fourth Gospel* (Cambridge: Cambridge Univ. Press, 1953) 407 (see also his *Historical Tradition in the Fourth Gospel* [Cambridge: Cambridge

cal function. The author gives every indication that the departure is
at hand, but he delays the telling of these events. The promise of
v. 30a, "I will no longer speak much with you," is temporarily frustrated as the reader moves on to further discourse. Tension and delay
enter the experience of the reader, who must work through further
elements of a farewell discourse before encountering, in 18:1-11, Jesus'
departure to meet the powers of darkness.[73] Tension and delay are also
the experience of the disciples living in the in-between time. The
reader and the characters in the story are drawn together as both experience frustrating delay. Jesus still has a great deal to tell the disciples;
thus, it is important that the action be "put on hold" lest these words
remain unsaid. The action must wait, as more must be said concerning
the future of the disciples, the difficulties and the blessings of living
in the in-between time. Similarly, more must be said concerning the
significance of the events of the departure for Jesus. Jesus' summons
to depart is a fitting conclusion to that section of the discourse that
has dealt with the fact of his departure and its consequences both for
himself and for his disciples.[74] The fact of the departure is now in
place, and the action that will set the departure in motion is unavoid-
ably imminent. However, the reader and the disciples experience a
delay. They must wait. Despite v. 30a, further words must be spoken
before the advent of *ho tou kosmou archōn* (v. 30b).

CONCLUSION

John 13:1-38 has made it clear that Jesus' self-gift in death will be a
consummate act of love (see especially 13:1, 18-20, 34-35), and 14:1-
31 has been entirely dedicated to the further, obvious clarification:
The death of Jesus will be his departure from the disciples. But the
departure of Jesus (14:1-6, 27b-31) must not be a moment for consternation or fear (vv. 1, 27b). Jesus returns to the Father (vv. 2-3, 6, 28)
to initiate an in-between time marked by the sending of another Paraclete who will be with the disciples, continuing the revealing task of
Jesus in his physical absence (vv. 16-17, 26). Thus, the departing Jesus

---

Univ. Press, 1965] 72; Léon-Dufour (*Lecture*, 3:144) argues that the words mean "up, let
us march to meet him." This is a spiritual acceptance of the conflict that lies ahead,
not physical movement; and it leads directly into chap. 15.

[73] See U. Schnelle, "Die Abschiedsreden im Johannesevangelium," *ZNW* 80 (1989)
70–73; W. S. Kurz, *Farewell Addresses in the New Testament* (Zaccheus Studies. New Testament; Collegeville, Minn.: Liturgical, 1990) 72 n. 59.

[74] See Simoens, *La gloire*, 128–29.

is both going away from the disciples and coming to them (see vv. 3, 18, 21, 23, 28). He has opened the way to the Father (vv. 6; 20-21). Before the promise of the Paraclete, and surrounding Philip's request that Jesus show the disciples the Father, Jesus has restated a central message of the Gospel: Jesus' oneness with the Father makes his words and his works the unique revelation of God (14:7-11). His going away from the disciples will not bring this revelation to an end. The gift of the Paraclete will continue this revelation *eis ton aiōna* (see v. 16); the oneness that exists between the Father and the Son will be revealed in the disciple who loves Jesus and keeps his commandments (vv. 18-21). The experience of the presence of the absent one during the in-between time, therefore, undermines all the reactions that one might expect from these disciples of a leader who is to depart by death.[75] In place of consternation and fear (see vv. 1, 27b), the Spirit-filled disciples will experience love (see vv. 15, 21, 23-24, 28), further belief (see vv. 15, 21, 23-24, 29) and joy (see v. 28). The gift of the departing Jesus to the disciples is his peace, a peace that cannot be matched by anything "the world" can provide (v. 27a).

Has the departure of Jesus initiated a utopia where life is made up of the abiding presence of the Spirit and the experience of the presence of the absent one, marked only by love, belief, joy, and peace, where the believer is swept into the oneness that unites Jesus and the Father? The reader in the text is united with the reader of the text, the Johannine community (and all subsequent Christians), in recognizing that the hostility of "the world" to Jesus (see 14:17, 19, 22, 24, 30) has not disappeared despite Jesus' claim that the prince of this world has no power over him (v. 30c). Indeed, there is a tension in the closing sentences of this first discourse. Jesus announces that he will no longer talk much (v. 30a), but that the prince of this world is coming (v. 30b). The reader is caught in a tension between the revelation of God in the word of Jesus—now no longer spoken, but available through the gift of the Paraclete (see v. 26)—and the ongoing presence of the prince of this world. This is the tension that lies behind Jesus' summons to rise (v. 31c) and face the prince of this world (v. 30c) and the need for further words from Jesus that will guide his disciples through the conflicts and hatred of the in-between time (see 15:1—16:3).

---

[75] Migliasso, *La presenza*, 207–26, has seen the centrality of this issue, but focuses on a somewhat forced reading of the death of Jesus as redemptive, creating a presence of the absent Jesus among redeemed disciples See especially 211–15.

Chapter Three

To Abide, to Love, and to Be Hated
John 15:1—16:3

JESUS HAS TOLD the disciples he would no longer say much to them (see 14:30), but he continues to speak of the vine, the vine-dresser, the branches, and the fruit (15:1-8).[1] Most major commentators and editions of the New Testament divide 16:4 into two parts, with v. 4a serving as a conclusion to 15:1—16:4a, and 16:4b opening the final section of the discourse proper: 16:4b-33.[2] There are

---

[1] R. Bultmann, *The Gospel of John: A Commentary* (trans. G. R. Beasley-Murray; Oxford: Blackwell, 1971) 524 n. 4, objects to the use of the expression "allegory." R. E Brown, *The Gospel according to John* (2 vols ; AB 29, 29A; Garden City, N Y.: Doubleday, 1966–70) 2:558–69, claims that the form of vv. 1-6 is best described as *mashal*. R. Borig, *Der wahre Weinstock· Untersuchungen zu Joh 15,1-10* (SANT 16, Munich: Kosel Verlag, 1967) 21–23 describes vv. 1-10 as a *Bildrede*, while D. A. Carson, *The Gospel according to John* (Grand Rapids: Eerdmans, 1991) 511–13, calls it an "extended metaphor." C K. Barrett (*The Gospel according to St John* [2d ed. London: SPCK, 1978] 470–71) suggests that it is a Johannine use of traditional material that defies classification. I will use the expression "metaphor," as this allows for "oscillation between literal and pictorial language" (Bultmann). See the survey of this discussion in F F. Segovia, *The Farewell of the Word: The Johannine Call to Abide* (Minneapolis. Fortress Press, 1991) 132–35, and J G. van der Watt, "'Metaphorik' in Joh 15,1-8," *BZ* 38 (1994) 68–71.

[2] See, e.g , the division of the text in such widely used editions as UBSGNT, RSV, JB, NAB, BJ, TOB J. Becker, "Die Abschiedsreden im Johannesevangelium," *ZNW* 61 (1970) 236–41, links 16:4b-15 with 15:18—16.4a because of the use of the Paraclete in both sections For a similar view, see B. Lindars, "The Persecution of Christians in John 15:18—16:4a," in W Horbury and B. McNeill, eds., *Suffering and Martyrdom in the New Testament* (Cambridge: Cambridge Univ. Press, 1981) 54–55; A. Niccaci, "Esame let-

grounds, however, for suggesting that 16:3 may conclude 15:1—16:3.[3] A theme basic to the latter section of 15:1—16:3 is stated in 15:21 and restated in 16:3. Read within the broader argument of the discourse, this formula suggests closure in both 15:21 and 16:3.

> But all this they will do (*tauta panta poiēsousin*) to you on my account, because they do not know (*hoti ouk oidasin*) him who sent me (15:21).
> And they will do this (*tauta poiēsousin*) because they have not known (*hoti ouk egnōsan*) the Father, nor me (16:3).

In both cases, the *tauta* looks back across the previous words of Jesus and brings a subsection to a close (15:18-21; 15:26—16:3).

A similar use of parallel expressions is found at the end of 15:1-11 and toward the end of the section on hatred: *tauta lelalēka humin hina* (see 15:11; 16:1). The second of these expressions, in 16:1, is a literary link that scholars use to close the discourse at 16:4a. This same expression (*tauta lelalēka humin hina*) is found there, and commentators see 16:1 and v. 4a as the beginning and the end of a literary inclusion forming a subsection, 16:1-4a. But the expression is introduced in v. 4a by an adversative, *alla,* and returns with the adversative in 16:6 (*all' hoti tauta lelalēka humin*). The identical expression, but without the adversative, reappears in 16:33 (*tauta lelalēka humin hina*).[4] It is possible that 16:4a and v. 33 form an inclusion, with the adversative *alla* in v. 4a separating 16:4-33 from 15:1—16:3, which leads into a subsection in its own turn determined by an inclusion between v. 4 and v. 6. These formal indications suggest that 15:1—16:3 may be a literary unit followed by 16:4-33.

THE SHAPE OF THE DISCOURSE

Many scholars trace the metaphor of the vine as far as v. 8, as the theme of the relationship between the Father and the Son becomes

---

terario di Gv 15–16," *Ant* 56 (1981) 53–62; C. H. Talbert, *Reading John: A Literary and Theological Commentary on the Fourth Gospel and the Johannine Epistles* (New York: Crossroad, 1992) 215; D. F. Tolmie, *Jesus' Farewell to the Disciples: John 13:1—17:26 in Narratological Perspective* (BibIntS 12; Leiden: Brill, 1995) 30–31. For further discussion, see F. F. Segovia, "John 15:18—16:4a: A First Addition to the Original Farewell Discourse," *CBQ* 45 (1983) 217 n. 37.

[3] See F. J. Moloney, "The Structure and Message of John 15.1—16.3," *AusBR* 35 (1987) 35–37, 41–44.

[4] See Y. Simoens, *La gloire d'aimer: Structures stylistiques et interprétatives dans la Discours de la Cíne (Jn 13–17)* (AnBib 90: Rome: Biblical Institute Press, 1981) 152–58; E. Delebecque, *Evangile de Jean: Texte Traduit et Annoté* (CahRB 23; Paris: Gabalda, 1987) 193.

dominant in v. 9.[5] Borig has developed vv. 1-10 as a unit, partly on the basis of chiastic structures in vv. 9-10 and 4b-5.[6] But the verb *menein* first appears as an imperative in v. 4, and recurs in various forms across vv. 1-11 (see v. 4 [three times], v. 5, v. 6, v. 7 [twice], v. 9, v. 10 [twice]).[7] The metaphor is not an end in itself but serves as a vehicle to articulate the importance of abiding. To abide means to bear fruit and to live in the love of Jesus (see vv. 4a, 5, 7, 9, 10); not to abide means to die and to be destroyed (see vv. 4b; 5b; 6).

There are indications that 15:1-11 is made up of three subsections. A close parallel between v. 1, "I am the true vine," and v. 5a, "I am the vine," marks a beginning and a closure. A similar parallel is found at the beginning and toward the end of the next subunit (vv. 5b-8) in v. 5b, "He who abides in me," and v. 7, "If you abide in me."[8] The remaining section (vv. 9-11) is not framed by such clear literary links but develops the notion of "abiding," adding the further direction: To abide in Jesus means to abide in his love. The central section (15:12-17) of John 15:1—16:3 is determined by literary indications and content, recalling Jesus' earlier command that the disciples love one another as he has loved them (see 13:34-35). The command that the disciples love one another frames a unit:

This is my commandment, that you love one another (v. 12).

This I command you, to love one another (v. 17).

As the content of the opening unit (vv. 1-11) is determined by the command "to abide," the following unit, made up of vv. 12-17, is framed by the command "to love." The opening and closing units insist on the disciples' loving one another as a result of Jesus' prior

---

[5] G. Segalla, "La struttura chiastica di Giov. 15,1–8," *BibOr* 12 (1970) 129–31, traces a chiastic structure that unifies vv. 1-8.

[6] Borig, *Weinstock,* 68–76.

[7] J. Becker, *Das Evangelium des Johannes* (2 vols.; OTK 4/1–2; Gütersloh: Gerd Mohn; Würzburg: Echter, 1979–81) 2:482, uses the presence of *menein* to unite vv. 1-17. But the verb appears 10 times in vv. 1-11, and only once (see v. 16) in quite a different fashion in vv. 12-17. See also L. Morris, *The Gospel According to John* (rev. ed.; NICNT; Grand Rapids: Eerdmans, 1995) 592–600. On the difference between v. 16 and vv. 1-11, see J. Heise, *Bleiben: Menein in den Johanneischen Schriften* (HUT 8; Tübingen: J C. B. Mohr, 1967) 81–82.

[8] Following many commentators, I see v. 8 as the conclusion of the subsection vv. 5b-8. For some, e.g., Bultmann, *John,* 546–47, Segovia, *Farewell,* 125–27, and Talbert, *Reading John,* 211–15, vv. 1-17 is a major unit, with vv. 1-8 and vv. 9-17 forming subunits Many separate 15.1-17 from 15:18—16:4a. See, e.g., R. Schnackenburg, *The Gospel according to St John* (3 vols.; HTCNT 4/1–3; London: Burns & Oates; New York: Crossroad, 1968–82) 3:113; Niccaci, "Gv 15–16," 43–53; T. Onuki, *Gemeinde und Welt im Johannesevangelium: Ein Beitrag zur Frage nach der theologischen und pragmatischen Funktion des johanneischen "Dualismus"* (WMANT 56; Neukirchen-Vluyn: Neukirchener Verlag, 1984) 119–30.

love for them (vv. 12-14; v. 17), while the central section addresses the change in the situation of the disciples and consequently the change in the way the disciples relate to Jesus, a consequence of Jesus' unsolicited choice of them (vv. 15-16).[9]

The theme of hatred marks the final section, 15:18—16:3. Verses 18-19b and vv. 20b-21 repeat sentences made up of a conditional clause (*ei* is used in all four conditions) and a principal statement (vv. 18, 19a; vv. 20b, 20c). They conclude with a sentence formed by a causal (*hoti* is used in both instances) and a principal statement (v. 19b; v. 21).[10] Between these carefully balanced conditional and causal statements (vv. 18-19b; vv. 20b-21) lies an imperative: "Remember the word that I said to you, 'A servant is not greater than his master'" (v. 20a). Verses 22-25 also have two flanking conditional (*ei* is used in both conditionals) and principal clauses, each one leading into a statement of a present situation (*nun* is used) of sin (vv. 22, 24). Between these two verses lies Jesus' assessment of those who have sinned: "He who hates me, hates my Father also" (v. 23). This section is rounded off by Jesus' informing the disciples that such an attitude to him and the Father fulfills the word of the Law: "They hated me without a cause" (v. 25). The formal elements that clearly mark vv. 18-21 and vv. 22-25 are not present in 15:26—16:3. However, the reader senses that themes from 15:18-21 return, especially in Jesus' words in v. 27b describing the disciples' situation: "because you have been with me from the beginning" (see v. 19b: "because you are not of the world"), and his insistence that the disciples recall his words to them in v. 16:1: "I have said all this to keep you from falling away" (see 15:20a: "Remember the word that I said to you"). What has been said in more general terms in vv. 18-21 is applied more specifically to the present and future experience of the Johannine readers in 15:26—16:3.

The shape of the discourse can be summarized as follows:

1. *15:1-11:* The need to abide in Jesus, the vine, to bear much fruit. The Father prunes the branches. A union of love flows from the Father and Jesus to the disciples.

---

[9] Although guided by Simoens, *La gloire,* 143, this threefold division of vv. 12-17 is a simplification of his five-step chiasm The role of vv. 12-17 is missed by Tolmie's division: vv. 9-15, vv. 16-17 (*Jesus' Farewell,* 212–13). A. Dettwiler, *Die Gegenwart des Erhohten: Eine exegetische Studie zu den johanneischen Abschiedsreden (Joh 13,31—16,33) unter besonderer Berucksichtigung ihres Relecture-Charakters* (FRLANT 169; Gottingen. Vandenhoeck & Ruprecht, 1995) 80, 86–100, notes the importance of the inclusion, but prefers to read vv. 1-17 as a unit, with vv. 9-11 introducing the love theme of vv. 12-17.

[10] The conditionals in vv. 18 and 20b are negative but real, while that of v. 19a is also negative but unreal. Only in v. 20c does the conditional indicate a positive possibility See Brown, *John,* 2:686–87.

2. *15:12-17:* The new situation of the disciples, which results from what Jesus has done for them, demands that they love one another as he has loved them.

3. *15:18—16:3:* The reality of the world's hatred for Jesus and the Father, which leads to the hatred the world has for the disciples of Jesus.

John 15:1—16:3 is dominated by three experiences crucial to the Johannine understanding of what it means to be disciples of Jesus: to abide in Jesus, to love one another as he has loved them, and to be hated.[11]

READING THE DISCOURSE

1. To Abide in Jesus (15:1-11)
a. Verses 1-5a: Abiding in Jesus   Jesus' opening affirmation lays claim to a uniqueness: *egō eimi hē ampelos hē alēthinē* (v. 1a). As in all other "I am" sayings with a complement (see 4:26; 6:35, 51; 8:12; 9:5; 10:7, 9, 11, 14; 14:6), Jesus' claim to be the vine indicates what he does rather than who he is. Jesus is a source of life and fruitfulness. He is however, "the *true* vine." The adjective is used emphatically, which leads the reader to suspect that these words are touched with polemic. Israel had been described as a vine or vineyard (see Jer 2:21; Ezek 19:10-14; Ps 80:18-19; Isa 5:1-7; 27:2-6).[12] A question hangs over the narrative: If Jesus is the one true vine, what can be said of the vine that is Israel? Another character enters the discourse as Jesus introduces his Father as the one who cares for the well-being and the fruitfulness of the vine (*ho geōrgos*). As throughout the Fourth Gospel, it is the Father who is ultimately responsible for all Jesus does and makes known.[13] Tending the vine and its branches is described as the action of the

---

[11] This logic is lost in the many studies that have traced various hands and redactions. See, e.g., two studies that predate the approach taken in *Farewell*, F. F. Segovia, "The Theology and Provenance of John 15:1-17," *JBL* 101 (1982) 115–28, and idem, "John 15:18—16:4a," 210–30.

[12] The image is used to speak both negatively (see Jer 2:21; Ezek 19:12-14) and positively (see Isa 27:2-6; Ezek 19:10-11; Ps 80:8-19; Qoh 24:27; *2 Bar* 39:7) of Israel. See especially A. Jaubert, "L'image de la vigne (Jean 15)," in F. Christ, ed., *Oikonomia: Heilsgeschichte als Thema der Theologie: Oscar Cullmann zum 65. Geburtstag gewidmet* (Hamburg: H. Reich, 1967) 93–96. For an indication of the widespread rabbinic use of the vine to describe Israel, see Str-B, 2:563–64.

[13] There would be no life in the vine if the vine-dresser did not tend it. See B. F. Westcott, *The Gospel according to Saint John* (London: Murray, 1908) 217; Heise, *Bleiben*, 82–83.

Father. The metaphor is best understood as reflecting the everyday reality of vines and vinekeeping. Such practices, however, also describe what Jesus is saying about himself, the Father, and—the reader guesses—discipleship. The Father cares for the fruitful branch on the vine, pruning it so that it will become more fruitful, and he destroys the branches that bear no fruit by separating them from the vine (v. 2). Jesus is the life-giver, but it is the Father who promotes growth and decides on destroying the branches.

Jesus moves from a description of the vine, the branches, and the vinedresser, and addresses the disciples directly: *ēdē humeis katharoi este* (v. 3a). The disciples gathered with Jesus at the table and listening to the discourse are regarded as fruitful branches united to the vine and pruned by their having heard the word of the sent one of the Father. Because they have heard and accepted the word of Jesus, the pruning process is already in place. The indications of 13:10, that the disciples are all *katharoi* are repeated, but now they are told they are made clean by the word of Jesus.[14] The rhetoric of "abiding" and "not abiding" presupposes that the discourse addresses the threat— or even the reality—of disciples of Jesus "not abiding."[15] Jesus has established the essential frame of reference in vv. 1-3. Jesus is the vine, the Father is the vinedresser, and disciples, made clean by the word of Jesus, can be fruitful branches of the vine.

Jesus' discourse moves from the indicative to the imperative, showing the crucial importance of abiding in Jesus for the continuation of a relationship between Jesus, the disciples, and the Father.[16] Jesus informs the disciples that it is not enough to be with him and to have received his word; they must abide in him, and he will abide in them (v. 4a: *meinate en emoi kagō en humin*). There must be an ongoing, life-giving mutuality created by the disciples' union with Jesus and Jesus' oneness with them.[17] Jesus continues to use the image of a vine to clarify the need for "abiding." No branch can ever bear fruit if it is separated from the vine, and no disciple of Jesus will ever bear fruit alone (*aph' heautou*). Abiding in Jesus is the sine qua non of fruitfulness (v. 4c: *ean mē en emoi menēte*). Jesus reaffirms his function as the

[14] To be made clean by the word of Jesus involves a receptivity to the revelation of God in Jesus. See Brown, *John*, 2.676–77; R. H. Lightfoot, *St. John's Gospel* (ed. C. F. Evans; Oxford· Oxford Univ. Press, 1956) 283.

[15] See Westcott, *St John*, 216: "The life of union is begun but not perfected."

[16] For the relationship between this "basic thought of the chapter" (Barrett, *St John*, 474) and the Israelite testament tradition, see E. Cortès, *Los Discursos de Adiós de Gn 49 a Jn 13–17* (Collectanés San Paciano 23; Barcelona: Herder, 1976) 436–38.

[17] On the reciprocal nature of the abiding, see Borig, *Weinstock*, 215–36.

vine, repeating v. 1a, and associating the disciples with his claim: "I am the vine, you are the branches" (v. 5a). But the reader is still wondering why Jesus' first words aggressively presented himself as the *true* vine.[18]

b. Verses 5b-8: The Results of Abiding or Not Abiding in Jesus   The insistence on the need to abide in Jesus is continued in v. 5bc. The teaching of v. 4 is repeated, as the image used in the metaphor for the fruitful relationship between the vine and the branch (see vv. 1-2) is applied explicitly to Jesus and a disciple. It is only by mutual abiding, the disciple in Jesus and Jesus in the disciple, that fruitfulness comes. Separated from Jesus (*chōris emou*), the disciple can do nothing (*ou dynasthe poiein ouden*). The reader senses that something fresh has been added to the metaphor, as the disciple is told by Jesus that separated from him the disciple can do nothing (v. 5c: *poiein ouden*). Union with Jesus, and fruitfulness, is not a matter of enjoying the oneness that exists between the disciple and the master; it also consists of *doing something,* which is impossible without abiding in Jesus. To bear fruit (v. 4b) means to do something actively (5c). That "something" has already been suggested to the reader in the command to love, which Jesus taught would be the hallmark of anyone who claimed to be his disciple (see 13:34-35).

Jesus has stated two possibilities in v. 5bc. He articulates them in greater detail in vv. 6-7, reversing v. 5bc, which presented the positive and negative results of abiding and not abiding in Jesus. Verse 6 develops the negative and v. 7 spells out the positive. The passive is used in v. 6 to describe the result of a disciple's not abiding in Jesus. The subject of v. 6 is always in the third person, and the verbs "cast out" and "withered" (*eblēthē . . . exēranthē*) are unexpectedly in the aorist tense. Jesus is not only warning the people at table with him, he speaks more generally about what happens to any person who does not abide in him.[19] The aorists are best read as gnomic, expressing a truth valid for all times.[20] Like the branch the Father takes away in

---

[18] See A Jaubert, "L'image de la vigne (Jean 15)," in *Oikonomia: Heilsgeschichte als Thema der Theologie: Oscar Cullman zum 65. Geburtstag Gewidmet* (ed. F. Christ; Hamburg. H. Reich, 1967) 96–97 .

[19] The reality of failure in the community addressed by the Gospel lies behind this warning. See, among many, Schnackenburg, *St John,* 3:101.

[20] For this possibility, see Brown, *John,* 2:661; X. Léon-Dufour, *Lecture de l'Evangile selon Jean,* (3 vols.; Parole de Dieu; Paris: Seuil, 1988–93) 3:170; BDF, 171, para 333, 1. Some scholars suggest that the aorist expresses the immediacy of the consequences of not abiding (see W. Bauer, *Das Johannesevangelium erklart* [3d ed.; HKNT 6; Tubingen: J. C B.

v. 2, the person not abiding in Jesus is "cast forth as a branch and withers" (v. 6a). The use of the passives continues as the destiny of the withered branches is further described as gathered and burned (v. 6b). Dead wood, no longer attached to its source of life, is destroyed by burning.[21] Jesus returns to the positive consequences of abiding in him. In v. 7 the privileged position of the disciples at the table, already made clean by the word of Jesus (see v. 3), returns. Jesus tells them that their abiding in him, and his words' abiding in them, will produce a situation where whatever they ask will be done for them. Jesus is the revelation of God, and it is this that abides and gives life to the disciple who abides in Jesus.[22] After the introduction of the Father as the vinedresser in v. 1 and the description of his fundamental role in v. 2, the dire results of the passive verbs in v. 6 and the asking in v. 7 suggest to the reader that it is the Father, even though never explicitly mentioned, who destroys the one who does not abide and answers the disciple who does.

This suggestion is confirmed in v. 8, concluding the outcome of abiding and not abiding in Jesus. To abide in Jesus is to make the *doxa* of the Father visible. The disciples who live in mutuality with Jesus can be identified as disciples of Jesus bearing much fruit. It is not Jesus who is glorified by the relationship that can exist between Jesus and his disciples; it is the Father. "There is only one mission shared by the Son and his disciples. In this one mission the Father has been glorified."[23] The revelation of God, made possible because of the mutual abiding of the disciple in Jesus and Jesus in the disciple produces true disciples involved in the mission of Jesus (*genēsesthe emoi mathētai*).[24] The reader recalls Jesus' earlier words on the criterion for discipleship. In 13:35 he spoke of the link between mutual love and the public recognition of Jesus' disciples: "By this everyone will know that you are my disciples, if you have love for one another" (13:35). A

Mohr, 1933] 191) while others argue for its use as proleptic, after an implied condition The result is so certain that it is described as having already happened (see M.-J Lagrange, *Evangile selon Saint Jean* (EB; Paris: Gabalda, 1927) 404; ZGB, para 257).

[21] The destruction by fire comes from usual practice with dry wood, and does not refer to an eschatological fire. Against, e.g., J. H. Bernard, *A Critical and Exegetical Commentary on the Gospel according to St John* (2 vols.; ICC; Edinburgh: T. & T. Clark, 1928) 2:482.

[22] On the interchangeability of Jesus and the words of Jesus, see Brown, *John*, 2:662.

[23] Ibid.

[24] With, among many, Barrett, *St John* 475, and Segovia, *Farewell*, 147 n 36, reading the future with Sinaiticus and Alexandrinus, against the well-attested subjunctive of Vaticanus, Claromontanus, Regius, Koridethi, and perhaps P[66].

question emerges for the reader: Is there a connection between 13:35 and 15:8, between mutual love and the glorification of the Father?

c. *Verses 9-11: Abiding in the Love of Jesus*   The return of explicit reference to the Father, glorified in the fruitful oneness between Jesus and the disciples in v. 8, leads into vv. 9-11.[25] In vv. 9-11 the reader learns that this "doing," which reveals the glory of the Father and shows discipleship, is associated with love and loving. The Johannine story of Jesus has unfailingly looked to God, the Father of Jesus, as the source and goal of all Jesus is and does (see 1:18). Thus, it is not surprising that Jesus announces to his disciples that the source of his love for them is the love his Father has for him (v. 9a). A unity of love bonds the Sender and the Sent One (see 3:35; 5:20; 10:17). In as much as (*kathōs*) the Father loves Jesus, Jesus commands his disciples to become part of that oneness by abiding in his love (v. 9b).[26] But this abiding in the love of Jesus must be shown in a way of life determined by his commandments. To be a disciple abiding in the love of Jesus means to do something, and that "doing" is keeping the commandments of Jesus (10a). Jesus, however, is not the source of this abiding in love. The relationship of love that exists between the Father and the Son is based on the Son's having kept the Father's commandments and his abiding in the Father's love (v. 10b). Jesus' relationship with the Father is expressed as his having always kept the commandments of the Father (perfect tense: *teterēka*), flowing into a never-ending abiding in the love of the Father (present tense: *menō*). The disciples are asked to repeat, in their relationship with Jesus, what Jesus has always had with the Father: a loving mutuality reflected in the unconditional observance of his commandments.

A sense of closure is experienced by the reader as Jesus announces *tauta lelalēka humin hina* (v. 11). The point of the abiding, the loving, and the keeping of the commandments is that the joy Jesus has from his loving oneness and obedience to the commandments of the Father might also be with the disciples. Then the joy of the disciples will be complete (vv. 11: *hē chara humōn plērōthē*).[27] There has been a gradual movement through the metaphor of the vine, which introduced the theme of abiding (vv. 1-5a, vv. 5b-8; see vv. 4, 5a, 5b, 6, 7), into an insistence that to abide in Jesus means to abide in his love. It calls the

---

[25] On the link between v. 8 and v. 9, see Schnackenburg, *St John*, 3 103

[26] On *kathōs* as "in as much as," see BDF, 236, para. 453, 2.

[27] The expression is best rendered "complete" rather than "full." There is a sense of the disciples' joy being what it should be. See Segovia, *Farewell*, 153

disciples to do something: to keep his commandments. The disciples' abiding in the love of Jesus and keeping his commandments unites them with Jesus' response to the Father, in whose love he abides and whose commandments he keeps.[28] But what are the commandments and how does one keep them? What does it mean to abide in the love of Jesus? Does abiding in love proclaim the uniqueness of the disciple of Jesus (see 13:35 and 15:8)? Jesus turns to these questions in the section that follows (vv. 12-17).

2. The Commandment to Love (15:12-17)

a. Verses 12-14: The Commandment to Love as Jesus Loved Verses 1-11 of Jesus' discourse closed with an introduction to themes that will dominate this section: the commandments of Jesus and love (vv. 9-11).[29] The linking of the commandment of Jesus and love for one another is not new for the reader who has already encountered it in 13:34-35.[30] In 15:12 the immediately previous context has raised a question for the reader: What are the commandments of Jesus that one must keep in order to abide in his love (see v. 10)? The disciples are to love one another with a love that is continuous and lifelong (v. 12a: present subjunctive: *agapate*), and the measure of their love is to be the supreme act of Jesus' love for them (v. 12b: aorist: *ēgapēsa*). The narrative of the self-gift of Jesus in the footwashing (13:1-17) and the gift of the morsel (vv. 21-38) comes into play. It is essential intertext for 15:12-17. The reader is aware that Jesus loves "his own" *eis telos* (13:1). The disciples are to love one another with an unconditional love, matching the love of Jesus for them, the *hypodeigma* given them in 13:1-38.[31]

[28] Described by Segovia, *Farewell*, 148–63, as "the chain of love."

[29] As W. Kurz, "Luke 22.14-38 and Greco-Roman and Biblical Farewell Addresses," *JBL* 104 (1985) 262–63, has shown, renewal of covenant is part of the farewell genre. See also Cortès, *Los Discursos*, 434–43; R. F Collins, "'A New Commandment I Give to You . . .' (Jn 13:34)," *LTP* 35 (1979) 249–52.

[30] On the relationship between the present order of the discourse and the Jewish testament tradition, see Cortès, *Los Discursos*, 427–30.

[31] I will highlight the link that exists between 13:1-38 and 15:1—16:4. See also Dettwiler, *Die Gegenwart*, 60–110 and his summary on 107–10. Some scholars have traced eucharistic language and practices behind 15:1-11. See, e.g., E. C. Hoskyns, *The Fourth Gospel* (2d ed., ed. F. N. Davey, London: Faber & Faber, 1947) 474–79; C. H. Dodd, *The Interpretation of the Fourth Gospel* (Cambridge: Cambridge Univ. Press, 1953) 138–39, 411–12, and especially B. Sandvik, "Joh 15 als Abendmahlstext," *TZ* 23 (1967) 323–28. These suggestions misinterpret the intended link between 13:1-38 and 15:1—16:3.

In vv. 12-14 Jesus reminds the disciples of the *quality* of his love for them.[32] The greatest of all loves (*meizona tautēs agapēn oudeis echei*) is shown by one who lays down his life for his friends (*tōn philōn autou*). While Jesus loves without limit, the disciples have not shown great signs of their love for him. Throughout the Gospel, and dramatically in the roles of Judas and Peter in John 13, disciples have been portrayed as not understanding, as still locked in their own way of seeing and doing things, betrayers and deniers. Yet the reader is aware that Jesus lays down his life for them as the Good Shepherd (see 10:11, 14, 18). Past and present failures will not be held against the disciples. Jesus is responding to the commandments of the Father in loving his recalcitrant *philoi*. He asks that they live up to this friendship by doing what he commands them (v. 14): Love one another as he has loved them (see v. 12; 13:34).

b. Verses 15-16: Jesus' Love Has Established a New Relationship   If in vv. 12-14 Jesus insisted on the *quality of his love* for the fragile disciples, in vv. 15-16 he draws back from this theme to tell them of the *priority of his love* for them. The reader, fresh from the story of John 13, which has been close to the surface in vv. 12-14, wonders why Jesus should show such love for his fragile "friends." The disciples, through no act of the will or physical effort on their part, have been drawn into a new relationship (v. 15). They are not servants (*douloi*) dependent on a master.[33] Indeed, never throughout the Gospel has either Jesus or the narrator called them such. They have always been followers, people who have been going through a learning process as disciples (*mathētēs*) of Jesus. They are no longer *douloi*, depending on the wishes

---

[32] This interpretation links vv. 12-13. Verse 13 is primarily christological, spelling out for the disciples how Jesus loved them (see v. 12b), thus indicating how much they should love one another (v. 12a) Some would link v 13 with vv. 14-15, and others would regard it as a later insertion. For the discussion, and the position adopted above, see T. Knoppler, *Die theologia crucis des Johannesevangeliums: Das Verstandnis des Todes Jesu im Rahmen der johanneischen Inkarnations-und Erhohungschristologie* (WMANT 69; Neukirchen: Neukirchener Verlag, 1994) 209–10, and especially H. Thyen, "'Niemand hat grossere Liebe als die, dass er sein Leben fur seine Freunde hingibt' (Joh 15.13): Das johanneische Verstandnis des Kreuzestodes Jesu," in C. Andresen and G Klein, eds., *Theologia Crucis—Signum Crucis: Festschrift fur Erich Dinkler zum 70. Geburtstag* (Tubingen: J. C. B. Mohr, 1979) 467–81.

[33] The word *doulos* can refer to either a slave or a servant. Whichever translation one adopts, the question of a radical change of status from a dependent *doulos* to an equal *philos* is clear. G. M. Lee, "John XV 14 'Ye are my friends'," *NovT* 15 (1973) 260, makes a link with the "friend of the bridegroom" in 3.29.

and the whims of a master, but *philoi*, intimate and equal associates of Jesus who loves them without limit (see 13:1: *eis telos*).

In a succinct statement central to this story's strengthening presentation of the love of God revealed in Jesus, the disciples are told, "You did not choose me, but I chose you" (v. 16a). Again the opening narrative of Jesus' final night with his disciples serves as intertext. At the heart of the footwashing and the gift of the morsel Jesus told his disciples: "I know whom I have chosen. . . . He who receives any one whom I send receives me; and he who receives me receives him who sent me" (13:19b, 20). Jesus has chosen disciples and established them (*kai etheka humas*) as the ones who will be sent out to bear fruit that will endure (v. 16b). The initiative lies with Jesus, but in the end the disciples must turn to the Father in their need, asking in the name of Jesus (v. 16c). As the ongoing mission of Jesus, now entrusted to his chosen ones, is described, the language of the metaphor of the vine returns. The disciples are the *philoi* of Jesus, for whom he lays down his life in love (see v. 13), and they are the branches abiding in the vine (see v. 5a), bearing much fruit (vv. 5b, 8), fruit that will endure. They, in the name of Jesus who has chosen them and commissioned them to "go and bear fruit" (v. 16b), will turn to the Father (16c; see v. 10). As they bear fruit, continuing the mission of the one who chose them, all they ask will be granted to them (v. 16c). The oneness that exists between Jesus and the Father will also be enjoyed by the disciples chosen (v. 16a) and sent out (v. 16b) by Jesus (see 13:18-20).[34]

c. Verse 17: The Commandment to Love   In v. 17 Jesus returns to the words of v. 12. This repetition, however, is not only an obvious literary closure. It is important to the argument that Jesus' words on his prior choice of the disciples (v. 16a), their being established as the bearers of a lasting fruitfulness (v. 16b) in their new situation as his friends (v. 15), conclude with the sine qua non condition of their status and mission. They must accept the commandment of Jesus; they must love one another (v. 17). The reader has experienced an increasing insistence on the love of Jesus for his own. It was explicitly stated in 13:1 and dramatically symbolized in the footwashing and the gift of the morsel reported in 13:1-38. It has returned as the leitmotif of 15:12-17, introduced by Jesus' call to the disciples to abide in his love in vv. 9-11. Across the latter part of Jesus' ministry and into the story

---

[34] Some critics read v. 16 as the Johannine version of the appointment of the foundational apostles. It applies to all disciples of Jesus. For the discussion leading to this conclusion, see Léon-Dufour, *Lecture*, 3:182–85.

of his final meal with the disciples, a close connection was made between the death of Jesus and the revelation of the glory of God (see
11:4; 12:23; 13:18-20, 31-32). Jesus' words on love are focusing on his
gift of himself for his disciples in death (see 13:1; 1-17, 21-38). Jesus'
death will be the manifestation of love, the revelation of God, and the
glorification of the Son (see 11:4; 12:23; 13:18-20, 31-32). The disciples have been told that by abiding in Jesus and bearing much fruit
they will join with Jesus in the glorification of the Father (see 15:8).
They have been chosen by Jesus to bear much fruit (v. 16ab). But the
disciples, the friends of Jesus whom he loves in a way that cannot be
surpassed (v. 13), must continue that quality of love in their love for
one another (vv. 12, 17). The reader traces a link between Jesus' mission to make God known through his loving self-gift, and the task of
the disciples to continue that mission in their obedience to his commandment that they love one another as he has loved them (13:34;
15:12, 17). The quality of their love for one another will mark them
out as disciples of Jesus (13:35; see 15:8).

3. To Be Hated by the World (15:18—16:3)
a. Verses 18-21: An Explanation for the Hatred of the World Jesus opens
his words on the hatred the disciples will experience by explaining
why it exists.[35] On four occasions he establishes possible conditions
that probably reflect the experience of the readers (vv. 18, 19a, 20b,
20c: *ei*). These conditions are in sets of two, and after each pair he
explains why these conditions have been fulfilled (vv. 19b, 21: *hoti*).
Between these sets of "if . . . if . . . because" (*ei . . . ei . . . hoti;* vv. 18-
19b; vv. 20b-21) he asks them to remember his word: "A servant is not
greater than his master" (v. 20a). The ultimate reason for the hatred
of the world for the disciples is that they are disciples of Jesus, the
sent one of the Father.

If the world hates the disciples, this is but the logical consequence
of its prior hatred of Jesus, well documented for the reader through
the response his ministry has met (v. 18). It has led to a decision that
Jesus must be slain (see, most recently, 11:49-50, 53). The reason for
the world's rejection of Jesus is his claim to come from God and to
make God known to a world that has its own ideas about who the
Christ should be and how to relate to God.[36] If the disciples had been
happy to reject Jesus' word and accept the worldview of his oppo-

---

[35] These warnings are a widespread feature of the farewell genre.

[36] This "world" (see vv. 18-19) is not to be identified with humanity as such. The
expression is theologically determined, rejecting both Jesus and the Father.

nents, they would be of the world and would be loved, not hated, by the world (v. 19). This condition has not been realized in the story of the disciples. Jesus, by associating his disciples with his own being "not of this world" (see 8:21-23), has led to the world's hating them because they are not of the world. He has chosen them (see v. 16a; 13:20) and they have been made clean by the word of Jesus (see 13:10; 15:3). The world's rejection of Jesus and the disciples' choice of Jesus over against the claims of the world is a first explanation of why the world hates the disciples (vv. 18-19). The disciples should not be surprised at this, as they have already been instructed by the word of Jesus when they gathered at table for the footwashing: "a servant is not greater than his master" (v. 20a; see 13:16a; also Matt 10:25; Luke 6:40).

If "they" persecuted Jesus, and they have, then "they" will persecute his disciples (v. 20b).[37] The shift from *ho kosmos* to the use of the third person plural indicates to the reader that this hatred and rejection have their source in a recognizable group in the narrative. The final conditional is rhetorical for both the disciples and the reader: If they had kept the word of Jesus, then they would also keep the word of the disciples (v. 20c). Disciples proclaim the word and teaching of Jesus under the direction and inspiration of the Paraclete (see 14:25-26). The first set of conditions for the hatred of the world is explained by the world's rejection of Jesus' chosen ones (see v. 19b). The second set of conditions for the world's hatred of the disciples reaches beyond the disciples themselves to the rejection of the one who chose them and sent them out: "They will do this on my account" (v. 21a).[38] However, such a rejection takes place because "they" do not know or recognize the one who had sent Jesus: "Because they do not know him who sent me" (v. 21b). A theme returns that has dominated the earlier account of Jesus' revelation of the Father among "the Jews." They failed to accept Jesus because they would not and could not recognize that he was the sent one of God (see especially 8:19, 27, 39-47, 54-55). "The world," which has become "they," must be "the Jews" of the earlier narrative. The hatred Jesus' disciples will experience flows from the world's rejection of Jesus, of his chosen ones, and its lack of recognition of the God who sent Jesus. However, the disciples are

---

[37] On this relationship between the experience of Jesus and the experience of the disciples, see Lindars, "Persecution of Christians," 59–62.

[38] For this interpretation, see Barrett, *St John*, 481. Literally "because of my name" (*dia to onoma mou*), and Brown attempts too much in suggesting that the disciples are hated because Jesus bears the divine name (*John*, 696–97).

comforted by the promise of Jesus' word: "A servant is not greater than his master" (v. 20). The disciples continue the presence of Jesus in a hostile world as told them earlier in the discourse (see 13:16), but they are not alone. As the disciples face their difficult future, they are comforted by his earlier word: "The Paraclete, the Holy Spirit, whom the Father will send in my name, he will teach you all things, and bring to your remembrance all that I have said to you" (14:26).

b. Verses 22-25: The Results of the World's Hatred   Those who accept the revelation of God in Jesus have power to become the children of God (see 1:12-13), but this light shines in the midst of darkness (see 1:5). The indications of the prologue have become real in the life and ministry of Jesus. He has "come and spoken to them" (v. 22a: *ei mē elthon kai elalēka autois*). The Word has dwelt among them (see 1:14); he has come unto his own, but they have rejected his word (see 1:11). If they had not been the privileged recipients of the revelation of God in and through Jesus, they would have no sin. They have hated and rejected the word of Jesus, however, and thus have no excuse for their sin (15:22).[39] The intimate link this statement from Jesus has with the story of 1:19—12:50 convinces the reader that the "they" who have rejected Jesus and the revelation of God in Jesus are "the Jews." Jesus' words to his disciples build on the story that has already been told (see especially 9:39-41).

The reader also knows that "the one who does not honor the Son does not honor the Father who sent him" (5:23b; see also 8:49), and is thus prepared for Jesus' words to his disciples about a further—and even more damning—result of the world's hatred. The hatred of Jesus indicates a hatred of his Father (15:23). But the Father of Jesus is the God of Israel. Thus, Jesus is developing a portrait of some who, in their hatred and rejection of him, have also hated the God of Israel. "The Jews," who have heard the word of Jesus and rejected it (see v. 21), are now being accused of hating the God of Israel (v. 22). Paradoxically, "the Jews'" defense of their understanding of God over against the revelation of that God in and through Jesus (see, e.g., 5:19-47; 8:12-20, 21-30, 39-47, 54-59; 9:24-34, 39-41), is a reflection of their hatred of God. The discourse continues to build on Jesus' teaching and ministry. Jesus made God known not only by his word, but also by his deeds. On several occasions "the Jews" have been urged to see

---

[39] On the use of *nun* in vv. 22, 24, see Brown, *John* 2:688. It is more an indication of the state of affairs than an indication of time. As Bernard, *St John*, 2:494, puts it: "but now, as things are."

the revelation of God in his works if they cannot accept his word (see 5:36; 7:21-24, 50-52; 9:24-34; 10:31-39). Jesus repeats what he said about his coming to reveal God by his word in v. 22 (*ei mē elthon kai elalēsan autois*) and points to the resulting sin of those who have rejected the revelation that took place among them in his works (v. 24a: *ei ta erga mē epoiēsa en autois*). The rejection of the revelation of God in the words and the deeds of Jesus manifests their hatred for both Jesus and the Father (v. 24b).

Jesus' threatening words to "the Jews" in 8:24 are being realized: "I told you that you would die in your sins, for you will die in your sins unless you believe that I am he." This subsection closes as Jesus points beyond his own words and actions as the revelation of God. Traditionally, God has spoken to his people in their Scriptures. The negative response of "the Jews" to the revelation of God, and their resulting hatred of the Father of Jesus, the God of Israel, fulfills the Law. Jesus tells the disciples that in their determined defense of the Law, "the Jews" can be accused by a word from their own Scriptures (Ps 35:19; see Ps 69:4-5).[40] God speaks through his Scriptures, accusing "the Jews" in the story of Jesus: "You have hated me without cause" (v. 25). Those who hate the disciples hate Jesus and his Father. They remain in their sin, having hated and rejected God, and are accused by the word of God in the Scriptures. Jesus does not refer to the Scriptures as "their Law" (*en tō nomō autōn*) in mockery, but ironically indicates that they are making a lie of the Law by which they claim to live.[41]

c. 15:26—16:3: A Further Explanation for the Hatred of the World The offense Jesus' words and works have offered the world will not disappear. Thus, the hatred of the world will continue, and the disciples will be the bearers of the offensive presence of Jesus' revelation of God. They need not fear, as the role of the Paraclete in the in-between

---

[40] Most commentators see Ps 35 19 as Jesus' reference to "the Law," taken in its broad sense of the Jewish Scriptures as a whole. Some (e.g., A. Obermann, *Die christologische Erfüllung der Schrift im Johannesevangelium: Eine Untersuchung zur johanneischen Hermeneutik anhand der Schriftzitate* [WUNT 2/83, Tubingen: J. C. B Mohr, 1996] 271–76; M. J. J. Menken, *Old Testament Quotations in the Fourth Gospel: Studies in Textual Form* [CBET 15; Kampen Kok Pharos, 1996] 139–45) suggest Ps 69:4-5. J. Marsh (*Saint John* [PNTC, Harmondsworth: Penguin, 1968] 531) and E. Haenchen (*John* [2 vols.; trans. R W. Funk; Hermeneia, Philadelphia Fortress Press, 1984] 2:138), suggest that both passages may be behind Jesus' words. See the discussion in Segovia, *Farewell*, 194 n. 40; B. G. Schuchard, *Scripture Within Scripture: The Interrelationship of Form and function in the Explicit Old Testament Citations in the Gospel of John* (SBLDS 133; Atlanta: Scholars, 1992) 119–23

[41] See Obermann, *Die christologische Erfüllung*, 271–82.

time has been spelled out for them. The other Paraclete will always be
with them (see 14:16-17) teaching them all things, reminding them
of all Jesus has said to them (see 14:25-27). The Paraclete's presence
creates a situation in the midst of difficulty that should take away all
fear. The disciples have been given a new peace over against the false
securities offered by the world, and they must not be afraid (see
14:27). In the midst of the hatred described by Jesus in 15:18-21, the
Paraclete sent from the Father will continue to bear witness to Jesus.[42]
The other Paraclete, the Spirit of truth whom Jesus will send from the
Father and who proceeds from the Father,[43] continues this revelation
(v. 26), along with the disciples, who have been with Jesus from the
beginning hearing his word and seeing his works.[44] The disciples, directed, reminded, and strengthened by the Spirit, give witness to Jesus
in the midst of a hostile world. As this section of the discourse draws
to a close, Jesus begins to speak of the future experience of the disciples. They suffer the same rejection as Jesus has suffered during his
earthly ministry (see vv. 18, 20). But the future suffering of the disciples will take place *after the departure of Jesus* described in 14:1-31. It
will be part of the in-between time. Thus, the Paraclete must play a
role, continuing the revelation of God that has taken place in and
through Jesus (*ekeinos marturēsei peri emou*) now that he is no longer
physically with his disciples.

Earlier in the discourse Jesus told his disciples that he was allowing
them into the mysteries that lay ahead—his suffering (see 13:19), the
gift of the Paraclete (14:25-26), and his going to the Father (14:28-
29)—so that when they take place, the disciples will understand and
believe. He now does the same thing in foretelling the ongoing hatred
of the world. The disciples are told that they will be joined by the
witness of the Paraclete and continue the revelation of God they have
heard and seen in and from Jesus (15:25-26). Like the great figures

[42] The appearance of a Paraclete saying in this context has often mistakenly been
regarded as a later, clumsy, insertion into the text. See, e.g., Bauer, *Johannesevangelium*,
195; Becker, "Die Abschiedsreden Jesu," 237–38.

[43] This insistence that the Paraclete comes from the Father (see 14.16, 26), even
though Jesus now involves himself in the sending of the Spirit of Truth (see 14:17),
points to the identity of the origin of the former Paraclete (Jesus) and the other Paraclete (see 14·16). Despite Lagrange, *Saint Jean*, 413, this passage is not to be read in the
light of fourth-century trinitarian debates. On the one who sends the Paraclete, Brown,
John, 2:689, comments "The variation is not really significant at the theological level,
for in Johannine thought the Father and Jesus are one (10.30)."

[44] Given the setting of this final meal (see 13:1), *ap' archēs* means that the disciples
have been with him from the beginning of his ministry (see 1.35-51) See Brown,
John, 2:690.

from Israel's past, Jesus instructs his followers that they must face the future hatred of the world and, because of his assuring word, not fall away (16:1).[45] Jesus' description of the hatred of the world shifted from the all-embracing term *ho kosmos* (see vv. 18, 19) to "they" (see vv. 20, 21, 22, 24, 25). The response of these people to the revelation of God in and through Jesus leads the reader to identify them with "the Jews," who fail to live up to their own Scriptures (see 15:25). This identification is now ratified, as Jesus tells of his disciples' future experience at the hands of "the Jews." They will suffer the experience of the man born blind (see 9:22, 34).[46] The time is coming when they will be put out of the synagogue (16:2a: *aposunagōgous poiēsousin humas*). This corresponds with the comment of the narrator earlier in the story that "the Jews" had already decided to put out of the synagogue (9:22: *aposunagōgos genētai;* see also 12:42) anyone who confessed that Jesus was the Christ.[47] "The Jews" are the only characters in the story who could be involved in such action, and Jesus' words reflect the experience of the disciples living the in-between time,[48] where some are falling away in the face of hatred, persecution, expulsion, and death.

More drastically, Jesus tells his future witnesses (see 15:27) that they will be slain by people who regard the killing of disciples of Jesus as offering service to God (16:2b: *latreian prospherein tō theō*). It is difficult to document an early Christian experience of persecution at the hands of Jews, which was regarded as an act of worship to God. Some scholars suggest that Jesus foretells two forms of future suffering, currently part of the readers' experience: expulsion from the synagogue

---

[45] Strong similarities with the Jewish testament tradition continue. The *tauta* of 16:1 looks back across 15:18-27, and not just to the witness of the Paraclete and the disciples of 15.26-27.

[46] See, among many, Lindars, "Persecution of Christians," 48–51; T. Onuki, *Gemeinde und Welt im Johannesevangelium: Ein Beitrag zur Frage nach der theologischen und pragmatischen Funktion des johanneischen "Dualismus"* (WMANT 56; Neukirchen: Neukirchener Verlag, 1984) 131–43. See also Lightfoot, *St John,* 284–86, for a series of links between John 9 and 15:18—16.3

[47] The use of *erchetai hora* does not have links with "the hour of Jesus." It is a reference to the coming of a critical time in the future. See Léon-Dufour, *Lecture,* 3:205.

[48] As in the earlier volumes of this study, I continue to regard the Johannine community as having experienced expulsion from the synagogue. There is no need to link this expulsion with the *birkat ha-minim* For a recent restatement of the position that links the Fourth Gospel with the post-Jamnian situation, see W. D. Davies, "Reflection on Aspects of the Jewish Background of the Gospel of John," in R. A. Culpepper and C. C. Black, eds., *Exploring the Fourth Gospel: In Honor of D. Moody Smith* (Louisville: Westminster/John Knox, 1996) 43–64

perpetrated by "the Jews" and martyrdom at the hands of Romans, who regarded the early Christians as being atheists and thus deserving of death.[49] Whatever may have been the exact identification of the experience of Jesus' disciples who originally read this Gospel, such acts repeat in the life of Jesus' disciples the hatred and rejection of their Master (see v. 20). He is hated because "they do not know who sent me" (v. 21). The rejection of Jesus is based on the nonrecognition of God. The rejection of Jesus' disciples takes place for the same reason: they do not know the Father. The disciples are the next generation, but their rejection is also the result of the world's not knowing Jesus: "They have not known the Father, nor me" (v. 3). The situation of sin continues in the rejection of the revelation of God that flows from the witness of the Paraclete and the Spirit-directed disciples of Jesus.

CONCLUSION

This section of the last discourse is unique. Only Jesus speaks, announcing at the heart of his departing discourse a message about abiding, loving, and being hated. The passage is formed by Jesus' words on two contrasting experiences bridged by his commandment of mutual love. The first section deals with the mutuality of "abiding" that should exist between Jesus and the disciples (15:1-11). The closing section spells out the hatred and violent separation that exists between "the world" and both Jesus and the disciples (15:18—16:3). Both the abiding and the hatred are grounded in the recognition or

---

[49] The possibility of a reference to Roman persecution is canvassed by Brown, *John*, 2:691, but the use of *latreia* suggests that "the Jews" are involved This may not necessarily be the case. On the pagan use of *latreia* as acts of piety done in the service of religion, see Augustine, *De Civitate Dei*, V:15 (PL 41:160) Most scholars look to Jewish practices (see *NumR* 21; *Sanh* 9 6; Josephus, *Antiquities* 20.200; *Martyrdom of Polycarp*, 13 1; Justin, *Dialogue*, 95:4; 133.6). See, e.g., Hoskyns, *Fourth Gospel*, 482–83; Carson, *John*, 531; M. C. de Boer, *Johannine Perspectives on the Death of Jesus* (CBET 17; Kampen: Kok Pharos, 1976) 61–62. This is an important element in de Boer's reconstruction of the community's *Sitze im Leben*. J. L. Martyn has suggested that it may be a memory of some form of persecution that took place while the community was still a Jewish-Christian sect. See J. L. Martyn, "Persecution and Martyrdom: A Dark and Difficult Chapter in the History of Johannine Christianity," in *The Gospel of John in Christian History: Essays for Interpreters* (New York: Paulist, 1978) 55–89. Lindars ("Persecution of Christians," 66) stresses the future tense of the verbs, and (with reference to attacks on Christians during the Bar Kokhba rebellion referred to in Justin's *Dialogue with Trypho*) writes of an "alarming possibility" (see 66, n. 32).

the nonrecognition of the one who sent Jesus, the Father (see vv. 15:1, 8-11, 21, 23; 16:3). They are positive and negative faces of the same truth: the all-determining function of God in the Johannine story.

This contrast between the call to abide in Jesus and the hatred for him and his disciples shown by "the world" has led some scholars to see, behind this Gospel, a highly sectarian group.[50] Read on their own, 15:1-11 and 15:18—16:3 could leave one with that impression. But the central section of the discourse, 15:12-17, must not be lost from view. All that touches the experience of being a disciple of Jesus, union with him, mutual love, and sharing his experience of hatred, rejection, and death, has its source in the initiative of Jesus (15:15-16). The disciple is only a disciple because of a gratuitous act of love on Jesus' part (see v. 13). This is the reality that must be shown to the world (see vv. 8, 12; see 3:16-17; 13:35). The last discourse opened with a statement from the narrator describing the consummate nature of Jesus' loving (13:1: *eis telos*). Jesus has instructed his disciples on the new commandment, that they love one another *as he has loved them,* and that they be recognized as his disciples by the quality of their mutual love (see 13:34-35). Jesus' love is reflected in his choice of disciples and, in turn, is experienced in the mutual love of disciples for one another, showing to the world that they are Jesus' disciples. Jesus continues to call and love fragile disciples (see especially 13:18-20) and to share himself with them (see 13:8). The loving initiative of Jesus is surrounded by hatred (see 13:2), ignorance (see 13:22, 28), betrayal (see 13:2, 10-11, 21-30), the prophecy of denials (see 13:36-38), and the threat of death (see 13:2, 18-19, 36). The reader has been told, however, that Jesus' death will lead to the glorification of the Son of Man (see 11:4; 12:23, 32; 13:31-32), and that the association of the disciple with Jesus in the midst of hatred glorifies God (see 15:8). This is the love the disciples of Jesus are to reveal (13:34-35; 15:25-26).

The use of the expression *aposunagōgos* indicates that this story re-

---

[50] See, e.g., Becker, *Johannes,* 2:451–56, E. Kasemann, *The Testament of Jesus: A Study of John in the Light of Chapter 17* (trans. G. Krodel; London: SCM, 1965); W. A. Meeks, "The Man from Heaven in Johannine Sectarianism," *JBL* 91 (1972) 44–72; F. F. Segovia, "The Love and Hatred of Jesus and Johannine Sectarianism," *CBQ* 43 (1981) 258–72; idem, "'Peace I Leave with You; My Peace I Give to You': Discipleship in the Fourth Gospel," in F. F. Segovia, ed., *Discipleship in the New Testament* (Philadelphia: Fortress Press, 1985) 76–102; N. R. Petersen, *The Gospel of John and the Sociology of Light: Language and Characterization in the Fourth Gospel* (Valley Forge, Pa.: Trinity Press International, 1993); W. H. Kelber, "Metaphysics and Marginality in John," in F. F. Segovia, ed., *"What is John?" Readers and Readings of the Fourth Gospel* (SS 3; Atlanta: Scholars, 1996) 129–54.

flects the experiences of an early Christian community. But there is more to it. The shift from "the world" to "they" in vv. 18-21 points to "the Jews" of the earlier parts of the narrative. The reference to exclusion from the synagogue confirms this. In v. 1 Jesus has claimed to be the *true* vine. The actions of those who hate, exclude, and kill Jesus and the disciples are associated with the synagogue, the gathering place of a people of God who also claim to be "the vine." A paradox emerges as the vine-synagogue hates, persecutes, and excludes (16:1-3) the vine-Jesus (15:1-5a). Who is persecuting whom? Who is excluding whom? By hating, the persecutor and the executor fall into sin (see vv. 22-25) and do not bear the fruit that is demanded from those who are branches of the *true* vine. They are thus pruned, cut off from the vine and the branches that are tended by the Father, the vinedresser (see 15:1-5a, 5b-8). As throughout the Johannine story, those who hate and reject Jesus and his disciples are not judged; they judge themselves by refusing to accept the words and the works of Jesus (see vv. 22, 24). Such a perspective was no doubt formed within the context of anger, rejection, and exclusion on the part of "the Jews." Jesus is silent on the response disciples should make to "the Jews." But "the Jews" are not Israel however strongly they may claim to possess the definitive understanding of God's way with the world.

Those who will not abide in Jesus and those who hate, rejecting the revelation of the love of God in and through Jesus, are in sin. They bring judgment on themselves. Despite this self-inflicted judgment, at the center of 15:1—16:3 (15:12-17) the reader discovers that the message of the love of God shown by Jesus' words and actions in the midst of ignorance, failure, betrayal, and denial, so central to the narrative of 13:1-38, continues. Jesus has chosen disciples. They did not choose him (v. 16). He has loved them and made them friends rather than servants (vv. 14-15), giving himself unto death out of love for them (v. 13). Thus, in the midst of hatred and violence, one reality endures: the sovereign freedom for both Jesus and the Father to love the world (see 3:16-17). The reader, already aware of the portrait of Jesus' love for his own in 13:1-38, concludes that Jesus, the *true* vine, has both shown (13:1-38) and taught (15:1—16:3) that God's love knows no boundaries. There is only one *true* vine (15:1: *hē ampelos hē alēthinē*) however much some from the synagogue (16:2: *aposunagōgous poiēsousin humas*) may have become a "degenerate plant, a bastard vine" (see Jer 2:21). Contrary to the actions of this degenerate vine, Jesus' words on abiding, loving, and being hated have contained no message of exclusion from the true vine. But they have stated the possibility that some will choose to exclude themselves by rejecting Jesus and the Father who sent him. The characters and the reader of the story are free to abide or not to abide (see vv. 5b-6). This is what is meant by the narrator's description of Jesus' love for his own *eis telos* (13:1). The message of 13:1-38 is crucial for the reader's understanding of 15:1—16:3.

Chapter Four

Departure
John 16:4-33

¶ AFTER THE MONOLOGUE of 15:1—16:3, the next section of the discourse (16:4-33) returns the reader to a more familiar dialogue form. In a way strongly reminiscent of 14:1-31, Jesus speaks of his departure (16:4-6, 25-31), the gift of the Paraclete (vv. 7-15), and the challenges of living in the in-between time (vv. 20-24). The reader has a sense of déjà vu as a reading experience returns that deals with Jesus' departure and "the consolation of the inner circle."[1] Several indications point to a link between 16:4 and 16:33. The expression "these things I have said to you that" (*tauta lelalēka humin hina*) in v. 4a is repeated in v. 33. In a return to the theme of departure, Jesus' opening words recall one of the basic motivations for the discourse: that the disciples will remember and understand the events that lie ahead (v. 4a; see also 13:19; 14:25, 29; 15:11; 16:1). His closing words pick up a theme crucial to the first instruction on the departure: the gift of peace (v. 33a; see 14:27a).

There is almost universal agreement that this final part of the dis-

---

[1] M. W. G. Stibbe, *John* (Readings: A New Biblical Commentary; Sheffield: JSOT Press, 1993) 170. See A, Dettwiler, *Die Gegenwart des Erhohten: Eine exegetische Studie zu den johanneischen Abschiedsreden (Joh 13,31—16,33) unter besonderer Berucksichtigung ihres Relecture-Charakters* (FRLANT 169; Gottingen: Vandenhoeck & Ruprecht, 1995), 266–92, for his "Relecture" of 13:31—14:31 in 16:4b-33.

course proper begins with v. 4b,[2] but this division separates the things Jesus has said (*tauta lelalēka*) in v. 4a and his reference to his not having said these things from the beginning (*tauta . . . ex archēs ouk eipon*) in v. 4b. The things (*tauta*) Jesus has said or not said to his disciples in both v. 4a and v. 4b look back to what has been said in the discourse thus far, especially the themes of his departure (14:1-6, 25-31) and the rejection the disciples will suffer because they are his disciples (15:18—16:3).[3] Over against this pain and suffering (see v. 4a: *alla*), Jesus' words of prophecy and assurance have been delivered in this final period of his being "with them" (see v. 4b: *de*), so that when he is no longer with them, they will remember them (v. 4a).[4] After what has been said about Jesus' love for his own (13:1, 18-20), the future gift of the Paraclete (14:16-17, 26, 15:26), the oneness that will exist between the Father, the Son, and the one who believes and loves Jesus (14:20-24), and those who abide in Jesus (15:1-11), the reader suspects that the rejection, suffering, and even death that has been foretold in 15:18—16:3 cannot be the end of the story. The adversative *alla* of 16:4a confirms the reader's suspicion. The theme of Jesus' departure is resumed, and a rich reflection on that turning point in the story of both Jesus and the disciples is developed in 16:4-33.

THE SHAPE OF THE DISCOURSE

Although the source of considerable discussion, 16:4-33 can be seen as unfolding around three major sections. As with 14:1-31, the first part of 16:4-33 is dedicated to the theme of Jesus' departure and the role of the Paraclete in the in-between time (vv. 4-20). A second section plays on the theme of "before" and "after," using the image of a woman in childbirth as a symbol of the experience of the disciples (vv. 21-24). The final section, again paralleling the structure of 14:1-31, returns to the theme of Jesus' departure and the peace he leaves

---

[2] As well as the vast majority of commentators, this division is taken for granted by the widely used editions of the Greek New Testament, *UBSGNT, NTG* (26th ed.), and many modern language translations See, e.g., RSV, NRSV, JB, NJB, TOB, NAB, and NEB.

[3] Most scholars and commentators claim that the *tauta* of v. 4a looks back to 15:1-16:3, and thus closes 15 1—16:4a, while the *tauta* of v. 4b looks forward to the theme of departure, and thus opens 16.4b-33.

[4] With Y Simoens, *La gloire d'aimer: Structures stylistiques et interprétatives dans la Discours de la Cène (Jn 13–17)* (AnBib 90· Rome: Biblical Institute Press, 1981) 134, reading the *alla* of v 4a as adversative and the *de* of v. 4b as continuing the thought of v. 4a

with his disciples as they face the tribulations of the in-between time (vv. 25-33).[5] These sections unfold in the following fashion:

Verses 4-20: Jesus speaks of his departure, telling his disciples that their ignorance is creating sorrow (vv. 4-6). This section is enclosed between two uses of *tauta lelalēka humin* (v. 4 and v. 6).[6] But his departure is to the advantage of the disciples; it leads to the sending of the Paraclete, who will see to the judgment of the world and the ongoing revelation of Jesus (vv. 7-15). Jesus returns to the theme of departure, again addressing disciples who remain ignorant. This subsection is dominated by the theme of the "little while" *(mikron)* (vv. 16-20).[7]

Verses 21-24: The image of a woman in childbirth develops the theme of "now and afterward." Jesus presents the image of a woman, who passes from tribulation to joy by means of "the hour" (v. 21). On the basis of this image, Jesus corrects and instructs the disciples on their need to pass through their own experience of sorrow "now" to joy "afterward" (vv. 22-23a), and the section concludes with another contrast between the "now" of the disciples who do not ask in the name of Jesus, and an "afterward" when whatever they ask of the Father will be given in the name of Jesus (vv. 23b-24).[8] As so often in the Johannine story, the section concludes with the double "amen" that introduces vv. 23b-24.

Verses 25-33: The final section is enclosed between v. 25a: *tauta . . . lelalēka humin* and v. 33a: *tauta lelalēka humin.* In the first subsection, Jesus returns to the theme of his departure, explaining openly that the departure is the return of the Son to the Father (vv. 25-28). The disciples' response shows they have come part of the way to a proper understanding of Jesus, but they have not grasped the significance of his departure (vv. 29-30). Re-

---

[5] See Simoens, *La gloire,* 151-67, for the overall division. Most commentators divide the material into a section dealing with the sorrow of the disciples (vv. 4b-7) and two sections on the Paraclete (vv. 8-11, vv. 12-20). See, for a survey, R E Brown, *The Gospel according to John* (2 vols ; AB 29, 29A; Garden City, N Y: Doubleday, 1966-70) 2 709 F. F. Segovia, *The Farewell of the Word: The Johannine Call to Abide* (Minneapolis: Fortress Press, 1991) 220-24, and M. W. G. Stibbe, *John* (Readings: A New Biblical Commentary; Sheffield. JSOT Press, 1993) 170-71, have three major divisions: vv. 4b-15, vv 16-24, vv. 25-33, depending upon the progressive role of the disciples (see vv. 5, 17, 29). On the unity of vv. 7-15, see R. Schnackenburg, *The Gospel according to St John* (3 vols , HTCNT 4/1-3; London: Burns & Oates; New York: Crossroad, 1968-82) 3:132-33, Segovia, *Farewell,* 227.

[6] Among other things, this formal indication of "closure" leads me to describe vv 4-6 as a unit rather than the more commonly accepted vv. 4b-7. See Simoens, *La gloire,* 153-54.

[7] Most commentators see vv. 16-33 as a unit and then subdivide it further. See Brown, *John,* 2:727-29; C. Dietzfelbinger, "Die eschatologische Freude der Gemeinde in der Angst der Welt," *EvTh* 40 (1980) 420-21

[8] See Simoens, *La gloire,* 163-67

sponding to their partial belief, Jesus points out that the hour of his departure may produce physical scattering, but it cannot take away the peace he
gives. He has overcome the world (vv. 31-33).

Many of the themes of Jesus' earlier words return: departure, the
Paraclete, the joy and peace that will be with the disciples in the in-
between time, and the oneness Jesus' departure will establish between
Jesus, the disciples, and the Father. There is an increased focus on the
disciples. They are told that their sorrow at Jesus' departure is misplaced. For their benefit Jesus is going away so that the Paraclete might
bring judgment against the world and further unfold the revelation
of God that has taken place in and through Jesus (vv. 7-15). But the
disciples must pass through "the hour," that they might overcome
their sorrow of the "now" of the narrative, to attain the perfect joy of
the "afterward" (vv. 22-23a). As the discourse comes to an end and
Jesus speaks plainly of his departure as the return of the Son to the
Father and of the future presence of the Father with the disciples, at
last they come to accept part of the author's christological point of
view: "We believe that you came from God" (vv. 29-30). The reader
wonders, however, have they only accepted half of the equation? Jesus
came from God, but he is now departing, returning to the Father, from
whom he came (see v. 28). The disciples have accepted his origins, but
how will they deal with his departure?

READING THE DISCOURSE

1. The Departure of Jesus (16:4-20)
a. Verses 4-6: A Departure That Creates Sorrow   Jesus informs his disciples that he has told them of many experiences that lie ahead of them,
so that *afterward*, when they happen,[9] the memory of Jesus' word will
be with them (v. 4a; see 13:19; 14:25, 29; 15:11; 16:1). Jesus has spoken of the difficult things that will happen to the disciples: The departure of Jesus will leave them bereft (14:1, 18, 27) and they will
experience suffering, hatred, and even death (15:18—16:3). Counter-
balancing the suffering that lies ahead, however, will be the gift of the
Spirit-Paraclete (see 14:16-17, 26; 15:26-27), already, for the reader,
associated with the moment of Jesus' glorification (see 7:37-39). Jesus
has not spoken to them in this way from the beginning of his ministry

[9] Reading *hē hōra autōn* as referring to the immediately preceding *tauta:* "When the
hour of these things comes   .." United, as the first verse in the division of 16:4–33,
the *tauta, autōn, autōn, tauta* of v. 4 all (logically) refer to coming events.

(ex archēs; see 15:27). It was not necessary and would not have been appropriate during those formative times as Jesus was with them. The days of Jesus' being "with them," however, are drawing to a close as the time of his departure is at hand (v. 4b).

A new situation is nigh, and in the "now" of the discourse, Jesus is telling them of the *afterward* that lies ahead (v. 4a: *hē hōra autōn*). An expression has been used across the major part of the story of Jesus' ministry, during which "the hour" (*he hōra*) was not yet at hand (see 2:5, 7:8; 7:30; 8:20). As some Greeks asked to see him, Jesus announced the arrival of "the hour" (12:23). In the solemn introduction to the final discourse in 13:1, the narrator reminded the reader that the hour of Jesus had come (*elthen*). The expression returns in v. 4a to refer to a series of events that will happen to the disciples as a consequence of Jesus' departure. The reader is aware that "the 'hour' of Jesus appears to mean his failure but is in fact his exaltation and glory; that of his enemies appears to be their victory but is in fact their defeat." [10] The disciples have been told often enough during this discourse that Jesus is going away, that the sent one is returning to the one who sent him (see 13:33, 36b; 14:2-4, 6, 12, 18, 19-20, 28, 31; 15:26), and so he rebukes them, as not one of them has asked where he was going (v. 5).

This is not entirely true, as the reader recalls Simon Peter's asking exactly that question (*pou hupageis*) in 13:36a.[11] The contexts of Peter's question (13:36a) and Jesus' rebuke (16:5) indicate that failure to un-

---

[10] C. K. Barrett, *The Gospel according to St John* (2d ed. London. SPCK, 1978) 485 See R. Bultmann, *The Gospel of John: A Commentary* (trans. G. R. Beasley-Murray, Oxford: Blackwell, 1971) 558, n.1.

[11] Commentators regularly point out that Philip's question in 14:5 is also a request to know where Jesus is going. I will focus my attention on 13:36a, as the reader finds the repetition of the exact words in 13:36a and 16:5. The contradiction has created difficulty for interpreters. Many attempts have been made to resolve it. Some rearrange the order of the text (J. H. Bernard, *A Critical and Exegetical Commentary on the Gospel according to St John* [2 vols.; ICC; Edinburgh: T. & T. Clark, 1928] 1:xx; Bultmann, *John*, 459–61), while others have argued that there is no contradiction (M.-J. Lagrange, *Evangile selon Saint Jean* [EB; Paris: Gabalda, 1927] 417–18; C. H. Dodd, *The Interpretation of the Fourth Gospel* [Cambridge: Cambridge Univ. Press, 1953] 412–13, n. 1; E. C. Hoskyns, *The Fourth Gospel* [2d ed.; ed. F. N. Davey; London: Faber & Faber, 1947] 483), and a slightly different text has been proposed (F. da Cagliari, "'... E nessuno di voi mi domanda: - dove vai?' - [Giov. 16,5]," *Laur* 10 [1969] 233–44). The most common contemporary explanation is that it is the result of the final editor's placing two versions of a discourse side by side. See, e.g., Brown, *John*, 2:710; Schnackenburg, *St John*, 3:126; G. R. Beasley-Murray, *John* (WBC 36; Waco: Word Books, 1987) 279. D A. Carson, *The Gospel according to John* (Grand Rapids: Eerdmans, 1991) 533, resorts to desperate measures when he asks whether Peter and Thomas were "really asking the question formally represented by their words "

derstand Jesus' destiny is in question in both places. Within the context of the footwashing (13:1-17), the promise that the revelation of God would take place in events that were near at hand (vv. 18-20), and the gift of the morsel (21-38), Simon Peter's mind is turned toward death. His question in v. 36a is totally conditioned by his concerns for Jesus' immediate future *within the world of human experience*. Jesus' attempts fail to transcend this horizontal, time-conditioned understanding of his destiny (vv. 33, 36b), as Simon Peter asks why he cannot follow *now*, swearing that he will lay down his life for Jesus (v. 37). But since then Jesus' description of his departure has eclipsed all suggestions that this moment can be limited to a traditional understanding of death. He will certainly depart through death (see 14:18), but the disciples have been told, "I go to the Father" (14:28; see 13:33, 36; 14:4, 5, 6, 7, 16:5). The disciples have been further instructed since 13:36-38, but still they are not asking the correct question. The use of the present tense (*erōtą*) focuses Jesus' accusation on the present context, a moment in the time of the narrative that is somewhat distant from Peter's question, but still the disciples are not asking the correct question. They are not questioning Jesus' destiny despite his consistent and clear instruction. They remain locked within the world they can understand and control: Departure is death.[12] They are not asking where Jesus is going (16:5), because they are unable to reach beyond the identification of departure with physical death. Thus, "grief has pervaded, taken possession of"[13] their hearts because Jesus continues to talk of these matters (*oti tauta lelalēka humin*) in a way they are unable to comprehend (v. 6). The reader knows that Jesus' death is the moment of his departure yet follows the disappointing response of the disciples. The misunderstanding of Simon Peter's earlier question (13:36a) has not been overcome.

b. Verses 7-15: The Role of the Paraclete   Though there may have been only three explicit references to the Spirit-Paraclete figure thus far (14:16-17, 26; 15:26-27), the shadow of the Paraclete is cast across all the farewell discourse. Jesus' words again open with *alla* (see v. 4a), contrasting the lack of belief among the disciples (vv. 4-6) with the truth he is telling them. Despite their desire to keep their master with

---

[12] The motivation for sorrow thus generated is eloquently described by H. van den Bussche, *Jean: Commentaire de l'Evangile Spirituel* (Bruges: Desclèe de Brouwer, 1976) 435: "Et que reste-t-il de leur rêve messianique? Une tristesse poignante étreint leur coeurs. Chacun considère les debris de ses illusions."

[13] Barrett, *St John*, 486, commenting on the strange use of *plēroun*.

them, it is to their advantage (*sumpherei humin;* see 11:50) that Jesus depart. Rather than adding to their sorrow (see 15:18—16:3), it will overcome their sorrow. At the heart of the benefits that will flow from the departure of Jesus is the gift of the Paraclete (see 14:15-16, 26; 15:26), but this gift is entirely dependent on the departure of Jesus (v. 7). The sending of the Spirit has been linked to the departure of Jesus since the narrator's remark in 7:39: "As yet the Spirit had not been given, because Jesus was not yet glorified." The narrative tension created by this prolepsis has not been resolved, but the link between the end of Jesus' life through death and departure, and his glorification, is being increasingly strengthened (see 11:4; 12:23, 32-34; 13:1, 31-32).

The first Paraclete saying informed the reader that the one who sent the Son, the Father, also lies behind the mission of the Paraclete, but as the result of Jesus' asking (14:16). Almost immediately, however, the reader has been informed that the Father and the Son are united in the sending of the Spirit: "whom the Father will send in my name" (14:26). From that point on, the author takes for granted that the reader is aware of the role of the Father and has Jesus speak predominantly of his own role in the sending of the Paraclete in 15:26 ("whom I shall send you from the Father") and 16:7 ("whom I shall send you"). The cumulative reading experience of the Paraclete sayings informs the reader that Jesus' active role in the sending of the Spirit is intimately linked with his departure. Nevertheless, "the other Paraclete" (see 14:16) is a sent one of the Father (see 14:26) just as "the former Paraclete," Jesus, is the sent one of the Father. The reader now meets two detailed descriptions of the roles the Spirit-Paraclete will play: judging the world (vv. 8-11) and further revealing God (vv. 12-15). Both roles are the prolongation of the person and work of Jesus into the in-between time.

Jesus first describes the role of the Paraclete in the world, further explaining for the reader why the world is unable to receive the Spirit of Truth (see 14:17). The Paraclete comes to expose the world concerning sin, righteousness, and judgment (v. 8). The text is made notoriously obscure by the use of the verb *elenchein,* a rich expression with a number of possible meanings across the semantic fields of blame, conviction, convincing, exposure, shame, and investigation.[14] On two

---

[14] See F. Buchsel, *"elenchō ktl,"* TDNT 2 (1964) 473–76; I de la Potterie, *La Vérité dans Saint Jean* (2 vols.; AnBib 73; Rome: Biblical Institute Press, 1977) 1·399–406, F Porsch, *Pneuma und Wort: ein exegetischer Beitrag zur Pneumatologie des Johannesevangeliums* (FThSt 16; Frankfurt· J. Knecht, 1974) 281–82; W Stenger, *"DIKAIOSUNE* in Jo XVI 18.10," *NovT* 21 (1979) 3–6.

earlier occasions this verb was used in contexts linked with the idea
of presenting for view, bringing out into the open. In 3:20 Jesus spoke
of the person who will not walk in the light lest evil deeds be brought
out into the open (*hina mē elenchthē ta erga autou*), while in 8:46 he
challenged his opponents to make evident that he was a sinner (*elenxei
me peri hamartias*). The reader is guided by this earlier use of the verb
when it appears in 16:8.[15] There is a further close link between this
role of the Paraclete, making obvious that the world is at fault concerning sin, righteousness, and judgment, and the parallel role of Jesus, who did not come to judge (see 3:17; 5:24; 8:15; 12:47), but whose
very presence as the revelation of God brought about *krisis* (see 3:19-
21; 5:22; 7:7; 8:24; 9:39; 12:31). Jesus' presence within the human
situation is the revelation of truth and light that exposes the surrounding darkness (see 12:45-47). The reader knows that the Paraclete
continues the revealing task of the word of Jesus (see 14:26). As well
as the mission of continuing the revelation of God to a world that has
never seen God (see 1:18; 3:13-14; 6:40), there is a further, negative
side to the task of the Paraclete: to expose the darkness of the world
and thus bring it to judgment. The Johannine story has been marked
by a trial during which Jesus is the accused, but all the time, ironically,
his accusers are judged (see 3:19; 5:22; 27, 30, 44-45; 8:16, 26; 9:39).
This process will continue after Jesus' departure.[16] The Paraclete continues the critical, judging function that flows from the revelation of
God, so clearly attributed to Jesus (see 5:27).[17] The ongoing presence
of this authority in the Paraclete is now described in more detail in
vv. 9-11.

[15] See Porsch, *Pneuma und Wort*, 282–83; Beasley-Murray, *John*, 280–81; B. Lindars,
"*DIKAIOSUNĒ* in Jn 16.8 and 10," in A. Descamps and A. de Halleux, eds., *Mélanges
Bibliques en hommage au R. P. Béda Rigaux* (Gembloux· Duculot, 1970) 279–80; Stenger,
"*DINAIOSUNE*," 5–6. D. A. Carson, "The Function of the Paraclete in John 16:7-11,"
JBL 98 (1979) 551–58, contests this understanding of the Johannine texts, and adds
many other NT passages to show that the meaning must be "to convict of" or "to
convince of."

[16] For the interpretation of *elenxei* as associated with the judging role of the Paraclete,
see Bultmann, *John*, 561–62; J. Blank, *Krisis: Untersuchungen zur johanneischen Christologie
und Eschatologie* (Freiburg: Lambertus, 1964), 335; de la Potterie, *La Vérité*, 1:410–16. On
the continuation of the legal process, which was behind much of John 5–12, in the
Paraclete who eventually reverses the process, judging those who have judged Jesus, see
X. Léon-Dufour, *Lecture de l'Evangile selon Jean*, (3 vols.; Parole de Dieu; Paris Seuil,
1988–93) 3:225–26.

[17] See Dettwiler, *Die Gegenwart*, 221–22. For the link between revelation and judgment
in 5:27, see F. J. Moloney, *The Johannine Son of Man* (2d ed.; BibScRel 14; Rome: LAS,
1978) 77–86.

The Paraclete will expose the sin of the world because (*hoti*) they have not believed in Jesus (v. 10).[18] The reader is sufficiently well schooled in the essential role of belief in Jesus to know that not to believe in Jesus must be judged as sin: "The one who rejects me and does not receive my word has a judge" (12:48a; see 8:44-47). The Paraclete will expose the false righteousness of the world because it is completely mistaken in its attempt to understand and judge Jesus in terms of "this world." Jesus' opponents have consistently failed to accept that Jesus is from the Father and that he is returning to the Father and will no longer be seen among his disciples (v. 11).[19] Yet they have laid claim to righteousness as children of Abraham (see 8:39-59), disciples of Moses (see 6:30-31; 9:28-29), and subject to Torah (see 5:16-18, 39-40, 45-47; 7:12, 18, 20-24, 48-49; 9:16, 24 8:58-59; 10:24-38; 11:48-50; 16:2).[20] The problem of 12:43 has never been overcome: The opponents of Jesus preferred the *doxa tōn anthrōpōn* to the *doxa tou theou*. In their *horizontally* determined understanding of a righteousness worked out within human history (Abraham, Moses, and Torah), they have rejected the *vertical* inbreak of the Son of God (the word become flesh, Jesus Christ).[21] The Paraclete will expose the false judgment of the world because, despite all appearances to the contrary, Jesus' departure through death is at the same time his being "lifted up" in exaltation (3:14; 8:28; 12:32-33), his revelation of the glory of God and his own glorification (11:4; 12:23; 13:31-32), his "gathering" of

[18] On the possible meanings of *hoti* in this context, see Barrett, *St John*, 487; Carson, *John*, 535-39; Idem, "The Function of the Paraclete in John 16:7-11," *JBL* 98 (1979) 561-63. Carson insists that *hoti* be understood in exactly the same way across vv 8-11.

[19] Jesus' words address the failure of the world to accept that Jesus departs to the Father. But the form of a discourse, where Jesus is speaking to "his own," enables him to speak of a consequence of his departure, in the second person future: *ouketi theōreite me*. See Lagrange, *Saint Jean*, 419.

[20] On this issue, see S. Pancaro, *The Law in the Fourth Gospel: The Torah and the Gospel, Moses and Jesus, Judaism and Christianity according to John* (NovTSupp 42; Leiden: Brill, 1975) 9-125. The use of *dikaiosunē* in v. 8 and v. 10 addresses "the Jews'" false sense of "righteousness," a mistaken understanding of "fulfilling the divine statutes" (BAGD, 196, s. v. *dikaiosunē*, para 2b). Against, e.g., B. Lindars, *The Gospel John*, (NCB; London: Oliphants) 502-3, who regards *dikaiosunē* as "the opposite of *hamartia*." See idem, "*DIKAIOSUNĒ*," 279-85. The negative meaning of *dikaiosunē*, adopted above, is what is meant by the immediately preceding 16:2: "Whoever kills you will think he is offering service to God." See B. F. Westcott, *The Gospel according to Saint John* (London: Murray, 1908) 229.

[21] See F. J. Moloney, *Signs and Shadows: Reading John 5-12* (Minneapolis: Fortress Press, 1996) 196-98. As Blank, *Krisis*, 336-38, insists, they are exposed concerning *dikaiosunē* because they cannot accept the *hupagein* of Jesus, and all that is associated with it. See also Stenger, "*DIKAIOSUNĒ*," 6-8, and Bultmann, *John*, 565.

the scattered (see 11:50, 52; 12:11, 19, 32), and the moment of his return to the Father (13:1). The apparent victory of the ruler of this world in the death of Jesus is to be exposed, as Jesus' death and glorification reverses the judgment of history (v. 11; see 14:30).

How will this exposure take place? Jesus has informed the disciples in 15:26-27 that during the in-between time marked by his physical absence, the Paraclete will testify on his behalf through Spirit-filled witnesses of Jesus. Until now the disciples have been largely instructed on how they will be comforted (14:16-17), further enlightened, and reminded of Jesus' teaching (14:26). And they have been told that they will testify, as the Paraclete will testify (15:26). This last saying, which comes toward the end of Jesus' instruction on the future suffering, rejection, and death of the disciples, introduces the reader to the need for the disciple to look realistically at the challenge of living in a hostile world. "The Spirit, not content with defending the believers, takes the offensive against the world,"[22] and this offensive is a challenge to the disciple of Jesus, living the in-between time in the presence of the Paraclete (see 14:16), rendering witness in the world (see 15:26-27), instructed, enlightened, and remembering the person and teaching of Jesus (see 14:26). "The Paraclete exposes the sin of the lack of faith of the world and shows that unbelieving world that it is guilty by confronting it with the faith of the community."[23]

The rhythmic repetition of important Johannine expressions appears here to inform the reader further on the parallel, but chronologically subsequent, revealing activity of the Paraclete who will speak (vv. 13: *lalēsei* [twice]) and declare all truth (vv. 13, 14, 15: *anangelei*).[24] The reader knows that the time of Jesus' presence with his disciples is coming to an end and senses both Jesus' urgency to communicate much to them (v. 12a) and the disciples' *present* inability to cope with all the implications of the revelation of God that takes place in Jesus (v. 12b: *ou dunasthe bastazein arti*). The temporal aspect of the narrative, indicated by the adverb *now* (*arti*) must be taken seriously. It is not as if more revelation is still to follow, to be delivered by the Para-

[22] Barrett, *St John*, 487.
[23] Schnackenburg, *St John*, 3 132.
[24] See Porsch, *Pneuma und Wort*, 295–97. The use of *legein* in the Fourth Gospel for Jesus' revealing word is widespread. This cannot be said for *anangellein* which, up to this point of the story has been found only twice (see 4:25; 5:15). Brown, *John*, 2.708, claims that its widespread use in the LXX, and especially in Isaiah, has provided background for the Johannine use. For Brown, it contains the idea of "seeking a deeper meaning in what has already happened." See also F. W. Young, "A Study of the Relation of Isaiah to the Fourth Gospel," *ZNW* 46 (1955) 224–26.

clete. The problem lies with the disciples "now." The reader has no
illusions about the fragility of the people at the table listening to Jesus'
words. God has been made known to these people in Jesus Christ (see
1:14-18), but in the Spirit-directed time, after the departure of Jesus,
the implications of this revelation unfold. This is yet another reason
that it is advantageous for Jesus to depart (see v. 7). Jesus must leave
the many things (*polla*) that he would like to tell them to the other
Paraclete (14:16), the Spirit of truth (vv. 12b-13a). This figure (*ekeinos*)
will guide the disciples (*hodēgēsei humas*) into the fullness of truth.
The careful choice of words highlights the author's concern to instruct
the reader that the journey to "all truth" (*en tēi alētheiai pasȩ̄*) has not
been completed. Jesus has been with the disciples as the way (14:6a:
hē hodos). He is about to depart, but "the way" goes on. The in-
between time will be marked by the ongoing revelation of the light
and the truth (see 14:6b) embodied in Jesus through the presence of
the Spirit of truth who will lead (*hodēgēsei*) disciples unerringly toward
the fullness of truth.[25] There is a dynamic sense of a steady unfolding
of a revelation that has not yet been fully grasped or experienced.
Given the guide, the traveler journeys on with unconditioned confidence (v. 13).

Neither Jesus nor the Paraclete is the ultimate source of the revelation they communicate. Jesus has not proclaimed himself or his own
word; he has made the Father known (see 3:32-35; 7:16-18; 8:26-29,
42-43; 12:47-50; 14:10). The Spirit also speaks whatever he hears (13b:
hosa akousei lalēsei). The reader is reminded that the period of the
Spirit is still an in-between time. As Brown insists:

> We find no evidence that Johannine theology ever abandoned the hope of
> the final return of Jesus in visible glory, although the Gospel clearly puts
> more emphasis on all the eschatological features that have already been
> realized in Jesus' first coming. The question is not one of the presence of

---

[25] The use of the expression *alētheia* links the mission of the Paraclete with the ongoing task of the revelation of God. Here, however, the stress is on *pasēi*. See the rich
study of J. Kremer, "Jesu Verheissung des Geistes. Zur Verankerung der Aussage von Joh
16,13 im Leben Jesu," in R. Schnackenburg, J. Ernst, and J. Wanke, eds., *Die Kirche des
Anfangs: Fur Heinz Schurmann zum 65. Geburtstag* (EThSt 38; Leipzig: St. Benno-Verlag,
1977) 247-73, claiming that John 16.13 is (along with Mark 13:11) legitimation for the
Christian community's ongoing interpretation of the message of Jesus in the post-Easter
period. Against Porsch, *Pneuma und Wort*, 294-95, and de la Potterie, *La Vérité*, 1 431-38,
among others, who read (following Vaticanus) *eis tēn alētheian pasan* as "to the very
heart of all truth." Most scholars accept the *lectio difficilior* adopted above (following
Sinaiticus, Cantabrigiensis, Freer Gospels, and others).

Jesus in and through the Paraclete *as opposed to* the coming of Jesus in glory, but one of the relative importance to be given to each.[26]

The author insists that there are things "yet to come" (*ta erchomena*).[27] The revealing task of the Paraclete points forward toward these things that are yet to come (v. 13b). The gift of the Spirit does not mark the end of the story but signals a new stage after the departure and glorification of Jesus, the period of the Spirit-filled community of worshiping disciples. But the expression also reminds the reader of *ta eschata*, of the Christian belief that this period will come to an end (see 4:36; 5:28-29; 6:40, 39, 54; 11:24-25; 12:25, 48; 14:1-3).

As promised in the prologue (see 1:14), Jesus' saving presence during the period of his ministry revealed his *doxa* (see 2:11; 11:40; 12:23, 43; 13:31), as the *doxa* of God could be seen at Sinai (see Exod 19:16-20). Despite Jesus' physical absence, his glory will be seen because the Paraclete will take what is of Jesus and further declare it to his disciples. The reader is told that Jesus' revealing mission, described biblically as the vision of the *doxa* (see 12:43), will continue in the revealing mission of the Paraclete, who will take all that is of Jesus and declare it (*ek tou emou lēmpsetai kai anangelei*), thus bringing to remembrance what Jesus has said to the disciples (v. 14; see 14:26). But this affirmation needs further clarification lest the disciples mistakenly think that all the Paraclete declares has its *source* in Jesus. Both Jesus and the Paraclete have been sent by the Father (see 14:16, 26; 15:26). To reaffirm this fundamental element in the story's theological

[26] Brown, "The Paraclete," 131 (stress original). See also E. Cortès, *Los Discursos de Adiós de Gen 49 a Jn 13–17* (Colectanea San Paciano 23; Barcelona: Herder, 1976) 445–50.

[27] Scholars have been divided over the interpretation of the role of the Paraclete, declaring *ta erchomena* Is it fully eschatological; i.e., the Paraclete points toward the end of time (so, e.g., Bernard, *St John*, 2:511; H. Windisch, *The Spirit-Paraclete in the Fourth Gospel* (Facet Books: Biblical Series 20; Philadelphia: Fortress Press, 1968); G. Johnston, *The Spirit-Paraclete in the Gospel of John* (SNTSMS 12; Cambridge: Cambridge Univ. Press, 1970) 38–39; O. Betz, *Der Paraklet: Fursprecher im haretischen Spatjudentum, im Johannesevangelium und in neu gefundenen gnostischen Schriften* (AGSU 2; Leiden: Brill, 1963) 191–92, an indication of the apocalyptic aspect of primitive Christian prophecy (see, e.g., W. Bauer, *Das Johannesevangelium erklart* [3d ed.; HKNT 6; Tubingen: J. C. B. Mohr, 1933] 198–99; Bernard, *St John*, 2:511; Lindars, *John*, 505), or is the reference to the events of "the hour," which are about to come in the story of Jesus (W. Thusing, *Die Erhohung und Verherrlichung Jesus im Johannesevangelium* [2d ed.; NTAbh 21, 2/1; Munster: Aschendorf, 1970] 149–53; J. Marsh, *Saint John* [PNTC; Harmondsworth: Penguin, 1968] 538–39)? The position taken above has the Paraclete pointing the disciples forward to the many things that will flow from the event of Jesus, from "the hour," and including "the hour," until the traditional end of time.

point of view, Jesus states that everything belonging to the Father also belongs to him. Something like this has been said in 5:19 and 5:30, but there Jesus claimed to have everything from the Father. While those earlier words are related to what Jesus is now saying (16:15), something more far-reaching is being claimed. Not only does Jesus receive everything from the Father, but *everything that the Father has* is his. The oneness between the Father and the Son (see 1:1-2, 18; 10:30, 38) is so complete that what is of the Father is also of the Son. What is "of God" is also "of Jesus." Jesus is thus the perfect and ideal revelation of the Father, and nothing of the Father can be hidden, as Jesus possesses everything of the Father (16:15; see 1:1c). This unique Johannine understanding of Jesus flows into the author's presentation of the Paraclete, who takes all that is from Jesus and will declare it (*ek tou emou lambanei kai anangelei*) to the disciples in the in-between time (v. 15).[28] The critical presence of the Paraclete over against the world is new, but it is the logical development of what has earlier been said about the inability of the world to receive the Paraclete (14:17). The reader has heard of the exposing *krisis* the Paraclete will bring into the world (see 15:18—16:3)[29] and the Paraclete's role as the ongoing presence of the revelation of God in the in-between time (vv. 12-15; see 14:1-31).

c. Verses 16-20: A Departure That Creates Confusion   In v. 16 Jesus repeats what he has already said several times (v. 5; see 7:33; 12:35; 13:33; 14:19). Using a motif familiar to the reader (*mikron*), the theme of his departure so that he cannot be *seen* (*ouketi theōreite me*) is coupled with a promise that the time will come when the disciples will see him again (*palin . . . opsesthe me*). The focus of the narrative shifts as the disciples fail to understand and accept Jesus' consistent teaching on the two brief times that lay ahead of them: the *mikron* after which they will no longer see Jesus, and the *mikron* after which they

---

[28] All the verbs that speak of the revealing task of the Paraclete in vv. 12-15 are in the future tense, with the exception of *lambanei* in v. 15. Is this present tense called for once the author has stated one of the consequences of the Prologue (see 1:1-2) in v. 15a: *panta hosa echei ho patēr ema estin?* All that is of Jesus always has been his, because of the oneness between God and the Logos. The Paraclete therefore *takes* (*lambanei*) that which *is* (*estin*).

[29] U. B. Muller, "Die Parkletenvortstellung im Johannesevangelium," ZTK 71 (1974) 66–75, has shown, convincingly, that the judging, forensic, role of the Paraclete, taken by many scholars as the original meaning of *paraklētos*, is a development within the Johannine tradition.

will again see him (v. 17bc).[30] Yet they recall Jesus' words on the deeper implications of his departure. In the questioning discussion among themselves (v. 17a: *ti estin touto ho legei hēmin*), they raise an issue not mentioned in Jesus' words to them in this immediate context but recalled from earlier statements on his departure. Without any prompting, they link Jesus' departure with his return to the Father. Not only do they question the meaning of the two "times," but also the "place" to which Jesus is going: to the Father (v. 18d; see 14:28). The disciples have heard of the relationship between Jesus' departure and his return to the Father but reject it as they plead total ignorance on the meaning of *mikron:* "we do not know what he means" (v. 18). The reader is aware that they have provided the answer to their own question by mentioning Jesus' departure (v. 17d). It is *because* Jesus is going away from them that they will see him again. It is for their benefit that he departs (see v. 7). Despite the eightfold use of *mikron* in vv. 16-19, the issue at stake is the *fact* of Jesus' departure, not simply its *timing.* Given the criteria for authentic faith (see 2:1—4:54), the disciples are judged by the reader to be like Nicodemus (see 3:1-11) and the Samaritan woman (see 4:16-30), unable to reach beyond their own categories to accept the word of Jesus.

The focus returns to Jesus, who knows the subject of their private conversation and their desire to ask him for the meaning of his words. Jesus takes the initiative by means of a double "amen," words that link all that went before with words that point forward to the next theme (see also 13:16, 20, 21; 14:12). In response to the disciples' lack of acceptance of his word (v. 19, repeating, almost verbatim, v. 16), he does not answer the precise question the disciples are asking. Jesus does not explain the meaning of *mikron* (see v. 18), nor does he elaborate on what he means when he tells them of his return to the Father (see v. 17d). He returns to the theme of the in-between time addressing the immediate future situation of the disciples and the experience through which they must pass as they broach this time. Jesus' words on the future of the disciples recall several earlier sayings that created a tension between the experiences of the present, which must be un-

---

[30] Scholarship is in wide agreement that these two "times" are the short time between the discourse and Jesus' death ("you will not see me"), and the time after the resurrection ("you will see me"). See, e g., Bauer, *Johannesevangelium,* 199; Hoskyns, *Fourth Gospel,* 487, Dietzfelbinger, "Die eschatologische Freude," 422–23. I am suggesting that the period of not seeing *Jesus* is—as the disciples correctly suggest—associated with the departure and his return to the Father (see v. 17d), and thus not the time between the discourse and the resurrection, and that the time of seeing him will be associated with the worshiping community in the time of the Paraclete (see 14:18-21).

dergone to produce belief, joy, memory, and peace in the future (see 13:18-20; 14:25-27, 29; 15:11; 16:1, 4). The shadow of the cross looms as Jesus tells his disciples they are approaching a moment when they will weep and lament (*klausete kai thrēnēsete*)[31] and the world will rejoice. The reader knows that a death through being lifted up on a cross lies in the immediate future (see especially 12:32-33). This death will bear all the appearances of a victory for the forces which are lining up against Jesus (see 11:49-50, 53, 57; 12:10-11). But their rejoicing will be short-lived as, for this author, the brute facts of history do not reflect the true significance of the death of Jesus. The departure of Jesus through the cross will create the *mikron* when Jesus will not be seen (see v. 16a), but the sorrow of the disciples will be turned into joy. How this will take place is still to be discovered, but the reader has every reason to suspect that the Paraclete will play a crucial role in the transformation and that it will be the result of Jesus' departure to the Father (see v. 7). Jesus' departure will be a genuine departure, and he will not return to be seen again as he was seen during his ministry. However, the absent one will be present in the worshiping community in the experience of the Paraclete (see v. 16b).[32] The cross may appear to be defeat, but enigmatically the opposite is the case. The lifting up of Jesus is also his exaltation (see 3:14; 8:28; 12:32), and it marks "the hour" of the judgment of the world (see 12:23, 27-33). But neither Jesus nor the disciples can avoid the experience of the cross. There is unavoidable loss and pain in the departure of death. The author is not about to rewrite the *events* of history, but this story of Jesus of Nazareth is an attempt to give these events new *meaning*.

2. Now and Afterward (16:21-24)
a. Verse 21: The Now and Afterward of the Woman
There is an easy progression from Jesus' closing words to the disciples' wonderings about

---

[31] The verb *thrēnein* is regularly linked with the singing of funeral dirges (see Matt 11:17; Luke 7:32; 23:27). See BAGD, 363. *Klaiein* is used in this Gospel only in connection with death (see 11:31, 33).

[32] I am thus suggesting that the times of not seeing and then seeing of v. 16 are the time of suffering produced by the departure of the former Paraclete, Jesus, through the cross, and the time of joy when the other Paraclete is sent, as a result of the departure of Jesus (see v. 7. See 14:18-21). See D. E. Aune, *The Cultic Setting of Realized Eschatology in Early Christianity* (NovTSup 28, Leiden: Brill, 1972) 132–33. T Onuki, *Gemeinde und Welt im Johannesevangelium: Ein Beitrag zur Frage nach der theologischen und pragmatischen Funktion des johanneischen "Dualismus"* (WMANT 56; Neukirchen-Vluyn. Neukirchener Verlag, 1984) 152–56, also makes the link with the Paraclete, but unnecessarily introduces the notion of Pentecost to explain two different points of time.

the meaning of "a little while" (v. 20) and his further instruction on how they are to live through the oncoming anxiety of broaching the in-between time (vv. 21-24). In v. 20 he has told them that they are about to pass through weeping, lamenting, and sorrow, eventually to experience joy. They have every right to ask: *How?* This question is answered in three stages. Fundamental to Jesus' explanation are the stages of the basic experience of a woman in childbirth (v. 21). There are contrasting moments in the woman's experience, neither of which can be avoided: before and after the birth of a child.[33] *Before* the birth, the woman experiences the sorrow of physical pain and anxiety, as she has come to her "hour" (v. 21a). The reader recalls the earlier association of this expression with a woman, the mother of Jesus, who was told that his "hour" had not yet come (2:4; see also 7:6, 30; 8:30). *After* her child has been born, the memory of this anguish (*tēs thlipseōs*) has disappeared (v. 21b). This takes place because a child (*anthrōpos*) has been born to the world (v. 21c). There is also a very close link between Jesus' words and Isa 26:16-19 and 66:7-14, where the prophet announced a messianic salvation to relieve the afflictions that must intervene before the final consummation.[34] The surface meaning of Jesus' affirmation is clear: the experience of a woman at the birth of a child serves as a symbol of the way in which joy can be the end result of sorrow and anxiety (see v. 20). But the reader wonders if there are hints of deeper meanings lurking behind the language of "the woman" (*hē gunē;* see 2:4), "the hour" (*hē hōra;* see 2:4), anxiety (*hē thlipsis*), and "a human being" (*anthrōpos*). A fundamental human experience is described, but its language is reminiscent of an earlier moment in the story (2:4). There is also a reminiscence of a widespread early Christian expression for the pains of the end time (*hē thlipsis;* see Matt 24:9, 21, 29; Mark 13:19, 24; Acts 14:22; 1 Cor 7:26; 10:11; 2 Cor 4:17; Rev 2:10; 7:14),[35] and a possible reference to one of the story's major expressions to speak of Jesus: the Son of Man (*ho huios tou anthrōpou;* see 1:51; 3:13-14; 5:27; 6:27, 53, 62; 8:28; 9:35; 12:23; 13:31-32). The use of the same imagery in Isa 26 and 66 also leads the

[33] The theme of "before and afterward" is crucial for my interpretation of vv. 21-24. See Simoens, *La gloire,* 163–67. It receives insufficient attention from Dettwiler, *Die Gegenwart,* 239–52. He strenuously excludes any reference to the parousia (see 240–41).

[34] For further biblical and Jewish background, see, among many, Bauer, *Johannesevangelium,* 199

[35] See H. Schlier, "*thlibō ktl,*" *TDNT* 3 (1965) 143–48. On *thlipsis* in the Hebrew testament tradition, see E. Bammel, "The Farewell Discourses of the Evangelist John and the Jewish Heritage," *TynBul* 44 (1993) 109.

reader to look beyond the surface reading of the image to suspect that something of messianic and final significance is being mooted.

b. *Verses 22-23a: The Now and Afterward of the Disciples*   Within the time of the story, *before* Jesus' departure (*nun*) the disciples wait in sorrow and anxiety just as the woman awaited the birth of her child (22a; see 21a). But *afterward* sorrow will be turned into joy, and they will no longer need to ask Jesus for anything (vv. 22c-23a; see v. 21c).[36] Jesus, whose departure is about to cause their sorrow, will see them again, and no one will be able to take their joy from them (v. 22b; see 21b). *When* will this time be? Although almost universally understood as a reference to Jesus' seeing the disciples again after the resurrection, this does not respond to the situation of the reader. This story is being read in the in-between time, marked by hatred, rejection, and murder (see 15:18—16:3). Can this "time" be described as a time when Jesus is seeing his disciples in a way that resolves all the difficulties disciples must face (v. 22bα), filling their hearts with a joy no one can take from them (v. 22bβ) so that there is no longer any need to ask anything of Jesus (v. 23a)?[37]

The traditional eschatological expression *en ekeinę tę hemerai* (see 14:20) retains some of its usual meaning (see Mark 13:11, 17, 19; 14:25; Acts 2:18; 2 Tim 1:12, 18; Heb 8:10; Rev 9:15). Jesus' coming back "to see" (v. 22b: *opsomai humas*) his disciples will produce a joy that no one will take away and will remove all need for them to turn to him in prayer. The disciples have just been told that they will

---

[36] Among others, Hoskyns, *Fourth Gospel*, 488–89, and Barrett, *St John*, 494, distinguish between the use of *erōtan* and *aitein* in vv. 23-24, with the former meaning "to ask a question" and the latter "to ask for something." See also Segovia, *Farewell*, 257–58. Given the Johannine stylistic tendency to couple words having the same meaning, I am reading both verbs in the sense of "to ask for something." As well as suiting the context, it eliminates the conflict between Jesus' saying that the disciples do not ask questions, when the discourse is studded with their questions.

[37] Schnackenburg, *St John*, 3:159, who claims that the time referred to is post-Easter, says that interpreters who read it as the end-time "have misunderstood the joy of the Johannine community." But what internal wrangling might lie behind the insistence on the need to abide in 15:1-11, and to love one another in 15:12-17? See F. F. Segovia, "The Theology and Provenance of John 15:1-17," *JBL* 101 (1982) 125–28. What is the reader to make of the suffering imposed upon the community by others, described in 15:18—16:3? See F. F. Segovia, "John 15:18—16:4a: A First Addition to the Original Farewell Discourse," *CBQ* 45 (1983) 225–30. What internal divisions lie behind the account of the disciples who left Jesus in 6:61? See Moloney, *Signs and Shadows*, 62–63. The joy of the Johannine community may represent the dream of the interpreter more than the world behind the text.

shortly *see* the revelation of God in Jesus continued in and through the presence of the Paraclete (see vv. 16b and 19c: *palin mikron kai opsesthai me*). But in v. 22b the reader is not told that Jesus will be seen by the disciple, but that *Jesus will see the disciple.*[38] Verses 22-23a contrasts the difficulties of that in-between time (v. 22a: *nun*) and the definitive return of Jesus at the end of time (*opsomai . . . charēsetai . . . ouden airei*). "On that day" they will no longer have need to ask for anything (v. 23a). The weight of the Johannine realized eschatology has not eliminated a traditional view of an end time. Jesus continues to speak of a time when the ambiguities of the in-between time will be finally resolved.[39]

c. Verses 23b-24: Living Between Now and Afterward   But the problems and difficulties of the in-between time remain (see 15:18—16:3). There is need for further instruction for the disciples as they face the time between "the hour" of the woman and the time when there will no longer be any need for prayer, and when no one will be able to take away their joy. The double "amen" opens the final statement of this subsection, bringing it to a conclusion and carrying with it all that has been said throughout vv. 21-23a (see also 13:16, 20, 21; 14:12). In the in-between time they are to turn to the Father, and whatever they ask of him will be given to them in the name of Jesus (v. 23b). The Jesus known to the disciples during the earthly ministry will be absent, but the Father will respond to the prayers of the disciples of Jesus and answer them in union with the absent Jesus who has now returned to the Father, just as the Father sends the Paraclete in the name of Jesus (see 14:26, 16:17). The exalted—and therefore absent—Jesus can be experienced in community worship as disciples pray in the name of Jesus. The in-between time will be marked by requests granted in the name of Jesus and by the Paraclete sent in the name of Jesus.

[38] Scholars generally remark on the importance of the initiative of God, or make true, but vague, generalizations about the use of *opsomai humas:* "It is better to be seen of God than to see him (cf. Gal 4:9)" (Bernard, *St John,* 2:515). Nothing is said of the disciples' seeing Jesus, although some commentators take it for granted that this is what is meant (see, e.g., T L Brodie, *The Gospel according to John: A Literary and Theological Commentary* [New York· Oxford Univ. Press, 1993] 500), or what is demanded by vv. 16, 17, 19 (so Carson, *John,* 545).

[39] See J Neugebauer, *Die eschatologischen Aussagen in den johanneischen Abschiedsreden: Eine Untersuchung zu Johannes 13–17* (BWANT 140; Stuttgart: Kohlhammer, 1995) 136–37. Dettwiler, *Die Gegenwart,* 248–49, is unconvincing in his attempt to describe a post-Easter experience of the community when there will be no need to ask for anything.

Having stated the situation that will exist in the in-between time, Jesus returns to his earlier use of the scheme of *before* and *afterward* (v. 24). Up until this time, as Jesus speaks to them at the meal table (*heōs arti*), the disciples have asked nothing in the name of Jesus. This situation *before* the events of "the hour" will change. *Afterward,* if they ask the Father in the name of Jesus, they will receive what they ask for, and their joy will be full. There is a difference, however, in the character of Jesus' words in v. 24 and his earlier words, which used this time scheme in vv. 21 and vv. 22-23a. In his earlier use of the scheme, Jesus was able to speak in an authoritative way. The pain of the woman *will be overcome* by the birth of the child (v. 21); the disciples' sorrow and their need to ask things of Jesus *will disappear* when he comes again and sees them (vv. 23b-24). These are truths that do not depend on the disciples' response. This is not the case in Jesus' final use of the before and after scheme. For the first time in the passage an imperative appears (*aiteite*) instructing the disciples on what they must do, followed by a subjunctive: so that their joy might be complete (*hina hē chara humōn ȩ peplerōmenē*). The truths of v. 21 and vv. 22-23a are an inevitable part of the Johannine story of God's involvement with the world. The imperative of v. 24 is an indication of how disciples living in the in-between time might be part of that involvement. Whether or not they respond to Jesus' imperative is entirely their concern as they face the ambiguities of the in-between time. The reader is aware that it is in the worshiping community that the exalted Jesus gives life to those who ask in his name (see 14:18-21). Jesus' word promises that a positive response will lead to a joy-filled experience of the in-between time. Belief in the word of Jesus (see 2:1—4:54) will lead to life in the midst of hatred, rejection, and murder.

3. The Departure of Jesus (16:25-33)
a. Verses 25-28: The Return of the Son to the Father   With direct reference to the immediately previous use of the image of the woman in childbirth (see v. 21), which has served as a basis for the instruction of the disciples in vv. 22-24, but reaching back across the long story of misunderstanding, Jesus tells his disciples that his communicating to them *en paroimias* will soon come to an end (v. 25a). There is to be a change in the way Jesus announces the Father: *ouketi en paroimias . . . alla parrēsia,* and this change is associated with the coming "hour" (*erchetai hōra*). The reader recognizes the depth and importance of what is being said in v. 25. The hour is coming when the limitations of words, which are always approximations of the reality that lies behind them, will be surpassed by a public proclamation of the Father (25b:

peri tou patros apangelō humas).[40] The reader has little difficulty in linking the promise of Jesus' public revelation of the Father with the hour of the death of Jesus on a cross: The glory of God will shine forth in and through the death of Jesus (see 11:4; 12:23, 32-33; 13:1, 31-32).

But the hour of this public revelation will not only be marked by a change in the way *Jesus is present to his disciples*. The way *they are present to him* will be radically altered. The coming hour of Jesus will transform everything. No longer will the disciples approach the Jesus they have known. Instead, they will make their requests in the name of Jesus (v. 26a). The reader presupposes that the requests will be made to God. This presupposition is confirmed as Jesus tells the disciples they will not need his intercession with the Father (v. 26b). The event of "the hour" and the revelation of God so closely associated with it will change the nature of the relationship between the Father of Jesus and the disciples of Jesus. In a way that recalls 14:23, Jesus tells his disciples that because they have loved him and believed he came from God,[41] they will be swept into the love of the Father himself (vv. 26-27).[42] This new situation is demanded by the central message of 16:4-33: the departure of Jesus to the Father. Jesus tells his disciples of his origins with the Father (*para tou patros*), from whom he once came in the event of incarnation (aorist: *exēlthon*). He has come into the world, and the significance of that coming endures (perfect: *elēlutha*).[43] Balancing the statement of his coming, he tells of his imminent departure from the world (*palin aphiēmi ton kosmon*) and return to the Father (v. 28b: *poreuomai pros ton patera*).[44] Jesus' departure to return to the person and the place of his origins leaves the disciples in an in-between time. The departure of Jesus (v. 28), linked with the public proclamation of the Father (v. 25), necessitates the oneness that will exist between the Father and the disciples in this in-between time (vv. 26-27). Jesus is already speaking *parrēsią*, but the fundamental truth of

---

[40] Some witnesses have *anangelō,* due to assimilation with vv. 13, 14, 15.

[41] There is a finely balanced textual problem in v. 27b: "from God", or "from the Father." Following Segovia, I have chosen the reading of, among others, P⁵, the first hand of Sinaiticus, Alexandrinus, "from God." See Segovia, *Farewell,* 265, n. 73.

[42] On the use of *autos gar ho patēr* in v. 27b as a classical way of emphasizing the Father himself, of his own accord, see Bernard, *St John,* 2:520.

[43] On the use of the aorist and the perfect tenses here, see Brown, *John,* 2:725.

[44] On the textual difficulties of a shorter reading, omitting *exēlthon ek tou patros* at the beginning of v. 28, and thus linking the belief of the disciples in v. 27 with Jesus' coming from God and into the world in vv. 27-28 (Bezae, Freer Gospels, Old Latin and the Sinaitic Syriac), see Barrett, *St John,* 496. In support of the longer reading, followed here, see Brown, *John,* 2:724–25; Lindars, *John,* 512.

Jesus' origins and destiny is not being revealed for the first time (see 1:1-18, 29-34, 51; 3:16-21, 31-36; 4:34; 5:19-30, 36-38, 43-44; 6:35-40, 46-51, 62-63; 7:14-18, 28-29, 33-36; 8:14-20, 23, 38, 47, 54-59, et al.).

b. *Verses 29-30: The Disciples' Knowledge and Belief*   With one voice (*legousin hoi mathētai autou*) the disciples acclaim Jesus' having spoken in clear words (*en parrēsią*), and not in a way that can be misunderstood (v. 29). The time of clarity (*nun*) has done away with the obscurities of the past (*paroimian oudemian legeis*). As a result of this clarity, the disciples think they can already (*nun*) lay claim to perfect knowledge and authentic belief (v. 30): Jesus knows all things, and no one can question him. The encounters of the past, especially as they are reported in the conflicts of chaps. 5–10, have been studded with sharp and unbelieving questions (see 5:12, 18; 6:5, 7, 9, 30-31, 34, 41-42, 52; 7:3-4, 20, 25-27, 31, 35-36, 40-42, 45-52; 8:13, 19, 22, 25, 33, 39, 41, 48, 52-53, 57, 9:40; 10:6, 19-21, 33). As recently as 16:19, the disciples have posed questions. They claim such a relationship with Jesus is a thing of the past. An awareness of Jesus' knowledge of everything is an admission that Jesus "is the only true revealer of God."[45] Their knowledge (v. 30a) leads them to state their belief: Jesus came from God (v. 30b).

Within this section of the discourse the disciples have earlier confessed their inability to understand what Jesus meant when he spoke of his return to the Father (see vv. 17-18). Jesus has indeed spoken openly to them about his having come from the Father and his return to the Father (v. 28). This issue, however, which stands at the heart of Jesus' words to them, still escapes their knowledge and belief, despite their claims. They have come to know that Jesus possesses all knowledge and to believe that he came from the Father. But they must also believe that he is returning to the Father. The reader senses the irony and judges the disciples as having arrived at a partial faith, parallel to that of Nicodemus and the Samaritan woman.[46] They are correct in

[45] Brown, *John*, 2:726. See Brown's survey of discussions that surround v. 30a on 725–26. See also H. N. Bream, "No Need to be Asked Questions: A Study of John 16:30," in J. M. Myers, O. Reimherr, and H. N. Bream, eds., *Search the Scriptures. New Testament Studies in Honor of Raymond T. Stamm* (Gettysburg Theological Studies 3; Leiden. Brill, 1969) 49–74. After surveying the discussion, Bream contrasts Jesus with revealers from the Greek and Jewish worlds, and shows that, unlike them, he does not need to be questioned, as he is the authentic revelation of God.

[46] See P. D Duke, *Irony in the Fourth Gospel* (Atlanta· John Knox, 1985) 57–59. Against Dettwiler, *Die Gegenwart,* 258–59, 262–63, who sees this as a climactic post-Easter confession of Johannine faith.

what they know and believe, but there is more to it, and the "more" in the present context is Jesus' return to the Father. As Jesus' words in v. 28 have indicated, both the incarnation and the return of Jesus to the Father must be accepted. The disciples are still not able to commit themselves to an unconditional acceptance of the word of Jesus (v. 30; see v. 28).

c. Verses 31-33: The Peace That Jesus Gives   The limited faith of the disciples is immediately laid bare, just as with Martha's confession in 11:26-27, by Jesus' penetrating question: *arti pisteuete* (v. 31).[47] The *nun* of the claim of the disciples in v. 29 is undermined by the *arti* of Jesus' response. The temporal aspect of this discussion has an obvious importance, as Jesus returns to his promise of v. 25, again informing the disciples of a time that is rushing upon them: *idou erchetai hōra kai elēluthen.* But while the oncoming hour was linked with Jesus' clear revelation of the Father in v. 25, some of the more externally apparent events that will surround that same "hour" are now listed. As a warning against the littleness of the knowledge and faith the disciples have just claimed (vv. 29-30), Jesus tells them that "the hour," which the reader links with the "lifting up" of Jesus (see 3:13-14; 8:28; 12:32), the glorification of Jesus and the Father (see 11:4, 40; 12:23; 13:1, 31-32), the gathering (see 10:16; 11:50-51; 12:11, 19, 32-33), and the gift of the Spirit (7:37-39; 14:16-17, 25-26; 16:7), will also lead the disciples to abandon Jesus and to scatter, fulfilling the prophecy of Zech 13:7 (v. 32ab).[48] Their flight *eis ta idia* is a rejection of the challenge of Jesus, as each "disciple is concerned with his own safety, and not at all with Jesus."[49] The reader has earlier met the expression *eis ta idia* in the prologue, in the rejection of Jesus by *hoi idioi* when he came *eis ta idia* (1:11). Are these two rejections to be linked? The question remains in the air, as the enigma of this author's understanding of the death of Jesus endures. "The hour" is at the same time Jesus' clearest revelation of the Father (v. 25) and a moment of fear, flight, and abandon (v. 32).[50] A partial explanation of the enigma is provided immediately. Jesus may be abandoned at "the hour," but he is not alone (see 8:16, 29). The oneness that has always existed between Jesus and the

<hr/>

[47] See Moloney, *Signs and Shadows*, 161–62.
[48] On the relationship between 13:32 and the use of the same background in Mark 14 27, see, among many, Brown, *John*, 2 736–37; Dodd, *Tradition*, 56–58.
[49] Schnackenburg, *St John*, 3:165.
[50] I am linking "the hour" of v. 25 and "the hour" of v. 32. They both refer to the cross, the "lifting up," the glorification, the gathering, and the gift of the Spirit.

Father will not be taken away by the violence that will surround Jesus' death (v. 32c).[51] Indeed, the reader is beginning to suspect that it may be at "the hour" that this oneness will become most visible (see 13:1).

Jesus' final words to his disciples repeat a theme that has been present across the discourse. He is using this discourse to inform them of "the hour" that is about to come, and of its significance, so that they may be aware of the riches that will flow from it (see 13:18-20 [belief]; 14:25-27 [peace]; 14:29 [belief]; 16:1 [to prevent failure]; 16:4a [that they might remember]). He has also reprimanded his disciples because his telling them of these things is leading to a sorrow rooted in unbelief (16:4b-6). He returns to this motif, telling them of the dramatic events that lie ahead of them and of their significance so that when these things take place the disciples will not remain in their flight and confusion but will have peace (v. 33a). Jesus' words recall the promises of 15:18—16:3 and no doubt reflect the experiences of the first readers of the story. He promises tribulation, but this should not become the all-determining element in their lives as his disciples. In the midst of their suffering they are to be of good cheer (see 14:1, 27), as they are disciples of Jesus who even in his darkest moment of abandonment and death is victorious. The oneness between Jesus and the Father (see v. 32) is Jesus' assurance of victory no matter how convincingly the forces of this world may appear to have won the day in the violence that will terminate Jesus' life (v. 33c). In the God-directed view of reality that is all-determining in this story, Jesus has overcome the world. This victory, made possible by his oneness with the Father, enables Jesus to promise the gift of peace to his failing (see vv. 29-30) and troubled (see v. 33b) disciples.[52] Within the context of these final words of Jesus, the disciples have been promised that the events of "the hour" will lead to an unequivocal revelation of the Father and unmediated oneness between the Father and the disciples. This revelation and oneness flow from their love of Jesus and their belief that Jesus came from the Father (see vv. 25-27). The peace and victory of Jesus, which flow from his oneness with the Father (v. 33), will also be granted to disciples who love and believe in Jesus even though, for the moment, they are unable to accept his departure (vv. 29-30). They are summoned to be one with Jesus (*en emoi*), rather than in the world

[51] On the possible relationship of 16:32c (correcting? reaffirming?) with Jesus' cry of abandon in Mark 15:34, see the summary in Brown, *John*, 2.737.

[52] G. R. O'Day, "'I Have Overcome the World' (John 16:33): Narrative Time in John 13–17," *Sem* 53 (1991) 162–64, pays too little attention to the function that Jesus' words in 16:33 *will have* in the future experience of disciples in the in-between time.

(*en tē kosmē*) if they are to be part of his victory. In the midst of their confusion (vv. 16-17) and limited faith (vv. 29-30), the disciples of Jesus have every reason for good cheer (v. 33, vv. 25-27).

CONCLUSION

In anticipation of the prayer of Jesus, which immediately follows, the need for the disciples to turn to the Father in the name of Jesus is central to this passage. Jesus addresses the experience of disciples *before* and *after* "the hour" (vv. 21-24). The in-between time will be highlighted by asking and receiving in the name of Jesus (v. 23b). *Before* this time the disciples have not prayed in the name of Jesus, but *after* the hour of Jesus their prayer will bring them the fullness of joy (v. 24). This time will come to an end, when Jesus will see his disciples once more, and they will no longer ask anything in his name (vv. 22b-23a). But during the time of the reader there is a fundamental need for disciples of Jesus to ask for things from the Father so that their joy may be full (vv. 23b-24). The ambiguities of the in-between time will be overcome because of the life-giving presence of the absent one to a worshiping community (see 14:18-21; 16:16-19, 23b-24).[53]

As they have believed that Jesus comes from the Father, the Father loves them (see vv. 25-27), but they are challenged to go further in their love and belief. Jesus came from the Father and is returning to the Father (v. 28), but the disciples are only able to accept half of that equation. They are not prepared to understand or accept that Jesus must depart (vv. 29-30). Between the "now" of the upper room and the "then" of perfect faith, when they will ask nothing of Jesus (see v. 23a), they must live through the anguish of the in-between time. During that period they will be scattered, abandoning Jesus in his "hour" (v. 31). But Jesus' suffering and loneliness is overcome by his oneness with the Father (v. 32). Jesus has overcome the world, and the disciples' eventual awareness of his victory should bring them courage and joy in the midst of their many tribulations (v. 33). Jesus has now finished his discourse with a cry of triumph and with a promise that his failing disciples can be associated with that triumph. He

[53] Dettwiler's study, well summarized in *Die Gegenwart,* 293–304, rightly interprets 13:31—16 33 as the fruit of a "Relecture" within the Johannine community, by means of which the absent Jesus is rendered present. However, he collapses the presence of the Paraclete in the post-Easter period into the presence of the glorified Christ and underestimates the importance of the *physical* absence of Jesus.

has instructed them on his departure, the conditions and the challenges that will face them, and the critical, yet revealing, presence of the Spirit-Paraclete during his absence.[54] He has promised them that despite his absence—indeed, *because of* his absence through departure (see v. 7)—love, faith, joy, and peace can be theirs.

---

[54] It is the Spirit-Paraclete who fills the post-Easter period, and not the risen Jesus, as so many insist. See, most recently, A. Stimpfle, *Blinde Sehen: Die Eschatologie im traditionsgeschichtlichen Prozess des Johannesevangeliums* (BZNW 57; Berlin: de Gruyter, 1990) and Dettwiler, *Die Gegenwart*. Both Dettwiler and Stimpfle overstate the centrality of Johannine realized eschatology, and underestimate the "in-between time" role of the Paraclete during the time of the physical absence of Jesus. Stimpfle is correct in claiming that Johannine eschatology cannot be described as a tension between the "now" and the "not yet" (see 278), but the notion of a final return of Jesus is still in place, however much the Johannine community already experiences "eternal life." As Brown has rightly commented: "The question is not one of the presence of Jesus in and through the Paraclete *as opposed* to the coming of Jesus in glory, but one of the relative importance given to each" ("The Paraclete," 131. Stress original). See above, n. 37.

Chapter Five

Making God Known
John 17:1-26

INTRODUCTORY WORDS from the narrator break into Jesus' discourse (17:1aα: *tauta elalēsen*) and then describe Jesus' raising his eyes to heaven, adopting a formal pose for prayer (v. 1aβ; see 11:41). Jesus addresses the Father directly (*pater;* see 11:41; 12:27), announcing that the hour has come, praying that he be glorified so that he might glorify the Father (v. 1b). Jesus continues to pray without interruption until v. 26. Although the disciples are regarded as present and hearing the prayer (see vv. 6-8, 9-19, 20, 24-26), they never speak. Jesus addresses the Father at all times (see vv. 1, 5, 11, 21, 24, 25) even though the bulk of the prayer concerns his listeners and those who believe in Jesus through their word (see v. 20). The prayer concludes Jesus' final discourse with his disciples.[1] In 18:1 Jesus sets out with them, crossing to a garden on the other side of the Kedron.

Some Jewish testaments end with a brief prayer of praise, rendering glory to God (see *Testament of Job* 43:1-17; *Testament of Isaac* 8:6-7; *Testament of Jacob* 8:6-9), and the doxological element is not lacking

---

[1] There have been long-standing debates about the *Traditionsgeschichte* of the prayer. For a survey, see H. Ritt, *Das Gebet zum Vater: Zur Interpretation von Joh 17* (FB 36; Wurzburg: Echter Verlag, 1979) 59–91. For a discussion of the possible liturgical origins of the prayer, see R E. Brown, *The Gospel according to John* (2 vols.; AB 29, 29A; Garden City, N Y: Doubleday, 1966–70) 2·745–47; D Marzotto, "Giovanni 17 e il Targum di Esodo 19–20," *RivBib* 25 (1977) 375–88; W. O Walker, "The Lord's Prayer in Matthew and John," *NTS* 28 (1982) 237–56.

in John 17 (see vv. 1-5, 24). Other biblical and Jewish literature shows that the practice of a final "prayer" was reasonably common. The song of Moses in Deut 32 honors God's rule in the history of his people.[2] Patriarchal prayers from the testament tradition can be found in *Jubilees* 1:19-21 (Moses); 10:3-6 (Noah); and 20-22 (Abraham), using the "form" of prayer to repeat many of the elements found in the more narrative sections of the testaments, especially admonitions and blessings (*Jubilees* 36:17). There is concern for the future of God's people, requests for God's mercy and an easing of his judgment in the apocalyptic literature; and in some cases, prayers also have the literary function of linking diverse sections of the apocalypse (see 4 Esdras 8:20-36; *Syriac Baruch* 21, 34, 48:1-24; 84-85). The "form" of prayer is present, and even though the prayers in the testamentary and apocalyptic traditions are "remote from the prayer of intercession,"[3] John 17 must be regarded not only as a prayer, but as a privileged insight into the inner relationship between Jesus and God.[4] As Westcott has rightly pointed out, John 17:1-26 is "at once a prayer and a profession and a revelation."[5] Closer parallels have been urged between John and the Hermetic writings (see *Poimandres* 1:31-32; *Corpus Hermeticum* 13:21-22)—in which God is praised and there are certain verbal similarities[6]—and the Mandean writings (see *Book of John*, 236–39; Mandean Liturgy [*Qolastâ* 58:9-20])—in which "the Great Life" is asked to raise up and to give the splendor of light to disciples and children who are locked in the darkness of the lower world.[7] Apart from the problem of the antiquity of the gnostic traditions, the mythological setting of these prayers from the Hermetic and gnostic world is very different

[2] See Brown, *John*, 2.744–45. For links between John 17 and the Targums on Deut 32, see F. Manns, *L'Evangile de Jean à la lumière du Judaisme* (SBFA 33; Jerusalem: Franciscan Printing Press, 1991) 394–96.

[3] R. Schnackenburg, *The Gospel according to St John* (3 vols.; HTCNT 4/1-3; London: Burns & Oates, New York: Crossroad, 1968–82) 3:198.

[4] There is no sense of a privileged gnostic access to mystical experience, as R. Bultmann, *The Gospel of John: A Commentary* (trans G. R. Beasley-Murray; Oxford: Blackwell, 1971) 486–87, would argue.

[5] B. F. Westcott, *The Gospel according to Saint John* (London: Murray, 1908) 293–94. See S. Agourides, "The 'High Priestly Prayer' of Jesus," *SE* 4 (1968) 137–45, E. Käsemann, *The Testament of Jesus: A Study of John in the Light of Chapter 17* (trans G. Krodel, London: SCM, 1965) 5. On John 17 as a farewell prayer, see Ritt, *Das Gebet*, 381–426.

[6] See W. Bauer, *Das Johannesevangelium erklärt* (3d ed.; HKNT 6; Tubingen: J. C. B Mohr, 1933) 207; C. H Dodd, *The Interpretation of the Fourth Gospel* (Cambridge. Cambridge Univ. Press, 1953) 420–22.

[7] See Bauer, *Johannesevangelium*, 207–8. See especially the documentation provided by the notes in Bultmann, *John*, 489–522.

from that of John 17, where Jesus is firmly located in a room with
his disciples on the night before his death (see 13:1-4). There is no
convincing evidence that John 17 *depended on* these traditions. Yet, as
Dodd has remarked, "the language and ideas would . . . be familiar
and acceptable."[8]

There are literary and theological contacts between Jesus' final
prayer and earlier shorter prayers of Jesus in the Fourth Gospel (see
11:41-42; 12:27-28). This form of prayer, in turn, is close to the so-
called "bolt from the Johannine sky" found in the Synoptic tradition
in Matt 11:25-27 (par. Luke 10:21-22). None of these elements, and
especially the Jewish testamentary traditions and pre-Johannine
Christian traditions, can be ruled out as having played their role in
the formation of John 17. Yet the strength and unifying principles of
Johannine theology have unquestionably played a determining function in the composition of John 17. Thus, as with the use of the Jewish testamentary tradition in the discourse section of the Johannine
report of Jesus' last evening with his disciples, so also in the composition of the final prayer "the author of the prayer had received ideas
from different directions, but . . . in the last resort he produced something quite distinctive and unique, firmly marked by the Johannine
Christology."[9]

THE SHAPE OF THE PRAYER

There is widespread agreement that the prayer unfolds in three stages:
vv. 1-5, vv. 6-19, and vv. 20-26. Critical studies of John 17 have
pointed to the unequal length of the three sections of the prayer and
the place of vv. 24-26.[10] Attempts to resolve these issues have led to

[8] Dodd, *Interpretation*, 422.
[9] Schnackenburg, *St John*, 3·200. For a thorough survey, see M. L. Appold, *The Oneness
Motif in the Fourth Gospel: Motif Analysis and Exegetical Probe into the Theology of John*
(WUNT 2/1; Tubingen: J. C. B. Mohr, 1976) 194–211.
[10] Some have opted for a fourfold division, seeing vv. 24-26 as a self-standing unit.
See, e g , M.-J. Lagrange, *Evangile selon Saint Jean* (EB; Paris: Gabalda, 1927) 436; C. K.
Barrett, *The Gospel according to St John* (2d ed. London: SPCK, 1978) 499 (vv. 25-26
as fourth unit), B. Lindars, *The Gospel of John* (NCB; London: Oliphants, 1972) 515.
M Balagué, "La oración sacerdotal (Juan 17,1-26)," *CultBib* 31 (1974) 69, proposes five
sections: vv. 1-5, 6-8, 9-19, 20-23, 24-26 R. Kysar, *John* (Augsburg Commentary on the
New Testament; Minneapolis: Augsburg, 1986) 254–55 suggests a threefold argument:
vv 1-5, 6-23, 24-26. For more detailed surveys see Ritt, *Das Gebet*, 92–147; J. Becker,
"Aufbau, Schichtung und theologiegeschichtliche Stellung des Gebets in Johannes 17,"
ZNW 60 (1969) 56–61

the application of formal criteria to the text: the use of *kai nun*,[11] tracing rhythmic figures,[12] linguistic structure,[13] and the explicit references to "Father."[14] Developing the suggestion of a number of earlier scholars,[15] Brown has proposed a structure based on three formal indications of prayer in 17:1-26.[16] In v. 1 the narrator describes Jesus' raising his eyes to heaven, adopting a position for prayer. In v. 9 Jesus says, "I am praying for them" (*egō peri autōn erōtō*), and in v. 20 he indicates that he is praying for another group: "I do not pray for these only [*ou peri toutōn de erōtō monon*], but also for those who believe in me through their word." These formal indications create three more evenly distributed sections: vv. 1-8, 9-19, 20-26.

As one division closes, it opens the way to the subject of the following section. Thus, in v. 4 Jesus tells the Father, "I glorified you on earth, having accomplished the work which you gave me to do." This theme is then exemplified in vv. 6-8, where Jesus does not pray for his disciples, but tells the Father that he has accomplished the work among the disciples (v. 6). Having *described* the situation of the disciples, he then begins to *pray* for them (vv. 9-19). As his prayer for the disciples draws to a close, Jesus parallels his own mission with the disciples' mission to make God known in a hostile world (vv. 17-19).

---

[11] A. Laurentin, "*We'attah—Kai nyn*. Formule charactéristique des textes juridiques et liturgiques (à propos de Jean 17,5)," *Bib* 45 (1964) 168–97, 413–32. See especially 426–32

[12] A. Malatesta, "The Literary Structure of John 17," *Bib* 52 (1971) 190–214.

[13] R. Schnackenburg, "Strukturanalyse von Joh 17," *BZ* 17 (1973) 67-78, 196-202.

[14] X. Léon-Dufour, *Lecture de l'Évangile selon Jean* (3 vols.; Parole de Dieu; Paris Seuil, 1988–93) 3 275–78. C. H. Talbert, *Reading John: A Literary and Theological Commentary on the Fourth Gospel and the Johannine Epistles* (New York: Crossroad, 1992) 224, suggests vv. 1-8; 9-24; 25-26. G Segalla, *La preghiera di Gesù al Padre (Giov. 17): Un addio missionario* (SB 63; Brescia: Paideia, 1983) 17–32, 384–89, proposes vv 1-5, 6-11a, 11b-16, 17-19, 20-23, 24, 25-26, as also does Manns, *L'Evangile*, 384–89 B. Rigaux, "Les destinataires du IVe Évangile à la lumière de Jn 17," *RTL* 1 (1970) 292–96, suggests vv 1-8, 9-23 (determined by the use of *kosmos*), and 24–26.

[15] See J. H. Bernard, *A Critical and Exegetical Commentary on the Gospel according to St John* (2 vols.; ICC; Edinburgh: T. & T Clark, 1928) 2:559, A. Loisy, *Le quatrième évangile* (Paris. Emil Nourry, 1921) 441; E. C. Hoskyns, *The Fourth Gospel* (2d ed ; ed. F. N. Davey, London: Faber & Faber, 1947) 496–97; R. H. Lightfoot, *St John's Gospel* (ed. C. F. Evans; Oxford: Oxford Univ. Press, 1956) 296–97; H. van den Bussche, *Jean: Commentaire de l'Evangile Spirituel* (Bruges: Desclèe de Brouwer, 1976) 448

[16] See Brown, *John*, 2:748–51. Schnackenburg, *St John*, 3:433, n. 3, is unjustifiably critical of this position, claiming that its motivation is "probably because of *erōtō* in v. 9." As the same verb appears in vv. 15 and 20, he simply affirms that it can "hardly be regarded as a factor on which to base a division " There is more to Brown's structure than the use of *erōtaō*, despite its importance. See Brown, *John*, 2:750, for a summary of five further features that mark his structure.

There are people in the world who believe in Jesus through the word of the disciples. Having *described* the mission of the disciples, the final part of the prayer indicates that Jesus also *prays* for "those who believe in me through their word" (v. 20). As the final section of the prayer comes to a close, Jesus prays for those whom God has given him (v. 24). This petition looks back across the prayer, that all who believe might be swept up into the love that unites the Father and the Son (vv. 25-26). This conclusion begs for a resolution. It will be provided for the reader by the rest of the story (18:1—20:31).[17] A tripartite shape emerges.

Part One: To Make God Known (17:1-8)
Jesus Prays to the Father
   a. Verses 1-5. Jesus asks for the consummation of both God's glory and his own glorification, to bring eternal life into the human story by making God known (vv. 1-5). Jesus' petition "glorify" (*doxason*) both opens and closes this subsection (see vv. 1, 5).
   b. Verses 6-8. Jesus has perfected the task the Father gave him to do: He has made God known. The disciples know and believe that Jesus is the sent one of the Father (vv. 6-8). This subsection is marked by the repeated use of the verb *didōmi*, "to give" (*edōkas* [twice in v. 6], *dedōkas* [v. 7], *edōkas, dedōka* [v. 8]).

Part Two: Keep Them and Make Them Holy (17:9-19)
Jesus Prays to the "Holy Father"
   a. Verses 9-11a. Jesus is about to depart from this world, and the disciples will remain. This subsection is highlighted by Jesus' negative words on "the world," which both open (v. 9: *ou peri tou kosmou erōtō*) and close it (v. 11a: *ouketi eimi en tō kosmō, kai autoi en tōi kosmou eisin*).
   b. Verses 11b-16. Addressing God as "holy Father" (*pater hagie*), Jesus first asks the Father to be "father" to them, keeping them safe (vv. 11b-16). This subsection opens with a petition that the Father "keep" the disciples (v. 11b: *tēreson autous*) and closes with the reason

---

[17] This responds to the objection raised by, among others, J. Becker, *Das Evangelium des Johannes* (2 vols.; OTK 4/1–2; Gutersloh: Gerd Mohn; Wurzburg: Echter, 1979–81) 1:509, concerning the place of vv. 24-26 in the structure adopted above. There are other features that support this proposal. Each unit has the theme of glory (vv. 1-5, 10, 22), an address to the Father (vv. 5, 11, 21), those given to Jesus by the Father (vv. 2, 9, 24), and Jesus' revelation of the Father to them (vv. 6, 14, 26) See Brown, *John*, 2:750.

for such a petition: that the Father might "keep" them from the evil one (v. 15: *hina tērēseis autous*).

c. Verses 17-19. Jesus asks that the Father extend his holiness and sanctify the disciples (v. 17: *hagiason autous*) that they may parallel the holiness of Jesus. They have been sent into the world as Jesus was sent into the world (vv. 17-19). This subsection both opens (v. 17: *hagiason autous*) and closes (v. 19: *hina ōsin kai autoi hēgiasmenoi*) with the use of the verb *hagiazein*.

Part Three: To Make God Known (17:20-26)
Jesus Prays to the Father
a. Verses 20-23. Jesus prays for those who will believe in him as a result of the ongoing presence of the disciples in the world. He prays that oneness among them might make God known to the world, *showing* that the love that drives the mission of Jesus also unites them. This subsection is highlighted by the prayer "that they may be one" (vv. 21: *hina pantes hen ōsin;* v. 22: *hina ōsin hen;* v. 23: *hina ōsin teteleiō-menoi eis hen*).

b. Verses 24-26. The prayer closes as Jesus points the disciples in the story and the readers of the story further into the narrative—and beyond. He asks that they might be swept into the oneness of love that unites the Father and the Son and makes God known (vv. 24-26). This subsection opens with a change of literary form. Jesus expresses his will (*thelō hina*) rather than his petition (see vv. 9, 20). It then refers to the love of God for Jesus (v. 24: *hoti ēgapēsas me*) and closes with a prayer that all be swept up into the love that exists between Jesus and the Father (v. 26: *hina hē agapē hēn ēgapēsas me en autois ē kagō en autois*).

The theme of the fragility of the disciples that flanked the central statement of chap. 13 (see 13:1-17; 21-38) returns at the center of 17:1-26. Jesus prays that they be kept safe and made holy (vv. 9-19). The reader finds that the theme of the central statement of chap. 13, making God known in a hostile world (see 13:18-20), flanks the center-piece of chap. 17. Jesus has made God known (17:1-8), and he passes on this task to his disciples and to subsequent generations who come to believe in Jesus because of their word (17:20-26). Despite the difference in literary form, ideas crucial to 13:1-38 return in 17:1-26.[18]

[18] Bultmann's recognition of the links between chaps 13 and 17 led to his reordering of the text. On these parallels, see G. Segalla, *Giovanni* (NVB; Rome: Edizioni Paoline, 1976) 416–17; M. W. G. Stibbe, *John* (Readings: A New Biblical Commentary, Sheffield: JSOT Press, 1993) 175–76.

READING THE PRAYER

1. To Make God Known (17:1-8)
The setting for the prayer continues the description of 13:1-4. Despite
14:31, Jesus and his company have not moved from the setting at
supper (see 13:1-2). It is there that he closes his discourse (17:1a: *tauta
elalēsen*) and takes up a formal position of prayer.[19] What follows is
uttered at a given time and place to a specific group of people. A link
is made with 13:1 in Jesus' words of address to the Father. As this final
encounter between Jesus and his disciples began, the narrator alerted
the reader, "Jesus knew that his hour had come" (13:1); as it comes to
an end, Jesus announces: "Father, the hour has come" (17:1b).[20] Because of the arrival of "the hour" of Jesus, the time of his glorification
has come. This is not new to the reader, who has already encountered
a link between the glorification of Jesus and "the hour" in earlier narratives. The "not yet" (see 2:4) was later associated with a future feast
(see 7:8), and violence was part of the mounting attempt on the part
of "the Jews" to eliminate Jesus (7:30; 8:20). The link between the
revelation of the glory of God and the glorification of the Son was
made explicit in 11:4, and its relationship with Jesus' oncoming death
was reinforced by the decisions taken by "the Jews," the final negative
response of this group to Jesus' words and actions (see 11:45-50, 57;
12:9-11). The reader's increasing association of "the hour" and the
glorification of Jesus has been confirmed by Jesus' words in 12:23:
"The hour has come for the Son of Man to be glorified." This was
further clarified in vv. 32-33 by the two most authoritative voices in
the Gospel: Jesus and the narrator. Jesus spoke of his being lifted up
to draw everyone to himself (v. 32), and the narrator added a clarify-
ing remark that associated the glorification (see v. 23), the lifting up
and the "drawing" (v. 32) to the crucifixion: "He said this to indicate
the way in which he was to die" (v. 33). These themes continue to
intertwine in a further identification of "the hour," the revelation of
the glory of God, and the glorification of the Son in 17:1b. The prayer
that follows this introductory statement will lead the reader more
deeply into the enigma of a crucifixion that is also the revelation of

[19] The *tauta* refers to the discourses of chaps. 14–16. Westcott, *St John*, 237, hypothe-
sizes that Jesus uttered the prayer in the temple courts. Léon-Dufour, *Lecture*, 3:273,
points out that Jesus' departure from "the Jews" and from the disciples opens with the
same words: *tauta elalēsen Iēsous* (see 12:36; 17:1).
[20] Jesus' recourse to intimate prayer to the Father hard on the heels of 16:4-33, is
proof of his claim in 16:32b: "I am not alone, for the Father is with me."

the glory of God and part of the process of Jesus' glorification. It unfolds under the shadow of "the hour."[21]

Jesus' role as the one who will glorify God and thus be glorified is associated with his having been given prerogatives traditionally belonging to God (see v. 2a: *kathōs*). Jesus' having *exousia* over all flesh so that he might give eternal life to all (*pan*) that God has entrusted to him (v. 2; see also 6:37 and Sir 17:1-4) conjures up memories of the prologue (see 1:12-13), further developed in Jesus' discourse on his authority as life-giver and judge in 5:19-30.[22] Jesus does nothing of his own authority, as "the Father loves the Son, and shows him all that he himself is doing" (5:20a). The glorification of the Father and the Son (17:1; see 5:23) flows from (*kathōs*) the Son's giving eternal life to those entrusted to him (17:2; see 5:21, 24).[23] But the author reinforces what has already been said in 5:19-30 and succinctly restated in 17:2 through the clarification of 17:3. Verse 3, widely regarded as a later editorial comment added to an original prayer, can also be taken as the leitmotif of the prayer.[24] The reader knows that the believer comes to knowledge of God in and through the sent one, Jesus Christ (see 1:14, 16-18; 3:14-15, 16-17, 31-36a; 4:13-14; 5:24-25; 6:35, 51; 7:37-38; 8:12; 9:5; 10:27-29; 11:42; 13:18-20; 14:6-7). This is no gnostic promise of a saving "knowledge," but the promise of life that can be had by those who believe that Jesus Christ has told the story of God (see 1:18).[25] The believer comes to life by knowing the God revealed by Jesus, the *logos* of God. Revelation, through which all flesh can

[21] See W. Thusing, *Herrlichkeit und Einheit. Eine Auslegung des Hohenpriesterlichen Gebetes Jesu (Joh. 17)* (2d ed.; Munster: Aschendorff, 1975) 10–13.

[22] The use of the neuter singular *pan* rather than the masculine plural suggests the oneness of the group of disciples, and the use of the aorist *edōkas* is associated with the incarnate one (see 1:14) being the sent one of God.

[23] Some limit the *hina*-clause to v. 2: "given him power . . so that." See Barrett, *St John*, 502; Lagrange, *Saint Jean*, 440. More likely, however, Bernard, *St John*, 2.560 and Brown, *John*, 2:740-41, among others, suggest that there is a link between "glorify . . so that" in v. 1 and "given . . so that" in v 2. The glorification of the Father is reflected in Jesus' gift of life. The use of *kathôs* in v. 2a supports this view.

[24] Verse 3 may well have been added to an original prayer. The use of "Jesus Christ" on the lips of Jesus is strange (for its only other use, see 1 17), and the expression *ton monon alêthinon theon* is found only here. But why was it added? See Barrett, *St John*, 503

[25] For the gnostic background, see Bultmann, *John*, 494–95; Kasemann, *Testament*, 6. On the widespread biblical background to "knowledge of God," see Barrett, *St John*, 503, and Brown, *John*, 2:752–53. For discussions of "the knowledge of God" in the Old Testament, see H W. Wolff, "'Wissen um Gott' bei Hosea als Urform der Theologie," *EvTh* 12 (1952–53) 533–44, and W. Zimmerli, "The Knowledge of God according to the Book of Ezekiel," in *I am Yahweh* (trans. D. W. Stott; ed W. Brueggemann; Atlanta John Knox, 1982) 29–98.

come to eternal life (vv. 2-3), has taken place in Jesus' words and works (*erga*).[26]

Jesus' indication at the beginning of his ministry that the fundamental orientation of his life was to complete the task given him by the Father (see 4:34: *teleiōsō autou to ergon*, and also 3:35; 5:36) is now regarded as accomplished (17:4: *to ergon teleiōsas*). A decisive turning point in the story of Jesus has been reached (*kai nun*). The revelation of God is complete, and thus Jesus can ask that the Father enter his story in a final way, glorifying him (*nun doxason me*) by restoring him to the Father's presence with the glory that was his before the world was made (see 1:1-2; 6:62; 8:58). Jesus' origin with God determined his ministry. Now, as the story comes to a close, Jesus asks that he come to his own glory by returning to his origin. But the reader knows this can only happen through "the hour" of the "lifting up" in an act of perfect love for his own so that God will be glorified and that Jesus might come to his glory (see 12:23, 32-33; 13:31-32). The hour is "now" (v. 1: *elēluthen hē hōra*). As Jesus crosses the threshold into his "hour," he looks back across his life and ministry to the people at the table with him (see vv. 6-8) and claims to have brought to completion the task given by the Father.[27] But the final moment for the revelation of the glory of the Father through which the Son will be glorified lies in the near future. The reader is again faced with the puzzling claim of this story that the "lifting up" on the cross is the event in time and space that reveals the *doxa* of God and by means of which the Son is glorified (see 3:13-14; 7:39; 8:28; 11:4; 12:23, 32-33; 13:18-20, 31-32).[28] At that time and place, the love of God revealed in Jesus' love for his Father and for his own will be seen (see 13:1, 18-20; 14:30-31; 17:1-2). Through the "hour," Jesus will return to the glory that was his before the world was made (17:5).

If the hour has come and its completion will not be achieved until

---

[26] Verse 3 is no doubt a traditional "summary," inserted here to make an important point. See D Marzotto, *L'Unità degli Uomini nel Vangelo di Giovanni* (SuppRivB 9; Brescia: Paideia, 1977) 172–73, Thusing, *Herrlichkeit*, 40–41.

[27] However much the later experience and thought of the Johannine community may be present in the prayer, its place in the narrative, *before* the death and resurrection of Jesus, must be kept in mind in a reader-oriented approach, as Jesus looks both backward and forward

[28] Many point to Phil 2 9-11 as parallel to John 17:1-5, but two different Christologies are involved. It is *as a consequence* of the humiliation of crucifixion that the Pauline Jesus is lifted up into glory (see Phil 2:9 *dio kai ho theos auton huperupsōsen*), while the Johannine *hupsôsis* takes place *on the cross* (see John 3:14; 8:28; 12:32-33)

Jesus passes through it, how can he claim to have perfected the task given to him by the Father (see v. 4)? As he concludes the first part of his prayer, Jesus provides the answer by looking to the fragile group of disciples sharing his table (vv. 6-8).[29] There is an intimate link between Jesus' words in vv. 3-5 and vv. 6-8. Jesus has said that eternal life flows from the knowledge of God, the result of an acceptance of the revelation that takes place in Jesus Christ (v. 3). Jesus has made God known, and his revealing ministry is at an end. He is about to return to the glory he had with the Father before the world was made (vv. 4-5). Nevertheless, Jesus is able to indicate to the Father the group around him, his disciples, given to him by the Father from "the world." A theme that stood at the center of the discourse (see 15:12-17, especially vv. 14-16) returns as the disciples at the table hear Jesus' words to the Father, recalling that they are disciples of Jesus because of the initiative of God. God "gave" them to Jesus (v. 6: *edōkas . . . edōkas*); they are part of God's larger gift of all things to Jesus (v. 7: *panta hosa dedōkas moi*), and Jesus, the Son of the Father, has "given them" (v. 8aβ: *dedōka autois*) the words the Father "gave" to him (v. 8aα: *edōkas moi*). Jesus' positive assessment of his disciples cannot be regarded as the result of their achievements.[30] Jesus has made known the name of God (v. 6: *ephanerōsa sou to onoma*) to them. The use of the aorist tense looks back and sums up Jesus' ministry (see v. 4). To reveal "the name" of God means to make known all that can be known of the reality of God. "The name stands for God's being and nature, his holiness, 'justice' and love."[31] Jesus has completed the task given to him by the Father because these people have kept this word. Made clean by the word of Jesus (see 13:10; 15:3), abiding in Jesus and in God, as Jesus abides in God (see 15:9-10), the disciples know that everything Jesus has passed on to them is from God (v. 7; see 15:15). "Gifted" in a remarkable way, they have now (v. 7: *nun*) reached a greater maturity of faith and knowledge. The disciples are described in terms that make them models of the Johannine believer: they have received from Jesus the revelation of God that comes to Jesus from God (*ta rhēmata ha edōkas moi dedōka autois*). They have accepted that Jesus is the sent one of the Father (v. 8).

---

[29] See Segalla, *Giovanni*, 419, who points to vv. 6-8 as "una esplicitazione del v. 4."

[30] See Rigaux, "Les destinataires," 300–302.

[31] Schnackenburg, *St John*, 3·175; Bultmann, *John*, 498. Barrett, *St John*, 505, points out that the language is both biblical and gnostic. There is no need to see the revelation of a particular name, as do Dodd, *Interpretation*, 417 n. 2, and Brown, *John*, 2:754–56.

The doxologies that concluded some of the Jewish testaments (see *Testament of Job* 43:1-17; *Testament of Isaac* 8:6-7; *Testament of Jacob* 8:6-9) rendered glory to the wonder of God in the midst of the ambiguity of Israel's situation. The reader is aware that the disciples' *knowledge* and *belief* reflect Jesus' accomplishment of the task that his Father gave him: He has made God known to them (see vv. 3-4). How they will respond to the challenges that lie ahead of them, the necessary consequences of their knowledge and faith (see 15:1—16:3), is yet to be seen. There is more to the story of Jesus (see 18:1—20:29), but an even longer story lies ahead of the disciples (see 13:1—17:26).[32] The future success or failure of the disciples of Jesus takes nothing away from Jesus' claim: "I have glorified you on earth, having brought to completion the task which you gave me to do" (17:4).

2. Keep Them and Make Them Holy (17:9-19)
Jesus' explanation of his claim to have brought to perfection the task given to him by the Father (v. 4) by making God known to the disciples (vv. 6-8; see v. 3) serves as a bridge into a new stage in the prayer. Jesus turns away from petitions for himself (see vv. 1, 5) to pray for these disciples (v. 9: *egō peri autōn erōtō*). Much of Jesus' description of the disciples' situation is familiar to the reader. The reader is not surprised that Jesus does not pray for the world (see 14:30; 15:18-19, 21; 16:3).[33] Jesus prays for those whom the Father has given to him (see vv. 6-8). In the closing stages of the discourse, developing his earlier words on the relationship between the Father and the Son in 5:19-30, Jesus told his disciples that everything belonging to the Father has been given to the Son (see 16:15). The disciples are part of this gift of the Father to the Son (v. 10a). But the disciples have their own responsibility: Jesus is glorified in them (v. 10b). The reader recalls Jesus' earlier challenge to the disciples. They are no longer *douloi;* they are *philoi* of Jesus (15:14-15). They will demonstrate their new status by doing what Jesus has commanded (15:14). Jesus' command has been that they love one another as he has loved them (see 13:34-35; 15:12, 17). The repetition in the life of the disciples of the loving self-

[32] The community reading the Gospel is marked by both success and failure. See R. A. Culpepper, *Anatomy of the Fourth Gospel: A Study in Literary Design* (Philadelphia: Fortress Press, 1983) 118–19. See also D. A. Carson, *The Gospel according to John* (Grand Rapids: Eerdmans, 1991) 559–60.
[33] The Johannine use of *ho kosmos* is ambiguous. See F. J. Moloney, *Belief in the Word: Reading John 1–4* (Minneapolis: Fortress Press, 1993) 37–38; C. R. Koester, *Symbolism in the Fourth Gospel: Meaning, Mystery, Community* (Minneapolis: Fortress Press, 1995) 249–53. Here the meaning is clearly negative.

gift of Jesus will reveal that they are disciples of Jesus (see 13:15; 35; 15:12). Initiating an argument that will gather momentum through the prayer, Jesus' words to the Father inform the reader and listener that, as his own gift of self in love glorifies the Father, so the ongoing presence of the same quality of love among his disciples glorifies Jesus (v. 10b).

At the threshold of "the hour," Jesus tells the Father he is no longer in the world (v. 11aα). In strictly physical terms, Jesus is at table with his disciples and thus still part of the human story. His presence to the world, however, has come to an end; his public revelation of God through word and deed came to a close as he "hid himself from them" (12:36b). The reader, nevertheless, waits for the inevitable end of Jesus' story, "the hour" (12:23, 31-32; 13:1; 17:1), the lifting up on the cross (3:14; 8:28; 12:32), the gathering of the whole world (10:16; 11:52; 12:11, 19, 32), which will also be the moment when he reveals the glory of God and begins his own glorification (11:4; 12:23; 13:31-32; 17:1, 5). Jesus' words of v. 11aα, concerning his no longer being in the world, do not remove him from the constraints of time.[34] Jesus has begun a prayer for his disciples (v. 9). They are in the world and will remain in the world (v. 11aβ), but Jesus is returning to the Father (v. 11aγ; see 13:1; 17:5). The present tense is used (*kagō pros se erchomai*) to indicate that Jesus has not yet returned to the Father but that a process has begun by means of which Jesus will be glorified (see 11:4; 12:23; 17:1, 5). He is passing from this world to the Father (see 13:1; 17:5) but has one further task. He is to love his own *eis telos* (13:1). Through the performance of that task, which will be the consummate revelation of love and the revelation of God in and through Jesus (see 13:18-20), he will return to the Father. The disciples will be the ongoing bearers of the mission of Jesus. They are to make God known by loving as Jesus has loved (see 13:15, 34-35; 15:12, 17; 17:10). Jesus' mission in and to "the world" has come to an end (v. 11aα; see 12:36), but that of the disciples is about to begin (v. 11aβ; see 10b).

Throughout the prayer, Jesus addresses God as "Father," but here he adds a qualification, addressing his prayer to his holy Father (v. 11b: *pater hagie*).[35] These two words, *hagios* and *pater*, are the determining

[34] There has been a presence of Jesus in "the world," teaching and doing "signs," which Jesus has brought to its completion (see v. 4, 12:36b). This presence "in the world" is past, however much the reader looks forward to a further "completion" in the lifting up of the Son of Man to reveal the glory of God and initiate the glorification of Jesus (3:14; 8:28; 11:4; 12:23, 31–33; 13 1; 17:1).
[35] This expression, based on a fundamental Hebrew concept of the holiness of God (see 2 Macc 14.36; 3 Macc 2:2 for use of *hagie* in addressing God in prayer), is found

elements of the remaining subsections of this central section of the prayer (vv. 11-16 [pater]; vv. 17-19 [hagios]). Applying the implications of the address, Jesus asks the Father to be "father" to the disciples. He asks that the Father care for them (tērēson autous).[36] However well Jesus might have spoken of the disciples in vv. 6-8, they are fragile (see 13:2, 10-11, 12, 18, 21-30, 36-38; 16:29-31). All Jesus is and does flows from his oneness with the Father (see 10:30, 38), a consequence of his being the sent one of the Father. The one sent is to be identified in every way with the one who sends.[37] There is a bond between the Son and the Father that Jesus describes as "in the name" the Father gave to him. Jesus has made the name of the Father—all that one can know of the reality of God—known to the disciples (see v. 6).[38] The oneness between the Father and the Son enables Jesus' authoritative revelation of "the name of" the Father, which does not belong to him by right but has been granted to him (hō dedōkas moi).[39] Jesus asks the Father to care for his fragile disciples by gathering them into all that can be known of the reality of God (tērēson autous en tō onomati sou), creating a unity among them, repeating the oneness that has always existed between Jesus and the Father.[40] Jesus used the expression "the name"

---

only here in the New Testament. See I. de la Potterie, La Vérité dans Saint Jean (2 vols ; AnBib 73; Rome. Biblical Institute Press, 1977) 2 737–40, for background for hagiazein as the presence of the holiness of God in the human sphere. "le fruit de l'active présence de Dieu au milieu de son peuple" (739, citing J. Roth, "Thèmes majeurs de la Tradition sacerdotale dans le Pentateuque," NRT 80 [1958] 718).

[36] For this meaning of têrein, see E. Delebecque, Evangile de Jean: Texte Traduit et Annoté (CahRB 23; Paris: Gabalda, 1987) 197.

[37] See J.-A Buhner, Der Gesandte und sein Weg im 4. Evangelium: Der kultur- und religions-geschichtlichen Grundlagen der johanneischen Sendungschristologie sowie ihre traditions-geschichtliche Entwicklung (WUNT 2/2; Tübingen: J. C. B. Mohr, 1977) 181–267, P. Borgen, "God's Agent in the Fourth Gospel," in Logos was the True Light and Other Essays on the Gospel of John (Relieff 9, Trondheim: Tarin, 1983) 121–32.

[38] See M. Rose, "Names of God in the OT," ABD 4:1001–11, esp. 1002.

[39] Reading the perfect tense, rather than the aorist found in some manuscripts. Also reading, along with P[66], the dative neuter singular relative pronoun, referring back to en tôi onomati sou See B. M. Metzger, A Textual Commentary on the Greek New Testament (2d ed.; Stuttgart· German Bible Society, 1994) 213.

[40] Some scholars regard "in the name of" here as "by the power of your name " See, e.g , W. Heitmuller, "Im Namen Jesu": Eine sprach- u. religionsgeschichtliche Untersuchung zum Neuen Testament, speziell zu altchristlichen Taufe (FRLANT 2, Gottingen: Vandenhoeck & Ruprecht, 1903) 132–34; Hoskyns, Fourth Gospel, 500; Bultmann, John, 503. Marzotto, L'Unità, 177–80, argues that it also has the notion of being in a sacred space. For the interpretation adopted above, reading it as "in adherence to what Jesus has revealed to the disciples of the character of God" (G. R Beasley-Murray, John [WBC 36; Waco: Word Books, 1987] 299), see Lagrange, Saint Jean, 445, Lindars, John, 524, Schnackenburg, St John, 3:180.

of God in v. 6 to indicate that he had made known all that can be known of God. Jesus was "gifted" with the knowledge of all that could be known of God, and this was the basis of his oneness with the Father (v. 11c). He prays that the disciples, to whom he has manifested the "name" (see v. 6), might be kept in that name by the Father and thus experience the same oneness (v. 11d).

After asking the Father to "keep" the disciples in his name, Jesus looks back on his own care for them. In the time he was with them he has done what he now asks the Father to do: He has kept them in God's name (v. 12a: *egō etēroun autous en tō onomati sou*). As he asks the Father to be "father" to the disciples, he points out that he has guarded them, surrounding them with care (v. 12b: *ephulaxa*) so effectively that not one of them has been lost (see 3:16; 6:39; 10:28), with the exception of "the Son of Perdition" (*ho huios tēs apōleias*).[41] This expression must be given the meaning it has in the only other place in the New Testament where it appears: Satan (2 Thess 2:3, 8-9). The only figure in the story Jesus could not care for is Satan, who planned a betrayal (see 13:2). But Jesus washed the feet and shared the morsel with Judas, despite Satan's designs. Nevertheless, Satan entered Judas (see 13:27) "that the scripture might be fulfilled" (17:12c), and the reader recalls 13:18. There is a divine order in the events of the life and death of Jesus beyond the control of Jesus.[42] The Son of Perdition is beyond the control of Jesus, but he was given the disciples to care for (see v. 6, 9, 10, 11). During their time with him, they have been made clean by his word (see 13:10; 15:3), which they have kept (17:6), and they have believed that he is the sent one of the Father (see 16:30; 17:8). He has manifested the name of God to them (17:6). Jesus has kept and cared for them all, including Judas. As his gestures in 13:1-17, 21-38 indicate, not even Judas can be judged as lost. The intervention of the Son of Perdition is part of the larger design of God manifested in the Scriptures, but so is the limitless love of God revealed in the unfailing love of Jesus for fragile disciples (see 13:18-20). He now asks the Father to be "father" to all the disciples, including Judas.

The time of Jesus' presence with the disciples is now at an end, as Jesus has begun the process of coming (*erchomai*) to the Father. Thus,

---

[41] The expression *ephulaxa* is stronger than *tērein;* but here "it is probably no more than a synonomous variation" (Barrett, *St John,* 508).

[42] J. Daniélou, "Le fils de perdition (Joh. 17,12)," in *Mélanges d'histoire des religions offerts à Henri-Charles Puech* (Paris: Presses Universitaires de France, 1974) 187–89, suggests that Judas anticipates the Antichrist. But the Antichrist is responsible for the betrayal of Judas, whom Jesus has loved and whom he continues to love and care for.

it is important that, while he is still speaking in the world,[43] the disciples hear this prayer, asking the Father to keep them after his departure. In this way, all anxiety about their future will be overcome, and their joy will be full, matching the joy of Jesus (v. 13). The promises of the discourse, that the disciples' openness to the Father in the in-between time will bring them a fullness of joy (see 15:7-11; 16:24), are now solidly based on a request that Jesus makes of the Father in the hearing of his disciples. This section of the prayer, asking that the Father "keep" and care for the fragile disciples, closes with the repetition of themes from across the last discourse and the earlier parts of the prayer itself (vv. 14-16). The disciples are not "of the world" (*ek tou kosmou*), as Jesus is not "of the world" (*ek tou kosmou*) (see 15:19).[44] This does not mean that the disciples are some sort of otherworldly enclave. The expression *ek tou kosmou* indicates that they do not belong to the prince of this world, to the Son of Perdition (see v. 12), to the power of darkness, to the forces of evil that are even now lining up against Jesus to kill him (see, most recently, 11:49-50, 57; 12:9-11). Jesus has come to make God known, but "the world" has rejected Jesus, the one who sent him, and his disciples (v. 14; see 15:18—16:3). In the face of this opposition and even violence (see 16:2), the revelation of God will continue. Jesus is departing from the world (v. 13), but he is leaving behind disciples who do not belong to this world, so that they may continue to glorify him (v. 10). The disciples will continue to make God known as they continue to glorify Jesus. Jesus does not pray that they be removed from their situation in the world, but that the Father keep them (*hina tērēsēs autous*) from the evil one.[45] The reader senses closure as the petition that began Jesus' prayer to the Father (v. 11b: *tērēson autous*) returns (v. 15: *hina tērēsēs autous*).

Jesus' disciples cannot simply bask in the protecting care of God as their Father (vv. 11b-16). They are to be made holy by a holy God (vv. 17, 19; see v. 11b: *pater hagie*). Jesus now prays that they be made

---

[43] This claim, that Jesus is still speaking "in the world" does not contradict v. 11a: "I am no longer in the world." Jesus is still firmly located in a room on the face of earth (v. 13), but he is no longer involved in his revealing mission to the world (v. 11a; see 12:36b)

[44] The phrase "as I am not of the world" in v. 14b is missing in P⁶⁶. This is the result of an accidental omission, through homoeoteleuton. See Metzger, *Textual Commentary*, 213.

[45] As the word is genitive (*ponērou*) it is impossible to be certain if "evil" (*ponēron*; see 3:19; 7:7) or "the evil one" (*ponēros*) is meant. In the light of 12:31; 14:30; 16:11, and 1 John 2:13-14; 3:12; 5:18-19, and especially the reference to Satan as "the Son of Perdition in v. 12, the "evil one" is likely.

holy in the knowledge of God, in the truth (*en tē̦ alētheia̦*) (v. 17). It is identification with the design of God that will make the disciples holy. To be *hagios* means to be one with a *pater hagios* (see v. 11b).[46] They are the recipients of the manifestation of God in Jesus, and they have come to believe that he is the sent one of God (v. 8). Jesus prays that they might live holy lives corresponding to the holiness of God revealed to them in and through Jesus.[47] As Jesus' association with the Father has determined his life, the disciples' association with Jesus, who has revealed the truth to them, determines theirs. The disciples are to become the sent ones of the Sent One. They are to make God known in the world.[48] As Jesus made God known in and through his mission as the sent one of a holy God, so must the disciples continue to make the same God known as the sent ones of Jesus (v. 18b). The revelation of a holy God calls for a holy sent one. It is a mission to make God known (v. 18) that determines the demand for holiness (vv. 17, 19).

[46] I am rendering the verb *hagiazō* as "make holy," rather than "consecrate," in the sense of setting apart for sacred things. The latter translation is closely associated with the tradition, which has its beginning at least as early as Cyril of Alexandria (*In Joannis Evangelium*, XI, 8; PG 74:545) and was made popular in the sixteenth century by David Chytraeus (1530-1600), that this prayer was priestly, associating the disciples with Jesus' self-oblation. Some, e.g., Hoskyns, *Fourth Gospel*, 501-4; Lindars, *John*, 528-29; Kysar, *John*, 261, argue that *hagiazō* means "make holy" in v. 17 and "consecrate" in v. 19. For a more detailed discussion, rejecting this shift of meaning, see de la Potterie, *La Vérité*, 2:740-46, and especially his rich study, "Consécration ou sanctification du chrétien d'après Jean 17?" in E. Castelli, ed., *Le Sacré: Etudes et Recherches. Actes du colloque organisé par le Centre International d'Etudes Humanistes et par l'Institut d'Etudes Philosophiques de Rome* (Paris: Aubier-Montaigne, 1974) 339-49. Against the sacrificial-priestly interpretation in general, see Appold, *The Oneness Motif*, 194-98. The use of *hagios* in v. 11b determines the meaning of *hagiazō*. In v 11b it does not mean that the "holy Father" is in some way consecrated and separated from the profane. A reader will give the same meaning to the uses of *hagios* and *hagiazein* across such closely related contexts. A. Feuillet, *The Priesthood of Christ and His Ministers* (Garden City, N.Y.: Doubleday, 1975) 37-48, traces the passage from the Suffering Servant in Isaiah 53 into the Jewish liturgy of *yôm kippur* to show that John 17:19 as both priestly and sacrificial. For a detailed discussion and rejection of this position, see J. Delorme, "Sacerdoce du Christ et ministère (A propos de Jean 17): Sémantique et théologie biblique," *RSR* 62 (1974) 199-219.

[47] See de la Potterie, *La Vérité*, 2:747-58, for a full discussion of *en tē̦ alētheia̦*, concluding that it serves as *place* of holiness, a *means* for sanctification, closely related to *en tôi onomati sou* of v. 11b.

[48] The mission of the disciples *eis ton kosmon* must be taken seriously and should not be explained away, as does Kasemann, *Testament*, 29-30, as aimed at church order, or, aided by a hypothetical source theory, because of a conviction that the Johannine community was a sectarian conventicle, as does Becker, *Johannes*, 2:524-25. See the critique of Segalla, *La preghiera*, 73-84.

Jesus has come to the moment of his final self-gift in love so that the glory of God might be revealed. For the sake of the disciples—those at the table, and all disciples—Jesus' consummate act of love will be accomplished. Jesus' total identification with the design of God (see 4:34; 17:4) and his being associated with the judging and life-giving actions of God (see 5:19-30) are the basis of his holiness. Thus, Jesus can lay claim to a final and consummate act of holiness (*egō hagiazō emauton*) in "the hour," the lifting up, the gathering, the revelation of the glory of God and the glorification of the Son, the final revelation of his love for his own (see 13:1). But Jesus' holiness is not an end in itself (see 3:16-17; 10:14-18; 13:1; 15:13). He thus commits himself to a final act of holiness for their sake (*huper autōn*), so that in his total self-gift, making known the love of God, he makes known to them the holiness that must be theirs.[49] The present tense of the verb *hagiazō* associates this moment of final revelation of holiness with the departure of Jesus, which has already been initiated (see 13:1; 17:1, 11, 13). As his oneness with the Father is the basis of his holiness, their oneness with the God who has been revealed to them (*en alētheią; see* v. 17) is the basis of their holiness.[50] Jesus prays that they be made holy in the truth (*hina hōsin kai autoi hēgiasmenoi en alētheią*). The holiness of God (v. 11b: *pater hagie*), visibly present in the human story in the holiness revealed by Jesus' gift of himself for his own (v. 19a: *huper autōn egō hagiazō emauton*), is to be matched by the holiness of the disciples (v. 19b: *hina kai autoi hēgiasmenoi*), as Jesus is sending them into the world to make God known just as God sent him (v. 18). To succeed in this mission, they must be holy as God is holy (see Lev 11:44; John 17:11b, 17, 19).

---

[49] It is this "made holy for their sake" that is often read as priestly. The reader is aware that Jesus' final act of holiness is an act of self-gift in love, in total obedience in the perfect fulfillment of his God-given task (see 4 34; 17.4), so that he can make God known, and thus enable eternal life (see 17:3). See Schnackenburg, *St John,* 3:187–88; J T. Forestell, *The Word of the Cross: Salvation as Revelation in the Fourth Gospel* (AnBib 57; Rome. Biblical Institute Press, 1974) 78–82, Thusing, *Herrlichkeit,* 79–85; de la Potterie, *La Vérité,* 2 761–67; Knoppler, *Die theologia crucis,* 210–15. Jesus' holiness flows from his oneness with God, whose love leads Jesus to lay down his life and take it up again (see 10:17-18). This is revealed to the disciples. He prays that they may be caught up in the same oneness, as a result of his manifestation of God to them (see v. 6) and thus holy as he is holy. See especially de la Potterie, *La Vérité,* 2:767–75. For some, this is a "priestly" concept

[50] In itself, the expression *en alētheią* would simply mean "indeed." However, the expression *en tę̄ alētheią* in the parallel v. 17 makes this more theological reading of v. 19 probable. See de la Potterie, *La Vérité,* 2:773–75.

3. To Make God Known (17:20-26)

Jesus prays not only for them (v. 20a: *ou peri toutōn de erōtō monon*), but also for those who will be fruit of the missionary activity of his sanctified disciples: "for those who believe in me through their word" (v. 20b: *alla kai peri tōn pisteuontōn dia tou logou autōn eis eme*). The situation at table must not be lost from view. While there has been no report in the Gospel story of the disciples' having successfully brought people to faith, such believers are presupposed by the narrative.[51] Jesus prays for those already believing (*peri tōn pisteuontōn*) because of the word of the disciples.[52] There is a double reading possibility in v. 20. Remaining strictly within the story time of the passage, Jesus prays for his disciples present with him at the table and for other believers not present. Jesus' reference to these believers is an analepsis, looking back to a nonreported event, now called into the narrative. Real readers across the generations, however, rightly read themselves into Jesus words "for those who believe in me through their word."[53] They are the continuing presence of those original believers who were part of the time of the story, fruit of the original disciples' preaching (see 4:35-38).

Jesus' having made God known to the disciples has opened a new possibility: They can share in the oneness that exists between the Father and the Son (see v. 11b). This petition is repeated in v. 21ab, and a further element is added in v. 21c. Jesus now prays that this group of believers be taken into the oneness that exists between the Father and the Son (v. 22ab). In a carefully structured prayer, Jesus first asks the Father that believers be united as one (21a: *hina pantes hen ōsin*). The juxtaposition of the many (*pantes*) and the one (*hen*) expresses the point of Jesus' request. But, as in the earlier part of the prayer for the disciples (v. 11b), a unique model of unity is given. As the Father is in the Son and the Son is in the Father, so also might it be among believers (v. 21b).[54] Throughout the Gospel, Jesus has revealed a one-

---

[51] See the limit of such activity, however, in 4:35-38. See Moloney, *Belief,* 163-68.

[52] Verse 20 is almost universally read as addressing the time of the church. Yet the present participle *pisteuontōn* could be a hint of the present disciples' mission (see 4:35-38).

[53] I am rejecting a theory of "timelessness" for the interpretation of the prayer, or a reading of the words of Jesus *entirely* from the point of view of the later Johannine church. For this perspective, see O'Day, "'I Have Overcome the World'," 153-66. The Gospel must be read from the perspective of the Johannine church, as from the perspective of every reader and community of readers. Nevertheless, the narrative has its own "time," which must be respected.

[54] For a comparison between this request for unity, and "the unity" (*yahad*) that was the Qumran community, see Brown, *John,* 2:777; Beasley-Murray, *John,* 302. On the twofold use of *hina .. kathōs . . . hina . . . hina* in vv. 21-23, see Brown, *John,* 2:769.

ness at the level of action between himself and the Father (see 4:34; 5:19-30; 10:30, 38; 17:4). As with the unity between the Father and the Son, the unity among believers is not an end in itself. The believers are to be one as the Father and the Son are one (*hina ho kosmos pisteuę hoti su me apesteilas*) (v. 21c). Jesus may not be praying for "the world" (v. 9), but he has been sent into the world (see 3:16; 17:18) and he sends his disciples into the world (17:18). Because of the mission of his disciples, others have come to believe in Jesus as the sent one of the Father (v. 20). The missionary chain, however, runs on unendingly. A further group of believers is to mirror in the human story the oneness between the Father and the Son that "the world" might be led to believe that Jesus is the sent one of God.

The theme of oneness and mutuality that leads to the world's coming to know that Jesus is the sent one of the Father (v. 21) is expressed in another way in v. 22. There is a slight deviation from the form of a prayer as Jesus tells the Father, in an aside heard by the disciples listening to the prayer, that the mutuality between himself and the Father that he passes on to believers is the *doxa* (v. 22). Consistent with the use of this expression across the Gospel, the biblical idea of the revelation of God returns. God was made known through the gift of the covenant at Sinai and has continually been made known throughout Israel's history in the *kabôd* YHWH, especially in and through the Law. But the love and oneness existing between the Father and the Son from all time (see 1:1-2; 17:5) have been made visible in and through the gift of the Son (see 1:14; 3:16). Jesus' life and teaching and his signs have been the revelation of the *doxa* of God (see 2:11; 5:44; 7:18; 8:50-54; 11:4, 40), a *doxa tou theou* rejected by "the Jews" because they preferred the *doxan tōn anthrōpōn* (see 12:43). But there are some to whom the love of God, made visible in the *doxa* of Jesus, has been given (see vv. 6-8). Jesus has already prayed for their oneness (see v. 11b). He now prays for oneness among those who have come to believe through their word that Jesus is the sent one of God (see v. 20). Jesus has given the love and oneness shared by the Father and the Son to the believers. The *doxa*, which is the love bestowed on the Son by the Father (*tēn doxan hēn dedōkas moi*), is present in the human story in the *doxa* Jesus has given to the believers (*dedōka autois*). The love the believers bear one another reflects the love that exists between the Father and the Son.[55]

---

[55] The position taken here is only one of many possible. Westcott, *St John*, 246–47, saw it as "the revelation of the divine in man realized through Christ." For Bultmann, *John*, 515–16, the *doxa* is to be paralleled with the name of God and the words of God given to Jesus (see vv. 8, 11, 14). Schnackenburg, *St John*, 3:191–92, sees it as the antici-

After this brief pause describing the uniting love between the Father and the Son and the Son and the believers as *doxa*, the form of prayer returns (see v. 21). But a chain of relationships continues into v. 23. Jesus now *prays for* the interrelated mutual indwelling *stated* in v. 22. This prayer takes the reader back to 15:1-11. Jesus asks the Father that the mutual abiding be realized in a mutual indwelling between Jesus and believers and the Father and Jesus (v. 23a). The realization of this indwelling will have two results, one internal and the other external. First, it will produce a situation in which the Father enables the perfection of oneness among a newer group of believers (v. 23b: *hina ōsin teteleiōmenoi eis hen*).[56] But, as throughout the prayer, Jesus does not make intense communion among disciples an end in itself. There is to be a quite different consequence: *that God might be made known*. The gift of the *doxa* given to Jesus by the Father and passed on to the believers by Jesus (see v. 22) reaches beyond the bounds of the believers and into the world. The end result of Jesus' request for a oneness between the Father, Jesus, and the believers is that the glory of the love that unites them makes God known to the world (v. 23c). The unifying love that should exist between the believers makes known that the Father so loved the world that he sent the Son (3:16) who loved his own *eis telos* (see 13:1). This love that Jesus has shown for his own and the love they have for one another make known, not only the love of Jesus and the mutual love of believers, but also the love that lies behind the sending of the Son: God. God so loved the world that he sent Jesus (see 3:16), and it is this same love that produces oneness among the believers (*kai ēgapēsas autous kathōs eme ēgapēsas*). Jesus' loving his own is not for their comfort and encouragement. It inevitably leads to a mission, matching the mission of Jesus (see vv. 17-19) to make God known (v. 23b; see 17:3).[57]

---

pation of eternal life, and Barrett, *St John*, 513, suggests that it is unity with the death and resurrection of Jesus, from which life flows. My reading depends upon the principle that the reader will regard the use of *doxa* and *doxazô* across the story as having the same basic meaning, linked to the revelation of God.

[56] The passive participle *teteleiōmenoi* indicates that the Father is the agent who enables this oneness. See Westcott, *St John*, 247. The use of this verb associates the "perfection" with Jesus' accomplishment of the task given him by the Father (see 4:34; 5:36; 17:4). See Rigaux, "Les destinataires," 312–16.

[57] On the identity between *hina ho kosmos pisteuȩ* (v. 21) and *hina ginōskȩ ho kosmos* (v. 23), see, among many, Rigaux, "Les destinataires," 304–5. I am reading the *hina* associated with the mission to the world as an expression of a purpose of the petition. See M. Rodríguez Ruiz, *Der Missionsgedanke des Johannesevangeliums: Ein Beitrag zur johanneischen Soteriologie und Ekklesiologie* (FB 55; Wurzburg Echter, 1987) 247–55, and especially Appold, *The Oneness Motif*, 157–193, 227–35, 287–89.

Jesus has already asked the Father that he be restored to the glory that was his before the world was made (see 17:5; see 1:1-2). The reader senses a change of tone. Jesus expresses a desire (*thelō hina*) that all those whom the Father has given him may be with him "there" (*hopou eimi egō kakeinoi ōsin met'emou*) (v. 24a). The expression "whom you gave me" could be limited to the disciples, described in this way in vv. 6-7. This might exclude those who have come to believe because of the disciples' teaching that Jesus is the sent one of God (v. 20), but the cumulative effect of the prayer makes such a reading improbable. Jesus prays for all who have been touched by his love, which makes known the union existing between the Father and the Son (see vv. 21-23). He expresses his desire that the gulf between the union of the Father and the Son and the ambiguous situation of fragile disciples and believers *in* the world but not *of* the world (see vv. 11, 14-15, 16) be bridged. In a transformed situation, all fragility will be overcome, and they will join Jesus in a new "place" (see 14:2-3) to behold the *doxa* Jesus had as a result of the Father's love from before all time (v. 24). Such a transformation is, for the moment, impossible for the disciples *in the story* of Jesus. They have seen the *doxa* in Jesus' revealing life and actions (see 2:11; 11:4, 40). They wait for its consummation in the lifting up, the gathering, the revelation of the glory of God, and the glorification of the Son. They also wait for the return of Jesus, as he has promised to take them to the place he has prepared for them (14:1-3). But believing readers *of the story* of Jesus are also involved. The prayer draws to an end and brings the story closer to Jesus' death with a message of transcendent hope. Jesus' words to the Father open the mind and heart of the reader to the possibility of "a world" that lies beyond "the world": the vision of the glory of Jesus that existed "before the foundation of the world" (v. 24b) as the result of the Father's love for the Son.[58]

Earlier the reader encountered Jesus' prayer to a "holy Father" (v. 11b: *pater hagie*), followed by his request that God be both "father" and "sanctifier" to the disciples. Jesus now addresses God as *pater dikaie* (v. 25; see v. 11b). As a holy God is asked to make holy all those to whom he is Father (vv. 17-19), so also a just God will act justly with the world that does not know him. The reader recalls the exposing

---

[58] The difficulties and challenges of the in-between time, so much a part of chaps. 14–16, will be finally overcome. For A. Stimpfle, *Blinde Sehen: Die Eschatologie im traditionsgeschichtlichen Prozess des Johannesevangeliums* (BZNW 57; Berlin: de Gruyter, 1990) 217–43, this is not so. The Johannine "insider" is aware that they are already part of a predestined elect, while the "outsider" mistakenly waits for an end-time solution.

task of the Paraclete, bringing righteousness (*dikaiosunē*) and judgment (*krisis*) into a hostile world (16:7-11). Despite the world's rejection of Jesus' Father as God, Jesus never failed in his knowledge of his Father. Disciples, in the world but not of the world, have come to know the one true God in and through their belief in Jesus. The sound of a single theme tolls across all three sections of the prayer: to make God known.[59] Jesus stated in v. 3 the principle that eternal life comes from knowing God and Jesus Christ whom he has sent. He affirmed in v. 8 that his disciples had come to know God and the one whom he had sent. In the final section of the prayer, in vv. 21 and 23, he asks the Father that such knowledge be the fruit of a oneness among believers. Jesus has made God known, and his disciples and other believers have come to know the God and Father of Jesus as their God and Father (v. 25). Jesus has made known all that can be known of God (v. 26a: *to onoma sou;* see vv. 6, 11), and this revealing task will continue in the brief time that remains for Jesus (v. 26b).[60] Indeed, the reader is aware that the high point of Jesus' revelation of the love of God still lies ahead (see 13:1; 19; 34-35; 15:12-13). The enigma of the revelation of love on a cross looms large (see 13:1; 15:13).

Jesus has made God known to the disciples so that the love that bonds the Father and the Son might bond the disciples, that they might be loved by God in the same way that the Father has loved the Son, and that this love will be their experience of the never-failing presence of Jesus to his own (17:26c). It is crucial to the ongoing story of disciples who will be known as followers of Jesus: Only through God's being Father to them by bonding them in the love that unites the Father and the Son will disciples make God known. They are to live in the world in a way that responds to the commandment of Jesus: "By this they shall know that you are my disciples, if you love one another, as I have loved you" (13:34-35; 15:12, 17).

Jesus' first request in this closing passage (v. 24) offers hope to all believers. It transcends their life in the world and their mission to the world: that they might behold the glory the Son possessed before the

[59] See A. Jaubert, "Jean 17,25 et l'interprétation gnostique," in *Mélanges d'histoire des religions offerts à Henri-Charles Puech* (Paris: Presses Universitaires de France, 1974) 347–53.

[60] Jesus is situated at the end of his ministry, during which he has revealed the *doxa*. He will shortly consummate that revelation (see 13:1). There is a parallel between the past revelation of the name of God and its shortly to be accomplished future revelation of 17:26, and Jesus' proclamation of his past revelation of the glory of God (*edoxasthē . . . edoxasthē*) and God's future glorification of the Son of Man (. . *doxase auton*) in 13:31-32.

foundation of the world. Jesus' closing prayer (v. 26bc) missions the disciples for the world, united by the same love that unites the Father and the Son, making God known in loving self-gift as Jesus has made known the name of his Father. Between these requests lie words of Jesus telling of his having made God known (vv. 25-26a). The first two sections of 17:1-26 (vv. 1-8; vv. 9-19) closed with a subsection that served as a bridge from one section of the prayer into the next (vv. 6-8; vv. 17-19). The final section of the prayer (vv. 20-26) closes with words that end Jesus' prayer to his Father (vv. 24-26). They point the reader into the remaining moments of *the story of Jesus* (see vv. 25-26a), into *the future story of Jesus' disciples* (v. 26b), and into *a place that transcends the story time of both Jesus and his followers,* beyond the in-between time, contemplating the glory given to the Son by the Father before the world was made (v. 24; see 14:2-3).

CONCLUSION

Jesus has completed the task the Father gave him (17:4). *He has made God known* (v. 3), and there is a group of people given to Jesus by the Father who are the fruit of Jesus' *having made God known* (vv. 6-8). They believe that Jesus is the sent one of God (v. 8). He has also completed his prayer for these first believers, the disciples at the table (vv. 9-19). He has asked that they may be one as the Father and the Son are one (v. 11b) and that they be both protected and made holy in a hostile world so that they may perform their mission (vv. 11-19). As Jesus was sent into the world, Jesus sends them into the world (v. 18). The revealing task of Jesus is passed on to the disciples, whose performance of that task, *making God known,* glorifies Jesus (v. 10). They too have been successful in this mission, and thus Jesus has prayed for a newer group of believers who have come to believe that Jesus is the sent one of God through their word.[61] They too must be one as the Father and the Son are one, so that they might *make God known* (vv. 20-23). The love that unites them will reveal to the world the love that unites the Father and the Son and continues to make known that Jesus is the sent one of God. Jesus, the disciples, and the believers have an identical mission: *to make God known* (see vv. 3; 10, 18; 21, 23). The prayer comes to a close as all those for whom Jesus

[61] This is further reason for seeing the believers in v. 20 as absent contemporaries of the people at the table. As Jesus' mission (see v. 4) was successful (see vv. 6-8), so also is the disciples' mission (see v. 18) successful (see v. 20).

has prayed are recalled. The final words of Jesus' prayer reach beyond the limits of the time and place of the prayer into the proximate glorification of Jesus (v. 24), and the desired future glorification of the disciples and the first believers, through their association with his love and the love that unites him and the Father. Jesus *has made God known* to the disciples, and the believers' loving oneness with the Father and the Son will further *make God known* to a world that *has not known God* (vv. 25-26).

A rich interweaving of themes has been present throughout 17:1-26. However, one theme predominates: the mission *to make God known*.[62] Jesus prays for himself now that he has made God known (vv. 1-8). He prays to his holy Father for his fragile disciples so that in the midst of a hostile world, cared for and made holy, they might make God known (vv. 9-19), thus continuing their initial success (see v. 20). He also prays that all who believe in Jesus as the sent one of God might make God known (vv. 20-26) until such time as they are with Jesus in the place he has prepared for them (see 14:2-3) beholding the glory that was his before the foundation of the world (17:24). This is eternal life, that they know God, a knowledge now possible through the revelation that has taken place in and through Jesus Christ, whom God has sent (see v. 3).

A reading of the events and words that took place at a table the night before Jesus was "lifted up" has come full circle. The evening begins with the footwashing and the gift of the morsel, even to Judas (13:26). Jesus makes God known in the perfect love that he shows for his fragile disciples. In and through his loving, Jesus is glorified, and God is glorified in him. The disciples are to be recognized as the sent ones of Jesus by the unity created by the love they have for one another (13:1-38). As the discourse opens, Jesus instructs his failing disciples on his departure and the conditions and challenges that will face them. Guided by the Paraclete in his physical absence, love, faith, joy, and peace should be theirs as they are swept up into the love that unites the Father and Jesus, the sent one (14:1-31). At the center of the discourse, the reader hears the voice of Jesus, without interruption, telling of abiding, loving, and being hated. He proclaims that oneness and joy can be experienced by the disciple who abides in Jesus, the true vine. The disciple will be swept up into Jesus' abiding oneness with the Father (15:1-11). *The disciples of Jesus are to love as he has loved*

---

[62] For readings of John 17 which stress this missionary aspect, see Manns, *L'Evangile*, 396–400; J. F. Randall, "The Theme of Unity in John 17," *ETL* 41 (1965) 384–88, and especially Segalla, *La preghiera*, 193–207.

as a consequence of all that he has done for them (15:12-17). Hatred, rejection, expulsion, and slaying of the disciples will highlight the response of "the Jews," the false vine that has rejected Jesus and the Father (15:18—16:3). The voices of the disciples are again heard as the themes and the form of 14:1-31 return. Jesus instructs his failing disciples on his departure and on the conditions and challenges that will face them. They will be guided by the Paraclete in his physical absence; joy and confidence should be theirs as they are loved by the Father who sent Jesus (16:4-33). A prayer of departure instructs the reader that Jesus makes God known in the perfect love and unfailing care he shows for his fragile disciples, even Judas (see 17:11-12). In and through his loving, Jesus is glorified, and God is glorified in him. The disciples are to be recognized as the sent ones of Jesus by the unity created by the love they have for one another (17:1-26).[63]

The account of Jesus' final evening with his disciples encourages the reader to look further into the story for the resolution of the many questions that flow from this insistence that *Jesus' loving is the revelation of God.* In short, the reader must read on to discover how this happens in the life (and death) of Jesus. But the narratives, discourses, and prayer of John 13–17 also make a statement and raise questions that point the readers beyond the boundaries of the Jesus story.[64] The reader *in the narrative* is instructed that Jesus has made God known in a consummate act of love. But only the reader *of the narrative* can answer the question posed at the structural heart of the story of Jesus' last encounter with his disciples (15:1—16:3). Is God still being made known by fruitful disciples of the Johannine Jesus? Are they abiding in him (15:1-11) in the midst of a hostile world (15:18—16:3)? Does their love for one another proclaim that they are no longer servants (15:12-17)? This should be the case, as they have been chosen by Jesus and have heard all that the Father made known to him (15:15-16).

[63] Using of Dettwiler's language, and some of his conclusions, 17:1-26 is a "relecture" of 13:1-38; 16:4-33 is a "relecture" of 14 1-31, while 15.1—16:3 is an initial "relecture" of 13:1-38. There is an ongoing "relecture" of 13:1-38 into 15:1—16:3, climaxing in 17:1-26.

[64] This is part of the genre of the farewell discourse. As W. S Kurz, *Farewell Addresses in the New Testament* (Zacchaeus Studies: New Testament; Collegeville, Minn.: Liturgical Press, 1990) 15, remarks: "Farewells .. explicitly look ahead beyond the time of the narrative itself "

Chapter Six

Consummation
John 18:1—19:42

¶ JESUS' SUFFERING has its place in the Johannine tradition,[1] but the Johannine story must do more than repeat the earlier story. The reader expects an interpretation of the passion of Jesus that will resolve questions posed by the preceding narrative. The reader is aware that Jesus of Nazareth died by crucifixion, but much of this story has looked toward the event as the high point of Jesus' human experience, his being "lifted up" (see 3:14; 8:28; 12:32-33). Associated with this lifting up is the notion of Jesus' "hour," which during the major part of the public ministry has pointed the reader to some future moment (see 2:4; 7:6; 30; 8:20). Jesus announces that the hour has "come" as the ministry draws to an end (see 12:23) and as the final encounter between Jesus and his disciples opens (13:1) and closes

---

[1] On this, see W. Thusing, *Die Erhohung und Verherrlichung Jesus im Johannesevangelium* (2d ed.; NTAbh 21, 2/1; Munster· Aschendorf, 1970) 78–82; C. R Koester, *Symbolism in the Fourth Gospel: Meaning, Mystery, Community* (Minneapolis· Fortress Press, 1995) 188–91. For M. W. G. Stibbe, *John as Storyteller: Narrative Criticism and the Fourth Gospel* (SNTSMS 73; Cambridge· Cambridge Univ. Press, 1992) 129–47, although the main literary feature of the Johannine passion account is irony, it is also marked by *pathos*, and has the tragic genre of the "killing of the king" as evidenced in the *Bacchae*. For E. Kasemann, *The Testament of Jesus: A Study of John in the Light of Chapter 17* (trans G. Krodel, London: SCM, 1965) 6–8, tradition is the *only* reason for the telling of a Johannine passion story, but see M. M. Thompson, *The Humanity of Jesus in the Fourth Gospel* (Philadelphia Fortress Press, 1988) 87–115.

127

(17:1).[2] There have also been more subtle suggestions in the narrative
of a future time when the Son of Man would give a gift that will not
perish (see 6:27), the disciples would come to understand the words
of Jesus, the Spirit would be given, and Jesus would be glorified (see
2:22; 7:39; 12:16). Toward the end of Jesus' ministry a close link
emerges between Jesus' death and the glorification of God and Jesus'
being glorified (see 11:4; 12:23, 28). During the final meal, these suggestions are further confirmed (see 13:31-32; 17:1-5). The lifting up of
Jesus on a cross will lead to a gathering of many who were formerly
"dispersed" (see 10:16; 11:52; 12:11, 19, 32). During his final night
with his disciples, he has instructed them on the need for a oneness
of love (see 13:34-35; 15:12-17), the fruitfulness of being swept up into
the love that exists between the Father and the Son (see 14:23; 15:9-
11; 16:26-27). And he has prayed to the Father that this oneness might
be such that others would come to believe that Jesus was the sent one
of God (see 17:23-24, 26).

THE SHAPE OF THE NARRATIVE

The reader has regularly been introduced to new episodes in the story
by descriptions of the place and the characters involved in each particular event (see 2:1-2, 13-14; 3:1-2a; 4:1-7a; 5:1-5; 6:1-4; 7:1-14; 9:1-5;
10:22-23; 11:1-4; 12:1-2). On the basis of this formal criterion, supported by changes of place, character, and action,[3] the passion story
can be divided into five distinct scenes:

---

[2] For a detailed study of the *Traditionsgeschichte* of the Johannine passion narrative,
see A. Dauer, *Die Passionsgeschichte im Johannesevangelium: Eine traditionsgeschichtliche
und theologische Untersuchung zu Joh 18,1—19,30* (SANT 30; Munich: Kosel-Verlag, 1972)
21–227. For recent more theological studies of the text as it stands, see I. de la Potterie,
The Hour of Jesus· The Passion and Resurrection of Jesus according to John: Text and Spirit
(Slough· St. Paul Publications, 1989), D Senior, *The Passion of Jesus in the Gospel of John*
(The Passion Series 4; Collegeville, Minn.: Liturgical Press, 1991); Knoppler, *Die theologia
crucis,* 242–68, and J. P. Heil, *Blood and Water: The Death and Resurrection of Jesus in John
18–21* (CBQMS 27, Washington. The Catholic Biblical Association of America, 1995).
For a number of contemporary readings of John 18–19 (practical criticism, genre criti-
cism, sociological reading, narrative-historical reading), see Stibbe, *John as Storyteller,*
95–196. The most important study of the Johannine passion narrative is R E. Brown,
*The Death of the Messiah: From Gethsemane to the Grave. A Commentary on the Passion
Narratives in the Four Gospels* (2 vols.; ABRL, New York: Doubleday, 1994).

[3] See the same criteria, producing the same five scenes, in C. H. Giblin, "Confrontations in John 18,1-27," *Bib* 65 (1984) 211–12. I am unable to take into account the
reading of John 18.28—19·42 by J. L. Staley, *Reading with a Passion: Rhetoric, Autobiography, and the American West in the Gospel of John* (New York. Continuum, 1995) 200–234.

1. *18:1-11:* Jesus and his enemies in a garden (see vv. 1-3 for the introduction)
2. *18:12-27:* Jesus' appearance before "the Jews" (see vv. 12-16 for the introduction)[4]
3. *18:28—19:16a:* Jesus before Pilate (see v. 28 for the introduction)
4. *19:16b-37:* The crucifixion of Jesus (see vv. 16b-18 for the introduction)
5. *19:38-42:* The burial of Jesus in a garden by his newfound friends (see vv. 38-39 for the introduction)[5]

This shape begins and ends with scenes in a garden and has the report of the trial before Pilate at the heart of the story.

READING THE NARRATIVE

1. Jesus in a Garden with His Enemies (18:1-11)
Commentators generally refer to John 18:1-11 as "the arrest" of Jesus,[6] but this does not reflect what happens in Gethsemane. The events in the garden (vv. 1-11) are dominated by the initiative of Jesus.[7] Jesus

---

Staley introduces his biographical experience of dogs and postmodern literary theory to undermine the traditional reading of Johannine language and metaphors. One corpse has been cut down and lies on the ground mouthing a traditional interpretation of the passage. Jesus hangs on the cross subverting that interpretation. See also J L Staley, "Reading Myself, Reading the Text: The Johannine Passion Narrative in Postmodern Perspective," in F. F. Segovia, ed., *"What is John?" Readers and Readings of the Fourth Gospel* (SS 3; Atlanta. Scholars, 1996) 59–104. My reading is largely represented in Staley's story by the man cut down.

[4] "The Jews" are here—as throughout the rest of the Gospel—one side of a christological debate.

[5] This division is largely followed by almost all commentators. Some (e.g., A. Dauer, *Die Passionsgeschichte im Johannesevangelium: Eine traditionsgeschichtliche und theologische Untersuchung zu Joh 18,1–19,30* [SANT 30; Munich: Kosel-Verlag, 1972] and F Genuyt, "La comparution de Jésus devant Pilate: Analyse sémiotique de Jean 18,28–19,16," *RSR* 73 [1985] 133–34) follow this overall structure, but read larger blocks of material as units. Heil, *Blood and Water*, 4–12, proposes three major sections (18:1-27; 18.28—19·11; 19.12-42), each one formed by six scenes that are determined—in each case—by four sandwich constructions. Major changes of place and characters are ignored (e.g., 18 12, 19:16b-17, 38).

[6] See, e.g., W. Bauer, *Das Johannesevangelium erklärt* (3d ed.; HKNT 6, Tubingen: J. C. B. Mohr, 1933) 208; M. W. G. Stibbe, *John* (Readings: A New Biblical Commentary; Sheffield: JSOT Press, 1993) 180.

[7] This is recognized by commentators who include v 12 with vv. 1-11 as "the arrest of Jesus." See, e.g., R. E. Brown, *The Gospel according to John* (2 vols.; AB 29, 29A, Garden City, N.Y. Doubleday, 1966–1970) 2:805; B. Lindars, *The Gospel of John* (NCB, London.

and his disciples move to a known location, "where there was a garden [*hopou ēn kēpos*]," as opposing forces, Judas, a cohort of Roman soldiers (*tēn speirēn*), and some temple officers (*hupēretas*) gather and move against Jesus bearing lanterns, torches, and weapons (vv. 1-3). Such a combination is historically improbable, but the author indicates that Judas, the Romans, and "the Jews" combine against Jesus.[8] The reader is aware that Jesus is the light of *the world* (see 8:12; 9:5) and that he has challenged his listeners at the close of the ministry to walk in the light while they have the light (see 12:35-36a). Armed for violence, Jesus' enemies, Romans and Jews representing "the world," come in search of the light of the world, carrying their own light, lanterns, and torches (v. 3).[9]

Knowing what will befall him (v. 4a), Jesus comes forward asking whom they are seeking, only to level them to the ground with his self-identification as *egō eimi* after their request for "Jesus of Nazareth."[10] Again using the formula of self-revelation, *egō eimi*, Jesus *informs* his opponents that their designs upon Jesus of Nazareth can be pursued if they allow the disciples to go free (v. 8). The narrator nudges the reader to recall Jesus' words to the Father from the immediately previous context: "Of those whom thou gavest me, I lost not one" (v. 9; see 17:12; also 6:69; 10:28). Not even Judas, the betrayer, is excluded from those who must be allowed to go free. The fact that, even in this hostile context, no exception is made in Jesus' words in v. 9: "I lost not one," is indication that this Gospel makes no *final* judgment on the disciple Judas.[11] However bad his performance, he has now been

---

Oliphants, 1972) 537. Senior, *Passion,* 46, accurately calls 18:1-11. "Jesus confronts his enemies."

[8] See the full discussion of both the historical and theological possibilities of the grouping in Brown, *Death,* 1:248–52.

[9] See R. A. Culpepper, *Anatomy of the Fourth Gospel: A Study in Literary Design* (Philadelphia: Fortress Press, 1983) 192; C. H Giblin, "Confrontations in John 18,1-27," *Bib* 65 (1984) 216–17; Koester, *Symbolism,* 186, Heil, *Blood and Water,* 19–20.

[10] On the use of *egō eimi* in 18:4–8a, see Brown, *Death,* 1:259–62. Not all would accept that *egō eimi* is anything more than self-identification for the people who have come to arrest him. But the context demands more See J. Bligh, *The Sign of the Cross: The Passion and Resurrection of Jesus According St John* (Slough, England St Paul Publications, 1975) 18–19. D. M. Ball, '*I Am' in John's Gospel: Literary, Function, and Theological Implications* (JSNTSS, 124, Sheffield· Sheffield Academic Press, 1996) 137–45, 201, claims that in themselves the words say little, but the reader has by now (and especially after 13:19) come to recognize that Jesus is applying Isaian ideas of Yahweh as God and Savior to himself.

[11] This a further indication that the reference to the Son of Perdition in 17:12 is not Judas, but Satan (see 2 Thess 2·3, 8-9).

given into the care of the Father, whose remarkable love has been revealed by Jesus (see 17:11-12). Judas is "with them" (v. 5: *met' autōn*), but he plays no active role in the arrest (cf. Mark 14:42-45). Jesus prayed for his disciples (see 17:9-19) and for those who have heard the word through their ministry (vv. 20-26), that they might be swept up into the oneness of love that existed from all time between the Father and the Son "so that the world may know that you have sent me, and have loved them even as you have loved me" (v. 23). As Jesus initiates the process that will lead to his being lifted up (see 3:14; 8:28; 12:32), he demands that his disciples go their way so that they may perform their missionary task (see 13:20, 34-35; 15:5-8, 16, 26-27; 17:18-19, 20-23). Peter fails to understand the significance of the events about to take place, using a sword in a violent attempt to change the course of events (18:10). But he is rebuked, as the passion story must now begin.[12] The reader is aware that Peter is thwarting God's design as Judas is thwarting that design. The prophecies of 13:1-17, 21-38 are being fulfilled. But Jesus willingly drinks the cup the Father gives him (v. 11; see 12:27). The Johannine passion story begins because Jesus allows it to begin. He is the master of the situation. However, from the first scene, 18:1-11, the disciples are singled out for special attention. Unlike the parallel scene in the Synoptic tradition, where Jesus' loneliness is stressed (see Mark 15:32-42; Matt 26:26-46; Luke 22:40-46), Jesus is in the garden with his disciples (John 18:1). They are mentioned three times in two verses (vv. 1-2), while Judas, another disciple of Jesus, is described as standing with Jesus' enemies (v. 5: *eistēkei de kai Ioudas ho paradidous auton met' autōn*). In the face of hostility and violence, Jesus demands that the disciples be free. The passion of Jesus may not only be about what happens to Jesus but may also determine the future of the community. Jesus' never-failing love for his disciples, including Judas and Peter, makes God known (see 13:18-20).

2. Jesus' Appearance Before "the Jews" (18:12-27)
Verses 12-14 introduce Jesus and Peter in a way unparalleled in the Synoptic tradition.[13] Jesus is seized (v. 12) and led to the house of

---

[12] On Peter's failure, see Stibbe, *John*, 181; Senior, *Passion*, 54–55. J. P. Heil, "Jesus as the Unique High Priest in the Gospel of John," *CBQ* 57 (1995) 736–37, understands Peter's gesture as a misguided attempt to stop Jesus' high priestly sacrifice.

[13] For Synoptic contacts, see Dauer, *Passionsgeschichte*, 62–63, 91–99; K. Quast, *Peter and the Beloved Disciple: Figures for a Community in Crisis* (JSNTSS 32; Sheffield: JSOT Press, 1989) 71–76; Brown, *Death*, 1:78–79 (Mark), 87–88 (Luke), 418–19 (synoptic chart).

Annas (v. 13a), and the author takes this occasion to link Annas and Caiaphas to remind the reader that Jesus' death is not for himself but for the nation, and to gather into one the children of God who are scattered abroad (vv. 13b-14; see 11:49-52).[14] The reader is told that two disciples followed Jesus (v. 15: *ēkolouthei de tō Iēsou*). Simon Peter, well known as a leading disciple (see 1:41-43; 6:8, 68-69; 13:6-9, 24, 36-38), and an anonymous disciple who has also appeared earlier in the narrative (see 1:37-42).[15] The reader is told of the presence of two *mathētai* in the court of the high priest, along with Jesus (v. 15). Peter gains entry to the court through the mediation of the other disciple who is a *gnōstos* of the high priest.[16] Peter's being one of the *mathētai* of Jesus is the focus of the question of the maid who kept the door: "Are you not also one of this man's disciples?" Peter's first denial reverses the words of Jesus, who revealed his identity at Gethsemane with the words *egō eimi* (see vv. 5, 8). Peter responds *ouk eimi* (v. 17). A lie has been told. Without comment the narrator moves on to describe the action of the *hupēretai* and some servants who have prepared a charcoal fire against the cold. The reader recalls that the *hupēretai* had come out to arrest Jesus, the Light of the world (see 8:12; 9:5), carrying lanterns and torches (18:2); had seized him; and had bound him and taken him to Annas (18:12-13a). In a way that parallels the situation of Judas in the garden, Peter is described as *met' autōn* (v. 18; see 18:5).[17] He approaches the warmth and light created by characters who have sided with the powers of darkness. This irony is

[14] J L. Staley, "Subversive Narrator/Victimized Reader: A Reader Response Assessment of a Text-Critical Problem, John 18,12-24," *JSNT* 51 (1993) 91–98, uses this first reference to the *archiereus* as the beginning of the narrator's design to victimize the reader. Only in v. 24 does the reader discover that it was Annas, not Caiaphas. See also Idem, *Reading with a Passion*, 85–109. On the continuing use of *archiereus* for former high priests, see Brown, *John*, 2:820–21; S. Pancaro, *The Law in the Fourth Gospel: The Torah and the Gospel, Moses and Jesus, Judaism and Christianity according to John* (NovTSupp 42; Leiden: Brill, 1975) 66–67.

[15] There is some debate over the identification of "another disciple" with the Beloved Disciple, exhaustively surveyed by J. H. Charlesworth, *The Beloved Disciple: Whose Witness Validates the Gospel of John?* (Valley Forge, Pa.: Trinity Press International, 1995) 336–59. The issue is further complicated by textual confusion. Some manuscripts add a definite article before *allos mathētēs* in v. 15. Others read "that disciple," while some have neither "other" nor "that " S. van Tilborg, *Imaginative Love in John* (BibIntS 2; Leiden: Brill, 1993) 93–94, perhaps rightly, suggests that it is "poly-interpretable."

[16] There has been much speculation around the relationship that might exist between this disciple and the high priest. See Brown, *John*, 2:822–23.

[17] Knoppler, *Die theologia crucis*, 220–27, studies the role of Judas but does not see the uniqueness of the Johannine point of view. He points to Judas' being "with" the Romans in 18:5 (227), but fails to notice that Peter joins him in 18:18, 25

implicit commentary on the narrative. Peter is joining Judas, moving away from the light toward the darkness (see 13:30). In the telling of Peter's first denial (vv. 15-18), the term *disciple* is used four times. In addition to the technical term *mathētēs*, the name *Peter*, well known to the reader as an important (see 1:41-42), faithful (see 6:68-69), but misunderstanding and fragile (13:6-9, 24, 36-38) disciple, appears five times. In six brief sentences the theme of the disciple of Jesus appears nine times, focusing the reader's attention on the theme of disciple-ship. But, as he associates himself with Judas, it is a story of disciple-ship denied.

The reader is next told that Jesus is asked *peri tōn mathētōn autou kai peri tēs didachēs autou* (v. 19). Jesus' answer reverses the order of the issues raised. He first speaks of his *didachē* (v. 20) and then of "those who have heard me" (*tous akēkootas*), those who know what Jesus has said (v. 21).[18] Jesus looks back on that public revelation of God through word and deed, which closed in 12:36b, and informs his in-terrogator of two events, both in the past, but described with different forms of the past tense.[19] In v. 20b Jesus looks back over his preaching to "the Jews." The reader recalls the events and encounters of 1:19—12:36b, and especially the intensifying conflict of 5:1—10:42 that led to the decision that Jesus must die for the nation (11:50), as Jesus responds, "I have always taught in the Synagogue and in the Temple, where all Jews come together" (18:20b). He has taught, but he will do so no longer. There can be no going back on the definitive separation between Jesus and "the Jews" established for the reader through the narrator's comment in 12:36b. This is implied in the use of the aorist tense of the verb *edidaxa* ("taught"). Jesus devoted himself to a period of teaching in temple and synagogue in the past, but this stage has come to an end.[20]

But "I have spoken openly to the world . . . I have said nothing secretly" (v. 20a.c). Although the teaching (*didachē*) of "the Jews" has ended, the word of Jesus has been proclaimed in the world (*lelalēka*). This Gospel's rich use of *ho kosmos* can never be simply equated with

[18] The link between the interrogation over the *mathētai* and the *didachē* in v. 19, and Jesus' response in vv. 20-21 is rarely noticed. See, e.g., Giblin, "Confrontations," 221–30; Heil, "Unique High Priest," 739–40. C. K. Barrett, *The Gospel according to St John* (2d ed. London: SPCK, 1978) 523, states that Jesus "refuses to answer."
[19] Pancaro, *Law*, 64–71, rightly points out that 18:19-24 cannot be regarded as a trial. All "trials" (Jesus by "the Jews" and "the Jews" by Jesus) have taken place during the public ministry. See also Brown, *Death*, 1:423–26.
[20] The aorist is complexive. See BDF, 171, para. 332.

"the Jews."[21] The world, which is the object of God's saving love, is in question in 18:20a. This is indicated by the use of the perfect tense for the verb *lelalēka* ("spoken"). A word has been spoken in the world, which is *parrēsia* ("openly"). Jesus' historical presence as a teacher, proclaiming his word, has come to an end (12:36b). But his word, spoken in the past, was never hidden or limited (18:20c: *en kruptōi elalēsa ouden*).[22] The perfect tense, placed in close proximity with the aorist *edidaxa* indicates that although the teaching of Jesus to "the Jews" has come to an end, the word of Jesus is still available. Something began in the past, and its consequences are still abroad.[23]

Jesus has answered the question concerning his teaching. He is no longer prepared to teach "the Jews" who are now interrogating him. They have already been taught, and they have rejected his teaching.[24] Yet the word of Jesus is alive in the world. But if the presence of Jesus "in Synagogues and in the Temple" (v. 20b) is no longer available (see 12:36b), where is this word to be found, spoken so openly to the world (v. 20a.c)? One must ask those who have heard him (*tous akekootas*) what he said (*elalēsa*) to them. During the ministry of Jesus, the word was spoken (complexive aorist) to "those who have heard." They are in possession of the word to the world, and anyone who wishes to hear that word must ask them (v. 21b). They know (*oidasin*) what Jesus said (v. 21c). According to many commentators, Jesus' reply simply insists that his accusers "take testimony in the legal manner."[25] But the reader understands that they are the followers of Jesus (see v. 15a), the *mathētai*, the ones who have learned at the school of Jesus.[26] Jesus is no longer available to speak his own word. He has spoken it to followers and disciples who know what he said. The high priest's question concerning Jesus' disciples has been answered, as the *didachē* and the *mathētai* belong together. The "teaching" of Jesus is to be found among his "disciples" (see v. 19).[27]

One of the *hupēretai* (see vv. 2, 12, 18), out of loyalty to the high priest, slaps Jesus. He refuses to accept the promise of Jesus (18:22).

---

[21] On this, see Koester, *Symbolism*, 249–53.

[22] The aorist *elalēsa* is another complexive aorist, referring to the whole period of Jesus' once-and-for-all revelation of the Father during his ministry.

[23] See *BDF*, 175–76, paras 340–41

[24] The experience of the Johannine community (see 9:22; 12:42; 16:2) lies behind this assessment of the situation of "the Jews" who are not the Jewish people

[25] Barrett, *St John*, 528.

[26] For the importance of this feature of a *mathētēs*, see K Rengstorf, "*manthanō ktl.*," *TDNT* 4 (1967) 444–50.

[27] See E. C. Hoskyns, *The Fourth Gospel* (2d ed.; ed. F. N. Davey; London Faber & Faber, 1947) 514.

But Jesus' response to this rejection returns to the true significance of the events. If Jesus has spoken evilly (*ei kakōs elalēsa*), he asks his assailant to bear witness; but if he has spoken well (*ei kalōs elalēsa*), the officer must explain his action (v. 23). *Kakōs lalein* is used in the LXX with reference to blasphemy (see Exod 22:7; Lev 19:14; 20:9; Isa 8:21; 1 Macc 7:42). If the slap is punishment for blasphemy, witnesses must be brought. If such is not the case, and Jesus is proclaiming what is right (*kalōs*), a truthfulness that opposes blasphemy, then the officer stands condemned by his action.[28] The tradition of Jesus' guiltlessness, found in both the Synoptic and the Johannine trial before Pilate (see Matt 27:4, 19, 24; Mark 15:14; Luke 23:13-16, 22; John 18:38; 19:4, 6) emerges here. Jesus is not only guiltless; he has revealed the truth, he has spoken well (*kalōs*), and the truth has been rejected. The narrator immediately returns to a character whose performance interests him at least as much as that of Jesus: one of the founding members of the subsequent community of disciples, Peter, one of those who had heard what Jesus said (see v. 21) but who has joined Judas in the darkness (see vv. 1-5, 18).

The narrator resumes his presentation of Peter's denials. The "other disciple" has disappeared, but Simon Peter, still "with them" at the fire (see v. 18), is again asked whether he is *ek tōn mathētōn autou*. He repeats his first denial: *ouk eimi* (v. 25). The almost exact repetition in v. 25 of what was done and said in Peter's first denial in v. 17 creates a tight frame around Jesus' directions that those who wish to know his teaching must go to those who have heard him (vv. 20-21).[29] As Jesus points to the disciples as the ones who have heard him and are custodians of his word, one of them—indeed a leading disciple (see 1:41-43; 6:68-69)—has joined Judas with the representatives of the darkness (v. 18: *met' autōn;* see v. 5), denying his association with Jesus. On several occasions during the story of Peter and Jesus with "the Jews" (vv. 12-27), the immediately previous scene provides essential background for either the denials of Peter, his association with Judas, or the witness of Jesus (see vv. 5, 8 and vv. 17, 18, 25; v. 3 and vv. 12, 22). A further link emerges as Peter's active intervention with a sword to cut off Malchus' ear is recalled (v. 26; see v. 10). This accusation, made by a blood relative of the injured man, cannot be denied. Peter insists that he has no association with Jesus (v. 27a). The third denial

---

[28] See Brown, *Death,* 1:415–16.

[29] Scholars often complain that there are no changes of time mentioned throughout these alternating scenes. See Quast, *Peter,* 75, 85. By this process the author creates the impression that the events are happening simultaneously

implies that he never was in the garden, a place known to Judas because "Jesus often met there with his disciples" (v. 2). Peter, who has
drawn closer to the darkness represented by the *hupēretai*, falsely denies any link with Gethsemane, Jesus, and his disciples who often met
there. Peter denies something that even Judas acknowledged (see
vv. 2a, 26b-27a).

The report of Peter's threefold denial concludes: "And at once the
cock crowed" (v. 27b). The reader recalls Jesus' words from 13:38 and
is made aware that Jesus' promises are fulfilled. What Jesus said would
happen (13:38) does happen (18:27b). This is crucial for the reader's
appreciation of the present series of events. Jesus has indicated that
his word is abroad in the world (v. 20) and that it can be found among
those who have heard him; they know what he said (v. 21). One of
them is denying that he had anything to do with Jesus (vv. 15-18, 25-
27), and another has betrayed him (vv. 1-5), but the reader is assured
by the cock crow that what Jesus said would happen will happen.
However badly Peter and Judas may perform, Jesus' teaching can be
heard from those who—like Peter and Judas—have heard him.[30] The
reader also recalls the earlier promise of Jesus, made within the context of his prophecies of the betrayal of Judas and the denials of Peter
(13:1-17, 21-38): "I tell you this now, before it takes place, that when
it does take place you may believe *hoti egō eimi*" (13:19). It is in unconditional love for those who fail him that Jesus makes God known.

3. Jesus Before Pilate (18:28—19:16a)

The Synoptic tradition already used the trial of Jesus before Pilate and
the sign on the cross to proclaim Jesus as "King" (see Mark 15:2, 9, 12,
18, 26, 32; Matt 27:11, 29, 37, 42; Luke 23:2, 3, 27, 38), but in this
story the theme dominates the interrogation of Jesus by Pilate (see
18:33, 37, 39; 19:3, 12, 14, 15) and continues into the scene of the
crucifixion (19:19, 21).[31] The introduction sets the scene at the praetorium and presents the characters of Jesus, Pilate, and the Jewish lead-
ers, who—as the first light of the day breaks—ironically present the
Lamb of God for trial but remain outside the Praetorium to avoid ritual impurity on the eve of the Passover (v. 28).[32] The "trial" that fol-

---

[30] See F J Moloney, "John 18.15-27: A Johannine View of the Church," *DRev* 112
(1994) 231–48.

[31] For a useful list of the way in which John 18:28—19:16 has used earlier tradition,
see B. D. Ehrman, "Jesus' Trial Before Pilate," *BTB* 13 (1983) 124–26.

[32] See Senior, *Passion*, 77; Brown, *Death*, 1:744–46; Heil, *Blood and Water*, 47–48. The
dawning of the day may be a subtle hint of an ironic victory that is being initiated.

lows is marked by seven brief scenes that take place either inside or outside the praetorium.[33] The narrator uses verbs of motion to show that Pilate and/or Jesus comes out or goes in. There are two "trials" in progress: One flows from the encounter between the Roman authority of Pilate and "the Jews" (see 18:29-32, 38b-40; 19:5-7, 12-15) and the other from the encounter between Pilate and Jesus (18:33-38; 19:8-11).[34] For the reader, the deciding issue is how Pilate and "the Jews" respond to Jesus' royal status. There is only one scene, 19:1-3, where there is no verb of motion and no dialogue. In that scene, which takes place inside the praetorium, Jesus is crowned, dressed as a king, and ironically proclaimed: "Hail, the King of the Jews" (v. 3). Although the Synoptic tradition has a parallel scene (see Matt 27:29; Mark 15:18), only this Gospel has the soldiers use the definite article in addressing Jesus as "the King" in the ironic salutation: "*chaire ho basileus tōn loudaiōn*" (19:3).

The reader follows "the Jews" as their rejection of Jesus intensifies. They have already made up their minds that Jesus is an evildoer (see 18:30) and that he must die by being "lifted up."[35] He must be slain by the Roman method of execution: crucifixion (see v. 31). The narrator reminds the reader that this fulfills the earlier word of Jesus about the manner of his death: "When I am lifted up from the earth I will draw everyone to myself" (12:32). The reader is reminded that the death of Jesus will not be for himself, but for the "gathering" of others.[36] Pilate will have none of the Jewish stories of kings and messiahs (vv. 33-35),

---

[33] This pattern is widely recognized by scholars. See B. F. Westcott, *The Gospel according to Saint John* (London: Murray, 1908) 258. R. Baum-Bodenbender, *Hoheit in Niedrigkeit: Johanneische Christologie im Prozess Jesu vor Pilatus (Joh 18,28-19,16a)* (FB 49, Wurzburg: Echter Verlag, 1984) 28–96, uses the seven scenes in two acts (18:28—19:5 and 19 6-16a) in which the scenes "outside" (18:28-32; 38b-40, 19:6-8; 12b-16a) carry the supporting theme of "the Jews'" rejection of Jesus, and the scenes "inside" (18:33-38a; 19.1-5; 19:9-12a) form the main axis of the narrative, instructing the reader in Johannine Christology. While recognizing and accepting the seven scenes, C. H. Giblin, "John's Narration of the Hearing Before Pilate," *Bib* 67 (1986) 221–24, argues for a progression of mounting tension across two narrative sections, both of which conclude with *tote oun* and an action of Pilate· 19:1-3 and 19:16a

[34] See Brown, *Death*, 1:743. See also A. Janssens de Varebeke, "La Structure des scenes du récit de la passion en Joh. xviii–xix," *ETL* 38 (1962) 504–22. Giblin, "John's Narration," 226–27, 238, rightly rejects the interpretation of the encounter between Jesus and Pilate as State versus Christianity. See also D. Rensberger, *Johannine Faith and Liberating Community* (Philadelphia: Westminster, 1988) 87–106

[35] It is still debated whether or not the Jews could put people to death (see v. 31b) at the time of Jesus. See, for a survey, Brown, *Death*, 1:747–49. Pancaro, *Law*, 310–26, rightly claims that the motivation for 18:31 (and 19:6) is theological

[36] Here historical concerns are again subjected to Johannine theology.

but he is told of the nature of Jesus' messianic kingship: He exercises his royalty in making God known to the world, bearing witness to the truth, and drawing all who are of the truth into his kingdom (vv. 36-37). Although Pilate questions Jesus about his royal status, Jesus does not speak about himself, but about the *basileia*. There is a gratuitous offer of truth from Jesus to his Roman interrogator as he tells Pilate that he reveals the truth and draws the people of the truth into a kingdom of truth as they hear his voice. The reader recalls the only other use of *basileia* in the story, where Nicodemus was told of the need to be born again from above (*anōthen*), by water and the Spirit (*ex hudatos kai pneumatos*), in order to "see" and to "enter" the kingdom (3:3-5). The kingdom is a "place" where God reigns, a community, and those who are of God—that is, of the truth—respond to Jesus' voice, "see" (*idein*), and "enter into" (*eiselthein eis*) that kingdom (see again, 3:3, 5).[37] But Pilate rejects Jesus' revelation-invitation with his brusque refusal of the word of Jesus: "What is truth?" (v. 38).[38]

Despite Pilate's inability to step into Jesus' kingdom of truth, he goes out to "the Jews," proclaims Jesus' innocence, and—responding to a custom (*synētheia*)[39]—offers to free Jesus, "the King of the Jews" (v. 39). But "the Jews" ask for Barabbas, a *lēstēs*, a man of violence and a false messianic choice.[40] Ironically, at this stage of the story, without any notification of change of place or actors, Jesus is dressed and proclaimed as the King of the Jews (19:1-3). Gone are the blindfolding, the punches, the spitting, the mocking genuflections, and the striking on the head with a rod of the Synoptic tradition (see Matt

---

[37] See F J. Moloney, *Belief in the Word: Reading John 1–4* (Minneapolis: Fortress Press, 1993) 109–14. On the link between "hearing the voice" of Jesus, and the response of the sheep to the Good Shepherd in 10:10,3-4, 8, 16, see W. A. Meeks, *The Prophet-King: Moses Traditions and the Johannine Christology* (NovTSupp 14; Leiden: Brill, 1967) 66–67.

[38] The reader is aware that the criterion for authentic belief in Jesus is an openness to his word (see 2:1–4.54). Pilate fails.

[39] It is difficult to find evidence for this "custom." Some see it as a possible interpretation of *Pesahim* 8:6 and *bPesahim* 91a. For a comprehensive but inconclusive assessment of the evidence, see Brown, *Death*, 1:814–20.

[40] See Giblin, "John's Narration," 228. Josephus uses *lēstēs* of the Zealots, whose false messianic pretension—according to Josephus—caused God to abandon his people, and thus led to the destruction of the City and the Nation. On this, see A. J. Simonis, *Die Hirtenrede im Johannes-Evangelium: Versuch eine Analyse von Johannes 10,1-18 nach Entstehung Hintergrund und Inhalt* (AnBib 29; Rome: Biblical Institute Press, 1967) 130–39. Against this, see Brown, *Death*, 1:808. In 10:14-18 the celebration of Tabernacles (see 7:1–10-21) culminates with Jesus' self-identification of the messianic Good Shepherd. However, "the Jews" have chosen a *lēstēs*, a thief and a robber who came before him to plunder the sheep (see 10:1, 8). On this relationship between 18:40 and 10:1-18, see Meeks, *The Prophet-King*, 67–8. On the name of Barabbas, see Brown, *Death*, 1:796–800.

26:67-68; 27:27-30; Mark 14:65; 15:16-17; Luke 22:63-64). In their place there is a crowning, a clothing, and an ironic proclamation.[41] Despite the rejection involved in the scene, Jesus is crowned and acclaimed as "the King of the Jews."

Emerging from the praetorium, Pilate again declares that Jesus is innocent, and Jesus, crowned and dressed as a king, "came out" (*exelthen . . . exō*). He is not "led out." Still master of his own destiny, he comes out "bearing" (*phorōn*) the signs of his royal status.[42] The narrator never indicates that the royal trappings of crown and cloak are taken off Jesus to be replaced by his own clothing (contrast Matt 27:31; Mark 15:20). Jesus goes to the cross dressed as a king. This is the setting for Pilate's famous words: *idou ho anthrōpos*. Paralleling his earlier declaration of Jesus' innocence and his presentation of Jesus to "the Jews" as "the King of the Jews" in vv. 38b-39, Pilate again declares Jesus innocent and presents him to "the Jews" with another title of honor: "the Man." But as before Jesus' coronation and investiture "the Jews" had asked for Barabbas (see v. 40), they now demand that Jesus be crucified. This sequence of events leads the reader to recall Jesus' earlier words to "the Jews": "When you have lifted up the Son of Man, then you will know that I am he" (8:28). The first part of this prophecy is now being fulfilled: They are taking it upon themselves to "lift up" in crucifixion the royal figure presented to them as "the Man." As Greeks came to see Jesus, he announced, "Now is the hour that the Son of Man be glorified" (12:23). He further clarified the glorification by his words: "When I am lifted up from the earth I will draw everyone to myself" (12:32). The narrator comments: "He said this to show by what death he was to die" (v. 33). "The Jews" are demanding that the innocent Son of Man be lifted up,[43] because he challenges their

---

[41] On the irony of this scene, see P. D. Duke, *Irony in the Fourth Gospel* (Atlanta. John Knox, 1985) 131–32, and the references given there, especially J. Blank, "Die Verhandlung vor Pilatus Jo 18:28—19 16 im Lichte johanneischer Theologie," *BZ* 3 (1959) 73–74.

[42] For *phoreō* as a regal bearing of clothes or armor, see LSJ, 1950–51, s.v. The primary meaning of the verb is to bear regularly. See BAGD, 864–65.

[43] For a more detailed argument along these lines, see F. J. Moloney, *The Johannine Son of Man* (2d ed ; BibScRel 14; Rome: LAS, 1978) 202–7. See also Blank, "Verhandlung," 75–77; Dauer, *Passionsgeschichte*, 264–65; de la Potterie, *The Hour*, 79–80; Giblin, "John's Narration," 230; Stibbe, *John*, 191; Heil, *Blood and Water*, 64–65. R. Schnackenburg, *The Gospel according to St John* (3 vols.; HTCNT 4/1–3; London: Burns & Oates; New York. Crossroad, 1968–82) 1:532–33, is more cautious ("at most . . . an indirect illusion") R. Bultmann, *The Gospel of John: A Commentary* (trans. G. R Beasley-Murray; Oxford· Blackwell, 1971) 659, claims that Jesus' miserable state is the ultimate consequence of the word's becoming flesh. See also Brown, *Death*, 1:827–28. For J. Becker, *Das Evan-*

law in his claim to be the Son of God (v. 7). The real reason for their
rejection of Jesus has surfaced. Pilate is frightened, "more afraid," at
the suggestion that Jesus is the Son of God.[44] Thus, in his second encounter with Jesus, he asks the question fundamental to Johannine
Christology: "Where are you from?" but receives no answer from Jesus
(vv. 8-9).[45] The reader recalls Pilate's earlier encounter with Jesus when
Jesus openly and gratuitously revealed to him the possibility of being
drawn into the kingdom of truth by hearing his voice. This offer was
brusquely rejected (see 18:36-38). What is now happening to Pilate
matches Jesus' refusal to speak to "the Jews" in 18:20-21, as he has
already spoken to them *parrēsią* throughout his public ministry (v. 20).
He has also given witness *tę alētheią* to Pilate (18:37), but it has been
rejected (v. 38). Thus, he refuses to be drawn into any further self-
revelation to Pilate (19:9), who asks his question from a position of
human authority and nonbelief. He blusters against Jesus about his
political authority (v. 10), and the reader recognizes the truth of Jesus'
words, conceding that the one who handed him over (*ho paradous*)
has the greater guilt,[46] but informing Pilate that all authority comes
from above. In many ways Jesus has answered Pilate's question of
v. 9. He has everything "from above," because that is where he is from
(see v. 11).[47]

   This is beyond the Roman soldier, faced by "the Jews," who ironically attempt to teach the procurator a lesson on the universal author-

---

gelium des Johannes (2 vols ; OTK 4/1-2; Gutersloh: Gerd Mohn, Wurzburg: Echter,
1979-81) 2.572-73, Pilate presents Jesus as a "laughable King." Baum-Bodenbender,
Hoheit, 66-67, shows that both lowliness and majesty are present. C. Panackel, *IDOY
HO ANTHRŌPOS (Jn 19,5b): An Exegetico-Theological Study of the Text in the Light of the
Use of the Term ANTHRŌPOS Designating Jesus in the Fourth Gospel* (Analecta Gregoriana
251, Rome Gregorian Univ. Press, 1988) 215-338, claims too much. For him 19:5b is
the Fourth Evangelist's concluding use of *anthrōpos* to proclaim that in the humanity
of Jesus the Son of God is revealed.
[44] What is meant by Pilate's being "the *more* afraid" is widely discussed. See Brown,
Death, 1·830. Rightly Brown concludes: "Pilate is afraid because it becomes clearer and
clearer that he will not be able to escape making a judgment about truth."
[45] See L.-M. Dewailly, "'D'où es-tu?' (Jean 19,9)," *RB* 92 (1985) 481-96.
[46] This is not a reference to Judas, a disciple now consigned to the care of the Father
(see 17 12; 18:9). It is sometimes suggested that "the Jews" are to be held responsible
(see, e.g., Brown, *Death*, 1·842, Heil, *Blood and Water*, 73-4). The singular form of the
noun, however, points to an individual. Strictly in terms of the narrative it is Caiaphas
who made the final decision (see 11:49-53), and who is behind Jesus' being led to Pilate
(see 18:28). See G. R. Beasley-Murray, *John* (WBC 36; Waco: Word, 1987) 340. It may be
a further reference to Satan, the Son of Perdition of 17:12.
[47] See D. Zeller, "Jesus und die Philosophen vor dem Richter (zu Joh 19,8-11)," *BZ* 37
(1993) 88-92.

ity of the Roman emperor (v. 12).[48] Whatever may have been his fear on hearing the words of "the Jews," Pilate leads Jesus out and either sits on the judgment seat himself or (less likely) has Jesus take the seat (v. 13).[49] On the day of preparation for the Passover, Pilate proclaims Jesus as King: "Behold your King!" (v. 14). "The Jews" demand crucifixion while Pilate expresses surprise that they want to crucify their King. At the "sixth hour" (*hōra ēn hōs hektē*), precisely at the moment when the Passover lambs are being ritually slaughtered in the temple, "the Jews" scream out for the death of Jesus, the Lamb of God (vv. 14-15; see 1:29, 35). Despite Pilate's initial refusal to listen to "the truth" (18:38), Jesus' subsequent refusal to answer Pilate's questions concerning his origins (19:8-9), "the Jews'" baying for the blood of Jesus (v. 6), and their threat concerning Pilate's allegiance to Caesar (v. 12),[50] Pilate continues to insist on the kingship of Jesus (v. 14). This may not make much sense of Pilate's psychological coherence, but it enables the author to use Pilate's surprising insistence on Jesus' royal status to proclaim ironically the truth about Jesus. In the end Pilate capitulates to "the Jews" who betray the Mosaic tradition they have so stoutly used to accuse Jesus throughout the latter part of his ministry (see especially chaps. 5–10) and during this trial (see 19:7): "We have no king but Caesar" (v. 15). "The Jews" match their choice of Barabbas the *lēstēs* rather than Pilate's offer of the "King of the Jews" (see 18:39-40) when they choose Roman authority over against their King. They forsake all attachment to the promised kingdom of God and ask that a Roman form of execution be used to eliminate him (v. 15).[51]

As the account of Jesus before Pilate began with an introductory passage where "the Jews" led Jesus before the Roman authority (v. 28), it concludes with the Roman authority handing Jesus over to them so

[48] Dramatic irony, not history, is the major feature of the episode. See Duke, *Irony*, 134–36.

[49] There is the possibility that the verb *ekathisen* in v. 13 may be transitive, meaning that Pilate sat Jesus down, rather than the intransitive, indicating that Pilate sat down. For the transitive meaning, among many (Haenchen, Loisy, Lightfoot, Meeks, Brodie), see de la Potterie, *The Hour*, 108–11. Against such an interpretation, see Dauer, *Passionsgeschichte*, 269–74; Brown, *Death*, 1:844–45. The most likely meaning is that Pilate sat down, while the reader might suspect that the transitive meaning is possible. For a detailed survey of the discussion, concluding that Pilate sits on the judgment seat, see Brown, *Death*, 2:1388–93.

[50] On the possible reference to "friend of Caesar" as a technical term of honor, see Brown, *Death*, 1:843–44.

[51] See Beasley-Murray, *John*, 343; Brown, *Death*, 1:848–49, and especially Genuyt, "La comparution de Jésus," 133–46.

that they might lift up the Son of Man (v. 16a; see 8:28). The story has come full circle. Jesus has been proclaimed King both before (18:38b-40) and after (19:4-7) his coronation (19:1-3), but the response of "the Jews" has been to choose false messianic hopes (18:40 [Barabbas]; 19:12-15 [Rome]) and to seek the crucifixion of their King (18:29-32; 19:4-7, 13-15).[52] The trial of Jesus before Pilate, which has really been a trial of Pilate and "the Jews," comes to its conclusion as Pilate hands Jesus over to "the Jews" to be crucified (19:16a).

The reader is aware that a violent end to Jesus' life has been in the making from the earliest days of his ministry. Yet Jesus has spoken of the need for the Son of Man to be lifted up on several occasions (see 3:14; 8:28; 12:32). Jesus has also looked forward to this moment, associated with the "lifting up," as his glorification. At the Feast of Tabernacles the narrator informed the reader that the Spirit had not yet been given because Jesus had not yet been glorified (7:39). In 11:4 he informed his disciples that the illness of Lazarus would lead to the revelation of the glory of God and that the Son would be glorified through it. Further words of Jesus have indicated that such would be the case (see 12:16, 23; 13:31-32; 17:1). The reader is asked to accept that the crucifixion that must now follow will be a moment of royal glory. The reader looks forward to the resolution of a prolepsis that has been gathering from Jesus' first days. There can be no further postponement of the lifting up of Jesus (see 3:14; 8:28; 12:32), of the hour of his glorification (see 12:23), his enthronement as "King of the Jews."

4. The Crucifixion of Jesus (19:16b-37)
The scene is set at the place of the skull, or Golgotha (v. 17b), and the characters are introduced: Jesus, handed over by Pilate to "the Jews" (v. 16b),[53] carrying the cross, "the sole master of his destiny" (v. 17a).[54] He is crucified at Golgotha between two others. The Synoptic Gospels record that the two were bandits (see Matt 27:38; Mark 15:27) or evildoers (see Luke 23:39-43). This is not said in the Johannine narrative.

---

[52] Many scholars point to the chiastic nature of 18:28—19:16. See, e.g., Brown, *John*, 2:858–59; Stibbe, *John*, 187 But however obvious chiasms are to the scholar, readers do not read in chiasms. Senior, *Passion*, 68–71, warns against overplaying the chiasm, to the detriment of the linear "dynamism of the narrative" (69).

[53] "The Jews" were the ones who cried out that he be crucified in v. 15, to whom Jesus is "handed over," in v. 16 They are the subject of *parelabon* in v. 16b. See Senior, *Passion*, 101–2; Heil, *Blood and Water*, 84. Brown, *Death*, 1:856–57, insists that it is the Roman soldiers of v. 23.

[54] Brown, *John*, 2:917.

The narrator shows no interest in why two other people were being executed, but indicates that Jesus, now crucified, occupies a central place between them (*kai met' autou allous duo enteuthen, kai enteuthen meson de ton lēsoun*). The reader, who has waited so long for the event of the "lifting up" of Jesus finds it described in the briefest terms (v. 18b: *auton estaurōsan*). The narrator does not dwell on the bloody reality of a Roman crucifixion, but after making Jesus the centerpiece of a triptych of crucified people, moves immediately to the issue of the title on the cross: "Jesus of Nazareth the King of the Jews" (v. 19). Pilate continues to insist on Jesus' kingship, in Hebrew, Latin, and Greek (v. 20b), the languages of the "cultured world" of the Roman Empire. The kingship of Jesus is proclaimed universally and can be read by all who pass by (v. 20a). The multilingual proclamation of the crucified Jesus as King is the first indication to the reader that the theme of Jesus' drawing everyone to himself (see 10:16; 11:49-52; 12:32) is coming to a climax. "The Jews," as throughout the public ministry, reject this proclamation of the truth. But Pilate will not allow it to be changed, because what he has written, he has written. (vv. 21-22).

Romans (*hoi stratiōtai*) continue to play a role as they divide Jesus' garments into four parts but cast lots for the seamless inner garment so that it won't be torn asunder (vv. 23-24). Scripture is fulfilled as the soldiers do as Ps 22:19 had foretold.[55] But why this insistence on the fact that the intimate inner garment of Jesus is not to be torn asunder?[56] Is there something precious that belongs to Jesus whose unity must be maintained? The reader, coming from 17:20-26, is aware that Jesus has asked his Father to preserve the unity of his own and all those who will hear his word through their ministry so that the world might know that God has sent his Son and that God loves the world just as he loves his Son. The passion story has already told of Jesus' demand that his disciples be allowed to leave the garden freely (see 18:8-9), with a direct reference from the narrator back to Jesus' final prayer (see 17:12). Jesus has instructed his Jewish interrogators that they must ask *tous akēkootas* if they wish to know his *didachē* (see 18:21). Is this garment that cannot be torn apart, even when it falls

[55] See A Obermann, *Die christologische Erfüllung der Schrift im Johannesevangelium: Eine Untersuchung zur johanneischen Hermeneutik anhand der Schriftzitate* (WUNT 2/83; Tubingen: J. C. B. Mohr, 1996) 282–97, who suggests that 19:24 indicates that Jesus fulfills the psalm (LXX Ps 21:19) in his experience of rejection by God

[56] The clothes in general are called *ta himatia*, but this garment is called *ho chitōn*, a "tunic," an inner garment. On this, see Brown, *Death*, 2.955–56.

into the hands of Jesus' crucifiers, a symbol of the disciples, the ones who have heard what Jesus said—that is, the community of his disciples? The reader suspects that such may be the case.[57]

From his throne on the cross, Jesus speaks to the woman who was the first to commit herself unconditionally to his word (see 2:3-5),[58] and commands her to see (ide) the Beloved Disciple and to accept him as her son. He then turns to the Beloved Disciple, by now clearly indicated for the reader as the model disciple who has lain close to the breast of Jesus at the Last Supper (see 13:23), and commands him to see (ide) the mother of Jesus and to accept her as his mother.[59] Jesus' words are unquestioningly obeyed, as the narrator comments: *kai ap' ekeinas tēs hōras elaben ho mathētēs autēn eis ta idia.* The cross is "the hour of Jesus" (see 12:23; 13:1; 17:1), and there is a play of two possible meanings in *ap' ekeinas tēs hōras*. On the one hand, it has a temporal meaning: "from that particular time." But on the other, the

---

[57] There is a long and strong patristic interpretation of the passage in this sense. See, for a survey, M. Aubineau, "La tunique sans couture du Christ: Exégèse patristique de Jean 19:23-24," in *Kyriakon: Festschrift Johannes Quasten,* P. Grandfield and J. A. Jungmann, eds. (2 vols; Munster: Aschendorf, 1970) 1:100–127. See especially Cyprian, *De unitate ecclesiae,* 7 (PL 4:520–21), and Augustine, *In Joannem,* 118:4 (PL 35:1949). See also de la Potterie, *The Hour,* 124–32; B. G. Schuchard, *Scripture Within Scripture: The Interrelationship of Form and Function in the Explicit Old Testament Citations in the Gospel of John* (SBLDS 133; Atlanta: Scholars, 1992) 127–32. See the nuanced survey of the discussion, concluding that the communitarian interpretation is possible, in Brown, *Death,* 2:955–58. See also B. W. Longenecker, "The Unbroken Messiah· A Johannine Feature and Its Social Functions," *NTS* 41 (1995) 433–34. Against Schnackenburg, *St John,* 3:274, who points to the fact that Jesus' garment is taken from him, and is to be linked with Jesus' laying aside of his garments in 13:4, and the use of Josephus, *Antiquities* 3.161, to claim that there is reference to a priestly garment. See also Heil, *Blood and Water,* 89–92; idem, "Unique High Priest," 741–44, who broadens the discussion by more Old Testament and Jewish background, and by situating it at the conclusion of a number of other "high priestly" episodes. R. Kysar, *John* (Augsburg Commentary on the New Testament; Minneapolis: Augsburg, 1986) 288, rightly points out that clear signals to the right interpretation of the passage are missing. The reader must proceed further into the story to discover its significance within the context of the Johannine passion account.

[58] See, on the faith of the mother of Jesus in 2:3-5, Moloney, *Belief,* 80–85. R. G. Maccini, *Her Testimony is True: Women as Witnesses according to John* (JSNTSS 125; Sheffield; Sheffield Academic Press, 1996) 184–206, argues against this. He claims that she is one of four female witnesses at the cross. Attention is devoted to the relationship between 2:1-11 and 19:25-27 (see 191–99), but insufficient consideration is given to the ecclesial nature of the immediate narrative context.

[59] On 19:25-27 as a revelatory moment in the Fourth Gospel, see M. de Goedt, "Un Schème de Révélation dans le Quatrième Évangile," *NTS* 8 (1961–62) 145–50.

theological and dramatic significance of "the hour of Jesus" leads the reader to understand it as causal: "because of that hour."[60] As a result of the lifting up of Jesus on the cross, the Beloved Disciple and the mother of Jesus become one. The disciple leads the mother *eis ta idia*. The situation described in the prologue, where the Word came *eis ta idia* but was not received (*ou parelabon*), has now been reversed. Because of the cross, and from the moment of the cross, a new family of Jesus has been created. The mother of Jesus, a model of faith, and the disciple whom Jesus loved and held close to himself are one as the disciple accepts the mother (*elaben . . . autēn*). There have been exaggerated Mariological claims made for this passage,[61] but the reader of the Johannine story concludes that at the cross and because of the cross the lifted up Son of Man has established a new family.[62] The promise of the "gathering" that has been emerging from the closing scenes of Jesus' public ministry (see 10:16; 11:49-52; 12:11, 19, 20-24, 32-33) has been achieved as a new family is founded at the cross of the crucified King.[63]

The reader next encounters a series of statements that indicate fulfillment and perfection. Jesus knows that he has come to the end of his life (v. 28, *ēdē panta tetelestai*). The reader recalls the words of 13:1: "When Jesus knew that his hour had come to depart out of this world to the Father, having loved his own who were in the world, he loved them *to the end* [*eis telos*]." To fulfill (*hina teleiōthę̄*) the Scriptures, he cries out in his thirst and is assuaged with vinegar on "hyssop" (*hyssō-pǭ*).[64] He has drunk the cup the Father gave him (see 18:11), and there is a possible link with Jesus' role as the Passover Lamb in the explicit

---

[60] For this causal meaning of "because of" for *apo* with the genitive, see BDF, 113, para. 210.

[61] For surveys see R. F. Collins, "Mary in the Fourth Gospel—A Decade of Johannine Studies," *Louvain Studies* 3 (1970) 99–142; Senior, *Passion*, 108–13; Brown, *Death*, 2: 1019-26.

[62] Hoskyns, *Fourth Gospel*, 530. See also M. Gorgues, "Marie, la 'femme' et la 'mère' en Jean," *NRT* 108 (1986) 174–91; Koester, *Symbolism*, 214–19; Heil, *Blood and Water*, 94–98; S. Boguslazwski, "Jesus' Mother and the Bestowal of the Spirit," *IBS* 14 (1992) 106–29; J. Zumstein, "L'interprétation johannique de la mort du Christ," in F. van Segbroeck, C. M. Tuckett, G. van Belle and J. Verheyden, eds., *The Four Gospels 1992: Festschrift Frans Neirynck* (3 vols, BETL 100; Leuven: Leuven Univ. Press, 1992) 3:2131.

[63] See A. Serra, *Contributi dell'Antica Letteratura Giudaica per l'Esegesi di Giovanni 2,1-12 e 19,25-27* (Scripta Pontificiae Facultatis Theologicae "Marianum" 31; Rome: Edizioni Herder, 1977) 370–429.

[64] See L. T. Witkamp, "Jesus' Thirst in John 19:28-30: Literal or Figurative?" *JBL* 115 (1996) 492–502.

reference to "hyssop." Exod 12:22–23 instructs the Israelites to sprin-
kle their lintels by using a "hyssop" at the moment of the Exodus.[65]
There may also be an echo of LXX Ps 68, already used in 2:17 and
15:25, as Jesus said—to fulfill Scripture—"I thirst" (see LXX Ps
68:22).[66] Climaxing all these indications of fulfillment, Jesus cries out,
tetelestai ("It is finished"). This is an exclamation of achievement, almost of triumph. The task given to him by his Father (see 4:34; 5:36;
17:4), has now been consummately concluded.[67] He has now brought
everything to its perfect conclusion, and the narrator confirms this for
the reader by filling in a further consequence of the death of Jesus:
"He bowed his head and *paredōken to pneuma*" (v. 30). The reader recalls that earlier the Spirit had not yet been given because Jesus had
not yet been glorified (see 7:39). Now the Spirit is poured out. If the
seamless robe was a symbol of the church and if the gift of mother to
son, and son to mother, foreshadowed the unity of love and faith that
is the *ecclesia* of God, then it is upon that tiny church that the Spirit
is poured. The words of the narrator are not a euphemism for death.
The text does not say that Jesus gave up his spirit (RSV, NRSV, JB, NJB,
CEI; see, by way of contrast, Matt 27:50: *aphēken to pneuma;* Mark
15:37: *exepneusen* [par. Luke 23:46]). There is a deliberate choice of a
verb that has a primary meaning of "to hand over, to deliver, to en-
trust,"[68] and a definite article indicating "the Spirit." In bringing to
perfection the task the Father had given to him, Jesus hands over, or
entrusts, the Spirit to his new family, gathered at the foot of the Cross
(see vv. 25-27).[69]

[65] On this link, see Senior, *Passion,* 117–18; Stibbe, *John,* 196, F. G. Beetham and P. A. Beetham, "A Note on John 19:29," *JTS* 44 (1993) 163–69. R. L. Brawley, "An Absent Complement and Intertextuality in John 19:28-29," *JBL* 112 (1993) 427–43, rightly argues that more than Exod 12:22-23 may be involved in the fulfillment of scripture. He helpfully suggests that Ps 69 serves as intertext, allowing the reader to sense the fulfillment of a scripture that spoke of opposition to Jesus, at the cross and in the experience of the later community But as the psalm is an absent complement, not mentioned in the text, it makes the reader aware that "the divine power that embraces the death of Jesus remains a mystery beyond understanding" (443).

[66] On this possibility, see Obermann, *Die christologische Erfüllung,* 350–364; Witkamp, "Jesus' Thirst," 502–9.

[67] See Dauer, *Passionsgeschichte,* 20; Brown, *Death,* 2:1077–78; Koester, *Symbolism,* 193–96; R. Bergmeier, TETELESTAI Joh 19:30," *ZNW* 79 (1988) 282–90; Obermann, *Die christologische Erfüllung,* 362–63, Witkamp, "Jesus' Thirst," 489–510.

[68] See BAGD, 614, s.v. *paradidōmi.*

[69] See F. Porsch, *Pneuma und Wort: ein exegetischer Beitrag zur Pneumatologie des Johannesevangeliums* (FThSt 16; Frankfurt: J. Knecht, 1974) 327–32; Hoskyns, *Fourth Gospel,* 532; C Bampfylde, "John 19 28· A Case for a New Translation," *NovT* 11 (1969) 247–60;

The fifth and final scene at the Cross has two major elements.[70] In a first moment, the day of preparation for the Passover necessitates that the crucified be removed from their place of torture. The concern for cultic purity, evident in "the Jews'" unwillingness to enter the Praetorium in 18:28, is ironically pursued to the end of the passion story (v. 31). The two others crucified with Jesus have their legs broken, but this does not happen to Jesus. As he is already dead, his side is pierced with a lance, and blood and water flow from his pierced side (vv. 31-34). Scripture is fulfilled as the Passover Lamb is slain without a bone being broken (see Exod 12:10, 46; Num 9:12; Ps 34:20-21). Once allowance is made for the fulfillment of the Scriptures concerning the Passover Lamb,[71] this simple narrative could be no more than a reporting of facts, as everything could have taken place, even the blood and the water flowing from Jesus' side.[72] But the narrator unexpectedly launches into a personal comment that has no parallel in the rest of the Gospel story.[73] The narrator insists on personal witness and on the truthfulness of his testimony. It is important that the reader accept this witness—"that you also may believe" (v. 35). The blood and the water must mean something to the reader, and the narrator is anxious that the reader has no doubts about the fact that blood and water flowed from the crucified Jesus. Jesus has entrusted the Spirit to

Gorgues, "Marie," 187–88; Beasley-Murray, *John*, 353; de la Potterie, *The Hour*, 163–65; Heil, *Blood and Water*, 102–3; J. Swetnam, "Bestowal of the Spirit in the Fourth Gospel," *Bib* 74 (1993) 563–67.

[70] For chiastic readings of 19:17-37, see Brown, *Death*, 2:907–9; Stibbe, *John*, 193–94. Senior, *Passion*, 99–100, rightly insists on "the forward motion of the story."

[71] There may also be a reference to the righteous sufferer (see Ps 34 20-21). M J. J. Menken, "The Old Testament Quotation in John 19:36. Sources, Redaction, Background," in *The Four Gospels 1992*, 3:2101–18, shows that elements from the Psalm and the Pentateuchal texts have been combined in a way common in contemporary Jewish and Christian exegesis. Ps 34:21 is the primary text, but the addition of the Pentateuchal texts indicate the Evangelist's understanding of Jesus as *both* the righteous sufferer *and* the paschal lamb. See also M. J. J. Menken, *Old Testament Quotations in the Fourth Gospel: Studies in Textual Form* (CBET 15; Kampen: Kok Pharos, 1996) Menken, 147–66.

[72] For explanations of the blood and water, see J. Wilkinson, "The Incident of the Blood and Water in John 19.34," *SJT* 28 (1975) 149–72.

[73] The concluding words of 20:30-31 come close, but they are to be expected as the story comes to its solemn conclusion. The narrator's direct addressing of the reader in 19:35 occupies no such place in the story and comes as a surprise to the reader Many scholars have linked it with 21:24 and thus regard it as an editorial addition to the Gospel Once this step has been taken, there is no need to explain *why* v. 25 is in its present place, and *what it means* within that context See, e.g., Bultmann, *John*, 678; Brown, *John*, 2:945; Becker, *Johannes*, 2:600; Beasley-Murray, *John*, 354

the community; now he entrusts the blood and the water of Eucharist and Baptism.[74] The promise of Jesus' words and the narrator's comment in 7:37-39 is realized: "'If any one thirsts, let him come to me, and let the one who believes in me drink. As the scripture has said, "Out of his heart shall flow rivers of living water."'" Now this he said about the Spirit, which those who believed in him were to receive; for as yet the Spirit had not been given, because Jesus was not yet glorified." The "not yet" is "now," as Spirit (v. 30) and water (v. 34) are given to the community of Jesus' disciples by the crucified one.[75]

The author presupposes the reader's knowledge and experience of the "water" of Baptism (see 3:5) and the "blood" of Eucharist (see 6:53, 54, 55-56), and links them with the cross. The Johannine passion account deals both with what happened to Jesus and how this effects the community of Jesus' followers. Where is the pierced one in the life of a such a community that looks back over at least two generations to the events of Jesus' death? It is precisely the *absence* of the physical, historical Jesus to the community that lies behind the narrator's passionate intervention in v. 35. Despite his *physical* absence, Jesus is still present in the blood and the water of their community practices.[76] The narrator tells the reader that Jesus has fulfilled the Scriptures in two ways.[77] He is the perfect Paschal Lamb, as not one of his bones were broken (v. 36; see Exod 12:10; 12:46; Num 9:12). The earlier indi-

[74] See Zumstein, "L'interpétation johannique," 3:2132-33. On this passage as a late baptismal addition, see M. C. de Boer, *Johannine Perspectives on the Death of Jesus* (CBET 17, Kampen: Kok Pharos, 1976) 292-303. Rather than a sacramental reference, it is often suggested that the narrator is opposing a docetic stream in the community which claims that Jesus did not really die. See, e.g., Kysar, *John,* 292.

[75] See Thusing, *Herrlichkeit,* 50-52.

[76] This sacramental reading is often challenged. See, e.g., G. Richter, "Blut und Wasser aus der durchbohrten Seite Jesu (Joh 19,34b)," *MuTZ* 21 (1970) 1-21. C. H. Dodd, *The Interpretation of the Fourth Gospel* (Cambridge: Cambridge Univ. Press, 1953) 428, claims that the blood and water from the side of Jesus is a "sign" of the life that flows from the crucified and risen Christ. Attention must be given to the fact that it is from the crucified Jesus that the water and blood flow. The members of the new family of Jesus receive life from the pierced one, upon whom they will gaze (see 19:37); and this "life" includes Eucharist and Baptism, where the absent one is present to them. See Heil, *Blood and Water,* 105-13.

[77] See Brown, *Death,* 2:1184-88; Schuchard, *Scripture Within Scripture,* 133-40. For Pancaro, *Law,* 331-363, not only is there a literal fulfillment of biblical prophecies, but Jesus' death as the Son of God can be regarded as *kata ton nomon.* See also Schuchard, *Scripture Within Scripture,* 140. For Obermann, *Die christologische Erfüllung,* 298-310 (19:36), 311-25 (19:37), the Johannine community both looks to the Scriptures as a source for understanding Jesus, and recognizes that its members are the privileged recipients of the fulfillment of Scripture.

cations of John the Baptist, that Jesus was the Lamb of God (see 1:29, 35), are brought to their conclusion here. Second, despite his absence, the community of his disciples of all generations will be able to rediscover the presence of the absent one and thus gaze upon the one whom they have pierced (v. 37; see Zech 12:10).[78] God has been revealed in the pierced one, and this revelation of God continues in the flowing water and the spilled blood of Baptism and Eucharist. Thus, the worshiping community experiences the presence of the absent one. The urgency of this question for a community that no longer sees Jesus has led to the intervention of the narrator in v. 35: "He who saw it has borne witness—his testimony is true, and he knows that he tells the truth—*that you also may believe.*"

5. Jesus in a Garden with His Friends (19:38-42)
The story of Jesus' burial, told in gentler tones by the narrator, closes the passion story and points the reader to events that will take place beyond Jesus' tomb. The narrator links these closing events with all that has gone before (v. 38: *meta de tauta*): a community founded at the cross comes to life. Two characters emerge, one of whom is known to the reader: Nicodemus. He had earlier come to Jesus by night for fear of "the Jews" (see 3:1). As the other figure is not known to the reader, he is introduced by the narrator as another secret disciple of Jesus due to his fear of "the Jews." Both of these *secret* disciples of Jesus now become *public.*[79] Joseph of Arimathea goes to the person who had handed over Jesus to be crucified and successfully asks for Jesus' body. Nicodemus brings a very large quantity of myrrh and aloes (vv. 38-39). Together they anoint and bind Jesus' body in a way that is unknown to the Synoptic tradition. Jesus, proclaimed and crowned as a king before Pilate (18:28—19:16a), further proclaimed as a king by the sign on the cross (19:19-22), and who acted as a king in founding a new people of God from the cross (vv. 25-27), is anointed with an exaggeratedly large quantity of spices, bound in burial cloths, and placed in a new tomb. He is buried as a king (vv. 40-42).[80] But the

---

[78] This interpretation reads "they" who shall gaze upon the pierced one as the Johannine community and all who will later believe through them. See Schnackenburg, *St John*, 3:292–94; Dauer, *Passionsgeschichte*, 277; Senior, *Passion*, 127–29; Obermann, *Die christologische Erfüllung*, 320–23, and especially Menken, *Old Testament Quotations*, 167–85.

[79] This may be an encouragement for the so-called crypto-Christians (see 7:13; 9:22; 12:42-43). See Brown, *Death*, 2:1265–68.

[80] See Schnackenburg, *St John*, 3:296–97; Brown, *John*, 2:259–60; Senior, *Passion*, 130–33. Against those who read Nicodemus's gesture as indicating that he has not pro-

reader finds that these events take place in a garden (v. 41: *ēn . . . hopou . . . kēpos*), and recalls that the passion story began in a garden (see 18:1: *hopou ēn kēpos*).[81] There, however, Jesus encountered his enemies alone, betrayed by Judas and misunderstood by Peter (18:1-5, 10-11).

CONCLUSION

The reader is aware of close links between the first and final scenes (18:1-11; 19:38-42), where the same garden location witnesses a significant reversal made possible by the events that have happened during the passion story. The second scene, Jesus' interrogation by "the Jews," is framed by Peter's denials (18:12-27). It points to the future community of disciples, who had heard what Jesus had said, as the place where Jesus' teaching could now be found. This reference to the community is matched by the description of Jesus' crucifixion and death (19:16b-37): the royal moment of lifting up, the gathering, and the foundation of a community of faith and love. In death Jesus perfects all that he was sent to do, giving the Spirit and the blood and water that flowed from the side of the pierced one. The God who so loved the world that he gave his only Son (see 3:16) is now revealed to all who gaze upon the one who has laid down his life for his friends, the greatest gesture of love possible (see 15:13). The central scene (18:28—19:16a) stands alone. It is devoted to Jesus' proclamation and coronation as King, and the ironic judgment of those who appear to be judging. They show by word and deed that they do not belong to the truth. Many of the prolepses of the narrative have now been resolved: the lifting up (see 3:14; 8:28; 12:32), "the hour" (see 2:4; 7:6; 30; 8:20; 13:1; 17:1; 19:27), the gift of the Spirit (see 7:37-39), the

---

gressed beyond the limited faith he displayed in 3:1-11. See, e.g., Rensberger, *Johannine Faith*, 40, Duke, *Irony*, 110. For D. D. Sylva, "Nicodemus and His Spices," *NTS* 34 (1988) 148–51, the binding and the spices indicate that Nicodemus has no understanding of the possibility of a life after death. See 150–51, nn. 7, 12, for a comprehensive survey of scholarly opinion on Nicodemus' actions in the burial scene. Overstatements of the significance of the reception of the body of Jesus by Nicodemus, with possible eucharistic hints, are found in J. N. Suggit, "Nicodemus—The True Jew," *Neot* 14 (1981) 90–110, B. Hemelsoet, "L'ensevelissement selon Jean," in *Studies in John: Presented to Professor Dr. J. N. Sevenster on the Occasion of His Seventieth Birthday* (NovTSupp 24; Leiden: Brill, 1970) 47–65, J.-M. Auwers, "Le Nuit de Nicodème (Jean 3,2; 19 39) ou l'ombre du langage," *RB* 97 (1990) 481–503.

[81] There is a Jewish, patristic and scholarly association of "the garden" with Paradise and the crucified Jesus as a new Adam. See F. Manns, *L'Evangile de Jean à la lumière du Judaisme* (SBFA 33; Jerusalem: Franciscan Printing Press, 1991) 401–29.

revelation of a God who so loved the world that he gave his only Son (see 3:16).[82] The crucified Jesus has been proclaimed as King (see 18:28—19:16a) and has exercised his royal authority (19:16b-37). He has brought to completion the task given him by the Father (see 4:34; 17:4; 19:28-30). He has revealed the glory of God (see 11:4; 13:31-32; 17:1-5), and in doing so he has himself been glorified (see 11:4; 12:23).[83] The promise of the gift of the Spirit-Paraclete, which was not to take place until Jesus was glorified through his departure, returning to the Father by death (see 14:16-18; 15:26; 16:7), has now been fulfilled (see 19:30).

In the light of the farewell discourse (13:1—17:26), however, there are other prolepses that are partially resolved for the *reader in the story*. They require a time beyond the life and death of Jesus for their complete resolution and can only be resolved by the *reader of the story*. The "gathering" of all people around the one lifted up from the earth (see 10:16; 11:51-52; 12:11, 19, 32) has its beginnings in the foundation of a new community of faith and love at the foot of the cross (19:25-27), nourished by the blood and water that flow from the side of the pierced one (see 6:27; 19:31-37). Despite the ongoing frailty of those who have heard the word of Jesus, always capable of denying him (Peter) and betraying him (Judas), they are now the bearers of Jesus' teaching (see 18:12-27), cleansed by the word (see 13:10; 15:3), entrusted to the care of the Father (17:11-12), chosen and sent (13:18-20).[84] Their fragility has not disappeared. Indeed, Jesus' choice and sending of them is a further indication of a love that reveals God (13:19). These fragile disciples—no matter how much they have failed—are challenged to love as he has loved (13:34-35; 15:12-17) so that they might be swept into the oneness of love that unites the Father and the Son (see 14:23; 15:9-11; 16:26-27; 17:24-26). Gazing upon the one whom they have pierced, future generations of believers will see the revelation of the glory of God and the glorified Jesus (see 19:37). In Jesus' absence they will always have the Paraclete, the Spirit of Truth (14:16-17; 16:7), who will teach them and call to their remembrance all that Jesus has taught them (14:26). The Spirit will witness to Jesus, along with Jesus' disciples, in his absence (15:26-27),

---

[82] For a summary of the proleptic nature of the early part of the Gospel, which looks toward the death of Jesus for its resolution, see Zumstein, "L'interprétation johannique," 3·2119–27. On the cross as the manifestation of God's love, see Koester, *Symbolism*, 196–200

[83] See Knoppler, *Die theologia crucis*, 154–83.

[84] See Koester, *Symbolism*, 214–19.

laying bare the falseness of a world that has become an end unto itself
(16:8-10) and continuing the revelation of God initiated by Jesus
(16:12-15). There is an in-between time filled by the presence of the
"other Paraclete," during which the followers of Jesus confidently
await the fulfillment of another of his promises: "I will come again
and will take you to myself, that where I am you may be also" (14:3).
Jesus has told the story of God (see 1:18), but the reader is aware that
the cross is not the end of his story. A community of his disciples, the
founding group for a later community, is reading this particular version of Jesus' story (see 17:20). They are divided (see 6:60-71), hated,
excluded, and even slain (see 15:18—16:3). A story of suffering and
death that is at the same time *doxa*, addresses this situation.[85] Yet despite the sense of completion the passion story provides for the reader,
some questions remain unresolved.

[85] See Zumstein, "L'interprétation johannique," 3:2134–38.

Chapter Seven

A Journey Completed
John 20:1-31

THE JOHANNINE STORY *of Jesus* has come to a satisfying conclusion on the cross as Jesus perfects the task given him by the Father (see 4:34; 5:36; 17:4; 19:30). His exaltation and the revelation of the glory of God take place on the cross. But the story *of the disciples,* the other major characters in the story, is unresolved. Despite Jesus' challenging final discourse and prayer and his promise of the Paraclete who will be with them throughout the in-between time, they languish in misunderstanding (see 16:17-18, 29-31). They will not survive in the hostile world unless the holy Father of Jesus (see 17:11a) looks after them (17:11b-16) and makes them holy (17:17-19). The passion narrative has reinforced this presentation of the disciples. Judas has betrayed Jesus (see 18:1-5) and Peter has resorted to violence (see 18:8-11). Like Judas, Peter stands with Jesus' opponents (see 18:5, 18, 25), and denies any knowledge of him (vv. 15-18, 25-27). Yet as the passion story opens, Jesus' earlier words are recalled: "Of those whom you gave me I lost not one" (18:9. See 17:12). The first signs of the future role of the disciples appear as the Beloved Disciple is at the cross (see 19:25-27), and Nicodemus and Joseph of Arimathea emerge from the darkness for Jesus' burial (see 19:38-42). But the reader looks forward to a further resolution of the story of the larger group of the disciples who have been with Jesus from the beginnings of the narrative (see 1:35-51; 2:11).

153

The opening pages of this story of Jesus were highlighted by a hymn and a narrative that dealt with who Jesus is (1:1-18) and how one might respond to him (1:19—4:54). The story of the passion and death of Jesus has brought the story *of Jesus* to a close: The light has shone in the darkness, but the darkness has not overcome it (see 1:5). What of *the disciples'* response to Jesus? What of the response of *the readers* of the Gospel?[1] The implied reader recalls that, following the first disciples' hesitant and partial attempts to express their belief in him (1:35-51), there were stories dealing with a variety of responses to Jesus, the Word become flesh (see 1:14): the mother of Jesus (2:1-12), "the Jews" (2:13-25), Nicodemus (3:1-21), John the Baptist (3:22-36), the Samaritan woman (4:1-38), the Samaritan villagers (4:39-42), and the royal official (4:43-54).[2] It could be said that the Gospel of John *began* with a series of faith journeys through which various characters responded to Jesus in different ways. How does it close? The reader has become accustomed to the author's practice of opening and closing large sections of the narrative in a parallel fashion (see, e.g., 1:1-5 // 1:18; 2:1-12 // 4:43-54; 13:1-38 // 17:1-26; 18:1-11 // 19:38-42) and would not be surprised to find that this story ends by looking back to its beginning. It is often pointed out that the narrator's final words (20:30-31) look back to the first words of the book, which also came from the narrator (1:1-18),[3] but does the contact cease there? The *first reported episodes* of Jesus' life highlighted a journey of faith (1:19—4:54), and the reader might suspect that the *final reported episodes* will return to this theme.

THE SHAPE OF THE NARRATIVE

Scholars acknowledge that John 20:1-29, which leads to the concluding remarks of the narrator in vv. 30-31, is concerned with the theme of belief.[4] This closing narrative appears to have been constructed

[1] On the various readers of a text, see R. M Fowler, "Who is 'The Reader' in Reader-Response Criticism?" *Sem* 31 (1985) 5–23. On the Fourth Gospel, see C. R. Koester, "The Spectrum of Johannine Readers," in F. F. Segovia, ed., *"What is John?" Readers and Readings of the Fourth Gospel* (SS 3; Atlanta: Scholars, 1996) 5–19

[2] On this, see F J Moloney, *Belief in the Word: Reading John 1–4* (Minneapolis: Fortress Press, 1993); for a summary, see 192–99.

[3] Literary and theological links between 1:1-18 and 20:30-31 have often been noticed. See, most recently, G. Mlakuzhyil, *The Christological Literary Structure of the Fourth Gospel* (AnBib 117; Rome: Biblical Institute Press, 1987) 137–43, 238–40.

[4] See the following sample of works dedicated specifically to the resurrection stories: P. Seidensticker, *Die Auferstehung Jesu in der Botschaft der Evangelisten* (SBS 26; Stuttgart

from traditions associated with the resurrection: a woman at an empty tomb (20:1-2), appearances to individuals and to the disciples as a group (see vv. 11-18; 19-23), a command to women to announce the risen Jesus (see v. 17), and a missionary commission (see vv. 21-23). But these traditions have been thoroughly Johannized. Only Mary Magdalene is at the empty tomb, and she alone is commanded to announce the risen Lord. The missionary commission of John 20:21-23 is unlike Matt 28:16-20 or Luke 24:44-49.[5] The narrative of the disciples' running to the tomb may come from the same traditions that produced Luke 24:12 and 24,[6] the encounter with Mary Magdalene may be the Johannization of the Matthean report of Jesus' encounter with the women returning from the empty tomb (Matt 28:8-10), and the story of the doubting Thomas may be the dramatization of the theme of doubt that marks all the Synoptic resurrection stories (see Matt 28:8, 17; Mark 16:8; Luke 24:10-11, 19-24, 37-43; see also Mark 16:14).[7]

Valuable as analyses of the history of the passage are,[8] the present form of John 20 and its use of place, time, and characters indicate that

---

Katholisches Bibelwerk, 1968) 107–44; C. F Evans, *Resurrection and The New Testament* (SBT 2/12; London: SCM, 1970) 118–26, G. Ghiberti, *I racconti pasquali del capitolo 20 di Giovanni* (SB 19; Brescia: Paideia, 1972) 21–50, X. Léon-Dufour, *Resurrection and the Message of Easter* (London: Geoffrey Chapman, 1974) 169–90; R Fuller, *The Formation of the Resurrection Narratives* (London: SPCK, 1972) 133–45; D. Mollat, "La foi pascale selon le chapitre 20 de l'Évangile de Jean. Essai de théologie biblique," in *Etudes johanniques* (Paris: Editions du Seuil, 1979) 165–84; U. Wilckens, *Resurrection: An Historical Examination and Explanation* (Edinburgh: The Saint Andrew Press, 1977) 50–54; J H. Neyrey, *The Resurrection Stories* (Zacchaeus Studies. New Testament; Wilmington, Del.: Michael Glazier, 1988) 61–83; I. de la Potterie, "Genèse de la foi pascale d'après Jn 20," *NTS* 30 (1984) 26–49; R. E. Brown, "The Resurrection in John 20—A Series of Diverse Reactions," *Worship* 64 (1990) 194–206; F. Blanquart, *Le premier jour. Étude sur Jean 20* (LD 146; Paris: Cerf, 1992).

[5] See P. Perkins, *Resurrection: New Testament Witness and Contemporary Reflection* (Garden City, N. Y.. Doubleday, 1984) 169–80; G. Ludemann, *The Resurrection of Jesus History, Experience, Theology* (trans J. Bowden; London: SCM, 1994) 151–65.

[6] This question is complicated by textual doubts over Luke 24:12, a "Western non-interpolation." There is, however, growing support for its originality. See the full discussion in R. Mahoney, *Two Disciples at the Tomb: The Background and Message of John 20,1-10* (TW 6; Bern: Herbert Lang, 1974) 41–69 Mahoney decides against its originality. See Ludemann, *Resurrection*, 138–39, for a good summary of the case for its acceptance.

[7] See G. J Riley, *Resurrection Reconsidered: Thomas and John in Controversy* (Minneapolis: Fortress Press, 1995) 100–7

[8] See, e.g., B. Lindars, "The Composition of John XX," *NTS* 7 (1960–61) 142–47, G. Hartmann, "Die Vorlage der Osterbericht in Joh 20," *ZNW* 55 (1974) 197–220; Ghiberti, *I racconti pasquali*, 51–141; B. Rigaux, *Dio l'ha risuscitato: Esegesi e teologia biblica* (Parola di Dio 13; Roma: Edizioni Paoline, 1976) 292–95, 328–29, A. Dauer, "Zur Her-

there has been a careful plotting of the story. The structural importance of these narrative features can be seen in the following scheme.[9]

1. Verses 1-18: Scenes at the Tomb.
Two sets of characters are involved in these scenes: the two disciples who run to the tomb and Mary Magdalene. The events take place "on the first day of the week" (20:1).

a. Verses 1-10: Visits to the Empty Tomb   vv. 1-2: Mary Magdalene establishes the inexplicable emptiness of the tomb.

verses 3-10: Peter and the Beloved Disciple hasten to the tomb, find it empty, and the Beloved Disciple comes to faith (v. 8). The episode closes with an indication that this is not the end of possible journeys of faith (v. 9).

b. Verses 11-18: Jesus Appears to Mary Magdalene   vv. 11-13: Mary Magdalene looks into the tomb, but does not repeat the experience of the Beloved Disciple.

verses 14-18: The appearance of Jesus to Mary Magdalene leads her from no faith to a conditioned faith, until she finally accepts his command, returning to the disciples to announce: "I have seen the Lord" (v. 18).

---

kunft der Thomas-Perikope Joh 20,24–29," in H. Merklein and J. Lange, eds., *Biblische Randbemerkungen: Schulerfestschrift für Rudolf Schnackenburg zum 60. Geburtstag* (Wurzburg: Echter Verlag, 1974) 56–76, T Lorenzen, *Resurrection and Discipleship: Interpretive Models, Biblical Reflections, Theological Consequences* (Maryknoll: Orbis, 1995) 168–73.

[9] See the similar suggestion in R. E. Brown, *The Gospel according to John* (2 vols.; AB 29, 29A; Garden City, N.Y.. Doubleday, 1966–70) 2:965; S. M Schneiders, "John 20:11-18: The Encounter of the Easter Jesus with Mary Magdalene—A Transformative Feminist Reading," in F. F. Segovia, ed., *"What is John?"* 157. Some attempt to structure the account chiastically. See L. Dupont, C. Lash, and G. Levesque, "Recherche sur la structure de Jean 20," *Bib* 54 (1973) 482–98; I. de la Potterie, *The Hour of Jesus: The Passion and Resurrection of Jesus according to John: Text and Spirit* (Slough, England: St Paul Publications, 1989) 195–96; Mollat, "La foi pascale," 166–69; M. W. G. Stibbe, *John* (Readings: A New Biblical Commentary; Sheffield: JSOT Press, 1993) 200; B. Byrne, "The Faith of the Beloved Disciple and the Community in John 20," *JSNT* 23 (1985) 92; F. Manns, *L'Evangile de Jean à la lumière du Judaisme* (SBFA 33; Jerusalem: Franciscan Printing Press, 1991) 432–38. J. P. Heil, *Blood and Water: The Death and Resurrection of Jesus in John 18–21* (CBQMS 27; Washington: The Catholic Biblical Association of America, 1995) 6, 12–14, continues into 20:1-31 the pattern of six alternating scenes, each of which forms a sandwich with the following scene, has proposed: A¹: vv. 1-2; B¹: vv. 3-10; A²: vv. 11-18; B²: vv. 19-23; A³: vv. 24-25; B³: vv. 26-29. Unlike the sections in the Passion narrative, this passage closes with a coda, C: vv. 30-31.

2. Verses 19-29: Scenes in the House:
Two sets of characters again determine the shape of the narrative. Jesus appears to the disciples as a group and then to Thomas, who has joined the disciples. The two appearances, which both take place in the house, are separated by indications of a change of time: "On the evening of that day, the first day of the week" (v. 19) and "eight days later" (v. 26).

a. Verses 19-23: Jesus Appears to the Disciples   On the evening of the same day, Jesus appears to the disciples amid great joy. He gives them the Holy Spirit and the commission to forgive and retain sins.

b. Verses 24-29: Jesus Appears to the Disciples and to Thomas   Eight days later Jesus appears to the disciples, but the previously absent Thomas is now present. He did not share the faith and joy of the disciples, but the risen Jesus leads him from his conditioned faith until he finally proclaims: "My Lord and my God" (v. 28). Thomas is told that this moment of faith is not the end of possible journeys of faith (v. 29).

3. The End of the Story:
The narrator tells the readers, who have not seen, yet believe, that this account of the life, death, and resurrection of Jesus has been written for them that they might have life through their belief that he is the Christ, the Son of God.

The reader senses a pattern of growth across the story. In vv. 1-10 there is development in the objects seen. Mary Magdalene sees a stone that has been taken away (v. 1), the Beloved Disciple sees the linen cloths that had once encased Jesus' dead body (v. 5), and Peter sees the same linen cloths but also the napkin that had wrapped Jesus' head, lying apart from the linen cloths (vv. 6-7). Once the accounts of appearances begin (vv. 11-29), Jesus appears to an increasing number of people. He appears to a woman, Mary Magdalene (v. 14), and then to the disciples, but Thomas is absent (v. 24). Finally, he appears to all the disciples, including Thomas (v. 26). The account concludes with a universal blessing of all who will believe without seeing (v. 29).

READING THE NARRATIVE

1. Scenes at the Tomb (20:1-18)
a. Verses 1-10: Two Disciples at the Tomb   As Mary Magdalene comes to the tomb, the reader focuses on two aspects of time: the day of the

week and the time of the day. The first day of the week (v. 1a: *tē de mia tōn sabbatōn*) links the Johannine story with the earliest Christian tradition, that the tomb was found empty on the third day after Jesus' crucifixion on the day before the Passover, which that year fell on a Sabbath (see 19:31).[10] This story does not use the expression "on the third day" in its resurrection account but is at one with the tradition.[11] The indication of the time of the day (see also Mark 16:1) focuses on the fact that it was so early it was still dark (v. 1b: *prōi skotias*). This leads the reader to relate the setting of night and darkness with un-faith, as has been the case across the story (see 1:5; 3:2; 6:17; 9:4; 8:12; 11:10; 12:35, 46; 13:30; 19:39).[12] Mary Magdalene sees that the stone has been removed (*ton lithon ērmenon*) from the tomb. The use of the passive conveys a hint of the action of God for the reader.[13] The reader, aware of the tradition that Jesus was raised from the dead (see 2:22; 12:16), senses that God is acting. But Mary sees the open tomb and draws false conclusions about who is responsible for the removal of the stone.[14]

In the darkness, a setting of unfaith, Mary runs *away from the tomb* to the two most important disciples in the story: Peter (see 1:40-42; 6:8, 66-69; 13:5-11, 24, 36-38; 18:10-11, 15-18, 25-27) and the other disciple, the one whom Jesus loved (see 1:35?, 13:23-25; 18:15-16; 19:25-27).[15] On arrival she announces that the body has been taken

[10] The use of the cardinal number as an ordinal is Semitic. See BDF, para. 247, section 1, and the discussion in C. K Barrett, *The Gospel according to St John* (2d ed. London: SPCK, 1978) 562.

[11] See Brown, *John*, 2:980, R. Schnackenburg, *The Gospel according to St John* (3 vols.; HTCNT 4/1-3, London Burns & Oates, New York: Crossroad, 1968–82) 3.307–8; G Segalla, *Giovanni* (NVB; Rome. Edizioni Paoline, 1976) 462. The expression is found in 2:1, and is often interpreted there as having resurrection overtones See Moloney, *Belief*, 57–60, 77 D. A. Carson, *The Gospel according to John* (Grand Rapids· Eerdmans, 1991) 635, suggests that the use of "the first day" in all four Gospels (see Matt 28:1, Mark 16:2; Luke 24:1) presents the resurrection as "the beginning of something new." See also Blanquart, *Le premier jour*, 20–21.

[12] See, among many, R G. Maccini, *Her Testimony is True: Women as Witnesses according to John* (JSNTSS 125; Sheffield· Sheffield Academic Press, 1996) 207–8

[13] See D. Mollat, "La découverte du tombeau vide," in *Études johanniques* (Parole de Dieu; Paris: Editions du Seuil, 1979) 137–38.

[14] I. R. Kitzberger, "Mary of Bethany and Mary of Magdala—Two Female Characters in the Johannine Passion Narrative· A Feminist, Narrative-Critical Reader-Response," *NTS* 41 (1995) 564–86, links Mary of Bethany and Mary Magdalene by means of "con-figuration" and "interfigurality," in which a reader understands one character in terms of the other. See also J. H. Bernard, *A Critical and Exegetical Commentary on the Gospel according to St John* (2 vols.; ICC, Edinburgh: T & T. Clark, 1928) 2:657.

[15] This is the first time in the story that "the other disciple" has been linked with "the one whom Jesus loved." The latter expression has been added to the former in 20 2 so

away by an unnamed plural "they." She makes no suggestion of God's action or the possibility of resurrection. Further, she associates the two disciples with her lack of faith by creating another plural "we." For Mary Magdalene there are two groups involved: the "they" who have taken away (*ēran*) the corpse of the Lord[16] and the "we" who do not know (*ouk oidamen*) where they have laid it.[17] Most scholars argue that the plural *oidamen* is a remnant of an earlier tradition of other women associated with the finding of the tomb (see Matt 28:1; Mark 16:1; Luke 24:1, 10 [see Luke 8:2-3]).[18] Others suggest that it is a Semitic turn of phrase.[19] Would it not have been obvious to an author able to write such elegant passages as John 9, John 11, and John 18-19, that— whatever the source(s) may have said—this was an unpardonable error in Greek? The first person plural in v. 2 associates two other foundational figures from the Johannine story with Mary's situation of unfaith. The situation in vv. 1-2 is one of confusion and no faith, as the group of Mary Magdalene, Simon Peter, and the other disciple stand still in the darkness. Verses 1-2 "allow the view of the unbeliever to be stated."[20] A woman communicates the message of an empty tomb to the disciples, but she is an unbelieving character *with whom two disciples are intimately associated.* Thus, introduced and associated with an unbelieving Mary Magdalene, it is as unbelievers that the two disciples turn toward the tomb in v. 3.

There is a sense of a new beginning as Peter "came out" (*exēlthen oun*) with the other disciple and they "went" (*ērchonto*) toward the

---

that the reader will identify the two earlier descriptions (see 18.15-16 [the other disciple]; 13.23-26; 19:25-27 [the Beloved Disciple]) as the same disciple.

[16] Mary's description of Jesus as "the Lord" (*ton kyrion*) is to be read as a respectful title

[17] This detail may well reflect an early tradition, also found in Matt 28:11-15. The "them" and "us" language of John 20:2 reflects that situation. See also *Gospel of Peter* 5:30; Justin, *Dialogue with Trypho*, 108:2; Tertullian, *De Spectaculis* 30 (PL 1.737–738); *Apologeticus* 23 (PL 1:474). See P. Minear, "We Don't Know Where . . . Jn 20.2," *Int* 30 (1976) 125–39, who links the "we" with other "we-passages" in the Gospel (1:14, 3 11) reflecting a response of Johannine Christians to Jewish opponents

[18] See, e.g., W Bauer, *Das Johannesevangelium erklart* (3d ed ; HKNT 6; Tubingen: J C. B Mohr, 1933) 229; Maccini, *Her Testimony is True*, 208–10 For Kitzberger, "Mary of Bethany and Mary of Magdala," 564–86, on arrival at the account of Mary of Magdalene at the tomb, as well as the earlier reference to her at 19:25, the reader is also influenced by the other "Mary" who was at a tomb, Mary of Bethany, as she is portrayed in 11:1-46 and 12:1-8. The "we" in v. 2 is also a text-signal that evokes interfigurality with the Easter morning presence of other women at the empty tomb See 581–82

[19] See, e.g., R Bultmann, *The Gospel of John: A Commentary* (trans. G R. Beasley-Murray; Oxford: Blackwell, 1971) 684, n. 1.

[20] Evans, *Resurrection and the New Testament*, 120.

tomb. Initially, it is Simon Peter who leads the way, and the other disciple follows. The newness of the situation is reinforced by the reader's awareness that Mary *ran away from the tomb* to the disciples in v. 2, but the disciples' are *going toward the tomb* in v. 3. Much has been made of the running to the tomb, and it has sometimes been called a "race."[21] There is no race; rather, there is an indication that the disciples turn away from unfaith. The reader knows that God has entered the story of Jesus from the use of the passive and the reference to "the first day of the week" in v. 1. Two disciples turn their backs on the situation in which they found themselves through association with the unfaith of Mary Magdalene and move toward the place of the action of God: an empty tomb (vv. 3-4). They are now in a position of partial faith. Consistent with the priority accorded to the Beloved Disciple in 13:23-26 and 19:25-27, he is the one who arrives first at that place. The reader also knows, however, that Simon Peter is the one appointed to the position of "the Rock" (see 1:42), and that—with mixed success—he has represented other disciples on several occasions (see 6:66-69; 13:36-38; 18:10-11). The reader senses that there is a tension between these two figures. One is the disciple whom Jesus loved in a special way (see 20:2), while the other is the bearer of authority.[22] The tension is resolved as—in this situation of partial faith—the disciple whom Jesus loved demonstrates a greater urgency to come to a knowledge of the truth concerning the one who loved him, and thus arrives at the tomb before Simon Peter.[23] Although the Beloved Disciple initially followed Peter (v. 3) he arrives first at the tomb (v. 4). The two most important disciples in the Johannine story of Jesus experience unfaith (vv. 1-2) yet move away from that static situation toward the place where the action of God in Jesus can be seen (vv. 4-5).[24]

---

[21] See, e g , Bauer, *Johannesevangelium*, 229 ("Wettkampf"), and especially, S. van Tilborg, *Imaginative Love in John* (BibIntS 2; Leiden: Brill, 1993) 101–2.

[22] There is sufficient evidence within the Fourth Gospel to indicate that Simon Peter was understood as an authority and a spokesperson, however fragile he may have been. See R E Brown, K P. Donfried, and J. Reumann, eds., *Peter in the New Testament: A Collaborative Assessment by Protestant and Roman Catholic Scholars* (Minneapolis Augsburg; New York: Paulist, 1973) 129–47.

[23] Against Byrne, "Beloved Disciple," 86, who claims that "the race itself is not undertaken with any flickering of faith in the resurrection." See also 95, n. 12.

[24] R Mahoney, *Two Disciples*, 245–51, argues against any *personal* significance for Simon Peter and the Beloved Disciple, claiming that they only have a *function* within the narrative He argues that Simon Peter must establish the facts, while the Beloved Disciple, meaning disciples in general, must "see" these facts and "believe" (251–60).

Once at the tomb the other disciple stoops to look in and sees the
linen cloths (*ta othonia*). He does not enter the tomb, but waits for
Simon Peter (v. 5). As this scene began, Simon Peter led the way (v. 3).
This situation has been reversed: Simon Peter, now following the
other disciple,[25] arrives and penetrates further into the tomb. He not
only sees the *othonia*, but the napkin used to wrap Jesus' head (*to soudarion*). It is lying apart, carefully folded and placed to one side. The
reader recalls the brief description of the resurrected Lazarus, who
came forth from the tomb still wrapped in the clothing of death, his
face still covered with the *soudarion* (11:44). Not only is the tomb
empty, but the trappings of death are also empty. Lazarus was raised
from the dead, but he came forth bearing the clothing of death. The
risen Jesus has no such trappings.[26] Another use of the passive voice
(see 20:1) to indicate that the napkin that covered Jesus' head (*to soudarion*) had been folded (*entetuligmenon*) and that it was now lying to
one side separated from the cloths used to cover his body (*ta othonia*)
reinforces the reader's conviction: God has entered the story (vv. 6-
7).[27] Simon Peter enters the tomb and sees the evidence, but nothing
is said of his response. This delaying tactic leads the reader into the
climax of v. 8. The reader expects the disciples to recognize what the
reader has recognized: Jesus has been raised. The reader is reminded
of the greater urge to arrive at the tomb, which brought this disciple
there ahead of Simon Peter (v. 8a). The other disciple also sees the

[25] The description of Simon Peter as *akolouthōn autō* indicates that the Beloved Disciple must be "followed" no matter how important the follower might be.
[26] This has often been noticed. See, e.g., W. E. Reiser, "The Case of the Tidy Tomb: The
Place of the Napkins of John 11 44 and 20:7," *HeyJ* 14 (1973) 47–57, and B. Osborne, "A
Folded Napkin in an Empty Tomb· John 11:44 and 20:7 Again," *HeyJ* 14 (1973) 437–40.
The careful disposition of the cloths is probably also part of the apologetic against the
claim that the tomb was robbed. See Chrystostom, *In Joannem Homeliae* 85,4 (PG
59.465), for the early use of the Johannine text in this way.
[27] Byrne, "The Beloved Disciple," 87–89, rightly insists on the significance of the *soudarion* and its position, seen on entering the tomb, as the motive for the Beloved Disciple's faith However, he misses the divine passives, as he claims, on the basis of 10.18,
that while Lazarus was raised, Jesus "actively raised himself" (88). T L. Brodie, *The Gospel according to John. A Literary and Theological Commentary* (New York· Oxford Univ
Press, 1993) 562–63, argues, on the basis of Exod 34·33-35, that Jesus has put aside the
veil (see also S. Schneiders, "The Face Veil: A Johannine Sign," *BTB* 13 [1983] 94–97),
and on the basis of the undivided tunic in John 19:23-24, that what is seen in the tomb
suggests ascension (the veil) and unity (the clothes). J. P. Heil, *Blood and Water: The
Death and Resurrection of Jesus in John 18–21* (CBQMS 27; Washington: The Catholic
Biblical Association of America, 1995) 125, also makes a link with 19:23-24, and sees
the folded cloths as a symbol of the unity made possible by the death and resurrection
of Jesus.

vanquished signs of death: the empty tomb, the empty cloths, including the *soudarion*. The other disciple's sight of these things leads him
to faith: *kai eiden kai episteusen* (v. 8c).[28]

Paralleling the experience of several characters in the opening pages
of the Gospel who moved from no faith through partial faith to full
faith (2:1—4:54), the foundational disciple of the Johannine community and the model of Johannine discipleship has moved from no
faith (vv. 1-2) through partial faith (vv. 4-5) into the fullness of resurrection faith by seeing that God had overcome Jesus' death (vv. 7-8).
All the signs of death have been overcome. An aside from the narrator
tells the reader that as yet (*oudepō*) these disciples were not aware of
the Scripture that told that Jesus *must* rise from the dead (v. 9: *dei
auton ek nekrōn anastēnai*). The divine initiative reaches beyond the
experience of the two disciples in the narrative, now only a reported
memory for the readers of the Gospel. Two foundational disciples
have witnessed the action of God, and one of them has seen and believed.[29] But God also speaks through the Scripture: Jesus *must* rise
from the dead. The disciples do *not yet* know this truth: "As yet they
did not know the scripture."[30] They are in a "not yet" situation of
ignorance that will be overcome by a later generation of believers who

[28] Some scholars have questioned the significance of the Beloved Disciple's faith, especially in the light of v. 9 and then v 29. See, e.g., G. C. Nicholson, *Death as Departure.
The Johannine Descent-Ascent Scheme* (SBLDS 63; Chico. Scholars, 1983) 69–71, who joins
Augustine and other Fathers of the Church in seeing the disciple's belief as an acceptance of the witness of Mary Magdalene. Among others, de la Potterie, *The Hour*, 202–7,
argues that the faith of the disciple is only beginning, and has yet to be fully illumi-
nated (see v. 9) D A. Lee, "Partnership in Easter Faith: The Role of Mary Magdalene
and Thomas in John 20," *JSNT* 58 (1995) 39–40, argues that "v. 8 has no narrative
impact," and that v. 9 leaves both the Beloved Disciple and Peter in a situation of
unfaith not resolved until John 21. Brown, "John 20," 197–98, uses v 9 in support of
the great faith of the Beloved Disciple. He not only believed without seeing Jesus, but
he did not even need the help of the Scriptures.

[29] It is their significance as founding figures of the Christian community that leads to
their being singled out for this narrative, not their status as representatives of Jewish
(Peter) and Gentile (the Beloved Disciple), as Bultmann, *John*, 685, maintains. Nor do
they represent the pastoral ministry (Peter) and the prophetic ministry (the Beloved
Disciple) (A. Kragerud, *Der Lieblingsjunger in Johannesevangelium* [Hamburg: Osloer Universitatsverlag, 1959] 29–32) or the contemplative (the Beloved Disciple) and the official (Peter) faces of the church (Brodie, *John*, 563–64).

[30] It is the foundational importance of *both* Simon Peter and the Beloved Disciple that
necessitates the use of the plural verb *oudepō gar ēdeisan*. For a summary of scholarly
difficulty over this plural, see Brown, *John*, 2:987. On the prominent role of *both* disciples in the Johannine tradition, see Brown, Donfried, and Reumann, eds., *Peter*, 138–39;
M Hengel, *Die johanneische Frage: Ein Losungsversuch mit einem Beitrag zur Apokalypse von
Jorg Frey* (WUNT 67; Tubingen: J. C. B. Mohr 1993) 210–19.

will read the Scripture and recognize the revelation of God's action in the resurrection of Jesus. The Johannine narrative is itself "Scripture," but the characters *in the story* are not able to be *readers of the story*.[31] They are in a "not yet" situation as far as the *graphē* of the Johannine narrative is concerned. A later generation may not be able to penetrate the tomb and see the cloths, but it will have the Scripture, especially the Johannine story, and in every way match the faith experience of the Beloved Disciple.

The reader must not conclude that the Beloved Disciple had been given specially privileged access to a unique "sight" that made his belief superior to those who would never be able to match such an experience. The disciples did not know the "word of God" about the resurrection of Jesus from the dead, but the reader does! Having made this point, which leads the narrative away from the past and applies it to the broader worlds of the reader in the text and the readers of the text, the narrator dismisses the two disciples from the scene: they return to their homes (v. 10).[32] Both the Beloved Disciple and later generations believe without seeing *Jesus*. A later generation has no cause to lament the fact that they are living in the in-between time, in the time after Jesus' departure, and thus in his *absence*. During this time they are able to read the Scriptures under the direction of the Paraclete (see 14:25-26; 16:12-14), who will be with them until the final return of Jesus (14:16-17; see 14:2-3, 18-21). Faith motivated by the Scriptures, especially the Johannine version of the life, death, and resurrection of Jesus, matches the faith of the Beloved Disciple.[33] Those living in the absence of Jesus (see 14:2-3, 28; 16:5, 28), but in the presence of the Paraclete (see 14:16-17) have evidence that Jesus must rise from the dead (see v. 9b).

b. Verses 11-18: Mary Magdalene at the Tomb   There is no explanation for the appearance of Mary Magdalene at the tomb she had earlier

---

[31] On the Johannine understanding of its own story as *logos, graphē,* and *rhemata zōēs aiōniou,* see A. Obermann, *Die christologische Erfüllung der Schrift im Johannesevangelium: Eine Untersuchung zur johanneischen Hermeneutik anhand der Schriftzitate* (WUNT 2/83; Tübingen: J. C. B. Mohr, 1996) 109-22, especially 418-22

[32] For de la Potterie, *The Hour,* 205-7, v. 10 returns the disciples into the darkness with which the passage opened in v. 1. He regards it as a *reditus ad sua* in the sense of a turning back on themselves.

[33] See, among others, Seidensticker, *Die Auferstehung Jesu,* 122-25. The transferral of interest from the faith of the foundational disciple to the possibility of faith for future generations is missed by most commentators who attempt to identify some Old Testament references that may be implied here. Most suggest Ps 16:10. See, e g., B. F. West-

abandoned (see v. 2). The disciples have been dismissed (see v. 10), thus enabling the author to reintroduce the disconsolate Mary Magdalene into the story. Although one would expect an indication of Mary's return to the tomb, this is bypassed.[34] Another foundational character from the early Christian community (see Matt 27:56, 61; 28:1, 9-10; Mark 15:40; 16:1; Luke 8:2; 23:49, 55-56; 24:1-9, 10-11) is at center stage. Mary Magdalene and the two disciples who were dismissed from the story in v. 10 formed the "we" of v. 2, aware of the empty tomb but showing no recognition of resurrection. The reader knows that the disciples, and especially the Beloved Disciple, have gone beyond the experience of Mary, moving toward (vv. 3-4) and away from (v. 10) the empty tomb. As she returns to the stage, she is portrayed as stationary, standing still in the darkness of the unbelief she shared with them in vv. 1-2. Her tears show her continued inability to believe or understand what might have happened (v. 11a: *eistēkei pros tǭ mnēmeiǭ exǭ klaiousa*).[35] The reader recalls the faithless wailing (*klaiein*) accompanying the death of Lazarus (see 11:31, 33), which generated the deep frustration and weeping (*dakruein*) of Jesus (see 11:35).[36] Mary matches the initiative of both the Beloved Disciple (see 20:5) and Simon Peter (see v. 6), as she stoops and peers into the tomb for the first time (v. 10b). There is no mention of the cloths and the head band (see vv. 6-7). They have been replaced by two angels in white, one seated at the head and the other at the feet, in the place where Jesus had been laid (v. 11). The reader, already fully aware that God has entered the story, is not surprised by the presence of *angeloi*,[37]

---

cott, *The Gospel according to Saint John* (London: Murray, 1908) 290, M -J. Lagrange, *Evangile selon Saint Jean* (EB; Paris: Gabalda, 1927) 508–9.

[34] In almost every case the narrator in the Fourth Gospel informs the reader of the movement of characters. See, e.g., 2:1, 12, 13; 3:22; 4:3-6; 5:1; 6:1; 7:10; 8:59; 10:22; 11:5, 17, 38, 54; 12:1, 12, 36b. No doubt the present state of the text is the result of the insertion of the passage on the two disciples into what was originally a Mary Magdalene story For Kitzberger, "Mary of Bethany and Mary of Magdala," 582, the reader has supposed from the Lazarus story that Mary would come weeping to the tomb. But this is a misreading of 11.31. See F. J. Moloney, "The Faith of Martha and Mary: A Narrative Approach to John 11.17-40," *Bib* 75 (1994) 480–83.

[35] The *exō* is omitted by several manuscripts, but it should be regarded as original

[36] See F. J Moloney, *Signs and Shadows: Reading John 5–12* (Minneapolis: Fortress Press, 1996) 167–69 Against T. Okure, "The Significance Today of Jesus' Commission to Mary Magdalene," *IRM* 81 (1992) 180, and Lee, "Partnership in Easter Faith," 41, who see the weeping as revealing love and determination.

[37] On their white garments as "the symbol of the heavenly world," see Bernard, *St John*, 2:663. It is fanciful to link the angels with the cherubim at the two ends of the

and shares the sentiments of the angels' question: "Woman, why are you weeping?" (v. 13a).

Mary answers the angels with almost the same words as she used to tell the disciples of the open tomb: "They" have taken away (*ēran*) the body of Jesus, whom she calls her "Lord." There is a slight change from her earlier words. In v. 2 she associated the disciples with her lack of faith and knowledge, claiming that "we" did not know (*ouk oidamen*) where the body had been laid. Now she states, "I do not know" (*ouk oida*). The shift from the plural to the singular accurately reflects the present situation of the characters in the unfolding story. Now it is only Mary who does not know (v. 13b; see vv. 3-10). The portrayal of the depths of her unbelief is heightened as she turns to behold Jesus standing in front of her but is incapable of recognizing the figure as Jesus (v. 14).[38] Jesus repeats the question asked by the angels but adds, "Whom do you seek?" (v. 15a) recalling similar questions from earlier parts of the narrative (1:41; 18:4). The reader senses the irony as the one whom she seeks asks her whom she is seeking,[39] but her lack of faith is intensified as she mistakenly identifies Jesus as the gardener (*ho kēpouros*).[40] With deepening irony, the earlier "they" now becomes "you." Jesus, the supposed gardener, is asked where he—a representative of the violent "they" who crucified Jesus—has laid his body! The one whose body she is seeking is asked for a solution to the mystery of the empty tomb. Mary persists in her belief that the body has been "taken away" (*airein:* see vv. 2, 13; *bastazein:* 15a). She asks that she might be the one who takes away the body: "Tell me

---

mercy seat on the ark of the covenant, as does P. Simenel, "Les 2 anges de Jean 20/11-12," *ETR* 67 (1992) 71-76

[38] Mary's turning around *eis ta opisō* simply indicates that the angels are in front of Mary, and on turning around, she sees another figure. See Bernard, *St John*, 2:665.

[39] For the irony, see Kitzberger, "Mary of Bethany and Mary of Magdala," 582-83, who, like others, rightly makes a link with 1:37-38.

[40] This is perhaps the earliest literary evidence of a Jewish response to the Christian story of the resurrection that claimed that the gardener stole the body. For this suggestion, see H. von Campenhausen, "The Events of Easter and the Empty Tomb," in *Tradition and Life in the Church: Essays and Lectures in Church History* (trans. A. V Littledale London: Collins, 1968) 66-69. There is a trace of this legend in Tertullian, *De Spectaculis* 30 (PL 1:662A). E. C. Hoskyns, *The Fourth Gospel* (2d ed.; ed. F. N Davey; London: Faber & Faber, 1947) 542, sees the use of "the gardener" as a hint of "the true, life-giving ruler of the Paradise (Garden) of God." See also Blanquart, *Le premier jour*, 64-66, and the study of Jewish literature in support of this position by N. Wyatt, "'Supposing Him to Be the Gardener' (John 20,15): A Study of the Paradise Motif in John," *ZNW* 81 (1990) 21-38.

where you have laid him, and *I will take him away (kagō auton arō)"* (v. 15b). There is no suggestion of resurrection, and there is no recognition of the risen one. Mary Magdalene remains in a situation of unbelief as she concerns herself with the removal of a corpse.

Mary's unbelief has been described with considerable detail across vv. 1-2 and 11-15.[41] Her transformation, although not immediate, is reported more rapidly. Fulfilling the promise made in the Good Shepherd discourse (see 10:3, 14), Jesus calls Mary by her name: "Mariam." She turns again,[42] recognizes him, and knows him, addressing him with the Aramaic name used throughout Jesus' ministry, attaching the first person possessive ending, *Rabbouni:* "my master" (v. 17; see 1:38, 49; 3:2; 4:31; 6:25; 9:2; 11:8).[43] The first (1:38) and the last (20:16) appearances of this title in the story are followed by implicit commentary from the narrator: "which means teacher." The reader recognizes that Mary has made a partial confession of faith. She recognizes Jesus as the Rabbi whom she had known throughout his ministry. "Both by her address to Jesus as a teacher, and physical contact, she is trying to recapture the past."[44] Like Nicodemus and the Samaritan woman, used to exemplify the journey of faith at the beginning of the story (3:1-21; 4:16-26), Mary Magdalene has arrived at a partial faith, a belief in the Jesus who best responded to her present hopes and needs.[45]

Associated with this confession is a desire to cling to Jesus. Jesus' words "do not cling to me" (*mē mou aptou*), instruct her that she must desist from her attempt to reestablish the relationship she once had with him.[46] The hour is still in progress, and Jesus not only forbids

[41] See also Schneiders, "John 20:11-18," 161–62.

[42] There is no call for symbolic readings of this second "turning." See B. Lindars, *The Gospel of John* (NCB, London Oliphants, 1972) 606.

[43] *Miryam* is Aramaic. Thus the name Jesus calls Mary and her response *"Rabboni"* are Greek transliterations of Aramaic, although the narrator informs the reader that it is Hebrew (v. 16). There is a level of intimacy implied by the recourse to an original language in both the naming and the response. See Maccini, *Her Testimony is True,* 212–13. Some mistakenly argue that *Rabboni* is quasi-divine. See, e.g., J. Marsh, *Saint John* (PNTC; Harmondsworth Penguin, 1968) 637, Westcott, *St John,* 292.

[44] Barrett, *St John,* 565.

[45] Against those who regard this expression as an authentic declaration of faith. See e g , Hoskyns, *Fourth Gospel,* 542; Marsh, *St John,* 633, 636–37; Rigaux, *Dio l'ha risuscitato,* 324–25, Schneiders, "John 20:11-18," 162–64. A. Feuillet, "La recherche du Christ dans la Nouvelle Alliance d'après la Christophanie de Jo 20,11-18," in *L'homme devant Dieu* (2 vols , ed., H. de Lubac, Paris: Aubier, 1963) 1 93–112; Stibbe, *John,* 205, and Okure, "Jesus' Commission," 181, trace in this passage the experience of the bride seeking the spouse in the early hours of the dawn in Song of Songs 3:1-3.

[46] Bernard, *St John,* 2 671, emends the text to *mē ptoou:* "do not be afraid" (see Matt 28:10) For the translation of "do not cling to me," see BAGD, s.v *haptō,* para. 2a;

her to cling to him, but explains why all clinging should cease. In and through the cross, Jesus has revealed God and has brought to perfection the task given to him (see 4:34; 5:36; 17:4; 19:30). The disciples are yet to experience the fruits of Jesus' glorification, but the days of being associated with the historical Jesus are over. An entirely new situation is being established through the hour that is in progress. Jesus has "not yet" (*oupō*) fulfilled his promises to the disciples (see see 14:12, 28; 16:10, 28) that he would return to the Father.[47] It is about to take place.[48] But Jesus' words to Mary go further than the promises made before the hour of Jesus. Throughout the earlier part of the narrative there has been a studied avoidance of any relationship between Jesus' disciples and the Father of Jesus *as their Father*. Although the reader has been told that those who believe in Jesus have the *exousia* to become *tekna theou* (see 1:12), this has never been said to the disciples. Only Jesus is "the Son of God." Jesus' words to Mary indicate that this situation is about to change. He is ascending to the Father (v. 17a), and Mary is to inform the disciples, now called Jesus' brethren (v. 17b: *tous adelphous mou*), that he is ascending *pros ton patera mou kai patera humōn kai theon mou kai theon humōn* (v. 17c). The hour of Jesus, shortly to culminate in Jesus' ascension to the Father, will create a new situation where the God and Father of Jesus will also be the God and Father of Jesus' brethren. Because of this new

---

E. Delebecque, *Evangile de Jean: Texte Traduit et Annoté* (CahRB 23, Paris· Gabalda, 1987) 210. The conflict between the prohibition of touch in v. 17 and its encouragement in v. 27 is often overplayed, as the long history of critical discussion of this matter shows The verbs are different in the two encounters (v. 17: *haptō*; v. 27ab: *pherein*, 27c *ballein*), and the significance of the touching, or clinging (my preferred reading), is entirely determined by its immediate context. "To cling" simply indicates an ongoing holding of someone See Lee, "Partnership in Easter Faith," 42 n. 10.

[47] The "not yet" of v. 17 is to be associated with the conclusion of the hour in Jesus' return to the Father. It is not to be linked with a time "later on," reflected in the Thomas episode, when it will be possible to cling to Jesus (see v. 27).

[48] The importance of the "process" of the hour is highlighted by the use of the perfect tense to indicate that Jesus has "not yet" ascended, and the present tense of Jesus' instruction to Mary concerning the report that she must make to the disciples Jesus has not yet ascended, but is in the midst of a process that will come to its conclusion once he has returned to the Father. This is what the brethren must be told See Lagrange, *Saint Jean*, 511–2; Hoskyns, *Fourth Gospel*, 542–43, G. M Burge, *The Anointed Community The Holy Spirit in the Johannine Tradition* (Grand Rapids· Eerdmans, 1987) 136–37; Maccini, *Her Testimony is True*, 214–16. Carson, *John*, 641–44, 652–54, argues that the resurrection and ascension must be kept distinct, as 20·22 is a "symbolic promise" from Jesus, assuring the disciples of the gift of the Spirit at Pentecost, see. See, however, T. R. Hatina, "John 20,22 in Its Eschatological Context: Promise or Fulfillment?" *Bib* 74 (1993) 196–219.

relationship, made possible by Jesus' passing from this world to the Father through the hour (see 13:1), they are no longer Jesus' disciples, but his brethren.[49]

Mary does exactly as Jesus commanded: She "went and said to the disciples" (v. 18a. See v. 17b). This episode began with a tearful Mary stationary at the tomb, still in the darkness of unfaith. It closes as she moves again, away from the tomb. Responding to the command of Jesus who tells her to go *pros tous adelphous mou* (v. 17), she went (*erchetai*). This renewed movement indicates to the reader that Mary has reached another stage in her journey of faith. This is confirmed by her words. In vv. 2, 13, and 15 Mary used the respectful term *ho kyrios* to speak of the dead body of the man she had followed during his public ministry. The meaning of this term is transformed as she is the first to tell the disciples of Jesus' resurrection: "I have seen the Lord [*ton Kyrion*]" (v. 18b). Her journey of faith has come full circle. From the darkness of unfaith (vv. 1-2, 11-15) she has passed through the conditioned faith that led her to recognize Jesus as her Rabbi (vv. 16-17a). She now announces that she has seen the risen Lord.[50] Mary informs the disciples of the words Jesus had spoken to her concerning his return to the Father, and the establishment of the oneness between Jesus' Father and God and the Father and God of the disciples (v. 18c; see v. 17c). Mary was incapable of understanding the words of the *angeloi* as this scene at the tomb began (vv. 12-13), but as it closes she becomes the messenger, announcing (*angelousa*) the words of Jesus to the disciples (v. 18).[51] The reader has followed another foundational character from the earliest Christian community from the darkness of unfaith through a partial faith into perfect belief.

2. Scenes in the House (20:19-29)
c. Verses 19-23: Jesus Appears to the Disciples   There are indications for the reader that vv. 19-23 form a bridge between the scenes at the tomb

---

[49] See, among many, Mollat, "La foi pascale," 173–74. See, however, Barrett, *St John*, 566, who rightly points out that there are still two forms of sonship, that of Jesus and that of the Christian The Lukan and the Johannine ascensions are not to be compared or contrasted. As Bernard, *St John* 2:668–69, points out, for the Fourth Gospel *anabainein* is "practically equivalent" to the more frequently used verbs *hupagein* and *poreuesthai* to speak of Jesus' return to the Father.

[50] The Greek of v. 18 is a strange blend of direct speech ("I have seen the Lord") and indirect speech ("these things he said to her"), and it has prompted a number of attempts to correct the text (see Lagrange, *Saint Jean,* 513). It is probably an attempt to avoid the need to repeat Jesus' words from v. 17 in direct speech.

[51] See Maccini, *Her Testimony is True,* 225–33.

and the final scene in the house reported in vv. 24-29.[52] Mary obediently responds to Jesus' command (vv. 17-18). The following events take place "on the evening of that day [*ousēs oun opsias tȩ hēmerą ekeinȩ*]" (v. 19). As Mary went *from* the tomb to announce Jesus' message *to* the disciples (v. 18a), the place was now "*where* the disciples were [*hopou ēsan hoi mathētai*]" (v. 19a). Thus, Mary's presence at the tomb ends (v. 18) where the following scene begins (v. 19): with the characters to whom Mary announced Jesus' message. The day, place, and characters involved in the events of vv. 19-23 were already part of the closing moments of the immediately previous scene reported in vv. 11-18. The conclusion of the report of Mary Magdalene's experience of the risen Jesus is sufficiently "missionary" (vv. 17-18) to suggest to the reader that the faith experience of Mary Magdalene might be communicated beyond the boundaries of the characters and the time of the present story.

Jesus has been briefly present in the story to send Mary Magdalene to the disciples (vv. 17-19). Despite their having heard Mary's message from the risen Lord, they are locked in a room "for fear of the Jews" (v. 19a). There are no names given to the *mathētai* present in the upper room, nor is there a number. The Beloved Disciple and Peter are not part of this group. They are in their homes (see v. 10: *pros autous*). From the beginning of this brief scene "disciples" as such are the focus of attention. Matching the experience of many early Christians, the proclamation of the message of resurrection does not dispel the disciples' fears. All disciples of Jesus share in this narrative.[53] The "we" and the "they" of v. 2 are still active forces in the account. The disciples ("we") have not overcome the fear "the Jews" ("they") have created throughout the story of Jesus. The assembled disciples of Jesus know of the resurrection (see vv. 17-18), but the fear of "the Jews," who might subject them to hatred, insult, and death, remains (v. 19a). Jesus comes into this situation proclaiming his peace (v. 19b).[54] The

---

[52] For a series of links between vv. 19-23 and the earlier parts of the Johannine resurrection story, and the rest of the Gospel, see Heil, *Blood and Water*, 133–36.

[53] See Barrett, *St John*, 568. Against Rigaux, *Dio l'ha risuscitato*, 367–68, who sees the disciples as "the apostolic college," who will transmit all that they receive to the community at large. See also Blanquart, *Le premier jour*, 107–9.

[54] Against several commentators [e.g., Bultmann, *John*, 691–92; G. R. Beasley-Murray, *John* (WBC 36, Waco: Word, 1987) 379, C. H. Talbert, *Reading John: A Literary and Theological Commentary on the Fourth Gospel and the Johannine Epistles* (New York: Crossroad, 1992) 253–54; Heil, *Blood and Water*, 134–35)], this coming to the disciples is not the fulfillment of the promises made during the last discourse, that he would come to them (see 14:18, 22–23; 16:20-22).

greeting *eirēnē humin* may be a regular form of greeting, but within the present setting of Jesus' sudden physical presence among his fear-filled disciples (see 15:18—16:3), it brings into effect Jesus' promises of 14:27 and 16:33.[55] The disciples are now able to be of good cheer (see 16:33: *tharseite*); the risen Jesus is among them. His presence among them, despite the locked doors, is an indication of his victory over the limitations human circumstances would impose, evidenced earlier in the story by the empty cloths in an empty tomb (see vv. 5-7).[56] The reader suspects doubt among the disciples: is this really the crucified Jesus? The disciples may need proof that the figure they see before them is the same Jesus of Nazareth whom they followed. Thus, closely associating a gesture with the greeting of peace (v. 20a: *kai touto eipōn*), he shows them his hands and his side (v. 20b). The risen Jesus is the person whom they had seen lifted up on a cross and whose side had been pierced with a lance (19:18, 34).[57] Immediately the disciples respond with joy (v. 20c). Jesus' greeting, in vv. 19 and 21, brings peace in the midst of turmoil (see 14:27). The certain proof that Jesus of Nazareth, the crucified one, is among them as risen Lord brings joy in the midst of confusion and suffering (see 16:33). The situation of all disciples is reflected in the experience of these disciples. Now the message of Mary Magdalene has been confirmed by their own experience. The Beloved Disciple and Mary journeyed from unbelief, through conditioned faith, to an unconditional acceptance of the risen Lord (see vv. 3-9; vv 11-18). This is not the case with the assembled disciples. They have heard Mary's message, have had it confirmed, and now they respond with peace and joy.[58]

The author uses this first scene in the locked room to continue the account of Mary's journey of faith, bringing it to a conclusion that

[55] There is no verb, and thus the expression should be rendered "Peace to you." Jesus declares that peace is already among them. See especially W C. van Unnik, "*Dominus Vobiscum*: The Background of a Liturgical Formula," in A. J. B. Higgins, ed., *New Testament Essays: Studies in Memory of Thomas Walter Manson 1893–1958* (Manchester: Manchester Univ. Press, 1959) 270–305, especially 283–84.

[56] Jesus' victory over the constraints of human conditioning is the point at issue in the reporting of both the empty cloths and Jesus' appearance in the room, not a miraculous power. See Léon-Dufour, *Resurrection*, 183.

[57] As D. Mollat, "L'apparition du Ressuscité et le don de l'Esprit," in *Études johanniques* (Parole de Dieu; Paris: Editions du Seuil, 1979) 152–54, and J. Becker, *Das Evangelium des Johannes* (2 vols.; OTK 4/1–2; Gutersloh: Gerd Mohn; Wurzburg. Echter, 1979–81) 2:620–21, point out, unlike Luke 24:38-39, the showing of the pierced body in John 20:20 has no trace of apologetic but is above all an act of revelation.

[58] Mollat, "L'apparition," 148–50; Léon-Dufour, *Resurrection*, 182, and I. de la Potterie, "Parole et Esprit dans S. Jean," in M. de Jonge, ed., *L'Évangile de Jean: Sources, rédaction,*

parallels the conclusion of the experience of the Beloved Disciple (see v. 9). The linking of time, place, and characters across vv. 1-18 and 19-23 by means of vv. 17-19 enables the reader to find in the latter scene the conclusion of the former. Jesus' appearance among the rejoicing disciples is not told purely to inform the reader that the promises of 14:27 and 16:33 have been fulfilled. They are not only to be at peace and rejoice, in the midst of their fear, at the physical presence of the risen Lord; they are to be the bearers of the fruits of Jesus' victory to the world beyond the characters and the time of the story of Jesus (vv. 21-23). Again bestowing his peace on them, Jesus indicates to the disciples that his prayer for them on the night before he died was not a fancy. Jesus prayed to his Father: "As thou didst send me into the world, so I have sent them into the world" (17:18). He has gone through his total self-gift that makes God known (see 17:19), and now he sends them out. They are to be to the world what Jesus has been to the world (see 13:20; 17:18).[59] But the reader also recalls Jesus' awareness of the frailty of the disciples and of their need that Jesus' holy Father be Father to them (see 17:11b-16) and make them holy, for they must be holy as Jesus was holy (see 17:17-19). Such holiness is only possible through the presence of the Paraclete, the Holy Spirit (see 14:16-17; 26; 15:26-27; 16:7-11, 12-15).

Much of the earlier narrative floods back as intertext to the passage. The reader recalls the Paraclete sayings of Jesus' last discourse and also his prayer for the disciples, but the words of the narrator in 7:39 are also present: "As yet the Spirit had not been given, because Jesus was not yet glorified." At his death Jesus poured down the Spirit upon the tiny community at the foot of the cross (see 19:30). At the cross the promise of the narrator on the occasion of the Feast of Tabernacles is fulfilled: Jesus has been glorified, and the Spirit is given (see 7:39; 19:30). What is the point of this solemn second bestowal of the Spirit?[60] The Paraclete sayings, and especially 15:26-27, indicate to the reader that the Spirit was not only to dwell with the new family of Jesus founded at the cross; as risen Lord he further gifts his disciples

---

théologie (BETL 44; Gembloux: Duculot, 1977) 196–200, suggest that the scene is a diptych of vv. 19-20 and 21-23, both of which conclude with the fruits of resurrection faith: sight of the Lord (v. 20) and Spirit-filled mission (vv. 22-23).

[59] The identity of the mission of Jesus and the mission of the disciples is expressed by means of *kathōs . . . kagō* See Bernard, *St John,* 2:675–76; Barrett, *St John,* 569–70.

[60] Most comentators point to the parallel use of "he breathed upon" (*enephusēsen*) in Gen 2:7 (see also Ezek 37:9-10; Wis 15:11), marking this gift of the Spirit in the beginning of the new creation.

with the Spirit that they may be to the world what he has been.⁶¹
The reader is aware that the Spirit is *with* the community and *in* the
community and will remain with the community forever (see 14:16-
17). But the community must reach beyond its own borders to continue the mission of Jesus so that the world might know and believe
that he is the sent one of the Father (see 17:21, 23). The Spirit will
bear witness to Jesus in his absence so that the disciples, who have
been with him from the beginning, might also be witnesses (see 15:26-
27). There are not two "gifts of the Spirit." As there is only one hour
of Jesus, there is only one Spirit given to the members of the community (see 19:30) so that they might be witnesses to Jesus (20:22).⁶² At
the hour of the cross and resurrection, Jesus pours down the Spirit
upon the community of his followers (19:30) and breathes the Spirit
into its members so that they might be in the world as he was in the
world (20:22).⁶³ The oneness of the hour and all that is achieved by
and through it is nowhere clearer to the reader than in these two episodes that take place at the hour: the founding gift of the Spirit (19:30;
see 14:16-17) and the commissioning of the disciples who have been
with him from the beginning to be his witnesses empowered by the
Spirit (20:22; see 15:26-27).⁶⁴

⁶¹ Even though the recipients of the mission of the disciples are not mentioned, "the
world" is presupposed from 13:20, and especially 17:18 See Mollat, "L'apparition," 156.
⁶² See Manns, *L'Evangile*, 462. For this reason alone it is crucial that there be no suggestion of Jesus' having returned to the Father after his encounter with Mary Magdalene,
and then having appeared from there to his disciples so that he might give them the
Spirit See, e.g., M. R. D'Angelo, "A Critical Note. John 20.17 and the Apocalypse of
Moses," *JTS* 41 (1990) 529–36, who describes Jesus' appearance to Mary Magdalene as
an indication of the numinous state he is in prior to the completeness of his ascension.
He is no longer in this state when he appears to Thomas. There is no hint of this in
the text.
⁶³ Most scholars discount 19:30, and thus regard 20:22 as the *only* Johannine gift of
the Spirit in some way paralleling the Lukan Pentecost. See, e.g., Burge, *Anointed*, 116–
31, 147–49. De la Potterie, *The Hour*, 217–219, who regards 19:30 as the gift of the Spirit
(see 163–65), argues on several grounds that 20:22 is to arouse Easter faith in the disciples, and thus overcome their fear and hesitation For the more detailed study behind
this conclusion, see idem, "Parole et Esprit," 195–201. Heil, *Blood and Water*, 137–38,
who also holds that 19·30 marks the gift of the Spirit (see 102–3), plays upon the earlier
use of *paredōken* (19:30) as the moment of the gift of the Spirit, and Jesus' subsequent
command in 20:22 as his instruction that believing disciples receive (*labete*) the Spirit.
J. Swetnam, "Bestowal of the Spirit in the Fourth Gospel," *Bib* 74 (1993) 571–74, claims
that 19:30 is a bestowal to help all believers (symbolized by the mother and the Disciple) to discern the meaning of Jesus' life and death, while 20:22 is a specific empow-
erment to a restricted group for the forgiveness of sins.
⁶⁴ The issue of the relationship between this view of the gift of the Spirit and the
Lukan tradition of Pentecost cannot be resolved here. For a full discussion, see Burge,

The disciples who have been with Jesus from the beginning (see 15:27) will continue the presence of Jesus to a later generation. Again the author leads the reader away from those who have had the physical experience of the risen Lord toward those who have not. The disciples have failed to believe and commit themselves unconditionally to the one whom the Father sent. However much they have failed Jesus, they have never been failed by the love of God made manifest in Jesus. This author's presentation of Jesus' unfailing love for both Peter *and Judas* makes this point most dramatically. The immensity of the love of God has shone forth in Jesus' loving gift of self in the midst of their failure (see especially 13:19). Yet there is a positive side to the disciples who have been with him from the beginning. Jesus describes them as having received the manifestation of the name of God, having kept God's word and having known that everything Jesus had came from God. They know he is the sent one of God (see 17:6-8). It is for this group, whose story has been marked by a mixture of success and failure, that Jesus prays to his Father, asking that he keep them in his name (see 17:12) and make them holy as Jesus is holy (see 17:19). Their experience in the locked room encapsulates their response throughout the Gospel. They are at the one time full of fear yet joyful in the presence of the risen Jesus. Against this background Jesus' words to the frightened yet joyful disciples on their future mission must be understood. Through their ministry, sins are to be forgiven and to be retained. They are to render present the holiness of the absent Jesus (see 17:17-19). Another use of the passive (see vv. 1, 6-7) makes it clear that the disciples are missioned to do God's work, not their own.[65] They are to bring the peace and joy, received on the evening of that first day of the week from the risen Jesus (see v. 19), to later generations of frightened disciples of Jesus (see 15:18—16:3). The Paraclete's

---

Anointed, 114–49. Léon-Dufour, *Resurrection,* 186, aptly summarizes my position: "John sets forth an essential dimension of the Easter mystery which Luke has deliberately extended in time."

[65] For a discussion of the possibility that John 20:23 is a variant form of Matt 16.19; 18:18, see C. H. Dodd, *Historical Tradition in the Fourth Gospel* (Cambridge: Cambridge Univ. Press, 1965) 347–49; Brown, *John,* 2:1039–41. Both decide that the two traditions are probably independent. For the division that the understanding of this verse has created among Christian churches, see Brown, *John,* 2:1041–43. On the strange use of the verb *kratein* to refer to the retention of sins, see Bauer, *Johannesevangelium,* 232, who rightly points to its close association with *aphienai,* "to let go" (see Mark 7:8) For J A. Emerton, "Binding and Loosing—Forgiving and Retaining," *JTS* 13 (1962) 325–31, an original Aramaic saying, based on Isaiah 22:22, said "close-open," but was interpreted in the Matthean tradition as "bind-loose" and in the Johannine tradition as "retain-forgive."

ongoing—yet divisive—revelation will lay bare sin, righteousness, and judgment (see 16:7-11). Thus, the disciples, empowered by the Spirit, in the midst of their fear and joy, will be the agents for the future sanctification of generations of believers. The reader recalls Jesus' instruction of the disciples during the farewell discourse that the gift of the Spirit-Paraclete would render present the absent Jesus within the worshiping community (see 14:18-21), sharing their experience so that the world might know and believe that Jesus is the sent one of the Father (see 17:21-23). The mission of the disciples renders present the holiness of the absent Jesus. They will bring God's forgiveness for all sin that is to be forgiven and lay bare all sinfulness (v. 23).[66] This latter aspect may ring harshly for the reader, but it flows naturally from the story of Jesus. Brown aptly describes this element in the new situation established through the hour of Jesus: "the power to isolate, repel and negate evil and sin, a power given to Jesus by the Father and given in turn by Jesus through the Spirit to those whom he commissions."[67] Sanctification may lead to blessedness before God, but it also has the hard edge of exposing all that rejects the love lavished upon a world so loved by a God who sent his only son (see 3:16-17).

The reader finds that, as the Beloved Disciple's journey of faith led to an indication from the narrator that there would be a later generation of believers (vv. 3-10), so also does Mary Magdalene's journey of faith (vv. 11-23). Jesus commissioned Mary to announce the message of a new situation initiated by Jesus' return to the Father. She goes to the disciples, now the brethren of Jesus (vv. 17-18). Despite their fear, the disciples are blessed with the peace of Jesus and respond with joy when their crucified and risen Lord appears in their midst. The story of a journey of faith did not recommence with the introduction of a new set of characters, as these characters conclude Mary's journey. They are the ones who will bring the holiness of Jesus to a further generation, thus enabling the ongoing experience of the peace and joy only faith in Jesus can bring (see 14:27; 16:33). Despite the struggle of foundational characters in the Christian story to move from no faith through partial faith into unconditional belief, they stand at the

[66] The difficulties involved in understanding what is meant by the disciples' mission to forgive and retain sin are eased by its association with the mission of the Paraclete to "lay bare" the goodness and evil of the world (see 16:7-11). A further connection must be made with the Johannine understanding of the response to the revelation of God in and through Jesus. Some come to the light, but some turn away and the wrath of God rests upon them (see 3:11-21, 31–36).

[67] Brown, *John*, 2:1044.

beginning of a further generation of believers. The reader in the Gospel and the readers of the Gospel have come to believe in the resurrection of Jesus. They do so through the Scripture, including the Johannine Gospel (v. 9), and through the holiness, peace, joy, and judgment made possible by the Lord's gift of the Spirit and Jesus' sending disciples to bring forgiveness of sin to a later generation (v. 23).

d. Verses 24-29: Jesus Appears to the Disciples and to Thomas   The narrative continues: "Thomas, one of the twelve, called the Twin, was not with them when Jesus came" (v. 24).[68] The narrator gives no indication of a change in time or place. It is still that "first day of the week" (see vv. 1, 19), and the place is the upper room, where an atmosphere of peace and joy prevails among Spirit-filled disciples who have been commissioned to bring the holiness of God to the world. Thomas is not part of this. He is absent (v. 24: *Thōmas de eis tōn dōdeka . . . ouk ēn met' autōn*) and thus has not been part of Mary Magdalene's message (vv. 17-18) nor Jesus' appearance and commissioning (vv. 19-23).[69] This is understood by the reader as the first moment in this character's journey of faith. Surrounded by peace and joy, signs of Easter faith (see vv. 19, 20, 21), Thomas, like Peter, the Beloved Disciple, and Mary Magdalene in vv. 1-2, is in the darkness of unfaith (v. 24). His fellow disciples attempt to communicate their Easter faith with him (*elegon oun autǭ*), repeating the confession of Mary Magdalene: "We have seen the Lord" (v. 25a; see v. 18).[70] The earlier parts of the narrative are present to the reader but not to Thomas. His response to the other disciples marks a second stage in his journey of faith. He is only prepared to lay aside his unfaith if the risen Jesus meets *his* criteria. "Unless" (*ean me*) Jesus fulfills his conditions, he will remain in his present situation of unbelief (*ou mē pisteusō*).[71]

---

[68] The expression "the Twelve" has become a standard formula. See Brown, *John*, 2:1024. For Riley, *Resurrection Reconsidered*, 108–10, the author, who is addressing Thomas disciples to bring them into line with Johannine thought (just as he earlier addressed Baptist disciples), refers to "the Twelve" to link Thomas with Judas, the only other disciple to be associated with "the Twelve" (see 6:70-71). For the possibility that *didymos* carries the idea of duplicity, see Bauer, *Johannesevangelium*, 232. For Riley, *Resurrection Reconsidered*, 110–14, the reference to "the twin" identifies Thomas for the Thomas community.

[69] On the contrasting effect of the *de* in v. 24, see Heil, *Blood and Water*, 139. On Thomas's "not being with them," see Blanquart, *Le premier jour*, 116–19; Riley, *Resurrection Reconsidered*, 107–8.

[70] Brown, *John*, 2 1025, suggests that the *elegon* is a conative imperfect (see BDF, para. 326) indicating that the other disciples "tried to tell him "

[71] For the strength of this negative (*ou mē* with the future), see BDF, para. 365.

Thomas demands that Jesus be "touchable." As Mary wished to cling to Jesus' body, Thomas asks that he experience the risen body of the crucified one by seeing the nail marks and placing his finger into (*balō*) the wounds and his hand in (*balō*) Jesus' side.[72] Of the three journeys of faith told in this narrative, the conditioned response (v. 25: *ean mē*) of Thomas is the most dramatic. The author uses it as a final example of partial faith among foundational disciples stumbling toward faith. Thomas does not refuse the possibility of resurrection. He insists that the risen body of Jesus fulfill his requirements (v. 25; see v. 17). He has progressed from his situation of absence (see v. 24), but the imposition of his own criteria for belief in the resurrection of Jesus indicates his conditioned commitment.[73]

"Eight days later" (*kai meth' hēmeras oktō*) Jesus again stands among his disciples. Much of the detail that surrounded Jesus' earlier appearance returns.[74] The doors are shut, and he greets them with his peace: *eirēnē humin* (v. 26; see v. 19). The indication of time, eight days later, is also an association with the earlier appearance. Scholars have rightly suggested that the rhythmic reference to "the first day of the week" (v. 1), "the evening of that same day" (v. 19), and "eight days later" (v. 26) deliberately situates all these events on the day of the Lord. The only new element in v. 26, in comparison with v. 21, is the crucial indication: "Thomas was with them." Following hard on the heels of Thomas' arrogance in v. 25, the reader waits for Jesus' response. Surprisingly, Jesus offers to fulfill Thomas' conditions (v. 27ab). But he does more as he commands Thomas to reach beyond his conditioned faith: *mē ginou apistos alla pistos*. The risen Jesus is the crucified Jesus. If Thomas wishes to have physical proof, he can have it, but there is more at stake: "Do not be faithless but believing" (v. 27c).[75] There is no indication in the text that Thomas performed a

[72] The use of the verb *ballein* conveys the physical idea of an energetic thrust. See Brown, *John*, 2:1025.

[73] Léon-Dufour, *Resurrection*, 188, points out that the criteria imposed by Thomas are not his own: "He rigorously applies the categories of Jewish thought concerning the resurrection of the dead. He requires a strict continuity between the two worlds." In a provocative recent study, Riley, *Resurrection Reconsidered*, 126–75, argues that the Thomas community (see *The Gospel of Thomas, The Book of Thomas* and *The Acts of Thomas*) represents a widespread early Christian and Jewish understanding that continued a traditional Greco-Roman understanding of the risen body as substantial but disembodied. This false view is reflected in Thomas' words in John 20:25 (114–19)

[74] Reference to the fear of the disciples (see v. 19) is omitted. There is no place for fear after vv. 19-23.

[75] Agreeing with Brown, *John*, 2:1026, that Jesus' words summon Thomas away from unfaith into faith. Against those [e.g., Westcott, *St John*, 296; A. Loisy, *Le quatrième évan-*

touching ritual. The requested ritual is forgotten as Thomas accepts the challenge of faith, responding: "My Lord and my God!" Scholars differ in their evaluation of this act of faith. For some it is the "supreme Christological pronouncement of the Fourth Gospel."[76] Others claim that Jesus' remarks in v. 29, "You have believed because you have seen me. Blessed are those who have not seen and yet believe," show that there is a quality of faith without sight surpassing the faith that generated Thomas's confession.[77] A confession that recognizes Jesus as Lord and God at a climactic moment in the narrative corresponds to the Christology developed across the earlier parts of the story. It recognizes the implications of the narrator's teaching on the *logos* in 1:1-2, Jesus' unique use of the absolute *egō eimi* (see 4:26; 8:24, 28, 58; 13:19), and his claim, "I and the Father are one" (10:30; see also 10:38). The reader recalls the journeys of the Beloved Disciple and Mary Magdalene to full faith (see vv. 8, 18) and sees the final statement of faith in Jesus as a conclusion to Thomas's journey of faith. It also brings to an end three parallel resurrection experiences and the Gospel as a whole.

The faith journeys of the Beloved Disciple and Mary Magdalene looked beyond *the characters in the story* to further generations: *the readers of the story*. They believe on the authority of the Scripture, including the word of the Gospel itself, that Jesus rose (see v. 9), and they are the recipients of a holiness made possible by Jesus' commissioning fragile but peace-filled and joyful disciples (v. 23). There is a generation of believers reading the Gospel for whom the physical Je-

---

gile (Paris: Emile Nourry, 1921) 511; Barrett, *St John*, 476, H. van den Bussche, *Jean: Commentaire de l'Évangile Spirituel* (Bruges: Desclée de Brouwer, 1976) 553–54, H. Wenz, "Sehen und Glauben bei Johannes," *TZ* 17 [1961] 17–25)] who suggest that Thomas has never been an unbeliever, on the basis of the use of *pistos* and *apistos*, both hapax legomenoi, read as nouns: "Do not be an unbeliever but a believer." For Riley, *Resurrection Reconsidered*, 119–24, the author addresses the unbelievers in the Thomas community, using the figure of Thomas as a literary device to summon them away from their false understanding of resurrection.

[76] Brown, *John*, 2:1047. Has Johannine tradition taken this from Domitian's (81–86 C.E.) claim to be worshiped *Dominus et Deus noster* (see Suetonius, *Domitian*, 13)? For other classical references, see Bauer, *Johannesevangelium*, 233. On this, see B. A. Mastin, "The Imperial Cult and the Ascription of the Title to Jesus (John 20,28)," *SE* 6 (1973) 352–65. Recently R. J. Cassidy, *John's Gospel in New Perspective: Christology and the Realities of Roman Power* (Maryknoll: Orbis, 1992), has argued this case with some force. See especially 13–16, 69–88. At best, the rejection of emperor worship serves as background. The confession is not *against* something, but a final affirmation of the Christology of the Gospel.

[77] For Bultmann, *John*, 695–96, Thomas is used as a vehicle to criticize faith built on signs (v. 29a) rather than the word (v. 29b)

sus is *absent.* Their faith is based on the Scriptures, including the Johannine story (v. 9), and on the holiness administered by the
Christian community (v. 23). Addressing the last of the foundational
figures from the story who have stumbled to faith, Jesus says: "You
have believed because you saw me. Blessed are those who have not
seen yet believe" (v. 29).[78] As the Gospel closes, Jesus points to two
different eras. Some—not without difficulty—have made their journey of faith *in the physical presence of the risen Jesus:* Mary Magdalene,
and Thomas. Nevertheless, the experience of these disciples is past
history for the readers of the Gospel who have been summoned by
the narrative to believe that Jesus is the saving revelation of God. How
are they, a new generation, to believe *in the absence of Jesus?* With the
Scripture and this Gospel in hand (v. 9), and blessed with the holiness
that only God can give (v. 23), they are to regard their situation as
equally privileged to that of the foundational disciples. Indeed, they
are blessed in their belief without seeing (v. 29).[79]

On arrival at Jesus' blessing of those who believe without seeing
him, the reader recalls that one of the foundational disciples believed
without seeing Jesus. The Beloved Disciple had to make his journey
out of the darkness (see vv. 1-2) and came to faith without seeing Jesus
(v. 8). As one of the three characters used by the storyteller to portray
the necessity for a journey of faith, he, like those blessed in v. 29,
came to see and believe without seeing Jesus. He returned home, not
to reappear in the narrative (v. 10).[80] The foundational figure of the
Johannine community led the way: He believed without seeing *Jesus.*[81]
This was not the case for the two other characters in the story. Their
dependence on *the physical presence of Jesus* is evident in Mary Magdalene's wish to cling to Jesus (see v. 17) and Thomas' demand to touch
Jesus' wounds and place his hand in Jesus' pierced side (v. 25).[82] The

[78] For the translation of *hoti heōrakas me pepisteukas* as a statement rather than a question, see Barrett, *St John,* 573.
[79] See P. J. Judge, "A Note on Jn 20,29," in F. van Segbroeck, C. M. Tuckett, G. van
Belle and J. Verheyden, eds., *The Four Gospels 1992: Festschrift Frans Neirynck* (3 vols.;
BETL 100. Leuven: Leuven Univ. Press, 1992) 3:2183–92, Riley, *Resurrection Reconsidered,*
124–26. Most commentators cite *Tanhuma* 6:32a (c. 250 C.E.), where Rabbi Simeon ben
Laqish is reported as eulogizing the one who takes on the yoke of the kingdom of God
without having seen the events of Sinai
[80] This is not the case if John 21 is taken as integral to the narrative structure of the
Fourth Gospel (see 21 7, 20–23, 24).
[81] See Byrne, "Beloved Disciple," 89–91, 93–94
[82] For a study of the many ways in which the Mary Magdalene and the Thomas events
parallel each other, see Lee, "Partnership in Easter Faith," 40–46. On the relationship
between the Thomas story and v 29, and the characterization of Thomas and the reader

risen Jesus led these fragile disciples through their hesitation into authentic belief, yet the faith of those who believe without seeing
matches that of the greatest disciple (v. 29. See v. 8). They have come
to faith *in the absence of Jesus.*

3. The End of the Story (20:30-31)

The Johannine story of Jesus has come full circle. It opened with the
narrator's instructing the reader about *who* Jesus was and *what* he did
(1:1-18). The life story of Jesus has further developed that instruction,
but it has, above all, been concerned with telling the reader *how* Jesus
was who he was and *how* he achieved his mission. As Jesus dies upon
the cross, the narrator again interrupts the story to speak directly to
the reader. Although the prologue was dedicated to sophisticated instruction, the clumsily passionate intervention of the narrator into
the passion story makes his intentions clear. The author's chief concern is the faith of the reader (see 19:35). This theme returns as the
narrator resumes direct address to the readers to bring the book to its
end. Readers who have not seen yet believe are told that this account
of the life, death, and resurrection of Jesus has been written for them
(20:30-31).[83] The Jesus proclaimed in the prologue has lived, been
slain, and has risen through the story. But the narrative exists so that
the readers of the Gospel might go further in their faith. It is not a
recollection of things past, but a proclamation addressing the present.
Foundational disciples were summoned to reach beyond their unfaith
and their partial faith into genuine belief (20:1-29). The Gospel has
been written that the readers who believe without seeing might similarly go further in their belief in Jesus (vv. 30-31).[84]

---

of a later generation, see J. Kremer, "'Nimm deine Hand und lege sie in meine Seite!'
Exegetische, hermeneutische und Bibeltheologische Uberlegungen zu Joh 20,24-29," in
The Four Gospels 1992, 3:2153-81.

[83] On *tauta de gegraptai* (v. 31) as a rubric that includes the story now coming to its
end as part of the *graphē* of v. 9, see Obermann, *Die christologische Erfüllung*, 418-22

[84] I am reading the present subjunctive in v 31, rather than the aorist subjunctive.
The external evidence is very evenly balanced. See Brown, *John*, 2:1056, Schnackenburg,
St John, 3.337-38; G. D. Fee, "On the Text and Meaning of John 20,30-31," in *The Four
Gospels 1992*, 3:2192-205; B. M Metzger, *A Textual Commentary on the Greek New Testament* (2d ed ; Stuttgart: German Bible Society, 1994) 219-20 Brown, Schnackenburg,
and Fee opt for the present subjunctive Schnackenburg suggests that even if the original was in the aorist tense, it would not be "ingressive," as claimed by those who would
see the Fourth Gospel as something of a missionary tract (e.g , W. C van Unnik, "The
Purpose of St John's Gospel," *SE* [1959] 382–411; J. A. T. Robinson, "The Destination
and Purpose of St John's Gospel," *NTS* 6 [1959–60] 117–31; D. A. Carson, "The Purpose

The promise of a possible journey of faith in 2:1—4:54 comes to its completion in 20:1-29. As the public ministry of Jesus began, the reader encountered a series of episodes describing characters who demonstrated the possibility of authentic Johannine belief (2:1—4:54). At the end of the story the reader meets the foundational experience of the Beloved Disciple, Mary Magdalene, and Thomas. Faced with the evidence of God's victory (see 20:5-7) or the person of their risen Lord (see vv. 14-17; vv. 26-27), each foundational disciple journeyed from no faith to authentic belief (20:2-8, 11-18, 24-28). The readers of a story that began and ended in this fashion are the result of the missionary activity of the foundational members of the Christian community (see 17:20-23). The disciples have reaped a harvest they did not sow (see 4:36-38), the gathering associated with Jesus' glorification (10:16; 11:52; 12:11, 19, 32; 19:25-27). The readers are this "gathering," the fruit of Jesus' glorification and departure. Despite the absence of Jesus, they are blessed in their believing (see 20:9, 23, 29). No doubt, like the foundational members of the Christian community, they will struggle through experiences of no faith and partial faith toward true belief, but they should not be discouraged. Even the Beloved Disciple, so dear to the Johannine storyteller, had to struggle toward belief. If such was the case from the beginnings of the Christian community, the readers have no cause for anxiety as they face their own struggles and hesitations (see 6:60-71; 15:18—16:3). As a consequence of the gift of the Spirit-Paraclete, the absent Jesus is present to the members of the community in their mutual loving (see 13:34-35; 15:12, 17; 17:21-23), their mission (see 13:34-35; 15:12; 17:17-19), their sanctifying ministry (17:17-19; 20:22), and especially in their worship: cult (see 4:23; 14:18-21), prayer in the name of Jesus (see 14:12-14; 15:16; 16:23-24, 25-26), and celebration of Baptism and Eucharist (see 3:5; 6:51-58; 13:1-38; 19:34-37). But they do not *see Jesus*.

The readers of the story, members of a Christian community coming to faith in the in-between time, the time of the absence of the physical Jesus, are being summoned to recognize that they are as blessed in their belief as were those who believed on the basis of what they saw (see v. 29). Like the Beloved Disciple (see v. 8), they believe without

---

of the Fourth Gospel: John 20:31 Reconsidered," *JBL* 106 [1987] 639–51). If originally aorist, Schnackenburg suggests, it was a summons to "a new impulse in their faith," with reference to such a use in 11:15, 40 (*St John*, 3:338). For the use of *hina*-clauses in the Johannine literature for community instruction, see H. Riesenfeld, "Zu den johanneischen *hina*-Satzen," *ST* 19 (1965) 213–20.

seeing Jesus (v. 29). It is the desire of the author that all those who read this book or hear its proclamation be a community of Beloved Disciples![85] The book was written so that a narrative telling the reader *how* Jesus has lived his story might confirm *what* was proclaimed in the prologue. The author believes passionately that Jesus' life story proves the claims made for him in the prologue. Thus, he has written this account, confessedly a selection from the many stories that could have been told (v. 30),[86] so that the reader might share this passionate belief. Jesus is the Christ, but the Christ who is the Son of God. A belief that reaches beyond all historical and cultural conditioning accepts that Jesus is the long-awaited Christ, but only in so far as he has come from God and returns to God, the Son of God, the sent one of the Father, the one who has made God known. Eternal life is possible for those who come to know God through Jesus Christ, the one whom God has sent (see 17:3). Jesus' being the Christ is entirely conditioned by the greater truth: He is the Son of God. The author has shared his belief in Jesus, the Christ, the Son of God, by means of the story from which the reader now rises. The journey of Jesus and the journey of the reader have been completed. But the storytelling is successful only if the one rising from the story has become part of it, led more deeply into belief in Jesus and all that he made known about God, and comes to life as a result of the reading experience (v. 31).

[85] See Byrne, "Beloved Disciple," 94.

[86] With majority opinion, taking the *sēmeia* as a "look back over the *whole* book" (Schnackenburg, *St John,* 3:337) rather than the recently reported resurrection appearances. Advocates of the existence of a pre-Johannine Signs Source behind the Fourth Gospel see the reference to *sēmeia* in v. 30 as the original conclusion to the source. For a recent persuasive demolition of the Signs Source theory, see U. Schnelle, *Antidocetic Christology in the Gospel of John* (trans. L. M. Maloney; Minneapolis: Fortress Press, 1992) 150–64

Chapter Eight

But the Journey Continues
John 21:1-25

¶ JOHN 21·1-25 is widely regarded as an addition to a Gospel that closed with the author's words to the reader in 20:30-31.[1] The following might indicate that an original story ended at 20:31:

1. The ending of 20:30-31 reads like·a solemn conclusion to a story.
2. Many words, expressions, and literary peculiarities are found for the first and only time in the Fourth Gospel in 21:1-25.[2]

---

[1] As well as the majority of commentaries, see M -E. Boismard, "Le chapitre xxi de saint Jean· essai de critique littéraire," *RB* 54 (1947) 473–501; R. Mahoney, *Two Disciples at the Tomb: The Background and Message of John 20,1–10* (TW 6; Bern: Herbert Lang, 1974) 12–40; E. Delebecque, "La mission de Pierre et celle de Jean: note philologique sur Jean 21," *Bib* 67 (1986) 335–42; J. Zumstein, "La rédaction finale de l'évangile selon Jean (à l'exemple du chapître 21)," in J.-D. Kaestli, J.-M Poffet, and J. Zumstein, eds., *La Communauté Johannique et son Histoire* (Geneva: Labor et Fides, 1990) 207–30, and idem, "Der Prozess der Relecture," 401–4; F. Blanquart, *Le premier jour: Étude sur Jean 20* (LD 146; Paris: Cerf, 1992) 139–52; G. Reim, "Johannes 21: Ein Anhang?" in J. K. Elliott, ed., *Studies in New Testament Language and Text: Essays in Honor of George Dunbar Kilpatrick on the Occasion of His Sixty-Fifth Birthday* (NovTSupp 44; Leiden: Brill, 1976) 330–37.

[2] See especially Boismard, "Le chapitre xxi de saint Jean," 473–501. R. E. Brown, *The Gospel according to John* (2 vols.; AB 29, 29A; Garden City, N.Y.: Doubleday, 1966–70) 2:1079, expresses concern over many features singled out for attention, as this is the only fishing scene in the Gospel. Yet, on 2:1079–80, he develops his own list.

3. The narrative of John 21 shows a concern for mission and authority within the community that exceeds the interest shown these issues throughout John 1:1—20:31.[3]
4. The sequence of the story becomes confused. After Mary Magdalene's mission to announce the resurrection (see 20:18), and the subsequent mission of the disciples in vv. 19-23, why do the disciples return from Jerusalem to Galilee and to their former occupations, seemingly somewhat bored by their present situation (see 21:2-3)?
5. There is an obtuseness among the disciples that makes nonsense of the joy, the mission, and the gift of the Spirit of 20:19-23. After having twice seen Jesus in the upper room (vv. 19-23, 26-29), why do they fail to recognize him when he appears for the third time (21:14)?
6. Is this the third time? If one includes the appearance to Mary Magdalene (see 20:10-18), it is the fourth appearance.
7. The final words in 21:25 form a literary conclusion similar to other conclusions from ancient literature.[4] These words repeat in a less theological and a less reader-oriented fashion the conclusion of 20:30.

To the best of our knowledge, there has never been a textual tradition that did not contain John 21.[5] Whatever scholarship may decide about the origins of John 21 as an "addendum" or an "epilogue" to an original Gospel, this collection of postresurrection stories was important to the Christians who first wrote and passed down the Gospel to later generations.[6] This fact has led to a recent reassessment of the place of John 21. Although there have always been some who de-

---

[3] See, among many, E. Ruckstuhl, "Zur Aussage und Botschaft von Johannes 21," in R. Schnackenburg, J. Ernst, and J. Wanke, eds., *Die Kirche des Anfangs. Festschrift für Heinz Schurmann zum 65. Geburtstag* (EThSt 38; Leipzig St. Benno-Verlag, 1977) 339–62; R. E Brown, "The Resurrection in John 21—Missionary and Pastoral Directives for the Church," *Worship* 64 (1990) 433–45.

[4] See Brown, *John*, 2:1130.

[5] See, however, M. Lattke, "Joh 20:30f als Buchschluss," *ZNW* 78 (1987) 288–92. Lattke suggests, on the basis of Tertullian, *Adversus Praxean* (25,4), that the second century knew a Gospel ending at 20 30-31, and also traditions found in John 21. But Brown, *John*, 2:1057, claims that Tertullian may have anticipated the modern idea of the addition of chap. 21.

[6] For this reason alone, it must be regarded as an "epilogue," something that belongs to the Gospel as we have it, and not just an "addendum" or a "postscript." On this, see Brown, *John*, 2:1077–82; Zumstein, "Der Prozess der Relecture," 401–4

fended its place on historical grounds,[7] the rise of canonical and literary approaches to biblical narrative has led to increased effort among a newer generation of scholars to explain John 1:1—21:25 as a literary and theological unit. Most contemporary narrative approaches to the Fourth Gospel take this position.[8] In conclusion to my study of the narrative of the Fourth Gospel, I will briefly outline the shape and

[7] See, e.g , M.-J. Lagrange, *Evangile selon Saint Jean* (EB; Paris: Gabalda, 1927) 520–21 (but he transposes 20.30–31 to follow 21:23 so that it still remains as a conclusion to the Gospel), E. C Hoskyns, *The Fourth Gospel* (2d ed.; ed. F. N. Davey; London: Faber & Faber, 1947) 550; J A. T. Robinson, "The Relation of the Prologue to the Gospel of St John," *NTS* 9 (1962–63) 120–29; S S. Smalley, *John: Evangelist and Interpreter* (Exeter: Paternoster, 1978) 92–97; P. Minear, "The Original Function of John 21," *JBL* 102 (1983) 85–98, D. A Carson, *The Gospel according to John* (Grand Rapids: Eerdmans, 1991) 665–68; Morris, *The Gospel according to John* (rev. ed.; Grand Rapids: Eerdmans, 1995) 757–58

[8] See L Hartman, "An Attempt at a Text-Centered Exegesis of John 21," *ST* 39 (1984) 29–45; J L. Staley, *The Print's First Kiss. A Rhetorical Investigation of the Implied Reader in the Fourth Gospel* (SBLDS 82, Atlanta Scholars, 1988) 50–73; P. F. Ellis, *The Genius of John: A Composition-Critical Commentary on the Fourth Gospel* (Collegeville, Minn.: Liturgical Press, 1984) 13–15, 310–12; idem, "The Authenticity of John 21," *SVTQ* 36 (1992) 17–25; M. Franzmann and M Klinger, "The Call Stories of John 1 and John 21," *SVTQ* 36 (1992) 7–16, J Breck, "John 21· Appendix, Epilogue or Conclusion?" *SVTQ* 36 (1992) 27–49, R Kieffer, *Le monde symbolique de Saint Jean* (LD 137; Paris: Cerf, 1989) 17, 90–95; F. F. Segovia, "The Journey(s) of the Word of God· A Reading of the Plot of the Fourth Gospel," *Sem* 53 (1991) 23–54; idem, "The Final Farewell of Jesus: A Reading of John 20 30–21 25," *Sem* 53 (1991) 167–90; T L. Brodie, *The Gospel according to John: A Literary and Theological Commentary* (New York Oxford Univ. Press, 1993) 574–76; M. W. G. Stibbe, *John* (Readings: A New Biblical Commentary; Sheffield: JSOT Press, 1993) 206–10, D. A. Lee, "Partnership in Easter Faith: The Role of Mary Magdalene and Thomas in John 20," *JSNT* 58 (1995) 40; C H Talbert, *Reading John: A Literary and Theological Commentary on the Fourth Gospel and the Johannine Epistles* (New York Crossroad, 1992) 248, 258; S. M Schneiders, "John 21.1-14," *Int* 43 (1989) 70–75; T. Okure, *The Johannine Approach to Mission A Contextual Study of John 4:1–42* (WUNT 2/32; Tubingen: J C. B. Mohr, 1988) 194–95, 224–26; H. Thyen, "Entwicklungen innerhalb der johanneischen Theologie und Kirche im Spiegel von Joh. 21 und der Lieblingsjungertexte des Evangeliums," in M de Jonge, ed , *L'Évangile de Jean: Sources, rédaction, théologie* (BETL 44; Gembloux: Duculot, 1977) 259–99; A. Stimpfle, *Blinde Sehen: Die Eschatologie im traditionsgeschichtlichen Prozess des Johannesevangeliums* (BZNW 57; Berlin de Gruyter, 1990) 248–72; U. Busse, "Die 'Hellenen' Joh 12,20ff. und der sogennante 'Anhang' Joh 21," in F van Segbroeck, C M. Tuckett, G. van Belle, and J. Verheyden eds., *The Four Gospels 1992· Festschrift Frans Neirynck* (3 vols.; BETL 100; Leuven. Leuven Univ. Press, 1992) 3:2083–100; W S. Vorster, "The Growth and Making of John 21," in *The Four Gospels 1992,* 3:2207–21; G. Korting, *Die esoterische Struktur des Johannesevangeliums* (2 vols.; BU 25; Regensburg: Pustet, 1994) 1:425–47, 2:72–76; D. F. Tolmie, *Jesus' Farewell to the Disciples John 13:1–17:26 in Narratological Perspective* (BibIntS 12; Leiden: Brill, 1995) 45–46; J P. Heil, *Blood and Water: The Death and Resurrection of Jesus in John 18–21* (CBQMS 27; Washington: The Catholic Biblical Association of America, 1995) 151–67.

message of 21:1-25. Are these resurrection stories part of the original literary and theological design of the Fourth Gospel?

READING JOHN 21.1-25

The narrative of John 21:1-25 unfolds in three sections determined by the characters and the action central to each section:[9]

   a. *Verses 1-14:* Jesus' appearance to his disciples beside the Sea of Tiberias leads to a miraculous draft of fishes and a meal by the lake.
   b. *Verses 15-24:* A discussion between Jesus and Peter clarifies the respective roles of Peter as the shepherd and the Beloved Disciple, the one who has told this story.
   c. *Verse 25:* Conclusion.

The reader, who rises from 20:31 under the impression that both Jesus (see 20:29) and the narrator (see vv. 30-31) have had their last say, is surprised by the laconic summary statement of 21:1 that Jesus revealed himself again. After blessing those who believe without sight (20:29), are there to be more appearances?

a. Verses 1-14
Disciples gather at the Sea of Tiberias and set out on their normal occupation of fishing (vv. 2-3). The risen Jesus appears to them, and a large catch of fish results from his directions (vv. 4-6). At the miracle, the figure on the shore is recognized by the Beloved Disciple, who tells Simon Peter: "It is the Lord" (v. 7). The main theme of this section of the narrative concerns the Christian community, the disciples, and

---

[9] Most would place v. 24 with v. 25 as a conclusion to the chapter. See Brown, *John,* 2:1065 (but see 2·1126-27, where he shows the links between v 24 and vv 15-23) I prefer to read v. 24 as a conclusion to the episodes that deal with the different roles of Peter and the Beloved Disciple (vv. 15-19, 20-24), as does R. E. Brown in his later article, "John 21 and the First Appearance of the Risen Jesus to Peter," in *Resurrexit Actes du Symposium International sur la Rèsurrection de Jèsus (Rome 1970),* ed. E Dhanis (Rome. Libreria Editrice Vaticana, 1974) 434-35. See also Ruckstuhl, "Zur Aussage," 352 n. 22, Delebecque, "La mission de Pierre et celle de Jean," 339-41. T. Wiarda, "John 21 1-23· Narrative Unity and Its Implications," *JSNT* 46 (1992) 53-71, traces the appearances of Peter across the narrative, and argues that the author is concerned with Peter and discipleship rather than with the Beloved Disciple. But see I. de la Potterie, "Le temoin qui demeure· le disciple que Jésus aimait," *Bib* 67 (1986) 343-59, for the importance of vv. 20-25 in the narrative, and Ruckstuhl, "Zur Aussage," 360-61, for the significance of both disciples.

their mission as the sent ones of Jesus. But the question of the relationship between the Beloved Disciple and Simon Peter is also present. It is the Beloved Disciple who recognizes Jesus and confesses that he is "the Lord." The reader is not told of Simon Peter's faith, but of his actions. He leaps into the sea as the other disciples come to the shore in the boat dragging the heavy catch (vv. 7-8). On arrival, they find a charcoal fire already lit with fish on it, and bread as well (v. 9). On Jesus' command to "them" (*legei autois ho Iēsous*) that some of the freshly caught fish be brought, it is again Simon Peter who acts (*anebē Simōn Petros*), hauling the net containing 153 fish ashore.[10] The issue is not the number but the fact that despite the great number of fish, *the net is not torn* (vv. 10-11). The symbolism is clear. Simon Peter leads, enthusiastically taking action in response to the Beloved Disciple's announcement that the Lord is present (v. 7: *ho kyrios estin*), and at the word of the risen Jesus. Large numbers are drawn into the net, but it is not damaged. The church is a boat under the direction of the Lord, "gathering" large numbers under the inspiration of the Beloved Disciple and the leadership of Peter.[11] The Lord and his disciples share a meal. The man who shared meals with them during his ministry is still with them at the table (vv. 12-13). The identity and the mission of the Christian community are founded on the *presence* of the risen Jesus who has now appeared to his disciples three times (see v. 14) and who remains with them.

b. Verses 15-24
If Peter is the leader, what of his earlier failures? True to the criterion of authentic discipleship demanded by Jesus throughout the Gospel (see 13:34-35; 15:12, 17), Peter must thrice confess his love for Jesus and commit himself to shepherding the flock of Jesus. His threefold denial (18:15-18, 25-27) is overcome by his threefold profession of love (21:15-17). On the basis of his love for Jesus, he is entrusted with the mission of shepherding the sheep. He must be to the community

[10] Whatever the hidden secret behind the number might be (allegory, gematria, or a mathematical symbol), it has led such diverse critics as Brown, *John*, 2:1075–76, and Staley, *The Print's First Kiss*, 113, to conclude that it is impossible to give it a meaning. For a recent attempt to explain it on the basis of the number 17, see Brodie, *John*, 587–88.

[11] See Ruckstuhl, "Zur Aussage," 340–51; Schneiders, "John 21 1–14," 72; D. Marzotto, *L'Unità degli Uomini nel Vangelo di Giovanni* (SuppRivB 9; Brescia: Paideia, 1977) 215–19, Talbert, *Reading John*, 260; M. Rodriguez Ruiz, *Der Missionsgedanke des Johannesevangeliums· Ein Beitrag zur johanneischen Soteriologie und Ekklesiologie* (FB 55; Wurzburg: Echter, 1987) 290–304; Heil, *Blood and Water*, 157.

what Jesus was—a good shepherd (see 10:14-18). Peter is told that he will, like Jesus, lay down his life for his sheep (21:18-19; see 10:16). So much for Peter, but what of the Beloved Disciple? He has already led the way by telling Simon Peter: "It is the Lord" (21:7). How does Peter, in the light of the challenge he has accepted in vv. 15-19, relate to this figure? It is Peter who asks: "Lord, what about him?" (v. 21). The Beloved Disciple is no longer alive. The community is told not to be surprised at this (vv. 22-23). This disciple, possibly the unnamed disciple who appears during Jesus' first days (see 1:35-40), was at Jesus' side at the supper table (13:23), during the trials (18:15-16), at the cross (19:25-27), and at the empty tomb (20:2-8).[12] At the cross he was singled out by the exalted Jesus as one of the foundational figures for the new family of Jesus that has its birth at—and because of—that "hour" (see 19:27). Peter may be the shepherd who will lay down his life for the sheep (see 21:15-19), but the Beloved Disciple is the authority behind this community's story of Jesus (v. 24). Peter is the appointed shepherd of the flock of Jesus (see vv. 15-17), and the Beloved Disciple is the bearer of the Jesus tradition (see v. 24).

c. Verse 25
The reader must not, however, suspect that the story just read exhausts all that could be said about Jesus. Adopting a literary form used by other writers of the period (see Qoh 12:9-12; Minor Tractates of the Talmud, *Sopherim* 16:8; Philo, *Poster. C.* 43:144; *Ebr.* 9:42; *Vit. Mos.* 1:38,213), the author of John 21 repeats what the author of 20:30 said more briefly concerning the many other unrecorded signs Jesus did in the disciples' presence. A selection has been made. However, while 20:30-31 motivated that choice by further words to the readers telling them *why* a certain selection and a certain ordering of events has taken place, no such motivation is given in 21:25. Perhaps none was needed. It is sufficient for this readership to know that the book they have completed has the Beloved Disciple as its author (21:24).

DOES JOHN 21 BELONG TO THE STORY?

Interest in the integrity of John 1:1—21:25 concentrates on perceived gaps in the narrative of the Gospel. Some of these are the disappear-

---

[12] See F. Neirynck, "John 21," *NTS* 36 (1990) 330–36

ance of the Beloved Disciple and Peter in 20:10,[13] the need for clear indications of the mission of the Christian community,[14] and the relationship between the evangelist and the Beloved Disciple.[15] This case has been reinforced by literary considerations. For example, P. S. Minear suggests that 20:30-31 does not conclude the Gospel as a whole, but only 20:1-31, and opens the narrative to the events that follow.[16] F. F. Segovia has developed this further by drawing a link between 20:30-31 and 21:24-25, and showing that 21:1-23 is an example of a final farewell, common in the literature of the time.[17] C. H. Talbert sees 20:30-31 as an example of a technique used by the evangelist in 12:36b-37. There is an apparent "ending," but the story goes on.[18] J. L. Staley points to the literary contacts between the use of *agapaō* and *phileō* in 11:1-5 and 21:15-17, as well as the geographical parallels between 11:1—12:11 and 21:1-25. Both take place outside Jerusalem.[19] R. Kieffer makes a different geographical link, pointing to the fact that the Gospel closes (21:1-25) where it began (1:19-51): in Galilee.[20] U. Busse argues that the coming of the Greeks (12:20-22) set within

[13] Hoskyns, *Fourth Gospel*, 556–61, Carson, *John*, 666–67; J. Bligh, *The Sign of the Cross: The Passion and Resurrection of Jesus According St John* (Slough, England: St Paul Publications, 1975) 89–90; Hartman, "An Attempt," 37–39; Minear, "John 21," 91–94; Segovia, "The Final Farewell," 173–74, Schneiders, "John 21:1-14," 73–74; Talbert, *Reading John*, 260–63; Brodie, *John*, 581; Heil, *Blood and Water*, 154–56; Lee, "Partnership in Easter Faith," 40.

[14] Hoskyns, *Fourth Gospel*, 552–56, and Heil, *Blood and Water*, 156–59, associate the mission with a sacramental reading of the meal. For a more general reference to mission, see Hartman, "An Attempt," 41–42; Morris, *John*, 758; Segovia, "The Final Farewell," 176–82, Okure, *The Johannine Approach*, 194–95; Brodie, *John*, 579–81

[15] Minear, "John 21," 95, Thyen, "Entwicklungen der johanneischen Theologie," 273–99, Stimpfle, *Blinde Sehen*, 248–72; Segovia, "The Final Farewell," 183, Tolmie, *Jesus' Farewell*, 45–46 But see U Schnelle, *Antidocetic Christology in the Gospel of John* (trans. L M Maloney, Minneapolis: Fortress Press, 1992) 12–21, who rightly points to the different presentations of Peter and the Beloved Disciple in John 1–20 and in John 21

[16] Minear, "John 21," 87–90. See also Vorster, "The Growth," 2217–21. Segovia, "The Final Farewell," 174, has a variation on this. He attempts to weaken the link between 20:30-31 and 20.1-29, arguing that these verses are not addressed to the reader, but to the narratee, and thus 21:1-25 allows the author to tell the reader of "the final farewell."

[17] Segovia, "The Final Farewell," 174–75. See also Breck, "John 21," 29.

[18] Talbert, *Reading John*, 258. See also Ellis, "The Authenticity," 20–21. The parallels between 12 36b-37//20·30-31 and 12·38-50//21 1-25 cannot bear the weight of such an argument. Talbert traces the same practice in 1 John (1 John 5:13, followed by 5:14-21), which he regards as prior to the Gospel (see 3–7) and Revelation (Rev 22:5, followed by 22:6-21) These parallels are irrelevant in a discussion of the Gospel's ending.

[19] Staley, *The Print's First Kiss*, 67–69. It is far-fetched to see Bethany near Jerusalem (see 11.18) and Galilee (21:1) as being parallel because they are "outside Jerusalem."

[20] Kieffer, *Le monde symbolique*, 17, 90–95.

the context of 11:55—12:36 looks to the miracle of the 153 fish and Peter as the good shepherd in John 21 for narrative resolution.[21] A chiastic structure is proposed by P. F. Ellis, who finds parallels between 1:19-51, Jesus' first coming, the witness of the Baptist, Simon, two unnamed disciples and Nathanael, with 20:19—21:25, which treats Jesus' second coming, Thomas's witness, Simon Peter, two unnamed disciples and Nathanael.[22] Both Staley and Segovia locate 21:1-25 at the end of a series of physical and metaphorical journeys.[23] G. Korting structures the Gospel on the basis of a communication through "threes," and John 20:1—21:25 forms the final third of the section 13:1—21:25.[24] T. L. Brodie argues that John 21 is a culminating point in the theological argument of the Gospel as a whole. A mission of daily self-giving, especially in the church, watched over by a provident risen Lord brings the Gospel to a fitting conclusion.[25]

Much erudition and imagination has been given to explanations of the role 21:1-25 plays as the Gospel's conclusion. The number and variety of very different hypotheses weaken the likelihood of any one of these explanations, or even a combination of them, being true. However subtle such explanations are, they are overly ingenious. A crucial issue dominates the narrative of 20:1-31. The author desires that readers respond to a summons to greater faith (20:31) so that they might know of Jesus' resurrection from their reading of the Scriptures (v. 9), from their experience of the Spirit and the holiness granted to them through generations of disciples who retain and forgive sin (see vv. 22-23), and from their recognition of their blessedness in believing without seeing (v. 29). The story closes with a frank recognition of the situation of the readers: They are living in the in-between time, and they are blessed because they believe without seeing (see v. 29). The final chapter instructs a community of Christians on their blessedness and exhorts them to greater faith (vv. 30-31) even though they are living in the period of the physical absence of Jesus.

Earlier parts of the narrative have prepared the reader for this final instruction on the presence of the one who is now physically absent.

[21] Busse, "Die 'Hellenen' Joh 12,20ff.," 3:2097-100.
[22] Ellis, *The Genius of John,* 13-15, 310-12; "The Authenticity," 23-25; Breck, "Appendix?" 36-39; Smalley, *John,* 92-97; Robinson, "The Relation of the Prologue," 120-29. Franzmann and Klinger, "The Call Stories," 7-16, trace links between 1·25-50 and 21:15-23 and 1·37-39 and 21:19b-23. Franzmann, against Klinger, sees 21:1-25 as the addition of a skilful redactor to strengthen the Gospel's portrayal of Peter (14-15).
[23] See Staley, *The Print's First Kiss,* 72-73; Segovia, "The Journey(s)," 50-51
[24] Korting, *Die esoterische,* 1:425-47, 2:72-76
[25] Brodie, *John,* 579-82.

This is particularly obvious in those few places where the reading experience depends on the community's sacramental practices. This storyteller shows no overt interest in those rituals that came to be known as sacraments. On several occasions the storyteller takes Eucharist and Baptism for granted. Living without the physical presence of Jesus, the Christian reading in the in-between time asks: "How do I see and enter into this kingdom? Where do I find this Jesus in whom I must believe? How am I to have part in Jesus? Upon which crucified one must I gaze? The author responds by introducing material that reminds the reader of the presence of the one who is physically absent (3:3-5; 6:51-58; 13:1-38; 19:34-37).[26] The sacraments are not understood as in themselves in this Gospel; they are taken for granted by the storyteller as part of the life of the reader. Allusion to Baptism and Eucharist at critical moments in the narrative reminds the reader of the presence of the physically absent one. The Johannine Jesus and the narrator have insisted that Jesus must depart to the Father (see 7:32-36; 8:14, 13:1, 33, 36; 14:2-3, 28; 16:6-7, 16, 28; 17:1-5, 11a, 13, 24), leaving the disciples in the world (13:1; 14:2-3, 18-20, 29; 15:18—16:3, 16:21-24; 17:11b, 13-16). His departure, however, is not final. He will come to them (see 5:28-29; 6:40, 54; 14:3, 18, 23; 16:16), but during the in-between time he will not leave them orphans (14:18). He will send them another Paraclete to dwell with them throughout the in-between time (see 14:15-17), guiding, strengthening, reminding, and teaching them during his absence (see 14:26; 16:12-15), enabling them to bear courageous witness in a hostile world (see 15:26-27), and continuing the judgment of Jesus in the world (see 16:7-11). Because the departed Jesus lives, the disciples will live in the unity of Father, Son, and believer (14:18-21). The reader has been well prepared for the risen Jesus' final words in the original story: "Blessed are those who have not seen and yet believe" (20:29).

But, according to 21:1-25, the risen Jesus is not absent! This subverts the impact 1:1—20:31 should have made on readers living in the in-between time in Jesus' absence. The addition of the appearance stories of 21:1-25 contradicts the the storyteller's original narrative design. The story came to a conclusion with a blessing from Jesus in 20:29

---

[26] See F J Moloney, *Belief in the Word· Reading John 1–4* (Minneapolis: Fortress Press, 1993) 109–14, idem, *Signs and Shadows Reading John 5–12* (Minneapolis: Fortress Press, 1996) 58–59; idem, "A Sacramental Reading of John 13·1-38," *CBQ* 53 (1991) 237–56; idem, "The Johannine Passion and the Christian Community," *Sal* 57 (1995) 44–47. If 21:9-14 is eucharistic (see Hoskyns, *Fourth Gospel*, 552–56; Heil, *Blood and Water*, 156–59) it is unlike any other use of sacramental material in the Fourth Gospel, despite Brown's suggestion that there are similarities with John 6 (*John*, 2:1099–100).

and closing words from the narrator in vv. 30-31. While the author of
1:1—20:31 creates in the reader a satisfactory sense of closure as a
journey is completed in 20:1-31, the author of 21:1-25 tells the reader
that the journey goes on. John 21 undermines the implied author's
message on the absence of Jesus by telling the infant church of the
presence of Jesus.[27] This is not the place to discuss the identity of the
real authors involved in the storytelling. It is quite possible that the
addition of chapter 21 was the work of the same author at a later stage,
faced with unforeseen difficulties in the ongoing life of the community. It may not have been enough to exhort believers to go on believing more so that their experience of the risen one might match
that of the original disciples despite his physical absence. It is equally
possible that John 21 came from another Johannine Christian.[28] The
one (or those) responsible for the epilogue of John 21 belonged to
the same Christian community as the original author. The undeniable
literary links between John 1:1—20:31 and John 21:1-25 and the fact
that there is no manuscript tradition without John 21 show this con-
clusively.

CONCLUSION

The Johannine story of Jesus comes to an end in 20:30-31, but that
was not the end of the story of Johannine disciples. Troubled by the
unanswered questions concerning the nature and mission of the community, and questions of leadership and authority, someone had to
tell the readers that although the story of Jesus had come to an end,
another story had begun. To tell this further story, the author called
upon other Johannine traditions concerning the risen Jesus.[29] But *the
absent one has returned!* The addition of the epilogue was pastorally
effective, as the ongoing presence of John 21 within accepted Chris-

---

[27] Against Schneiders, "John 21:1-14," 74–75, who sees John 21 as the fulfillment of
Jesus' promise in 14 20-21, 23 that he will return to the disciples. See also Heil, *Blood
and Water*, 152. Reim, "Johannes 21," 335, incorrectly claims that the *only* difficulty for
accepting John 21 as part of the Gospel as a whole is the conclusion in 20·30-31. The
issue is more complex.

[28] For the debate over the identity of the historical author of John 21, and the reasons
for this epilogue, see R A. Culpepper, *John, the Son of Zebedee· The Life of a Legend* (Studies on Personalities of the New Testament; Columbia: Univ. of South Carolina Press,
1994) 297–325.

[29] See Brown, *John*, 2.1085–95, R E. Brown, "John 21," 246–65; Neirynck, "John 21,"
321–29, Vorster, "The Growth," 2207–14.

tian literature indicates, but it altered the design of the original narrative.[30] The Christian reader, who has been led from 1:1 to 20:31 to see the blessedness of the one who believes despite the absence of Jesus, has difficulty with a further narrative in which Jesus is again present. After the story told in John 1:1—20:31, there is no place for the return of the ascended Jesus to guide the church with Peter, the Beloved Disciple, and the other disciples,[31] however helpful this may have proved to be for the ongoing life of the Johannine community. Jesus has ascended to the Father to establish a new situation in which his disciples are his brethren, sons and daughters of the same Father (see 20:17). Another Paraclete is with the followers of Jesus and will be with them (see 14:16-17) until Jesus returns to take them to his Father's dwelling place (see 14:2-3).

Some who lived in a community that had produced a Jesus story sensed the need to give further instructions from the risen Lord to guide them as they lived in the in-between time. Thus, the Fourth Gospel appeared in its present form. John 21:25 hints that the early Christian community that listened to and read John 1:1—20:31 could not resist the temptation to add more to the book it had as a treasured part of its storytelling tradition. But there is only one book that rightly tells the Johannine story of Jesus, and it ends: "Blessed are those who have not seen and yet believe. . . . These things are written that you may go on believing that Jesus is the Christ, the Son of God, and that believing you may have life in his name" (20:29, 31).

---

[30] John 21 is not a "*mere* appendix." To regard it as an epilogue is not to devalue its importance in the Johannine and the Christian tradition. I am impressed by the suggestions of B. R. Gaventa, "The Archive of Excess: John 21 and the Problem of Narrative Closure," in R. A. Culpepper and C. C. Black, eds., *Exploring the Gospel of John: In Honor of D. Moody Smith* (Louisville: Westminster/John Knox, 1996) 240–52, who rightly points to 20:30-31 as the ending of the Gospel, but claims that 21:1-25 is an "excess," as are the details of the story (the fish, the breakfast, the strong nets, Jesus' repeated questions, and the limitless character of Jesus' deeds). Following John 19, John 20 circles back to the Prologue, while John 21 "signals that this narrative cannot close on a world whose equilibrium is restored or only modestly altered" (249). John 21 informs the reader that the journey of Johannine disciples goes on, however satisfactorily the Jesus-story has concluded in 20:30-31. See also Zumstein, "La rédaction finale," 214–30.

[31] Thus, Brodie, *John*, 582.

Bibliography

REFERENCE WORKS AND SOURCES

Aland, B.; K. Aland; J. Karavidopoulos; C. M. Martini; and B. M. Metzger, eds. *The Greek New Testament*. 4th ed. Stuttgart: United Bible Societies, 1993.

Aland, K., and B. Aland, eds. *Novum Testamentum Graece*. 26th ed. Stuttgart: Deutsche Bibelstiftung, 1979.

Bauer, W.; W. F. Arndt; and F. W. Gingrich. *A Greek-English Lexicon of the New Testament and Other Early Christian Literature*. 2d ed. rev. and aug. F. W. Gingrich and F. W. Danker. Chicago: University of Chicago Press, 1979.

Bietenhard, H. *Midrasch Tanhuma B.: R. Tanhuma uber die Tora, genannt Midrasch Jelammcnedu*. 2 vols. Judaica et Christiana 5–6; Bern: Peter Lang, 1980, 1982.

Blass, F., and A. Debrunner. *A Greek Grammar of the New Testament and Other Early Christian Literature*. Rev. and trans. R. W. Funk. Chicago: University of Chicago Press, 1961.

Boismard, M. E., and A. Lamouille. *Synopsis Graeca Quattuor Evangeliorum*. Leuven and Paris: Peeters, 1986.

Brown, F.; S. R. Driver; and C. A. Briggs. *A Hebrew and English Lexicon of the Old Testament with an Appendix Containing the Biblical Aramaic*. Oxford: Clarendon, 1907.

Brown, R. E.; J. A. Fitzmyer; and R. E. Murphy, eds. *The New Jerome Biblical Commentary*. Englewood Cliffs, N.J.: Prentice Hall, 1989.

Charlesworth, J. H., ed. *The Old Testament Pseudepigrapha*. 2 vols. London: Darton, Longman & Todd, 1983, 1985.

Colson, F. H.; G. H. Whitaker; J. W. Earp; and R. Marcus, eds. *Philo*. 12 vols. Loeb Classical Library. London: Heinemann; Cambridge: Harvard University Press, 1929–53.

Danby, H. *The Mishnah Translated from the Hebrew with Introduction and Brief Expository Notes*. Oxford: Clarendon, 1933.

Elliger, K., and K. Rudolph. *Biblia Hebraica Stuttgartensia*. Stuttgart: Deutsche Bibelgesellschaft, 1983.

Epstein, I., ed. *The Babylonian Talmud*. 35 vols. London: Soncino, 1948–52.

Freedman, H., and M. Simon, eds. *Midrash Rabbah. Translated into English with Notes, Glossary and Indices*. 10 vols. London: Soncino, 1939.

Kittel, G., and G. Friedrich, eds. *Theological Dictionary of the New Testament*. 10 vols. Grand Rapids: Eerdmans, 1964–76.

Lake, K., ed. *The Apostolic Fathers. With an English Translation*. 2 vols. Loeb Classical Library. London: Heinemann; Cambridge: Harvard University Press, 1912, 1913.

Liddell, H.; R. Scott; and A. S. Jones. *A Greek-English Lexicon*. Oxford: Clarendon, 1968.

Lidzbarski, M. *Das Johannesbuch der Mandaer*. Giessen: Alfred Topelmann, 1915.

———. *Mandaische Liturgien*. Abhandlungen der Akadamie der Wissenschaften in Göttingen. Philologisch-historische Klasse. Neue Folge 17,1. Gottingen: Vandenhoeck & Ruprecht, 1970.

Lohse, E., ed. *Die Texte aus Qumran. Hebraisch und Deutsch*. 3d ed. Munich: Kosel-Verlag, 1981.

Metzger, B. M. *A Textual Commentary on the Greek New Testament*. Stuttgart: German Bible Society, 1994.

Minor, M. *Literary-Critical Approaches to the Bible. An Annotated Bibliography*. West Cornwall, Conn.: Locust Hill Press, 1992.

Moulton, J. H.; W. F. Howard; and N. Turner. *A Grammar of New Testament Greek*. 4 vols. Edinburgh: T. & T. Clark, 1909–76.

Nock, A. D., and A.-J. Festugière, *Corpus Hermeticum*. 4 vols. Collection des Universités de France. Paris: Société d'Édition, "Les Belles Lettres," 1945–54.

Pirot, L.; A. Robert; and H. Cazelles, eds. *Dictionnaire de la Bible Supplément*. Paris: Letouzey, 1928–.

Powell, M. A.; C. G. Gray; and M. C. Curtis. *The Bible and Modern Literary Criticism. A Critical Assessment and Annotated Bibliography*. New York: Greenwood, 1992.

Rahlfs, A. *Septuaginta. Id est Vetus Testamentum Graece iuxta LXX Interpretes*. 2 vols. 8th ed. Stuttgart: Wurttemburgische Bibelanstalt, 1965.

Schwab, M., ed. *Le Talmud de Jérusalem*. 11 vols. Paris: Maisonneuve et Cie, 1878–90.

Strack, H., and P. Billerbeck. *Kommentar zum Neuen Testament aus Talmud und Midrasch*. 6 vols. Munich: C. H. Beck, 1922–61.

Temporini, H., and W. Hasse, eds. *Aufstieg und Niedergang der romischen Welt*. Berlin: Walter de Gruyter, 1981–.

Thackeray, H. St. J.; R. Marcus; A. Wikgren; and L. H. Feldman, eds. *Josephus*. 9 vols. Loeb Classical Library; London: Heinemann; Cambridge: Harvard University Press, 1926–65.

van Belle, G. *Johannine Bibliography 1966–1985. A Cumulative Bibliography on the Fourth Gospel.* BETL 82. Leuven: Leuven University Press, 1988.

Zerwick, M. *Biblical Greek Illustrated by Examples.* Rome: Biblical Institute Press, 1963.

COMMENTARIES ON THE FOURTH GOSPEL

Barrett, C. K. *The Gospel according to St. John.* 2d ed. London: SPCK, 1978.

Bauer, W. *Das Johannesevangelium erklart.* HKNT 6. Tubingen: J. C. B. Mohr, 1933.

Beasley-Murray, G. R. *John.* WBC 36. Waco: Word, 1987.

Becker, J. *Das Evangelium des Johannes.* 2 vols. OTK 4/1–2. Gutersloh: Gerd Mohn; Wurzburg: Echter, 1979–81.

Bernard, J. H. *A Critical and Exegetical Commentary on the Gospel according to St John.* 2 vols. ICC. Edinburgh: T. & T. Clark, 1928.

Boismard, M.-E., and A. Lamouille. *L'Evangile de Jean.* Synopse des Quatre Evangiles en Français III. Paris: Cerf, 1977.

Brodie, T. L. *The Gospel according to John: A Literary and Theological Commentary.* New York: Oxford University Press, 1993.

Brown, R. E. *The Gospel according to John.* 2 vols. AB 29, 29A. New York: Doubleday, 1966–70.

Bultmann, R. *The Gospel of John: A Commentary.* Trans. G. R. Beasley-Murray. Oxford: Blackwell, 1971.

Carson, D. A. *The Gospel according to John.* Grand Rapids: Eerdmans, 1991.

Delebecque, E. *Evangile de Jean: Texte Traduit et Annoté.* CahRB 23. Paris: Gabalda, 1987.

Ellis, P. F. *The Genius of John. A Compositional-Critical Commentary on the Fourth Gospel.* Collegeville, Minn.: Liturgical Press, 1984.

Haenchen, E. *John 1–2.* 2 Vols. Trans. R. W. Funk. Hermeneia. Philadelphia: Fortress Press, 1984.

Hoskyns, E. C. *The Fourth Gospel,* ed. F. N. Davey. London: Faber & Faber, 1947.

Kysar, R. *John.* Augsburg Commentary on the New Testament. Minneapolis: Augsburg, 1986.

Lagrange, M.-J. *Évangile selon saint Jean.* EB. Paris: Gabalda, 1936.

Léon-Dufour, X. *Lecture de l'évangile selon Jean.* 3 vols. Parole de Dieu. Paris: Seuil, 1988, 1990, 1993.

Lightfoot, R. H. *St. John's Gospel,* ed. C. F. Evans. Oxford: Oxford University Press, 1956.

Lindars, B. *The Gospel of John.* NCB. London: Oliphants, 1972.

Loisy, A. *Le quatrième évangile.* Paris: Emile Nourry, 1921.

Macgregor, G. H. C. *The Gospel of John*. MNTC. London: Hodder and Stough-
ton, 1928.
Malina, B. J. and R. L. Rohrbaugh. *Social-Science Commentary on the Gospel of
John*. Minneapolis: Fortress Press, 1998.
Marsh, J. *Saint John*. PNTC. Harmondsworth: Penguin, 1968.
Moloney, F. J. *Belief in the Word: Reading John 1–4*. Minneapolis: Fortress
Press, 1993.
———. *Signs and Shadows: Reading John 5–12*. Minneapolis: Fortress Press,
1996.
Morris, L. *The Gospel according to John*. NICNT. Rev. ed. Grand Rapids: Eerd-
mans, 1995.
Schnackenburg, R. *The Gospel according to St John*. 3 vols. HTCNT 4: 1–3. Trans.
C. Hastings. London: Burns & Oates; New York: Crossroad, 1968–82.
Segalla, G. *Giovanni*. NVB 36. Rome: Edizioni Paoline, 1976.
Stibbe, M. W. G. *John*. Readings: A New Biblical Commentary. Sheffield: JSOT
Press, 1993.
Talbert, C. H. *Reading John: A Literary and Theological Commentary on the Fourth
Gospel and the Johannine Epistles*. London: SPCK, 1992.
van den Bussche, H. *Jean: Commentaire de l'Évangile Spirituel*. Bruges: Desclée
de Brouwer, 1976.
Westcott, B. F. *The Gospel according to Saint John*. London: Murray, 1908.
Witherington III, B. *John's Wisdom. A Commentary on the Fourth Gospel*. Louis-
ville: Westminster/John Knox Press, 1995.

OTHER LITERATURE

Agourides, S. "The 'High Priestly Prayer' of Jesus." *SE* 4 (1968): 137–45.
Alter, R. *The Art of Biblical Narrative*. New York: Basic Books, 1981.
Appold, M. L. *The Oneness Motif in the Fourth Gospel: Motif Analysis and Exeget-
ical Probe into the Theology of John*. WUNT 2. Reihe 1. Tübingen: J. C. B.
Mohr, 1976.
Ashton, J. *Studying John*. Oxford: Clarendon, 1994.
———. *Understanding the Fourth Gospel*. Oxford: Clarendon, 1991.
Aubineau, M. "La tunique sans couture du Christ. Exégèse patristique de Jean
19:23-24." In *Kyriakon: Festschrift Johannes Quasten*, ed. P. Grandfield and
J. A. Jungmann, 1:100–127. 2 vols. Munster: Aschendorff, 1970.
Aune, D. E. *The Cultic Setting of Realized Eschatology in Early Christianity*.
NovTSup 28. Leiden: E. J. Brill, 1972.
Auwers, J.-M. "Le nuit de Nicodème (Jean 3,2; 19,39) ou l'ombre du langage."
RB 97 (1990): 481–503.
Balagué, M. "La oración sacerdotal (Juan 17,1–26)." *CultBib* 31 (1974): 67–90.
Ball, D. M. *"I Am" in John's Gospel: Literary Function, Background and Theological
Implications*. JSNTSS 124. Sheffield: Sheffield Academic Press, 1996.
Ball, R. M. "S. John and the Institution of the Eucharist." *JSNT* 23 (1985):
59–68.

Bammel, E. "The Farewell Discourse of the Evangelist John and the Jewish Heritage." *TynBul* 44 (1993): 103–16.

Bampfylde, C. "John 19:28: A Case for a New Translation." *NovT* 11 (1969): 247–60.

Barrett, C. K. *Essays on John.* London: SPCK, 1982.

Baum-Bodenbender, R. *Hoheit in Niedrigkeit: Johanneische Christologie im Prozess Jesu vor Pilatus.* FB 49. Wurzburg: Echter Verlag, 1984.

Becker, J. "Aufbau, Schichtung und theologiegeschichtliche Stellung des Gebets in Johannes 17." *ZNW* 60 (1969): 56–83.

———. "Die Abschiedsreden im Johannesevangelium." *ZNW* 61 (1970): 215–46.

Beetham, F. G., and P. A. Beetham. "A Note on John 19:29." *JTS* 44 (1993): 163–69.

Behler, G. M. *The Last Discourse of Jesus.* Trans. R. T. Francover. Baltimore: Helicon, 1965.

Bergmeier, R. "TETELESTAI Joh 19:30." *ZNW* 79 (1988): 282–90.

Betz, O. *Der Paraklet: Fursprecher im haretischen Spätjudentum, im Johannesevangelium und in neu gefundenen gnostischen Schriften.* AGSU 2. Leiden: Brill, 1963.

Beutler, J. "Die Heilsbedeutung des Todes Jesu im Johannesevangelium nach Johannes 13,1–20." In *Der Tod Jesu: Deutungen im Neuen Testament,* ed. K. Kertelge, 188–204. Quaestiones Disputatae 74. Herder: Freiburg, 1976.

———. *Habt keine Angst: Die erste Johanneische Abschiedsrede (Joh 14).* SBS 116. Stuttgart: Katholisches Bibelwerk, 1984.

———. "Psalm 42/43 im Johannesevangelium." *NTS* 25 (1978–79): 33–57.

Bietenhard, H. "*onoma ktl.*" TDNT 5 (1967): 242–83.

Black, C. C., "The Grandeur of Johannine Rhetoric." In *Exploring the Fourth Gospel: In Honor of D. Moody Smith,* ed. R. A. Culpepper and C. C. Black, 220–39. Louisville: Westminster/John Knox, 1996.

Blank, J. "Die Verhandlung vor Pilatus Jo 19:28—19:16 im Lichte johanneischer Theologie." *BZ* 3 (1959): 60–81.

———. *Krisis: Untersuchungen zur johanneischen Christologie und Eschatologie.* Freiburg: Lambertus, 1964.

Bligh, J. *The Sign of the Cross: The Passion and Resurrection of Jesus according to John.* Slough, England: St Paul Publications, 1975.

Blanquart, F. *Le premier jour: Étude sur Jean 20.* LD 146. Paris: Cerf, 1992.

Boguslazwski, S. "Jesus' Mother and the Bestowal of the Spirit." *IBS* 14 (1992): 106–29.

Boismard, M.-É. "Le chapitre xxi de saint Jean: essai de critique littéraire." *RB* 54 (1947): 473–501.

Borgen, P. "God's Agent in the Fourth Gospel." In *Logos Was the True Light and Other Essays on the Gospel of John,* 121–32. Relieff 9. Trondheim: Tarin, 1983.

Borig, R. *Der wahre Weinstock: Untersuchungen zu Johannes 15,1–10.* SANT. Munich: Kosel Verlag, 1967.

Brawley, R. L. "An Absent Complement and Intertextuality in John 19:28-29."
    JBL 112 (1993): 427–43.
Breck, J. "John 21: Appendix, Epilogue or Conclusion?" *SVTQ* 36 (1992):
    27–49.
Brown, R. E. "John 21 and the First Appearance of the Risen Jesus to Peter."
    In *Resurrexit. Actes du Symposium International sur la Résurrection de Jésus
    (Rome 1970)*, ed. E. Dhanis, 246–65. Rome: Libreria Editrice Vaticana,
    1974.
———. *The Death of the Messiah. From Gethsemane to the Grave. A Commentary
    on the Passion Narratives in the Four Gospels.* 2 vols. ABRL. Garden City,
    N.Y.: Doubleday, 1994.
———. *The Epistles of John.* AB 30. Garden City, N.Y.: Doubleday, 1982.
———. "The Paraclete in the Fourth Gospel." *NTS* 13 (1966–67): 113–32.
———. "The Resurrection in John 20—A Series of Diverse Reactions." *Worship*
    64 (1990): 194–206.
———. "The Resurrection in John 21—Missionary and Pastoral Directives for
    the Church." *Worship* 64 (1990): 433–55.
Brown, R. E.; K. P. Donfried; and J. Reumann, eds. *Peter in the New Testament:
    A Collaborative Assessment by Protestant and Roman Catholic Scholars.* Min-
    neapolis: Augsburg; New York: Paulist, 1973.
Bruns, J. E. "A Note on John 16:33 and I John 2:13-14." *JBL* 86 (1967): 451–53.
Buhner, J.-A. *Der Gesandte und sein Weg im 4. Evangelium. Die kultur- und reli-
    gionsgeschichtlichen Grundlagen der johanneischen Sendungschristologie sowie
    ihre traditionsgeschichtliche Entwicklung.* WUNT 2. Reihe 2. Tubingen:
    J. C. B. Mohr, 1977.
Burge, G. M. *The Anointed Community: The Holy Spirit in the Johannine Tradition.*
    Grand Rapids: Eerdmans, 1987.
Busse, U. "Die 'Hellenen' Joh 12,20ff. und der sogennante 'Anhang' Joh 21."
    In *The Four Gospels 1992: Festschrift Frans Neirynck*, ed. F. van Segbroeck,
    C. M. Tuckett, G. van Belle, and J. Verheyden, 3:2083–100. 3 vols. BETL
    100. Leuven: Leuven University Press, 1992.
———. "The Beloved Disciple." *Skrif en Kerk* 15 (1994): 219–29.
Byrne, B. "The Faith of the Beloved Disciple and the Community in John 20."
    JSNT 23 (1985): 83–97.
Cancian, D. *Nuovo Commandamento Nuova Alleanza Eucaristica nell'interpretazi-
    one del capitolo 13 de Vangelo di Giovanni.* Collevalenza: Edizione "L'Amore
    Misericordioso," 1978.
Carson, D. A. "The Function of the Paraclete in John 16:7-11." *JBL* 98 (1979):
    547–66.
———. "The Purpose of the Fourth Gospel: John 20:31 Reconsidered." *JBL*
    106 (1987): 639–51.
Casurella, A. *The Johannine Paraclete in the Church Fathers: A Study in the History
    of Exegesis.* BGBE 25. Tubingen: J. C. B. Mohr, 1983.
Cassidy, R. J. *John's Gospel in New Perspective. Christology and the Realities of
    Roman Power.* Maryknoll: Orbis, 1992.

Charlesworth, J. H. *The Beloved Disciple: Whose Witness Validates the Gospel of John?* Valley Forge, Pa.: Trinity Press International, 1995.

Collins, R. F. "'A New Commandment I Give You . . .' (Jn 13:34)," *LTP* 35 (1979): 235–61.

———. "Mary in the Fourth Gospel: A Decade of Johannine Studies." *Louvain Studies* 3 (1970): 99–142.

Cortès, E. *Los Discursos de Adiós de Gn 49 a Jn 13–17.* Colectánea San Paciano 23. Barcelona: Herder, 1976.

Culpepper, R. A. *Anatomy of the Fourth Gospel: A Study in Literary Design.* Foundations and Facets. Philadelphia: Fortress Press, 1983.

———. *The Johannine School: An Evaluation of the Johannine-School Hypothesis Based on an Investigation of the Nature of Ancient Schools.* SBLDS 26; Missoula, Mont.: Scholars Press, 1975.

———. *John, The Son of Zebedee: The Life of a Legend.* Studies on Personalities of the New Testament. Columbia: University of South Carolina Press, 1994.

———. "The Gospel of John as a Document of Faith in a Pluralistic Culture." In *"What Is John?" Readers and Readings of the Fourth Gospel,* ed. F. F. Segovia, 107–27. SS 3. Atlanta: Scholars Press, 1996.

———. "The Johannine *hypodeigma:* A Reading of John 13:1-38." *Sem* 53 (1991): 133–52.

D'Angelo, M. R. "A Critical Note: John 20.17 and the Apocalypse of Moses." *JTS* 41 (1990): 529–36.

Danielou, J. "Le fils de perdition (Joh., 17,12)." In *Mélanges d'histoire des religions offerts a Henri-Charles Puech,* 187–89. Paris: Presses Universitaires de France, 1974.

Dauer, A. *Die Passionsgeschichte im Johannesevangelium: Eine traditionsgeschichtliche und theologische Untersuchung zu Joh 18,1-19,30.* SANT 30. Munich: Kosel Verlag, 1972.

———. "Zur Herkunft der Thomas-Perikope Joh 20,24-29." In *Biblische Randbermerkungen: Schulerfestschrift fur Rudolf Schnackenburg zum 60. Geburtstag,* ed. H. Merklein and J. Lange, 56–76. Wurzburg: Echter Verlag, 1974.

Davies, W. D. "Reflection on Aspects of the Jewish Background of the Gospel of John." In *Exploring the Fourth Gospel: In Honor of D. Moody Smith,* ed. R. A. Culpepper and C. C. Black, 43–64. Louisville: Westminster/John Knox, 1996.

de Boer, M. C. *Johannine Perspectives on the Death of Jesus.* CBET 17. Kampen: Kok Pharos, 1996.

de Goedt, M. "Un Schème de Révélation dans le Quatrième Évangile." *NTS* 8 (1961–62): 142–50.

de la Potterie, I. "Consécration ou sanctification du chrétien d'après Jean 17." In *Le Sacré: Etudes et Recherches: Actes du colloque organisé par le Centre International d'etudes humanistes et par l'Institut d'etudes philosophiques de Rome,* ed. E. Castelli, 333–49. Paris: Aubier-Montaignel, 1974.

———. "Genèse de la foi pascale d'après Jn 20." *NTS* 30 (1984): 26–49.

———. "La témoin qui demeure: le disciple que Jésus aimait." *Bib* 67 (1986): 343–59.

———. "La tunique sans couture, symbole du Christ, grand prêtre?" *Bib* 60 (1979): 255–69.

———. *La Vérité dans Saint Jean.* 2 vols. AnBib 73. Rome: Biblical Institute Press, 1977.

———. "Parole et Esprit dans S. Jean." In *L'Évangile de Jean: Sources, rédaction, théologie,* ed. M. de Jonge, 177–201. BETL 44. Gembloux: Duculot, 1977.

———. *The Hour of Jesus: The Passion and Resurrection of Jesus according to John: Text and Spirit.* Slough, England: St Paul Publications, 1989.

Delebecque, E. "La mission de Pierre et celle de Jean: note philologique sur Jean 21." *Bib* 67 (1986): 335–42.

Delorme, J. "Sacerdoce du Christ et ministère (A propos de Jean 17): Sémantique et théologie biblique." *RSR* 62 (1974): 199–219.

Dettwiler, A. *Die Gegenwart des Erhohten: Eine exegetische Studie zu den johanneischen Abschiedsreden (Joh 13,31—16,33) unter besonderer Berucksichtigung ihres Relecture-Charakters.* FRLANT 169. Göttingen: Vandenhoeck & Ruprecht, 1995.

Dewailly, L.-M. "D'où es tu? (Jean 19,9)." *RB* 92 (1985): 481–96.

Dietzfelbinger, C. "Die eschatologische Freude der Gemeinde in der Angst der Welt." *EvTh* 40 (1980): 420–36.

———. "Die grosseren Werke (Joh 14.12f.)." *NTS* 35 (1989): 27–47.

———. "Paraklet und theologischer Anspruch im Johannesevangelium." *ZTK* 82 (1985): 394–408.

Dodd, C. H. *Historical Tradition in the Fourth Gospel.* Cambridge: Cambridge University Press, 1965.

———. *The Interpretation of the Fourth Gospel.* Cambridge: Cambridge University Press, 1953.

Duke, P. *Irony in the Fourth Gospel.* Atlanta: John Knox, 1985.

Dunn, J. D. G. "The Washing of the Disciples' Feet in John 13:1-20." *ZNW* 61 (1970): 247–52.

Dupont, L.; C. Lash; and G. Levesque. "Recherche sur la structure de Jean 20." *Bib* 54 (1973): 482–98.

Ehrman, B. D. "Jesus' Trial Before Pilate: John 18:20—19:16." *BTB* 13 (1983): 124–31.

Ellis, P. F. "The Authenticity of John 21." *SVTQ* 36 (1992): 17–25.

Emerton, J. A. "Binding and Loosing—Forgiving and Retaining." *JTS* 13 (1962): 325–31.

Evans, C. F. *Resurrection and the New Testament.* SBT 2/12. London: SCM Press, 1970.

Fee, G. D. "On the Text and Meaning of John 20,30-31." In *The Four Gospels 1992: Festschrift Frans Neirynck,* ed. F. van Segbroeck, C. M. Tuckett, G. van Belle, and J. Verheyden, 3:2193–205. 3 vols. BETL 100. Leuven: Leuven University Press, 1992.

Ferraro, G. "'Pneuma' in Giov. 13,21." *RivBib* 28 (1980): 185–211.

Feuillet, A. "La recherche du Christ dans la Nouvelle Alliance d'après la Christophanie de Jo 20,11-18." In *L'homme devant Dieu*, 1:93–112. 2 vols. Mélanges H. de Lubac. Paris: Aubier, 1963.

———. *The Priesthood of Christ and His Ministers*. Garden City, N.Y.: Doubleday, 1975.

Fischer, G. *Die himmlischen Wohnungen: Untersuchungen zu Joh 14,2f*. Europaische Hochschulschriften XXIII/38. Bern: Herbert Lang, 1975.

Forestell, J. T. *The Word of the Cross: Salvation as Revelation in the Fourth Gospel*. AnBib 57. Rome: Biblical Institute Press, 1974.

Fowler, R. M. "Who Is 'the Reader' in Reader-Response Criticism?" *Sem* 31 (1985): 5–23.

Franzmann, M., and M. Klinger. "The Call Stories of John 1 and John 21." *SVTQ* 36 (1992): 7–15.

Fuller, R. H. *The Formation of the Resurrection Narratives*. London: SPCK, 1972.

Gardner, H. *The Business of Criticism*. Oxford: Oxford University Press, 1959.

Gaventa, B. R. "The Archive of Excess: John 21 and the Problem of Narrative Closure." In *Exploring the Gospel of John: In Honor of D. Moody Smith*, ed. R. A. Culpepper and C. C. Black, 240–51. Louisville: Westminster/John Knox, 1996.

Genette, G. *Narrative Discourse: An Essay in Method*. Ithaca: Cornell University Press, 1980.

Genuyt, F. "La comparution de Jésus devant Pilate. Analyse sémiotique de Jean 18:28—19:16." *RSR* 73 (1985): 133–46.

Ghiberti, G. *I racconti pasquali de capitolo 20 di Giovanni*. SB 19. Brescia: Paideia, 1972.

Giblin, C. H. "Confrontations in John 18,1-27." *Bib* 65 (1984): 210–32.

———. "John's Narration of the Hearing Before Pilate (John 18:28—19:16a)." *Bib* 67 (1986): 221–39.

Gourgues, M. "Marie, la 'femme' et la 'mère' en Jean." *NRT* 108 (1986): 174–91.

Grelot, P. "L'interprétation pénitentielle du lavement des pieds." In *L'homme devant Dieu: Mélanges H. de Lubac*, 1:75–91. 2 vols. Paris: Aubier, 1963.

Grossouw, W. K. "A Note on John XIII 1-3." *NovT* 8 (1966): 124–31.

Gundry, R. "In My Father's House Are Many *Monai* (John 14:2)." *ZNW* 58 (1967): 68–72.

Hartman, L. "An Attempt at a Text-Centered Exegesis of John 21." *ST* 39 (1984): 29–45.

Hartmann, G. "Die Vorlage der Osterbericht in Joh 20." *ZNW* 55 (1974): 197–220.

Hatina, T. R. "John 20,22 in Its Eschatological Context: Promise or Fulfillment?" *Bib* 74 (1993): 196–219.

Heil, J. P. *Blood and Water: The Death and Resurrection of Jesus in John 18–21*. CBQMS 27. Washington, D.C.: The Catholic Biblical Association of America, 1995.

———. "Jesus as the Unique Priest in the Gospel of John." *CBQ* 57 (1995): 729–45.

Heise, J. *Bleiben. Menein in den Johanneischen Schriften.* HUT 8. Tübingen: J. C. B. Mohr, 1967.

Heitmuller, W. *"Im Namen Jesu": Eine sprach- u. religionsgeschichtliche Untersuchung zum Neuen Testament, speziell zur altchristlichen Taufe.* FRLANT 2. Gottingen: Vandenhoeck & Ruprecht, 1903.

Hemelsoet, B. "L'ensevelissement selon Saint Jean." In *Studies in John: Presented to Professor Dr. J. N. Sevenster on the Occasion of His Seventieth Birthday,* 47–65. NovTSupp 24. Leiden: E. J. Brill, 1970.

Hengel, M. *Die johanneische Frage: Ein Lösungsversuch mit einem Beitrag zur Apokalypse von Jorg Frey.* WUNT 67. Tubingen: J. C. B. Mohr, 1993.

Hultgren, A. J. "The Johannine Footwashing (13.1–11) as Symbol of Eschatological Hospitality." *NTS* 28 (1982): 539–46.

Iser, W. *The Implied Reader: Patterns of Communication in Prose Fiction from Bunyan to Beckett.* Baltimore: Johns Hopkins University Press, 1978.

Janssens de Varebeke, A. "La structure des scenes du récit de la passion en Joh. 18–19." *ETL* 38 (1962): 504–22.

Jaubert, A. "Jean 17,25 et l'interprétation gnostique." In *Mélanges d'histoire des religions offerts à Henri-Charles Puech,* 347–53. Paris: Presses Universitaires de France, 1974.

———. "L'image de la vigne (Jean 15)." In *Oikonomia: Heilsgeschichte als Thema der Theologie. Oscar Cullmann zum 65. Geburtstag gewidmet,* ed. F. Christ, 93–99. Hamburg: H. Reich, 1967.

Johansson, N. *Parakletoi: Vorstellungen von Fursprechern fur die Menschen vor Gott in der alttestamentlichen Religion, im Spätjudentum und Urchristentum.* Lund: Gleerup, 1940.

Johnston, G. *The Spirit-Paraclete in the Gospel of John.* SNTSMS 12. Cambridge: Cambridge University Press, 1970.

Judge, P. J. "A Note on John 20,29." In *The Four Gospels 1992: Festschrift Frans Neirynck,* ed. F. van Segbroeck, C. M. Tuckett, G. van Belle, and J. Verheyden, 3:2183–92. 3 vols. BETL 100. Leuven: Leuven University Press, 1992.

Kaefer, J. Ph. "Les discours d'adieux en Jean 13:31—17:26." *NovT* 26 (1984): 251–82.

Kasemann, E. *The Testament of Jesus: A Study of John in the Light of Chapter 17.* Trans. G. Krodel. London: SCM Press, 1965.

Kelber, W. "Metaphysics and Marginality in John." In *"What Is John?" Readers and Readings of the Fourth Gospel,* ed. F. F. Segovia, 129–54. SS 3. Atlanta: Scholars Press, 1996.

Kieffer, R. *Le monde symbolique de Saint Jean.* LD 137. Paris: Cerf, 1989.

Kitzberger, I. R. "Love and Footwashing: John 13:1-20 and Luke 7:36-50 Read Intertextually." *BibInt* 2 (1994): 190–206.

———. "Mary of Bethany and Mary of Magdala—Two Female Characters in the Johannine Passion Narrative." *NTS* 41 (1995): 564–86.

Kleinknecht, K. T. "Johannes 13, die Synoptiker und die 'Methode' der johanneischen Evangelienuberliefrung." *ZTK* 82 (1985): 361–88.

Knoppler, T. *Die theologia crucis des Johannesevangeliums: Das Verstandnis des Todes Jesu im Rahmen der johanneischen Inkarnations- und Erhohungschristologie.* WMANT 69. Neukirchen: Neukirchener Verlag, 1994.

Koester, C. R. *Symbolism in the Fourth Gospel: Meaning, Mystery, Community.* Minneapolis: Fortress Press, 1995.

———. "The Spectrum of Johannine Readers." In *"What Is John?" Readers and Readings of the Fourth Gospel,* ed. F. F. Segovia, 5–19. SS 3. Atlanta: Scholars Press, 1996.

Korting, G. *Die esoterische Struktur des Johannesevangeliums.* 2 Teile. BU 25. Regensburg: Pustet, 1994.

Kovacs, J. L. "'Now Shall the Ruler of This World Be Driven Out': Jesus' Death as Cosmic Battle in John 12:20-36." *JBL* 114 (1995): 227–47.

Kragerud, A. *Die Lieblingsjunger im Johannesevangelium.* Hamburg: Osloer Universitatsverlag, 1959.

Kremer, J. "Jesu Verheissung des Geistes. Zur Verankerung der Aussage von Joh 16,13 in Leben Jesu." In *Die Kirche des Anfangs: Festschrift fur Heinz Schurmann zum 65. Geburtstag,* ed. R. Schnackenburg, J. Ernst and J. Wanke, 247–73. Erfurter Theologische Studien 38. Leipzig: St. Benno-Verlag, 1977.

———. "'Nimm deine Hand und lege sie in meine Seite!' Exegetische, hermeneutische und Bibeltheologische Uberlegungen zu Joh 20,24-29." In *The Four Gospels 1992: Festschrift Frans Neirynck,* ed. F. van Segbroeck, C. M. Tuckett, G. van Belle, and J. Verheyden, 3:2153–81. 3 vols. BETL 100. Leuven: Leuven University Press, 1992.

Kurz, W. S. *Farewell Addresses in the New Testament.* Zacchaeus Studies: New Testament. Collegeville, Pa.: Liturgical Press, 1990.

———. "Luke 22:14-38 and Greco-Roman and Biblical Farewell Addresses." *JBL* 104 (1985): 251–68.

Lattke, M. "Joh 20:30f. als Buchschluss." *ZNW* 78 (1987): 288–92.

Laurentin, A. "*We'attah—Kai nun:* Formule charactéristique des textes juridiques et liturgiques (à propos de Jean 17,5)." *Bib* 52 (1971): 190–214.

Lee, D. A. "Partnership in Easter Faith: The Role of Mary Magdalene and Thomas in John 20." *JSNT* 58 (1995): 37–49.

Lee, G. M. "John XIV 14 'Ye are my friends.'" *NovT* 15 (1973): 260.

Léon-Dufour, X. *Resurrection and the Message of Easter.* London: Geoffrey Chapman, 1974.

Lindars, B. "The Composition of John XX." *NTS* 7 (1960–61): 142–47.

———. "The Persecution of Christians in John 15:18—16:4a." In *Suffering and Martyrdom in the New Testament: Studies Presented to G. M. Styler by the Cambridge New Testament Seminar,* ed. W. Horbury and B. McNeill, 48–69. Cambridge: Cambridge University Press, 1981.

Loader, W. "The Central Structure of Johannine Theology." *NTS* 30 (1984): 188–216.

Lombard, H. A., and W. H. Oliver. "A Working Supper in Jerusalem: John 13:1-38 Introduces Jesus' Farewell Discourses." *Neot* 25 (1991): 357–78.

Longenecker, B. W. "The Unbroken Messiah: A Johannine Feature and Its Social Functions." *NTS* 41 (1995): 428–41.

Lorenzen, T. *Resurrection and Discipleship: Interpretative Models, Biblical Reflections, Theological Consequences.* Maryknoll: Orbis Books, 1995.

Ludemann, G. *The Resurrection of Jesus: History, Experience, Theology.* Trans. J. Bowden. London: SCM Press, 1994.

Maccini, R. G. *Her Testimony Is True: Women as Witnesses according to John.* JSNTSS 125. Sheffield: Sheffield Academic Press, 1996.

Mahoney, R. *Two Disciples at the Tomb: The Background and Message of John 20, 1-10.* TW 6. Bern: Herbert Lang, 1974.

Manns, F. *L'Evangile de Jean à la lumière du Judaïsme.* SBFA 33. Jerusalem: Franciscan Printing Press, 1991.

Martyn, J. L. *History and Theology in the Fourth Gospel.* 2d ed. Nashville: Abingdon, 1979.

―――. *The Gospel of John in Christian History: Essays for Interpreters.* New York: Paulist Press, 1978.

Marzotto, D. "Giovanni 17 e il Targum di Esodo 19–20." *RivBib* 25 (1977): 375–88.

―――. *L'Unità degli Uomini nel Vangelo di Giovanni.* SuppRivB 9. Brescia: Paideia, 1977.

Mastin, B. A. "The Imperial Cult and the Ascription of the Title to Jesus (John 20,28)," *SE* 6 (1973): 352–65.

McCaffrey, J. *The House with Many Rooms: The Temple Theme of Jn 14,2–3.* AnBib 114. Rome: Biblical Institute Press, 1988.

Meeks, W. A. "The Man from Heaven in Johannine Sectarianism." *JBL* 91 (1972): 44–72.

―――. *The Prophet-King: Moses Traditions and the Johannine Christology.* NovTSup 14. Leiden: E. J. Brill, 1967.

Menken, M. J. J. *Old Testament Quotations in the Fourth Gospel: Studies in Textual Form.* CBET 15. Kampen: Kok Pharos, 1996.

―――. "The Old Testament Quotation in John 19,36. Sources, Redaction, Background." In *The Four Gospels 1992: Festschrift Frans Neirynck,* ed. F. van Segbroeck, C. M. Tuckett, G. van Belle, and J. Verheyden, 3:2101–18. 3 vols. BETL 100. Leuven: Leuven University Press, 1992.

―――. "The Translation of Ps 41.10 in John 13.18." *JSNT* 40 (1990): 61–79.

Migliasso, S. *La presenza dell'Assente: Saggio di analisi letterario-strutturale e di sintisi teologica di Gv. 13,31-14,31.* Rome: Pontificia Universitas Gregoriana, 1979.

Minear, P. S. *John: The Martyr's Gospel.* New York: Pilgrim, 1984.

―――. "The Original Functions of John 21." *JBL* 102 (1983): 85–98.

―――. "We Don't Know Where . . . John 20:2." *Int* 30 (1976): 125–39.

Mlakuzhyil, G. *The Christological Literary Structure of the Fourth Gospel.* AnBib 117; Rome: Biblical Institute Press, 1987.

Mollat, D. "L'apparition du Ressuscité et le don de l'Esprit." In *Études johanniques,* 148–64. Parole de Dieu. Paris: Editions du Seuil, 1979.

———. "La découverte du tombeau vide." In *Études johanniques*, 135–47. Parole de Dieu. Paris: Editions du Seuil, 1979.

———. "La foi pascale selon le chapitre 20 de l'Évangile de Jean: Essai de théologie biblique." In *Études johanniques*, 165–84. Parole de Dieu. Paris: Editions du Seuil, 1979.

Moloney, F. J. *A Body Broken for a Broken People: Eucharist in the New Testament.* 2d ed. Peabody: Hendrickson, 1996.

———. "A Sacramental Reading of John 13:1-38." *CBQ* 53 (1991): 237–56.

———. "Johannine Theology." *NJBC* 1417–26.

———. "John 18:15-27: A Johannine View of the Church." *DRev* 112 (1994): 231–48.

———. "The Faith of Martha and Mary: A Narrative Approach to John 11:17-40." *Bib* 75 (1994): 471–93.

———. "The Johannine Passion and the Christian Community." *Sal* 57 (1995): 25–61.

———. "The Johannine Son of God." *Sal* 38 (1976): 71–86.

———. *The Johannine Son of Man.* 2d ed. BibScRel 14. Rome: LAS, 1978.

———. "The Structure and Message of John 15.1—16.3." *AusBR* 35 (1987): 35–49.

———. "When Is John Talking about Sacraments?" *AusBR* 30 (1982): 10–33.

Morgan-Wynne, J. E. "A Note on John 14.17b." *BZ* 23 (1979): 93–96.

Muller, U. B. "Die Parakletenvorstellung im Johannesevangelium." *ZTK* 71 (1974): 31–77.

Neirynck, F. "John 21." *NTS* 36 (1990): 321–36.

———. "The Anonymous Disciple in John 1." *ETL* 66 (1990): 5–37.

Neyrey, J. H. *The Resurrection Stories.* Zacchaeus Studies: New Testament. Wilmington, Del.: Michael Glazier, 1988.

Niccaci, A. "Esame lettarario di Gv 14." *EuntD* 31 (1978): 209–14.

———. "Esame Letterario di Gv 15-16." *Ant* 56 (1981): 43–71.

———. "L'unità letteraria di Gv 13,1-38." *EuntD* 29 (1976): 291–323.

Nicholson, G. C. *Death as Departure: The Johannine Ascent-Descent Scheme.* SBLDS 63. Chico: Scholars Press, 1983.

Niemand, C. *Die Fusswaschungerzahlung des Johannesevangeliums: Untersuchung zur ihrer Enstehung und Überlieferung in Urchristentum.* Studia Anselmiana 114. Rome: Pontificio Ateneo S. Anselmo, 1993.

Obermann, A. *Die christologische Erfüllung der Schrift im Johannesevangelium: Eine Untersuchung zur johanneischen Hermeneutik anhand der Schriftzitate.* WUNT 2. Reihe 83. Tübingen: J. C. B. Mohr, 1996.

O'Day, G. R. "'I Have Overcome the World' (John 16:33): Narrative Time in John 13–17." *Sem* 53 (1991): 153–66.

Okure, T. *The Johannine Approach to Mission: A Contextual Study of John 4:1-42.* WUNT 2. Reihe 32. Tubingen: J. C. B. Mohr, 1988.

———. "The Significance Today of Jesus' Commission to Mary Magdalene." *IRM* 81 (1992): 177–88.

Oliver, W. H., and A. G. van Aarde. "The Community of Faith as Dwelling

Place of the Faith: *Basileia tou theou* as 'Household of God' in the Johannine Farewell Discourses." *Neot* 25 (1991): 379–400.

Onuki, T. *Gemeinde und Welt im Johannesevangelium: Ein Beitrag zur Frage nach der theologischen und pragmatischen Funktion des johanneischen "Dualismus."* WMANT 56. Neukirchen: Neukirchener Verlag, 1984.

Osborne, B. "A Folded Napkin in an Empty Tomb: John 11:44 and 20:7 Again." *HeyJ* 14 (1973): 437–40.

Painter, J. "The Farewell Discourses and the History of Johannine Christianity." *NTS* 27 (1980–81): 523–43.

———. *The Quest for the Messiah: The History, Literature, and Theology of the Johannine Community.* 2d ed. Edinburgh: T. & T. Clark, 1991.

Panackel, C. *IDOY HO ANTHRŌPOS (Jn 19,5b): An Exegetico-Theological Study of the Text in the Light of the use of the term ANTHRŌPOS Designating Jesus in the Fourth Gospel.* AnGreg 251. Rome: Gregorian University Press, 1988.

Pancaro, S. *The Law in the Fourth Gospel: The Torah and the Gospel, Moses and Jesus, Judaism and Christianity according to John.* NovTSup 42. Leiden: E. J. Brill, 1975.

Perkins, P. *Resurrection: New Testament Witness and Contemporary Reflection.* Garden City, N.Y.: Doubleday, 1984.

Petersen, N. R. *The Gospel of John and the Sociology of Light: Language and Characterization in the Fourth Gospel.* Valley Forge, Pa.: Trinity Press International, 1993.

Porsch, F. "Der 'andere Paraklet'." *BK* 37 (1982): 133–38.

———. *Pneuma und Wort: Ein exegetische Beitrag zur Pneumatologie des Johannesevangeliums.* FThSt 16. Frankfurt: J. Knecht, 1974.

Quast, K. *Peter and the Beloved Disciple: Figures for a Community in Crisis.* JSNTSS 32. Sheffield: JSOT Press, 1989.

Randall, J. F. "The Theme of Unity in John 17." *ETL* 41 (1965): 373–94.

Reim, G. "Johannes 21: Ein Anhang?" In J. K. Elliott, ed., *Studies in New Testament Language and Text: Essays in Honor of George Dunbar Kilpatrick on the Occasion of His Sixty-Fifth Birthday,* 330–37. NovTSupp 44. Leiden: E. J. Brill, 1976.

Reiser, W. E. "The Case of the Tidy Tomb: The Place of the Napkins of John 11:44 and 20:7." *HeyJ* 14 (1973): 47–57.

Rengstorf, K. *"manthanô ktl."* TDNT 4 (1967): 390–461.

Rensberger, D. *Johannine Faith and Liberating Community.* Philadelphia: Westminster, 1988.

Richter, G. "Blut und Wasser aus der durchbohrten Seite Jesu (Joh 19,34b." *MuTZ* 21 (1970): 1–21.

———. *Die Fusswaschung im Johannesevangelium: Geschichte und Deutung.* BU 1. Regenburg: Pustet, 1967.

Riesenfeld, H. "Zu den johanneischen *hina*-Satzen." *ST* 19 (1965): 213–20.

Rigaux, B. *Dio l'ha risuscitato: Esegesi e teologia biblica.* Parola di Dio 13. Rome: Edizione Paoline, 1976.

———. "Les destinataires du IVe Évangile à la lumière de Jn 17." *RTL* 1 (1970): 289–319.

Riley, G. R. *Resurrection Reconsidered: Thomas and John in Controversy.* Minneapolis: Fortress Press, 1995.

Rimmon-Kenan, S. *Narrative Fiction: Contemporary Poetics.* New Accents. London: Methuen, 1983.

Ritt, H. *Das Gebet zum Vater: Zur Interpretation von Joh 17.* FB 36. Wurzburg: Echter Verlag, 1979.

Robinson, J. A. T. "The Destination and Purpose of St John's Gospel." *NTS* 6 (1959–60): 117–31.

———. "The Relation of the Prologue to the Gospel of St John." *NTS* 9 (1962–63): 120–29.

———. "The Significance of the Footwashing." In *Twelve More New Testament Studies,* 77–80. London: SCM Press, 1984.

Rodriguez Ruiz, M. *Der Missionsgedanke des Johannesevangeliums: Ein Beitrag zur johanneischen Soteriologie und Ekklesiologie.* FB 55. Wurzburg: Echter Verlag, 1987.

Rose, M. "Names of God in the OT." *ABD* 4:1001–11.

Roth, J. "Thèmes majeurs de la Tradition sacerdotale dans le Pentateuque." *NRT* 80 (1958): 696–721.

Ruckstuhl, E. "Zur Aussage und Botschaft von Johannes 21." In *Die Kirche des Anfangs: Festschrift für Heinz Schurmann zum 65. Geburtstag,* ed. R. Schnackenburg, J. Ernst, and J. Wanke, 339–62. EThSt 38. Leipzig: St Benno-Verlag, 1977.

Sandvik, B. "Joh 15 als Abendmahlstext." *TZ* 23 (1967): 323–28.

Schnackenburg, R. "Strukturanalyse von Joh 17." *BZ* 17 (1973): 67–78, 196–202.

Schneider, J. "Die Abschiedsreden Jesu: Ein Beitrag zur Frage der Komposition von Johannes 13:31—17:26." In *Gott und die Gotter: Festgabe fur E. Fascher zum 60. Geburtstag.* Berlin: Evangelische Verlagsanstalt, 1958.

Schneiders, S. M. "John 20:11-18: The Encounter of the Easter Jesus with Mary Magdalene—A Transformative Feminist Reading." In *"What Is John?" Readers and Readings of the Fourth Gospel,* ed. F. F. Segovia, 155–68. SS 3. Atlanta: Scholars Press, 1996.

———. "John 21.1-14." *Int* 43 (1989): 70–75.

———. "The Face Veil: A Johannine Sign." *BTB* 13 (1983): 94–97.

———. "The Footwashing (John 13:1-20): An Experiment in Hermeneutics." *CBQ* 43 (1981): 76–92.

Schnelle, U. *Antidocetic Christology in the Gospel of John.* Trans. L. M. Maloney. Minneapolis: Fortress Press, 1992.

———. "Die Abschiedsreden im Johannesevangelium." *ZNW* 80 (1989): 64–79.

Schuchard, B. G. *Scripture Within Scripture: The Interrelationship of Form and Function in the Explicit Old Testament Citations in the Gospel of John.* SBLDS 133. Atlanta: Scholars, 1992.

Segalla, G. *La preghiera di Gesù al Padre (Giov. 17). Un addio missionario.* SB 63. Brescia: Paideia, 1983.

———. "La struttura chiastica di Giov. 15,1-8." *BibOr* 12 (1970): 129–31.

Segovia, F. F. "John 13:1-20. The Footwashing in the Johannine Tradition." *ZNW* 73 (1982): 31–51.

———. "John 15:18—16:4a: A First Addition to the Original Farewell Discourse." *CBQ* 45 (1983): 210–30.

———. *Love Relationships in the Johannine Tradition: Agapē/Agapan in I John and the Fourth Gospel.* SBLDS 58. Chico: Scholars Press, 1982.

———. "'Peace I Leave with You; My Peace I Give to You': Discipleship in the Fourth Gospel." In *Discipleship in the New Testament,* ed. F. F. Segovia, 76–102. Philadelphia: Fortress Press, 1985.

———. *The Farewell of the Word: The Johannine Call to Abide.* Minneapolis: Fortress Press, 1991.

———. "The Final Farewell of Jesus: A Reading of John 20:30—21:25." *Sem* 53 (1991): 167–90.

———. "The Journey(s) of the Word of God: A Reading of the Plot of the Fourth Gospel." *Sem* 53 (1991): 23–54.

———. "The Love and Hatred of Jesus and Johannine Sectarianism." *CBQ* 43 (1981): 258–72.

———. "The Theology and Provenance of John 15:1-17." *JBL* 101 (1982): 115–28.

———. "The Tradition History of the Fourth Gospel." In *Exploring the Fourth Gospel: In Honor of D. Moody Smith,* ed. R. A. Culpepper and C. C. Black, 178–89. Louisville: Westminster/John Knox, 1996.

Seidensticker, P. *Die Auferstehung Jesu in der Botschaft der Evangelisten.* SBS 12. Stuttgart: Katholisches Bibelwerk, 1968.

Senior, D. *The Passion of Jesus in the Gospel of John.* The Passion Series 4. Collegeville, Pa.: Liturgical Press, 1991.

Serra, A. *Contributi dell'Antica Letteratura Giudaica per l'Esegesi di Giovanni 2,1-12 e 19,25-27.* Scripta Pontificiae Facultatis Theologicae "Marianum" 31. Rome: Edizioni Herder, 1977.

Siminel, P. "Les 2 anges de Jean 20/11-12." *ETL* 67 (1992): 71–76.

Simoens, Y. *La gloire d'aimer: Structures stylistiques et interprétatives dans la Discours de la Cène (Jn 13–17).* AnBib 90. Rome: Biblical Institute Press, 1981.

Simonis, A. J. *Die Hirtenrede im Johannesevangelium: Versuch eine Analyse von Johannes 10,1-18 nach Entstehung, Hintergrund und Inhalt.* AnBib 29. Rome: Biblical Institute Press, 1967.

Smalley, S. S. *John: Evangelist and Interpreter.* Exeter: Paternoster, 1978.

Spicq, C. "*Trōgein:* Est-il synonyme de *phagein* et d'*esthiein* dans le Nouveau Testament?" *NTS* 26 (1979–80): 414–19.

Staley, J. L. "Reading Myself, Reading the Text: The Johannine Passion Narrative in Postmodern Perspective." In *"What Is John?" Readers and Readings of the Fourth Gospel,* ed. F. F. Segovia, 59–104. SS 3. Atlanta: Scholars Press, 1996.

———. *Reading with a Passion: Rhetoric, Autobiography, and the American West in the Gospel of John.* New York: Continuum, 1995.

———. "Subversive Narrator/Victimized Reader: A Reader Response Assessment of a Text-Critical Problem, John 18,12-24." *JSNT* 51 (1993): 79–98.

————. *The Print's First Kiss: A Rhetorical Investigation of the Implied Reader in the Fourth Gospel.* SBLDS 82. Atlanta: Scholars Press, 1988.

Stenger, W. "*DIKAIOSUNE* in Jo. XVI 18.10," *NovT* 21 (1979): 2–12.

Sternberg, M. *The Poetics of Biblical Narrative: Ideological Literature and the Drama of Reading.* ILBS. Bloomington: Indiana University Press, 1985.

Stibbe, M. W. G. *John as Storyteller: Narrative Criticism and the Fourth Gospel.* SNTSMS 73. Cambridge: Cambridge University Press, 1992.

Stimpfle, A. *Blinde Sehen: Die Eschatologie im traditionsgeschichtlichen Prozess des Johannesevangeliums.* BZNW 57. Berlin: de Gruyter, 1990.

Suggit, J. N. "John 13:1-30: The Mystery of the Incarnation and of the Eucharist." *Neot* 19 (1985): 64–70.

————. "Nicodemus—The True Jew." *Neot* 14 (1981): 90–110.

Swetnam, J. "Bestowal of the Spirit in the Fourth Gospel." *Bib* 74 (1993): 556–76.

Sylva, D. D. "Nicodemus and His Spices." *NTS* 34 (1988): 148–51.

Thomas, J. C. *Footwashing in John 13 and the Johannine Community.* JSNTSS 61. Sheffield: JSOT Press, 1991.

Thompson, M. M. *The Humanity of Jesus in the Fourth Gospel.* Philadelphia: Fortress Press, 1988.

Thusing, W. *Die Erhohung und Verherrlichung Jesu im Johannesevangelium.* 3d ed. NTAbh 21, 1–2. Munster: Aschendorff, 1979.

————. *Herrlichkeit und Einheit: Eine Auslegung des Hohepriestlerlichen Gebetes Jesu (Joh. 17).* 2d ed. Munster: Aschendorff, 1975.

Thyen, H. "Entwicklungen innerhalb der johanneischen Theologie und Kirche im Spiegel von Joh. 21 und der Lieblingsjungertexte des Evangeliums." In *L'Évangile de Jean: Sources, rédaction, théologie,* ed. M. de Jonge, 259–99. BETL 44. Gembloux: Duculot, 1977.

————. "Johannes 10 im Kontext des vierten Evangeliums." In *The Shepherd Discourse of John 10 and Its Context,* ed. J. Beutler and R. T. Fortna, 116–34. SNTSMS 67. Cambridge: Cambridge University Press, 1992.

————. "'Niemand hat grossere Liebe als die, dass er sein Leben fur seine Freunde hingibt' (Joh 15:13): Das johanneische Verstandnis des Kreuzestodes Jesu." In *Theologia Crucis—Signum Crucis: Festschrift fur Erich Dinkler zum 70. Geburtstag,* ed. C. Andresen and G. Klein, 467–81. Tubingen: J. C. B. Mohr, 1979.

Tolmie, D. F. *Jesus' Farewell to the Disciples: John 13:1—17:26 in Narratological Perspective.* BibIntS 12. Leiden: E. J. Brill, 1995.

Valdés, M., ed. *A Ricoeur Reader: Reflection and Imagination.* Toronto: University of Toronto Press, 1991.

van Cangh, J.-M. *La Multiplication des Pains et l'Eucharistie.* LD 86. Paris: Editions du Cerf, 1975.

van der Watt, J. G. "'Metaphorik' in Joh 15,1-8." *BZ* 38 (1994): 67–80.

van Iersel, B. "Die Wunderbare Speisung und das Abendmahl in der Synoptischen Tradition (Mk VI 35–44 par., VIII 1–20 par.)." *NovT* 7 (1964): 167–94.

van Tilborg, S. *Imaginative Love in John.* BibIntS 2. Leiden: E. J. Brill, 1993.

van Unnik, W. C. "*Dominus Vobiscum:* The Background of a Liturgical Formula." In *New Testament Essays: Studies in Memory of Thomas Walter Manson 1893–1958,* ed. A. J. B. Higgins, 270–305. Manchester: Manchester University Press, 1959.

———. "The Purpose of St John's Gospel." *SE* (1959): 382–411.

von Campenhausen, H. "The Events of Easter and the Empty Tomb." In *Tradition and Life in the Church: Essays and Lectures in Church History,* 42–89. London: Collins, 1968.

Vorster, W. S. "The Growth and Making of John 21." In *The Four Gospels 1992: Festschrift Frans Neirynck,* ed. F. van Segbroeck, C. M. Tuckett, G. van Belle, and J. Verheyden, 3: 2208–21. 3 vols. BETL 100. Leuven: Leuven University Press, 1992.

Walker, W. O. "The Lord's Prayer in Matthew and John." *NTS* 28 (1982): 237–56.

Weder, H. "*Deus Incarnatus:* On the Hermeneutics of Christology in the Johannine Writings." In *Exploring the Gospel of John: In Honor of D. Moody Smith,* ed. R. A. Culpepper and C. C. Black, 327–45. Louisville: Westminster/John Knox, 1996.

Weiss, H. "Footwashing in the Johannine Community." *NovT* 41 (1979): 298–325.

Wenz, H. "Sehen und Glauben bei Johannes." *TZ* 17 (1961): 17–25.

Wiarda, T. "John 21.1-23: Narrative Unity and Its Implications." *JSNT* 46 (1992): 53–71.

Wilckens, U. *Resurrection: An Historical Examination and Explanation.* Edinburgh: St. Andrew Press, 1977.

Wilkinson, J. "The Incident of the Blood and Water in John 19,34." *SJT* 28 (1975): 149–72.

Winandy, J. "Les vestiges laissés dans le tombeau at la foi du disciple." *NRT* 110 (1988): 212–19.

Windisch, H. *The Spirit-Paraclete in the Fourth Gospel.* Facet Books. Biblical Series 20. Philadelphia: Fortress Press, 1968.

Witherington III, B. *Jesus the Sage: The Pilgrimage of Wisdom.* Minneapolis: Fortress Press, 1994.

Witkamp, L. T. "Jesus' Thirst in John 19:28-30: Literal or Figurative?" *JBL* 115 (1996): 489–510.

Wolff, H. W. "'Wissen um Gott' bei Hosea als Urform der Theologie." *EvTh* 12 (1952–53): 533–44.

Woll, D. B. "The Departure of 'the Way': The First Farewell Discourse in the Gospel of John." *JBL* 99 (1980): 225–39.

Wyatt, N. "'Supposing Him to Be the Gardener' (John 20,15): A Study of the Paradise Motif in John." *ZNW* 81 (1990): 21–38.

Young, F. W. "A Study of the Relation of Isaiah to the Fourth Gospel." *ZNW* 46 (1955): 215–33.

Zeller, D. "Jesus und die Philosophen vor dem Richter (zu Joh 19,8-11)." *BZ* 37 (1993): 88–92.

Zimmerlı, W. "The Knowledge of God according to the Book of Ezekiel." In *I am Yahweh*, trans. D. W. Stott; ed. W. Brueggemann, 29–98. Atlanta: John Knox, 1982.

Zumstein, J. "Der Prozess der Relecture in der ıohanneischen Literatur." *NTS* 42 (1996): 394–411.

——. "La rédaction finale de l'évangile selon Jean (à l'exemple du chapître 21)." In *La Communauté Johannique et son Histoire*, ed. J.-D. Kaestli, J.-M. Poffet, and J. Zumstein, 207–30. Genève: Labor et Fıdes, 1990.

——. "L'interprétation johannique de la mort du Christ." In *The Four Gospels 1992: Festschrift Frans Neirynck*, ed. F. van Segbroeck, C. M. Tuckett, G. van Belle, and J. Verheyden, 3:2119–38. 3 vols. BETL 100. Leuven: Leuven University Press, 1992.

——. "Mémoire et relecture pascale dans l'évangile de Jean." In *Le mémoire et le temps: Mélanges offerts à Pierre Bonnard*, ed. D. Marguerat and J. Zumstein, 153–70. Genève: Labor et Fides, 1991.

Index of Authors

213